Data Warehousing and Web Engineering

Shirley Becker, Ph.D.
Florida Institute of Technology, USA

IRM Press
Publisher of innovative scholarly and professional
information technology titles in the cyberage

Hershey • London • Melbourne • Singapore • Beijing

Acquisitions Editor:	Mehdi Khosrow-Pour
Managing Editor:	Jan Travers
Assistant Managing Editor:	Amanda Appicello
Copy Editor:	Amanda Appicello
Cover Design:	Tedi Wingard
Printed at:	Integrated Book Technology

Published in the United States of America by
   IRM Press
   1331 E. Chocolate Avenue
   Hershey PA 17033-1117
   Tel: 717-533-8845
   Fax: 717-533-8661
   E-mail: cust@idea-group.com
   Web site: http://www.irm-press.com

and in the United Kingdom by
   IRM Press
   3 Henrietta Street
   Covent Garden
   London WC2E 8LU
   Tel: 44 20 7240 0856
   Fax: 44 20 7379 3313
   Web site: http://www.eurospan.co.uk

Library of Congress Cataloguing-in-Publication Data

Becker, Shirley A., 1956-
   Data warehousing and web engineering / Shirley A. Becker.
      p. cm.
   ISBN 1-931777-02-0 (paper)
      1. Data warehousing. 2. Software engineering. I. Title.

QA76.9.D37 B44 2002
005.74--dc21   2001059445

eISBN: 1-931777-21-7

British Cataloguing-in-Publication Data
A Cataloguing-in-Publication record for this book is available from the British Library.

Other New Releases from IRM Press

Data Warehousing and Web Engineering

Table of Contents

Foreword

From a historical perspective, web engineering focused on information presentation of products and services via the Internet. Many of these early web sites made use of glitzy technology in order to draw attention to them. They had minimal or no search capabilities, and provided no means of customer interaction other than email capabilities. There was no need to link to existing legacy systems, as information sharing was unidirectional from the organization to the customer.

Then came the explosion of the e-commerce web sites, as companies rushed to "test the waters" for the online selling of products and services. The existing paradigm for web development didn't prove successful as Internet savvy customers focused on the overall web experience and not the flashy technology. Many of these early web sites were poorly linked to the information infrastructure of the organization. Security and reliability became major issues. Many web site designs were viewed as "unusable" from the customer's perspective in terms of search capabilities, navigation, design layout, performance, customer service, and other factors. As a result, many of the dot coms failed when customers failed to use them.

A lesson learned from the dot com crisis is that we need more effective tools, techniques, and practices for developing e-businesses that prove to be successful. This includes the development and integration of web applications, information architectures, legacy systems, and communication mechanisms, among others.

Web engineering and data warehousing are two integral areas for which technological advances are being made in the e-business arena. Web engineering tools and techniques are needed to help us design more user-friendly web sites that are secure, reliable, understandable, and easy to use. They are also needed to maintain design standards such that enhancements and modifications can be readily made without major redesign efforts. Web engineering plays an integral role in ensuring that the e-business information architecture supports existing and new data requirements.

Data warehousing is an important aspect of e-business as legacy systems have vast amounts of data ready for analysis and interpretation. This data, as part of the e-business information architecture, is important in gaining insight into financial, marketing, organizational, and other online success factors. Both historical and operational data are essential components in understanding e-business opportunities in local and international marketplaces.

New technological advances associated with the Internet are offering interconnectivity in a global marketplace like never before. Internationally, remote areas are being reached offering products and services that were previously unavailable. Wireless technologies offer the means for anyone to be online anytime and anyplace. New opportunities are being explored in health, education, government, as well as, in the commercial sector utilizing both wired and wireless technologies. Innovations in web engineering and data warehousing are needed to meet the challenges of this ever-changing environment.

Shirley Becker
Florida Institute of Technology, USA

Preface

Capturing and utilizing data is a top priority of most businesses. Databases are fundamental to both internal and external business operations, but they can prove to be an expensive proposition. Increasingly important data are tied to information stored or gained from a company's Web site. Understandably, businesses throughout the world are exploring new technologies to optimize their database and Web site performance. For many organizations, data warehousing and data mining techniques offer promising improvements for the use and capture of data. Additionally, Web-base engineering is a significant development in the process of Web page design and development. In order to get the most from these emerging technologies, business people, academics, researchers and students alike need to have access to the most up-to-date information about the development and implementations of these technologies. This timely new book addresses the important issues of justifying the cost of data warehousing techniques, data allocation, data model development and successful use of Web-engineering technologies. The authors represent a wide variety of perspectives and provide insights from many different cultures and organizational and industrial backgrounds.

Chapter 1 entitled, "An Introduction to Information Technology and Business Intelligence" by Stephan Kudyba (USA) and Richard Hoptroff (The Netherlands) provides a comprehensive introduction to the use of information technology within the concept of business intelligence. The chapter looks at the technologies currently in use, describes current economic theory and applies them both to developing effective business strategies.

Chapter 2 entitled, "Some Issues in Design of Data Warehousing Systems" by Ladjel Bellatreche and Kamalakar Karlapalem, the University of Science and Technology (Hong Kong), and Mukesh Mohania, Western Michigan University (USA), defines data warehousing and treats two major problems in data warehousing, namely data partitioning and the interaction between indexes and materialized views. The chapter discusses these problems in depth and provides practical solutions to solving these problems. Additionally, the authors discuss the impact of these problems on future strategies for data warehousing.

Chapter 3 entitled "Benchmarking Data Mining Algorithms" by Balaji Rajagopalan of Oakland University and Ravi Krovi of the University of Akron (USA) reports on a study which sought to test the theory that machine-learning algorithms, which are under no assumptions, should outperform their traditional counterparts when mining business' databases. The results presented in the chapter can be used as prescriptive guidelines for the applicability of data mining techniques.

Chapter 4 entitled, "Justifying Data Warehousing Investments" by Ram Kumar of the University of North Carolina-Charlotte (USA) outlines an approach to justifying data warehousing investments that is based on the concept of options in finance. The approach described is being increasingly recognized as superior to the traditional methods used by finance professionals.

Chapter 5 entitled, "Data Mining: A New Arsenal for Strategic Decision-Making" by Sufi Nazem and Bongsik Shin of the University of Nebraska-Omaha (USA) provides an overview of this emerging technology and related trends in the application of data mining. Because data mining activities are often confidential and highly proprietary in nature, they rarely enjoy an open discussion. This chapter addresses the issues associated with data mining from an organizational perspective.

Chapter 6 entitled, "What's in a Name? Exploring the Metaphorical Implications of Data Warehousing in Concept and Practice" by Elizabeth Davidson of the University of Hawaii-Manoa (USA) examines the metaphorical implications of the data warehousing concept and presents the findings of an empirical study of a data warehousing project that illustrated limitations of metaphor in practice. The authors discuss the implications of this metaphorical analysis for both theory and practice.

Chapter 7 entitled, "Incremental Data Allocation and Reallocation in Distributed Database Systems" by Amita Goyal Chin of Virginia Commonwealth University (USA) presents the Partial REALLOCATE and Full REALLOCATE heuristics for efficient data reallocation. By allowing only incremental introduction of servers into the distributed database system, complexity is controlled and costs are minimized. The authors use simple examples and a simulator to provide a framework for data reallocation in distributed database systems. The framework discussed produces nearly optimal solutions when compared with exhaustive methods.

Chapter 8 entitled, "Using Business Rules Within a Design Process of Active Databases" by Youssef Amghar, Madjid Meziane and Andre Flory of the National Institute of Applied Sciences (France) proposes a uniform approach to modeling business rules such as active rules, integrity constraints, etc. The authors then extend the state diagrams that are widely used for dynamic modeling. Additionally, the authors outline new functionalities of Computer Aided Software Engineering to take into consideration the active database specificities.

Chapter 9 entitled, "A Methodology for Datawarehouse Design: Conceptual Modeling" by Jose Maria Cavero and Esperanza Marcos of Universidad Rey Juan Carlos, Mario Piattini of Universidad de Castilla-La Mancha, and Adolfo Sanchez of Cronos Iberica (Spain) presents a multidimensional data warehouse development methodology based on and integrated with a Public software development methodology. This chapter is written in response to the need for a generally accepted complete methodology for data warehouse design.

Chapter 10 entitled "Assessing and Improving the Quality of Knowledge Discovery Data" of Herna Viktor and Niek du Plooy of the University of Pretoria (South Africa) discusses the use of data mining and data generation techniques including feature selection, case selection and outlier detection, to assess and improve the quality of data. In this approach, redundant, low quality data are removed from the data repository, and high quality data patterns are dynamically added to the set. The chapter also looks at the relationship between data capturing and the social aspects of office work.

Chapter 11 entitled, "Complementing the Data Warehouse with Information Filtered from the Web" by Witold Abramowicz, Pawel Jan Kalczynski and Krzysztof Wecel of The Poznan University of Economics (Poland) examines the requirements for profiling in the data warehousing environments. The authors explore many issues concerning personalization, information overflow, user models and situatedness. The authors then analyze the contributing factors of the filtering process and offer some points to be considered during the extension of the evaluated system.

Chapter 12 entitled, "Justification of Data Warehousing Projects" by Reinhard Jung and Robert Winter of the University of St. Gallen (Switzerland) analyzes the economic justification for data warehousing projects and presents the results of a large academia-industry collaboration in the area of the non-technical issues of data warehousing. The authors derive basic steps and responsibilities for the justification of data warehousing projects based on an analysis of traditional approaches to economic IT project justification.

Chapter 13 entitled, "A Survey of Spatial Data Mining Methods Databases and Statistics Point of View" by Karine Zeitouni of the University of Versailles (France) reviews the data mining methods that are combined with Geographic Information Systems (GIS) for carrying out spatial analysis of geographic data. The chapter looks at data mining functions applied to spatial analysis data and highlights their specificity compared with their application to classical data. The authors then discuss two current methods of implementing these data mining techniques and discuss the similarities and differences between the approaches.

Chapter 14 entitled, "Efficient Query Processing with Structural Join Indexing in an Object Relational Data Warehousing Environment" by Vivekanand

Gopalkrishnan and Qing Li of City University of Hong Kong and Kamalakar Karlapalem of University of Science and Technology, Hong Kong (China) demonstrates the efficacy of building semantic-rich hybrid data indexes incorporating Structural Join Index Hierarch (SJIH) and Object Relational Data Warehousing (ORDW) views. The authors demonstrate this technique by using a set of queries to use a hill-climbing heuristic algorithm to select optima SJIHs, thereby embedding query semantics into the indexing framework. The authors also analyze the effectiveness of their approach when compared to a pointer chasing approach.

Chapter 15 entitled, "An Electronic Commerce Framework for Small and Medium Enterprises" by Anne Banks Pidduck of the University of Waterloo-Ontario (Canada) and Quang Ngoc Tran of TurboLinux describes an electronic commerce framework for small businesses. The authors discuss various services that a typical small business may want to provide for its customers and offer possible technologies to implement the services. Finally, the authors propose a prototype to generate such a model.

Chapter 16 entitled, "The VLEG Based Production and Maintenance Process for Web-Based Learning Applications" by Jorg Schelhase and Udo Winand of Universitat GH Kassel, Fachbereich Wirtschaftswissenschaften (Germany) presents an application for the realization, management and maintenance of Web-based learning applications. The chapter looks specifically at the Web-engineering principles necessary for improving Web-based learning.

Chapter 17 entitled, "Specification of Components Based on the WebComposistion Component Model" by Martin Gaedke of the University of Karlsruhe and Klaus Turowski of the University of Federal Armed Forces (Germany) illustrates the benefits of the WebComposition Component Model in overcoming the gap between implementation and design models. This gap has proven to be quite a difficulty in the use of modern software engineering practices applied to Web-Engineering. The authors further illustrate the usefulness of their model by applying it to real world-applications.

Chapter 18 entitled, "The Development of Ordered SQL Packages to Support Data Warehousing" by Wilfred Ng of the Hong Kong University of Science and Technology (China) and Mark Levene of the University of London (United Kingdom) propose the enhancement of database languages in order to manipulate user-defined data orderings. The chapter further extends the relational model to incorporate partial orderings into data domains and describes the ordered relational model. The authors then discuss the details of the generic operations arising from OSQL packages called OSQL_Time, OSQL_INCOMP and OSQL_FUZZY.

Data warehousing and data mining techniques offer much to businesses. These important techniques can be used to optimize databases and get the most from a business's data collecting efforts. Additionally, these chapters discuss the emerging technology of Web-based engineering and discuss the practicalities of implementing Web-based engineering as a beneficial alternative to traditional software engineering practices. The chapters in this book address the issues important to businesses implementing these techniques, researchers investigating them, and students studying them. From how to assess the quality of the data and to justify the expense of these techniques to comparisons of various Web-based engineering techniques and specific languages and methods used to implement them, the chapters contained herein provide insightful theoretical discussion as well as practical examples and case studies illustrating the concepts discussed. This book is a must-have for all those interested in understanding and applying the most up-to-date research and practice in data warehousing, data mining and Web-based engineering.

IRM Press
December 2001

Chapter 1

An Introduction
to Information Technology
and Business Intelligence

Stephan Kudyba
Economic Consultant, USA

Richard Hoptroff
Consultant, The Netherlands

The world of commerce has undergone a transformation since the early 1990s, which has increasingly included the utilization of information technologies by firms across industry sectors in order to achieve greater productivity and profitability. In other words, through use of such technologies as mainframes, PCs, telecommunications, state-of-the-art software applications and the Internet, corporations seek to utilize productive resources in a way that augment the efficiency with which they provide the most appropriate mix of goods and services to their ultimate consumer. This process has provided the backbone to the evolution of the information economy which has included increased investment in information technology (IT), the demand for IT labor and the initiation of such new paradigms as e-commerce.

A DRIVING SOURCE OF PRODUCTIVITY:
(IT, Economic Theory and Business Strategy)

Over the past six years, the US economy has been in a state of expansion which has included impressive growth in Gross Domestic Product (GDP), increased demand for labor and surprisingly low inflation. In fact, this lack of rising prices in the face of prolonged expansion has perplexed many analysts, economists and business leaders since traditional theory implies that as growth increases and unemployment declines, there is an increased probability of price pressures. One potential reason behind this anomaly of today's situation incorporates the notion of productivity at the firm level.

Productivity generally refers to the process by which firms use productive inputs to generate output. If they can more effectively or intelligently incorporate labor, machinery or technology and materials, they can better manage their underlying costs and maintain moderate prices for goods and services to the ultimate consumer. Firms can achieve increased productivity by combining the power of today's information technology with the tools of economic theory and business strategy. This notion has been supported by recent statistics.

There is evidence that the US economy is in the early stages of a powerful new wave of innovation. The leading edge is the information revolution, which permeates every sector of the economy. Over the last year, for example, high tech has taken half a percentage point off of inflation and added almost a full point to growth…Since 1990, productivity of non-financial corporations has risen at a strong 2.1% rate, far above the 1.5% seen from 1973 to 1990. Manufacturing has done even better: Since 1990, factory productivity has been soaring at 3.6% annually, the fastest rate in the post-World War II era.[1]

Economic and business theory provide the fundamental underpinnings to firm level productivity as these disciplines address such issues regarding the utilization of optimal levels of resources (land, labor, capital and materials) in bringing a good or service to the market (Varian, 1996). Business strategy bridges off the more rigorous microeconomic theory by applying it within the corporate world. It addresses such issues as accurately identifying corresponding target markets, consumer preferences and effectively managing the process by which goods and services are produced and delivered to the consumer. Information technology enables corporate managers and decision makers to more effectively devise appropriate business strategy based on economic theory by facilitating the flow of information to decision makers and employees throughout an organization. Through effective use of IT, managers can more quickly analyze operations in the organization which include such areas as:

1) Production (inventory and process and supply chain management)
2) Marketing/advertising and optimal pricing
3) Customer relationship management applications (churn, response)

4) Distribution (wholesale, retail, e-commerce)

5) Finance

6) Human resources

7) Telecomm and network processes (call center effectiveness and network usage)

This notion of the enhancement of business efficiency through the use of IT has received increased attention from analysts and economists. In fact, Federal Reserve Chairman Alan Greenspan addressed this topic in his 1997 Humphrey Hawkins testimony to US Congress.

"A surge in capital investment in high tech equipment that began in early 1993 has since strengthened. Purchases of computer and telecommunications equipment have risen at…an astonishing rate of nearly 25 percent in real terms, reflecting the fall in the prices of this equipment. Presumably companies have come to perceive a significant increase in profit opportunities from exploiting the improved productivity of these new technologies.

What we may be observing in the current environment is a number of key technologies, some even mature, finally interacting to create significant new opportunities for value creation…Broad advancements in software have enabled us to capitalize on the prodigious gains in hardware capacity. The interaction of both of these has created the Internet.

An expected result of the widespread and effective application of information and other technologies would be a significant increase in productivity and reduction in business costs."[2]

Significant breakthroughs in computer processing capabilities (e.g., increases in speed and memory made possible by such processing from Pentium, AMD CYRX) have opened the door for a host of high powered, state-of-the-art software applications. Innovations in telecommunications technology, which has augmented the capabilities of the Internet, has further enabled the proliferation of vital information via intranets and extranets. The entire combination of the above technologies come together to create a vast information network that becomes the information pulse of a given enterprise. Essential components to such a system involves the following components:

Data warehouses	OLAP
Data marts	Data mining
Data extraction and storage technology	Internet-related technology for Web deployment (intranets and extranets)
Query and reporting software	

Of course all the above assumes essential core technology including server mainframes and the proliferation of personal computers to establish local and wide area networks and workstations.

For a more detailed application of economic theory and productivity refer to Appendix (1) at the end of this book.

AN INTRODUCTION TO BUSINESS INTELLIGENCE

The competitive forces prevailing in the world of commerce today require firms to operate as efficiently and productively as possible in order to maintain and enhance market share, profitability and shareholder value. An essential element to achieving success involves the continuous enhancement of knowledge and understanding of the business environment by employees at all levels. This is can be accomplished by implementing processes which augment the accessibility and communication of value added information throughout the organization. As a result there has been an increased demand for cutting-edge information technology by businesses in all industries. This increased demand has further resulted in an explosion in the development and implementation of technologies that store, retrieve, manipulate, report, analyze and communicate data. The increased availability of value-added information throughout the firm helps to augment the knowledge of the business to a variety of individuals. Decision makers can use information to better devise and implement business strategy based on Economic theory to more effectively manage available resources in order to best meet the needs of the ultimate consumer.

The BI Spectrum: Data Extraction & Report Writing, OLAP, Intranets, Extranets and the Internet

The above process has evolved into a philosophy referred to as "business intelligence." This topic is increasingly being adopted by management across industry sectors. Elaborate IT networks enable users to extract data (demographic and transactional) into structured reports, which can be distributed throughout an enterprise via intranets. As a result, information corresponding to particular functional areas is more readily available to consumers of the data.

For example sales managers can quickly view monthly sales activity by salesperson corresponding to particular products and in some cases the clients who have purchased. Of course, this seems like nothing new, however the true value-added of this process involves:

1) The speed at which reports are generated
2) The accuracy of the content
3) The degree of user friendly format
4) The ability to disperse the information to appropriate individuals

The next level of BI involves the organization of aggregate information that facilitates on-line analysis of corresponding business scenarios. OLAP or on-line analytical processing involves aggregating large volumes of data in a cube which can be accessed by information consumers in a user friendly manner. OLAP enables users to quickly view particular business applications:

1) Product/Service sales, cost and profits
2) Distribution information
3) Production processes (inventory, materials, parts and supplier information)
4) Advertising, marketing and promotion expenditures on products across regions of operations
5) Customer activities according to product or service.
6) Employee performance and activity rates
7) Financial details and many, many more.

By slicing, dicing and filtering on particular business application dimensions (e.g., cost of production according to a particular product line, corresponding to a production facility utilizing a particular supplier) "information consumers" can more accurately identify sources of successes or failures in particular processes and take appropriate action (e.g., apply a corresponding business strategy to enhance process efficiency). A very simple illustration of a cube is included below, but just think of it as a multi-dimensional viewing tool of various business attributes, where illustrations are both numeric and graphic and can be changed according to the users specifications in an on-line, timely manner.

Basic OLAP analysis which enables users to quickly analyze the operations of functional areas of a given firm can help initiate efficiency enhancing strategies.

Figure 1

Time	Region	Product	Supplier	Parts	Measure
Years	Division	Product Lines	Names	Types	Cost
Quarters	Branch	Brands			Defect Rate
Months					Delay Rates

In the above case, this may entail switching to more reliable, cost effective suppliers, implementing new automation to the production process, (that reduce time and labor costs), or potentially outsource particular activities that can be done more cost effectively by outside partnerships. However the cycle does not end here. Business intelligence entails a constant routine of extracting corresponding information, creating and distributing accurate reports, and updating cubes for information consumers to analyze, identify successes and failures and take appropriate actions. It is only the continuous process of implementing policy and reviewing how those policies either successfully or ineffectively achieved the goals they were set out to attain which results in increased efficiency for the organization.

This brings us to the next level of business intelligence, which incorporates analytical technology that produces forecasts and identifies cause and effect relationships corresponding to a particular business scenario. At this level business intelligence involves the utilization of data mining technology.

BUSINESS INTELLIGENCE EXTENDED: AN INTRODUCTION TO DATA MINING

The term *data mining* has evolved over the years. In fact, as early as 5-10 years ago, many had referred to OLAP analysis as data mining. As the information age continued to evolve, which facilitated the availability of greater amounts of higher quality data, business analysts began to demand more information from this data. The proliferation of customized reports and the ability to scan data by geographic region, functional area and product or process performance, gave end-users a better picture of what was happening in their respective organization. In other words, complex information systems give information consumers or decision-makers a static view of their business. The next logical inquiry increasingly included such topics as:

1) Are there statistical relationships between variables in my data and are they reliable?
2) How strong are the relationships between variables?
3) If I change certain explanatory variables, what corresponding changes can I expect in the variable in question?
4) What can I expect in the future?

The term "variable" in these cases corresponds to factors that comprise a particular business application, (e.g., price, units sold, advertising spent...).

The term *data mining* today is characterized as the technology which incorporates the application of statistical techniques in conjunction with mathematical formulas that attempt to identify significant relationships between variables in historical data, which can then be used to forecast, perform sensitivity analysis, (e.g., what happens to my target/dependent variable when I change one or more of my explanatory/independent variables) or just identify significant relationships that exist in the data at hand. Some of the common methodologies that make up the world of data mining include:

1) Clustering
2) Segmentation and classification
3) Neural networks
4) Regression
5) Association analysis

A related topic that is often associated within the data mining spectrum is visualization. In this book we won't formally include this as a key mining technique but will classify it more as a mining augmentation methodology.

The following section will give a brief introduction on some typical business problems that require some of the more widely used data mining techniques.

An Introduction to Data Mining Methodologies

For the remainder of this book the terms:

1) **Explanatory, Driving, Descriptive, Independent variables** are used interchangeably and refer to those variables that explain the variation of a particular target variable.
2) **Target, Dependent variable** refers to a particular measure you seek to explain, (e.g., sales, units sold, defect rate, probability.)

Regression

One of the most widely used forms of high-end data mining refers to the application of regression analysis to historical data. This technique involves specifying a functional form that best describes the relationship between explanatory, driving or independent variables and the target or dependent variable the decision maker is looking to explain. Business analysts typically utilize regression to identify the quantitative relationships that exist between variables and enable them to forecast into the future. Some common questions that regression can answer involve:

1) What can I expect my sales or unit demand to be over the next six months given seasonal factors?
2) How does advertising expenditure affect market share over time or sales over time?
3) How does the strength of the economy affect my business over time?

Regression models also enable analysts to perform "what if" or sensitivity analysis. Some common examples include price elasticity, or in other words, how does a 1% increase in price affect my product demand. Other examples include how response rates change if I launch a particular marketing or promotional campaign, or how certain compensation policies affect employee performance and many more.

Regression also incorporates a probabilistic measurement between particular driving variables and whether an event will occur. Common examples, which involve the application of logit regression, include such topics as customer churning, employee retention and risk profiles. Given a sample of historical data, logit regression mining will enable the analyst to determine the probability that a customer will cancel, an employee will leave or how the risk profile of a portfolio will change in relation to changing the profile of a customer, employee or characteristic of a particular portfolio. The applicability of this technique is far reaching. The following is a list of a number of examples of how it may be deployed in business.

- Employee turnover
- Customer churn
- Customer response rate (mailing, marketing campaigns)
- Risk profiling (companies or individual's propensity to default)
- E-business Web site (effectiveness...hit rates)

Neural Networks

The next technological component of high-end data mining involves the incorporation of neural network architecture, which is also referred to as artificial intelligence, that utilize predictive algorithms. This technology has many similar characteristics to that of regression in that the application generally examines historical data, and utilizes a functional form that best equates explanatory variables and the target variable in a manner that minimizes the error between what the model had produced and what actually occurred in the past and then applies this function to future data. Neural networks are a bit more complex as they incorporate intensive program architectures in attempting to identify linear, non-linear and patterned relationships in historical data. This topic will be addressed in more detail later in this book, but keep in mind that this data mining approach can be used for the same type of applications as those mentioned for regression.

Segmentation

Another major group that comprises the world of data mining involves technology that identifies not only statistically significant relationships between explanatory and target variables, but determines noteworthy segments within variable categories that illustrate prevalent impacts on the target variable. In other words, segmentation technology that incorporates CART (Classification and Regression Trees) or CHAID (Chi-Squared Automatic Interaction Detection) will not only identify a statistical relationship between an individuals age and the potential to respond to a particular product offering, but will identify significant age segments that are more or less likely to respond.

For example, A credit card offering of free airline miles may be more successful with a particular age group and income level. Typical applications for segmentation and classification mining technology include many of those mentioned in the regression section and are as follows:
- Credit profiles
- Response profiles
- Customer/employee churn profiles
- Profitability, cost, revenue profiles
- Process (operational profiles)

The key differentiator between classification and segmentation with that of regression and neural network technology mentioned above is the inability of the former to perform sensitivity analysis or forecasting.

Clustering

Another major category in the data mining spectrum involves the application of clustering technology. This methodology facilitates the identification of relationships between groups of data within the vast amounts of information in a data warehouse. Through the incorporation of statistics and algorithms, the clustering technique seeks to partition large data bases into distinctly different groups comprised of variables that are statistically similar within the same group. At first glance, the user may mistakenly seek to apply a segmentation application mentioned earlier, however, this would be inappropriate. Clustering applications are designed to identify groupings of similar variables without the incorporation of a target while segmentation identifies relationships between independent/explanatory variables and a given target. The resulting groups or clusters help the end user make some sense out of vast amounts of data. For example, clustering may identify significant customer or product groupings.

One of the most popular clustering techniques incorporates the K-nearest neighbor approach which examines each new case of data to identify which group or neighbor it most closely resembles. The drawback of this application is that there is no guarantee that resulting clusters provide any value-added to the end user. Resulting clusters may just not make any sense with regards to the overall business environment. Because of limitations of this technique, (no predictive, "what if" or variable/target connection), this topic will not be addressed in great detail in the remainder of this work. For more details regarding this method and other mining approaches see Berry (2000).

Association Analysis

Another major component of data mining that will be addressed involves the application of association analysis. The association technique generally involves the process of measuring probabilities or propensities of the occurrence of a particular event given the occurrence of other events. One of the most popular association applications deals with market basket analysis, (e.g., what is the probability or percentage occurrence that a consumer purchases product A if they also buy product B). This technique incorporates the use of frequency and probability functions to estimate the percentage chance of occurrences. Business strategists can leverage off of market basket analysis by applying such techniques as cross-selling and up-selling. Association analysis empowers the end user to identify purchasing patterns of customers, which permits them to more accurately offer complimentary products or services to perspective buyers. This topic will be addressed in greater detail in the following chapter and chapter 7.

A more recent extension of association analysis has been the addition of sequence analysis to the association methodology. This is particularly applicable in e-business for Web site analysis. As the information economy continues to evolve, not only (.com) enterprises rely on the internet but the more traditional brick-and-mortar style organizations are adopting e-business by implementing Web deployment into the market place. Both (B2B) and (B2C) strategies are becoming common infrastructure in organizations throughout the world of commerce. Association and sequence technology analyzes (B2C) buy facilitating a type of market basket analysis through various levels of a Web site, (e.g., what does a customer click on and in what order, to finally reach the destination level of a particular site).

Association and sequence techniques are not the only mining applications that are applicable to e-business or Web Site analysis. Regression, neural networks, segmentation and clustering may all play a role in analyzing the vast amounts of Internet-related data. This subject will be addressed in later chapters.

Visualization Tools For Reporting and Monitoring:
The Humble Chart

The final area in the data mining spectrum involves the implementation of visual aid methodologies to analyze patterns and relationships in your data. As was previously mentioned, this methodology is not grounded in statistics and mathematics but relies on graphic illustrations. Therefore, it not only plays a role in complementing data mining techniques but also provides a value added across the business intelligence spectrum (e.g., OLAP).

The graphical representation of complex data, often by no more than drawing a chart, is such a straightforward complement of data mining that it is often overlooked. It is extremely powerful because it provides a direct interface to the most powerful pattern finding mechanism in the world – your own eyes. The topic is covered in more depth in Neurath (1980), Tufte (1983), Zelazny (1996) and Horn (1998).

Application Areas

Graphical representations of data take a while to get used to. Typically, when you first look at a chart, a sequence of three things happen:
1. The patterns jump out at you.
2. You take a minute to find out what the axes represent.
3. You spend a few more minutes working out what the chart is saying.

The speed of the first step is the major advantage of visualization. The lack of speed in the next two steps are its main disadvantages. Visualization will therefore be most useful in applications such as reporting and monitoring, where the axes stay the same; only the numbers change. This eliminates the cumbersome steps 2 and 3.

Visualization is best applied for monitoring a regular stream of incoming data. Examples include financial market data and weekly/monthly corporate financial reports. In these situations, nothing will communicate the information more quickly than a chart, especially if the same chart format is used, day in, day out.

Basic Chart Types

A visualization should be kept as simple as possible. Axes should be labeled, units specified, and sources cited. Zelazny (1996) cites five basic chart types which people are familiar with and identifies the key types of patterns they attempt to convey. They include:
1) Pie charts
2) Bar charts (items, correlations, changes)

3) Column charts (distribution and time series)
4) Line chart (distribution and time series)
5) Scatter plots

Figure 2

The pie chart shows proportions: how a whole unit is divided up into components. For example, it is often used to show how big a slice of the market each competitor has, or how much each product line or region contributes to a company's revenues or profits. Negative values cause problems for this chart.

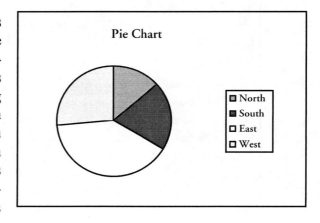

Figure 3

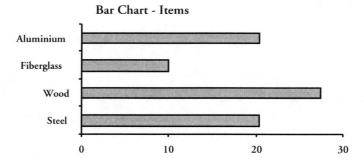

Simple bar charts are used to itemize quantities. Compound charts can be used to show correlations between variables or changes in variables over time.

Column charts, relying on the Western eye's tendency to see a flow from left to right, are useful for conveying quantities when the items being charted represent a logical sequence such as a time series or a frequency distribution.

Line charts serve the same purpose as column charts but are preferred if there are a large number of records or the records represent sample values of a continuously varying quantity.

Scatter charts are useful for showing correlations between variables when there are a large number of records.

In addition to the basic chart formats given above, an essential topic for effective visualization is a well-defined and logical color scheme. Color

Figure 4

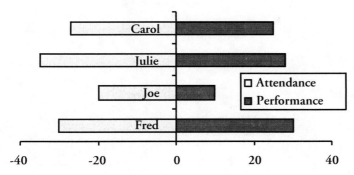

Bar Chart - Correlation

Figure 5

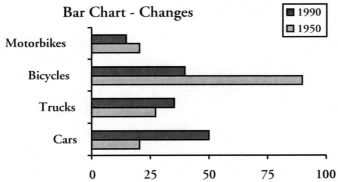

Bar Chart - Changes

Figure 6

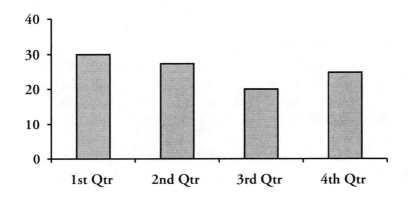

Column Chart - Time Series

Figure 7

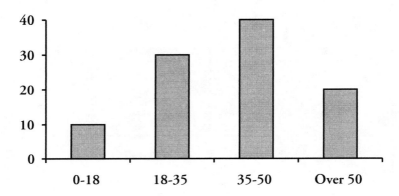

Column Chart - Distribution

Figure 8

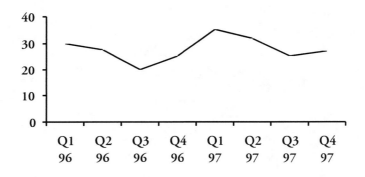

Line Chart - Time Series

schemes of corresponding variables and segments of variables should be designed to highlight important relationships and not introduce meaningless distractions that may render the visualization useless.

Visualization can also be used to complement other mining methodologies. For example, association analysis mentioned above, helps identify the quantitative relationships between customer activities regarding product purchases. Approaches such as Market Basket Analysis help decision makers identify customer affinities. The addition of visualization to this process can result in a significant value-added to the analytical process by providing a clear graphical view of existing relationships in the data. Figure 11 addresses this topic.

The analyst not only has the numeric indication of buying patterns but now can visually view the results. Within just a few minutes, the analysts

Figure 9

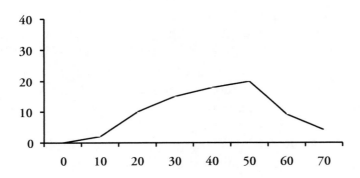

Line Chart - Distribution

Figure 10

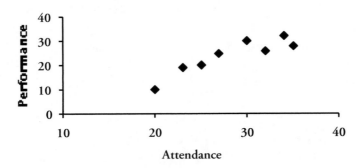

Scatter Chart - Correlation

Figure 11

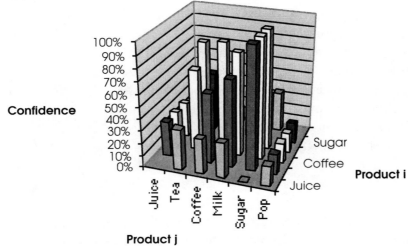

can determine the likelihoods of purchasing patterns that were uncovered by MBA.

Visualization Tricks and Gimmicks

The complexities and gimmicks which are often added to visualization software can be a distraction rather than an advantage. Exotic or interactive graphical representations are, because they are new to the viewer, an unnecessary effort to interpret. The most effective visualizations are often created using the basic charting capabilities of a spreadsheet or slice and dice tool (with some effort to choose pleasing rather than distracting colors).

One gimmick which can be effective is the ability to animate a chart. If this is used to show the evolution of data over time, trends can be spotted through the eye's ability to follow movement very well.

Although visualization techniques are often taken for granted, the closer look offered over the past few pages reminds users of the true value added this methodology offers to various forms of analysis. As a result, many of today's data mining and OLAP offerings incorporate robust graphic capabilities.

This completes the introduction to business intelligence and the various mining methodologies. The next sections will more closely tie the process of augmenting business intelligence through the interaction and effective utilization of software applications.

THE BUSINESS INTELLIGENCE CYCLE

The components of information technology mentioned above all come together to comprise vast IT systems. Data storage, extraction and report writing technology helps users access and transform vast amounts of information located in data warehouses to a more user friendly format which creates business related reports in a timely fashion. As a result, the vast number of consumers of static reports within an organization receive information that corresponds to their functional areas in a more timely manner.

These software applications also enable users to manipulate granular level warehouse data into more manageable aggregated data that can be stored in a multidimensional cube. Once again, information consumers can readily analyze data according to business related subject areas. Effectively created cubes provide the environment for users to quickly slice and dice and filter on particular dimensions in order to conduct static analysis both in a numeric and graphic view.

OLAP users can more easily work interactively with large amounts of data through user-friendly navigation to increase their knowledge according to their corresponding domain, functional area or strategic business unit.

The mining portion of this knowledge enhancing process augments the static OLAP approach in a number of ways. One of these entails a reliability check in the cube building process. The effectiveness of OLAP relies on well designed and constructed cubes. Many times cube designers miss the focus of the information a particular cube should include or may include too much information. Clustering, segmentation and potential neural network mining techniques can provide a statistical value added to the cube building process. These techniques give the cube designer a reliable view of what types of variables relate to each other and should perhaps, be grouped together in a cube environment. Clustering provides the more basic approach to identifying statistical relationships between groups of data, which is appropriate in applications where data volumes are extreme or users have little idea of potential relationships between variables.

Segmentation gives a bit more detailed approach to the cube building process. Users who want to construct a particular business centric cube (profitability cube) can set a particular target and run numerous potential drivers through CART or CHAID to identify the significant drivers or variables associated with the target. This process helps filter out useless or noisy information.

Using Mining to Extend OLAP

The next issue in which data mining augments the knowledge building process is that it enables the decision maker to better understand the interactions between related variables that drive a particular business application. OLAP provides a tremendous base for enlightening users on what potential drivers are and have been. Mining provides the next step, which validates the relationships between drivers and also quantifies the relationships. It complements/augments OLAP by providing a more rigid examination of business attributes. Mining validates relationships through statistical techniques, which can yield more concise and reliable analysis.

Segmentation quickly provides a statistically based picture of the profile of your particular application. For example, does age or income level really influence customers purchasing habits and if so what are the significant segments that require further analysis? Regression and neural networks on the other hand, not only identify statistically significant relationships between variables in a given application but also provide a resulting model or functional form that enables the user to forecast into the future or quantitatively identify how changing one variable actually changes a target variable. A very common example refers to how pricing policies effect demand. Segmentation will identify whether there is a statistical relationship between the two variables and which segments of pricing policies affect demand but regression and neural networks enable the user to "plug in" various prices and examine resulting changes in demand. This process can be done over time as well to determine demand schedules into the future.

The power of mining is extended as it facilitates not only the identification of relationships between one variable and its target but incorporate multivariate approaches, which in many cases, more accurately depicts the essential elements of business applications. In the above example, demand is not only a function of price but incorporates such factors as advertising and promotions and competitors behaviors. Segmentation, regression and neural nets facilitate the analysis of multivariate business applications. For example, common business practice incorporates product differentiation strategies, which may include charging a higher price for a given product in conjunction with aggressive advertising campaigns to establish a differentiation from competitors. Therefore, a more accurate analysis is not just price on product demand but price policies along with advertising expenditure on product demand.

CLOSING THOUGHTS ON BUSINESS INTELLIGENCE AND PRODUCTIVITY

You've read about complex IT systems that incorporate data extraction, reporting, on line analytical processing, data mining and the communication of information within companies and between companies and their customers, partners and suppliers. These systems generally facilitate a more streamlined flow of data throughout the world of commerce. State of the art software applications enable information users to store, extract, manipulate, analyze and communicate greater amounts of data more easily. But what does this really mean?

With a more timely and streamlined flow of more accurate, business related information, decision makers across the pyramid of the structure of the firm, have a better idea of what is happening in the world in which they operate. Not only do they more quickly receive reports that are more understandable, but many can navigate through business related cubes of data to answer a multitude of business questions in a timely manner. At the higher end of this spectrum, they can actually utilize models that quantify relationships between business drivers, which enable them to achieve a more accurate understanding of what to expect in the future. In other words, if certain events occur or are proposed there is less uncertainty regarding the corresponding results. The key to business intelligence is the reduction of uncertainty in the business environment. The ability to capture, access, manipulate, analyze and communicate relevant data helps reduce the unknown. For example, decision makers have a greater intelligence regarding which products are selling the best in a particular region, by a particular branch, by a particular consumer segment, and can have a more accurate idea of what to expect in the future given the implementation of corresponding business strategy.

Reducing Uncertainty by Minimizing the Variance

OK the process sounds Nirvana like...however it isn't. The process of storing data and extracting the correct variables in the correct format corresponding to a particular business application is by no means an easy task, and has nowhere near been perfected. In fact, the entire process of analyzing information, implementing appropriate business strategies and monitoring the success of those strategies is a continuous loop of data storage, retrieval, reporting, analyzing and implementing appropriate strategies. This core decision stage of this loop entails analyzing the results of policies against what was expected, identifying the sources of variance and taking the appropriate steps to minimize those variances. Variances in this case refer to uncertainty in the business process, or in other words, factors that have influenced your policies, which the decision-makers did not account for. The reduction of variance simply refers to the reduction of uncertainties or unknowns in the business process. By reducing variances, management has achieved a greater knowledge of their environment and has greater control over the operations of their enterprise.

Results Don't Happen Automatically (Technology must be utilized appropriately)

One pitfall that many organizations experience with regards to IT implementation and the resulting gains from business intelligence is that the link between technology and its effective utilization is not seamless, therefore enhanced business intelligence does not always occur. Appropriate systems, education/training and management skills are essential to achieving synergies from IT investment. (For a theoretical and empirical description see Weill, 1992).

Systems which can process appropriate volumes of data, which have natural integration both internally and with external partners and suppliers and are "user friendly" to the appropriate user are some core building blocks to an effective IT system. Once these fundamental issues have been achieved, which is not an easy process given differing needs according to functional areas within an enterprise, personnel must be trained or consultants utilized to achieve the full potential of the IT solution. Finally, and potentially of greatest importance, are effective management skills. Managerial skills require the know how to not only oversee the process just described (appropriate systems and user knowledge of them), they must be able to act on the information the systems are producing. Of course this process involves all tiers of management, from the lowest levels to the very top, from IT personnel to business strategists. Streamlining or optimizing this process should yield value added results. Investment in information technology alone does not insure firm-level productivity. IT must be used appropriately in order to extract the full benefits of its functionality. From data extraction and report writing, to OLAP and data mining, investment in education and training are essential to positive results.

Data mining involves the incorporation of more complex technology to help answer higher level enterprise problems, (how does advertising effect my market share?…how do pricing policies affect my demand?…what motivates my workers?). A requirement for effective data mining is the incorporation of accurate information with the appropriate methodology by individuals with the appropriate skills. The bottom line then is that with the proper IT infrastructure and worker skills to use them, business intelligence of the enterprise has a much greater chance to be enhanced. Decision makers can then ultimately apply the theoretical strategies of business and economics to enhance productivity and increase profitability and shareholder value.

ENDNOTES

[1]   Mandel M. "You Ain't Seen Nothing Yet," *Business Week Magazine*, McGraw-Hill, Feb, 1999.

[2]   Greenspan, Alan, Federal Reserve Board Humphrey Hawkins Testimony, July 1997.

REFERENCES

Berry, M. and Linoff, G. (2000). *Mastering Data Mining (The Art and Science of Customer Relationship Management)*, Wiley Computer Publishing.

Gujarati, D. (1988). *Basic Econometrics* (2nd ed.), McGraw-Hill.

Horn, R. E. (1998). *Visual Language,* Bainbridge Island, WA: Macro VU Press.

Neurath, M. (1990). *International Picture Language,* Dept of Typography & Graphic Communication, University of Reading, UK.

Tufte, E R. (1983). *The Visual Display of Quantitative Information*, Chesire CT: Graphics Press.

Varian, H. (1996). *Intermediate Microeconomics* (4th ed.), NY: W. W. Norton & Company.

Weill, P. (1992). The Relationship Between Investment in Information Technology and Firm Performance, *Information Systems Research,* December.

Zelanzy, G. (1996). *Say it With Charts,* McGraw-Hill.

Chapter VI

Some Issues
in Design
of Data Warehousing
Systems

Ladjel Bellatreche and Kamalakar Karlapalem
University of Science Technology, Clear Water Bay Kowloon, Hong
Kong, People's Republic of China

Mukesh Mohania
Western Michigan University, USA

INTRODUCTION

Information is one of the most valuable assets of an organization, and when used properly can assist intelligent decision-making that can significantly improve the functioning of an organization. Data warehousing is a recent technology that allows information to be easily and efficiently accessed for decision-making activities. On-line analytical processing (OLAP) tools are well studied for complex data analysis. A data warehouse is a *set of subject-oriented, integrated, time varying and non-volatile databases used to support the decision-making activities* (Inmon, 1992).

The conceptual architecture of a data warehousing system is shown in Figure 1. The data warehouse creation and management component includes software tools for selecting data from information sources (which could be operational, legacy, external, etc., and may be distributed, autonomous and heterogeneous), cleaning, transforming, integrating and propagating data

Figure 1. A Conceptual data warehousing architecture

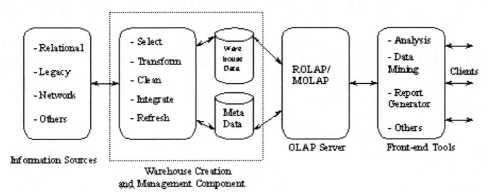

into the data warehouse. It also refreshes the warehouse data and meta-data when source data is updated. This component is also responsible for managing the warehouse data, creating indices on data tables, data partitioning and updating meta-data. The warehouse data contains the detail data, summary data, consolidated data and/or multidimensional data.

The meta-data is generally held in a separate repository. The meta-data contains the informational data about the creation, management and usage of the data warehouse. It serves as a bridge between the users of the warehouse and the data contained in it. The warehouse data is also accessed by the OLAP server to present the data in a multidimensional way to the front-end tools (such as analytical tools, report writers, spreadsheets and data-mining tools) for analysis and informational purposes. Basically, the OLAP server interprets client queries (the client interacts with front-end tools and passes these queries to the OLAP server) and converts them into complex SQL queries required to access the warehouse data. It might also access the data from the primary sources if the client's queries need operational data. Finally, the OLAP server passes the multidimensional views of data to the front-end tools, and these tools format the data according to the client's requirements.

There are two approaches to creating the warehouse data - bottom-up and top-down. In a bottom-up approach, the data is obtained from the primary sources based on the data warehouse applications and a profile of the likely queries which is typically known in advance. The data is then selected, transformed, and integrated by data acquisition tools. In a top-down approach, the data is obtained from the primary sources whenever a query is posed. In this case, the warehouse system determines the primary data sources in order to answer the query. These two approaches are similar to eager and lazy approaches discussed in Widom (1995). The bottom-up approach is used in data warehousing because user queries can be answered immediately and data analysis can be done efficiently, since data will always be available in the warehouse. Hence, this approach is feasible and improves the performance of the system. Another approach is a hybrid approach, which combines aspects of the bottom-up and top-down approaches. In this approach, some data is stored in a warehouse, and other data can be obtained from the primary sources on demand (Hull and Zhou, 1999).

The warehouse data is typically modeled *multi-dimensionally*. The multidimensional data model (Agrawal et al., 1997; Mohania et al., forthcoming) has proved to be the most suitable for OLAP applications. OLAP tools provide an environment for decision-making and business modeling activities by supporting ad-hoc queries. There are two ways to implement a multidimensional data model:

• by using the underlying relational architecture to project a pseudo-multidimensional model and
• by using true multidimensional data structures such as, arrays.

We discuss the multidimensional model and the implementation schemes in the next section.

The data fragmentation is a very well-known method used in the relational databases and aims to reduce the cost of processing queries. This technique can be adapted to the data warehouse environments, where the size of the fact tables is very large and there are many join operations. In the third section, we describe the fragmentation technique and show how it can be applied to data warehouse star/snowflake schemas.

Warehouse data can be seen as a set of materialized views, which are derived from the source data. OLAP queries can be executed efficiently over materialized views, but the number of views that should be materialized at the warehouse needs to be controlled, or else this can result to materialize all possible queries (this is known as *data explosion*).We then discuss the design issues related to warehouse views.

The technique of view materialization is hampered by the fact that one needs to anticipate the queries to materialize at the warehouse. The queries issued at the data warehouse are mostly *ad-hoc* and cannot be effectively anticipated at all times. Thus, answering these queries requires effective indexing methods since queries involve joins on multiple tables. The traditional indexing methods in relational databases do not work well in the data-warehousing environment. New access structures have been proposed for data warehousing environments. We investigate different types of indexing schemes in the next section.

The view and index selection problems are two problems mostly studied independently in data warehouses. This causes an inefficient distribution of resources (space, computation time, maintenance time, etc.) between views and indexes. In the final section, we discuss the problem of distributing space between views and indices in order to select two sets of materialized views and indexes to guarantee a performance.

DATA MODELS FOR A DATA WAREHOUSE

The data models for designing traditional OLTP systems are not well suited for modeling complex queries in data warehousing environment. The transactions in OLTP systems are made up of simple, pre-defined queries. In the data warehousing environments, the queries tend to use joins on more tables, have a larger computation time and are ad-hoc in nature. This kind of processing environment warrants a new perspective to data modeling. The *multidimensional* data model, i.e., the *data cube*, turned out to be an adequate model that provides a way to aggregate facts along multiple attributes, called dimensions. Data is stored as *facts* and *dimensions*, instead of rows and columns, as in relational data model. Facts are numeric or factual data that represents a specific business activity, and the dimension represents a single perspective on the data. Each dimension is described by a set of attributes.

A multidimensional data model (MDDM) supports complex decision queries on huge amounts of enterprise and temporal data. It provides us with an integrated environment for summarizing (using aggregate functions or by

Figure 2. A data cube.

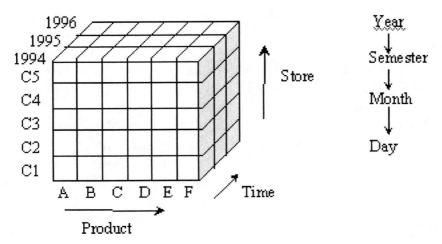

applying some formulae) information across multiple dimensions. MDDM has now become the preferred choice of many vendors as the platform for building new On-Line Analytical Processing (OLAP) tools. The user has the leverage to and the dimensions, thereby allowing him/her to use different dimensions during an interactive query session. The data cube allows the user to visualize aggregated facts multidimensionally. The level of detail retrieved depends on the number of dimensions used in the data cube. When the data cube has got more than three dimensions, it is called the *hypercube*. The dimensions form the axes of the hypercube, and the solution space represents the facts as aggregates on measure attributes (see Figure 2).

Implementation Schemes

The conceptual multidimensional data model can be physically realized in two ways: (1) by using traditional relational databases, called ROLAP *architecture* (Relational On-Line Analytical Processing) (example includes Informix Red Brick Warehouse (Informix Inc., 1997); or (2) by making use of specialized multidimensional databases, called MOLAP architecture (Multidimensional On-Line Analytical Processing) (example includes Hyperion Essbase OLAP Server). The advantage of MOLAP architecture is that it provides a direct multidimensional view of the data, whereas the ROLAP architecture is just a multidimensional interface to relational data. On the other hand, the ROLAP architecture has two major advantages: (1) it can be used and easily integrated into other existing relational database systems, and (2) relational data can be stored more efficiently than multidimensional data (Vasiliadis and Sellis, 1999).

We will briefly describe in detail each approach.

Relational Scheme

This scheme stores the data in specialized relational tables, called fact and dimension tables. It provides a multidimensional view of the data by using relational technology as an underlying data model. Facts are stored in the fact table, and dimensions are stored in the dimension table. Facts in the fact table are linked through their dimensions. The attributes that are stored in the dimension table may exhibit attribute hierarchy.

Example 1: Let us consider a star schema from Informix corporation (1997). It models the sales activities for a given company. The schema consists of three dimension tables CUSTOMER, PRODUCT and TIME, and one fact table, SALES. The tables and attributes of the schema are shown in Figure 3.

Figure 3. An example of a star schema

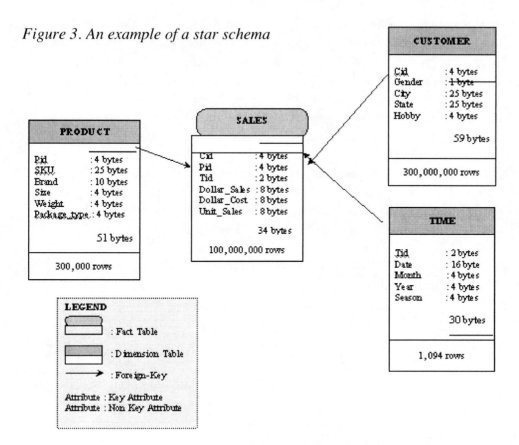

Star schema/snowflake schema is used to support multidimensional data representation. It offers flexibility, but often at the cost of performance because of more joins for each query required. A star/snowflake schema models a consistent set of facts (aggregated) in a fact table, and the descriptive attributes about the facts are stored in multiple dimension tables. This schema makes heavy use of de-normalization to optimize complex aggregate query processing. In a star schema, a single fact table is related to each dimension table in a many-to-one (M:1) relationship. Each dimension tuple is pointed to many fact tuples. Dimension tables are joined to fact tables through foreign key reference; there is a referential integrity constraint between fact table and dimension table. The primary key of the fact table is a combination of the primary keys of dimension tables. Note that multiple fact tables can be related to the same dimension table, and the size of dimension table is very small as compared to the fact table.

As we can see in Figure 3, the dimension table TIME is de-normalized and, therefore, the star schema does not capture hierarchies (i.e., dependencies among attributes) directly. This is captured in snowflake schema. Here, the dimension tables are normalized for simplifying the data selecting operations related to the dimensions, and thereby capture attribute hierarchies. In this schema, the multiple fact tables are created for different aggregate levels by pre-computing aggregate values. This schema projects better semantic representation of business dimensions. Figure 4 shows an example of snowflake schema after *TIME* dimension table in Figure 3 has been normalized.

A star schema/snowflake schema is usually a query-centric design as opposed to a conventional update-centric schema design employed in OLTP applications. The typical queries on the star schema are commonly referred to as star-join queries, and exhibit the following characteristics:

1) there is a multi-table join among the large fact table and multiple smaller dimension tables, and

Figure 4: Snowflake Schema Example

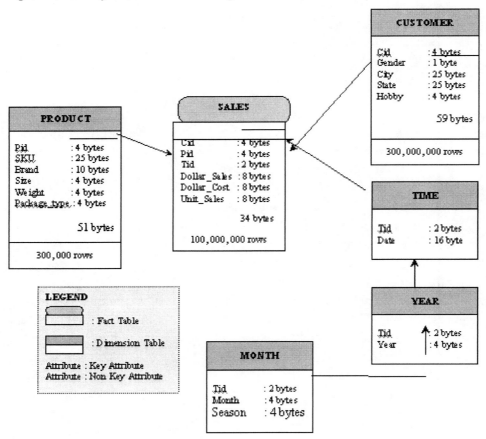

2) each of the dimension tables involved in the join has multiple selection predicates on its descriptive attributes.

Multidimensional scheme

This scheme stores data in a matrix using an array-based storage structure. Each cell in the array is formed by the intersection of all the dimensions, therefore, not all cells have a value. The multidimensional data set requires smaller data storage since the data is clustered compactly in the multidimensional array. The values of the dimensions need not be explicitly stored. The n-dimensional table schema is used to support multidimensional data representation, which is described next.

n-*dimensional table schema*

An n-dimensional table schema is the fundamental structure of a multi-dimensional database, which draws the terminology of the statistical data-bases. The attribute set associated with this schema is of two kinds: param-eters and measures. An n-dimensional table has a set of attributes R and a set of dimensions D associated with it. Each dimension is characterized by a distinct subset of attributes from R, called the parameters of that dimension. The attributes in R, which are not parameters of any dimension, are called the measure attributes. This approach is a very unique way of flattening the data cube since the table structure is inherently multidimensional. The actual contents of the table are essentially orthogonal to the associated structure. Each data cube can be represented in an n-dimensional table as table entries. These table entries have to be extended by certain dimensions to interpret their meaning. The current literature on an n-dimensional table, however, does not give an implementation of the MDDB, which is different from the implemen-tation suggested by the already existing schemas. This implementation breaks up the dimensional table into dimension tables and fact tables, which snowballs into snowflake schema and traditional ROLAP. The challenge with the research community is to find mechanisms that translate this multidimensional table into a true multidimensional implementation. This would require us to look at new data structures for the implementation of multiple dimensions in one table. The relation in relational data model is a classic example of an 0-dimensional table.

Constraints on the Cube Model

In a relational schema, we can define a number of integrity constraints in the conceptual design. These constraints can be broadly classified as key constraints, referential integrity constraints, not null constraint, relation-based check constraints, attribute-based check constraints and general assertions (business rules). These constraints can be easily translated into triggers that keep the relational database consistent at all times. This concept of defining constraints based on dependencies can be mapped to a multidimensional scenario.

The current literature on modeling multidimensional databases has not discussed the constraints on the data cube. In a relational model, the integrity and business constraints that are defined in the conceptual schema provide for efficient design, implementation and maintenance of the database. Taking a cue from the relational model, we need to identify and enumerate the constraints that exist in the multidimensional model. An exploratory research area would be to categorize the cube constraints into classes and compare them with the relational constraints. The constraints can be broadly classified into two categories: *intra-cube* constraints and *inter-cube* constraints. The intra-cube constraints define constraints within a cube by exploiting the relationships that exist between the various attributes of a cube. The relationship between the various dimensions in a cube, the relationships between the dimensions and measure attributes in a cube, dimension attribute hierarchy and other cell characteristics are some of the key cube features that need to be formalized as a set of intra-cube constraints. The inter-cube constraints define relationships between two or more cubes. There are various considerations in defining inter-cube constraints. Such constraints can be defined by considering the relationships between dimensions in different cubes, the relationships between measures in different cubes, the relationships between measures in one cube and dimensions in the other cube and the overall relationship between two cubes, i.e., two cubes might merge into one, one cube might be a subset of the other cube, etc.

Operations in Multidimensional Data Models

Data warehousing query operations include standard SQL operations, such as selection, projection and join. In addition, it supports various extensions to aggregate functions, for example, percentile functions (e.g., top 20 percentile of all products), rank functions (e.g., top 10 products), mean, mode and median. One of the important extensions to the existing query language is to support multiple 'group-by' by defining *roll-up*, *drill-down* and *cube* operators. Roll-up corresponds to doing further group-by on the same data object. Note that the roll-up operator is order sensitive, that is, when it is defined in the extended SQL, the order of columns (attributes) matters. The function of drill-down operation is the opposite of roll-up.

The hypercube, which involves joining of multiple tables to represent facts, needs a new set of algebraic operations. A new algebra needs to be proposed for the multidimensional environment. The idea of faster query processing requires an extension to existing SQL in the existing environment. New operators like *cube*, push, pull, restrict, star join and merge have been proposed in literature but all these operators are very specific to the schema for which they are designed (Agrawal, Gupta and Sarawagi, 1997; Lehner, Ruf and Teschke, 1996; Li and Wang, 1996; Bauer and Lehner, 1997).

DATA PARTITIONING
IN DATA WAREHOUSES

The data-partitioning concept in the context of distributed databases aims to reduce query execution tile and facilitates the parallel execution of queries. In this chapter, we use partitioning and fragmentation interchangeably. Partitioning is an important technique for implementing very large tables in data warehouse environments (Oracle Corp., 1999). The idea is to make a large table more manageable by dividing it in multiple tables. Oracle first introduced a limited form of partitioning with partition views in Oracle7 (Release 7.3). Fully functional table partitioning is available in Oracle8 (Oracle Corp., 1999).

Motivation

The main reasons that motivate us to use the partitioning in data warehouse environments are:

1. Building indices like join indices on the whole data warehouse schema can cause a problem of maintaining them, because whenever we need to execute a query, the whole indices should be loaded from the disk to the main memory. The sizes of this type of indices can be very huge (Bellatreche et al., 1999). But if we have a partitioned data warehouse with N sub-star schemas, we can build for each sub-star schema join indices that can be easier to maintain and to load. On the other hand, even though indexing can help in providing good access support at the physical level, the number of irrelevant data retrieved during the query processing can still be very high. The partitioning aims to reduce irrelevant data accesses (Bellatreche et al., 2000; O'Neil and Quass, 1997).

2. Since the OLAP queries use joins of multiple dimension tables and a fact table, the derived horizontal partitioning developed in the relational

databases can be used to efficiently process joins across multiple relations (Ceri et al., 1982).

3. Designing a warehouse database for an integrated enterprise is a very complicated and iterative process since it involves collection of data from many departments/units and data cleaning, and requires extensive business modeling. Therefore, some organizations have preferred to develop a datamart to meet requirements specific to a departmental or restricted community of users. Of course, the development of datamarts entails the lower cost and shorter implementation time. The role of the datamart is to present convenient **subsets of a data warehouse** to consumers having specific functional needs. There can be two approaches for developing the datamart--either it can be designed integrating data from source data (bottom-up approach) or it can be designed deriving the data from the warehouse (top-down approach) (Firestone, 1997) (see Figure 5). By advocating the top-down design for datamart and without partitioning, we need to assign to each datamart the whole data warehouse; even this datamart accesses only a subset of this data warehouse. By analyzing the needs of each datamart, we can partition the centralized data warehouse into several fragments that can be used as allocation units for datamarts.

4. parallelism is a good technique to speed up the OLAP query execution. With a partitioned sub-star schema, we can associate each star schema to one machine and execute queries in parallel. For example, MCI Telecommunications' IT data center in Colorado Springs is running a

Figure 5. The top-down flow from DWs to datamarts

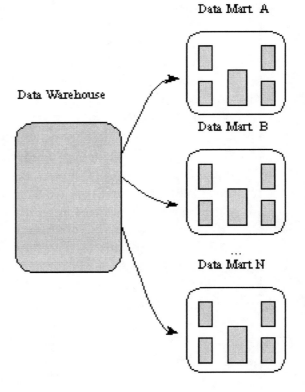

massive 2TB decision support data warehouse called warehouseMCI on a 104 node IBM RS/6000 SP massively parallel processing system. The database is growing at the rate of 100GB to 200GB per month (Simpson, 1996).

5. the main disadvantage of the horizontal partitioning in databases is that when update operations occur, some tuples may migrate from one fragment to another. The migration operation is sometimes costly. In the data warehouse environments, updates are not common (Karlapalem et al., 1994) compared to the append operations. Even if there are some update operations (Hurtado et al., 1999), the data warehouses are only periodically updated in a batch fashion (O'Neil and Quass, 1997), during the time where the data warehouses are unavailable for querying. This situation makes the utilization of horizontal partitioning feasible, as the reorganization of its fragments can be done off-line.

Partitioning plays an important role in the design of a distributed database system (Özsu and Valduriez, 1991). It enables the definition of appropriate units of distribution, which enhance query performance, by enabling concurrent and parallel execution of queries. Data partitioning involves using the application/query processing characteristics to fragment the database into a set of fragments. Each fragment contains data that is most relevant to one or more applications. Therefore, an application accesses only a subset of fragments (not the complete database) thus reducing the amount of irrelevant data accessed (Öszu and Valduriez, 1991).

Fragmentation Alternatives

Two types of partitioning are possible: vertical and horizontal.

Given a relation $R(K, A_1, A_2, ..., A_n)$, where $A_1, A_2, ..., A_n$ are the attributes and K is the key, each attribute Ai has a domain of values $dom(A_i)$. The vertical partitioning (VP) of R is given by $V^1(K, A^1_1, A^1_2, ..., A^1_{kl})$, $V^2(K, A^2_1, A^2_2, ..., A^2_{kl})$, ... $V^p(K, A^p_1, A^p_2, ..., A^p_{kl})$ where in each $A^i_j \in \{A_1, A_2, ..., A_n\}$. The set of vertical fragments $V_1, V_2, ..., V_p$ is disjointed if each attribute A_i ($1 \leq i \leq n$) of relation R belongs to one and only one vertical fragment. The key K is repeated in each fragment to facilitate the reconstruction of relation R from the vertical fragments. The original relation R is reconstructed by joining the p vertical fragments. The main advantage of vertical partitioning is that it reduces irrelevant attribute accesses of the user queries. The main disadvantage is that it requires the costly join operation to access two or more vertical fragments.

Each horizontal fragment of relation R is a subset of the tuples of R. The tuples of each fragment must satisfy a predicate clause. The horizontal partitioning (HP) of R is given by: $H_1 = \sigma_{cl1} (R) H_2 = \sigma_{cl2} (R)$, where cl_i is a predicate clause. The reconstruction of the relation R is obtained by uniting the original fragments with the union operation.

Two versions of HP are cited by the researchers (Ceri et al., 1982): primary HP and derived HP. Primary HP of a relation is performed using predicates that are defined on that relation. On the other hand, derived HP is the partitioning of a relation that results from predicates defined on another relation.

A lot of work has been done on the partitioning in the relational models (Özsu and Valduriez, 1991) and object models (Bellatreche et al., 1997, 1998, 2000; Ezeife and Barker, 1995) compared to the data warehouses. In this chapter, we will concentrate on HP because it is well adapted to data warehouses. Also, the TPC-D benchmark (TPC Home Page) in its implementation allows the utilization of HP, but it discards the utilization of the vertical partitioning.

Horizontal Partitioning Algorithms in Databases

Several algorithms were proposed in performing HP (Ceri and Pelagatti, 1984; Navathe et al., 1984; Navathe et al., 1995; Navathe and Ra, 1989; Bellatreche et al., 1997; Ezeife and Barker, 1995; Dewitt et al., 1986). These algorithms can be classified into two main categories: (1) query-driven algorithms and (2) data-driven algorithms.

Query-driven algorithms

These algorithms are performed based on a set of most frequently asked queries and their access frequencies for a specific application (Navathe et al., 1995). These queries respect the 80/20 rule, which considers that 20% of user queries account for 80% of the total data access in the database system. This category of algorithms is divided into two types:

- **Affinity based algorithms:** The most proposed algorithms for HP in the relational and object databases are affinity-based (Ceri and Pelagatti, 1984; Özsu and Valduriez, 1991; Navathe and Ra, 1989; Bellatreche et al., 1997; Ezeife and Barker, 1995). The affinities are used between predicates. Predicates having a high affinity are grouped together to form a horizontal fragment. The algorithm of Navathe et al. (1989) starts by performing an analysis on the predicates defined by a set of queries accessing a relation to be horizontally partitioned. From these queries, a predicate usage matrix is built. The rows and the columns of this matrix represent the queries and predicates, respectively. The value of this matrix *use* (Q_i, p_j) is equal to 1, if the predicate p_i is used by the query Q_j, otherwise it is equal to 0. This matrix is used to generate another matrix called predicate affinity matrix, where each value $(p_l, p_{l'})$ represents the sum of the frequencies of queries which access predicates p_l and $p_{l'}$, simultaneously. After that, the authors apply the graph-based algorithm defined in Navathe, Karlapalem and Ra (1995) to group these predicates into a disjointed subset of predicates. (Each subset of predicates can be a potential horizontal fragment.)

In each group, the authors optimize (if it is possible) by using implications between the predicates defined in queries, then they generate the horizontal fragments. Each fragment is defined by a Boolean combination of predicates using the logical connectives $(\wedge, \vee)$.

Özsu et al. (1991) developed a primary algorithm for HP. This algorithm has an input, a set of queries and their frequencies. Its steps are as follows:

1. Determine the set of *complete* and *minimal* predicates $P = \{p_1, p_2, ..., p_n\}$. A complete set of predicates is *minimal* if, and only if, all its elements are relevant.

2. Determine the set of *minterm predicates* M of P, which is defined as follow: $M = \{m_i \mid m_i = \wedge_{pj \in p} p^*_j\}$, where $p^*_j = p_j$ or $p^*_j = \neg p_j$ $(1 \leq j \leq n)$, $(1 \leq i \leq 2^n)$.

3. Eliminate the contradictory minterm predicates using the predicate implications.

This approach can generate 2^n horizontal fragments for n simple predicates.

- **Cost-based algorithms**: The main disadvantage of affinity-based algorithms is that they use affinity as a measure of grouping of predicates. This measure can *only express the affinity between pairs of attributes*, and cannot express the affinity among several (more than two) predicates (Bellatreche et al., 1998). On the other hand, all these algorithms ignore the physical costs corresponding to the savings in the amount of irrelevant data accessed. The utility of the HP can be measured by the amount of savings in disk accesses required for query execution. It is often argued that the advantage of the HP lies in the reduction in the amount of savings in disk accesses required for query execution (Karlapalem et al., 1994; Hevner and Rao, 1988). Although this argument is understandable from an intuitive point of view, not much work has been done to evaluate the impact of this type of partitioning on query evaluation on a quantitative basis. According to Karlapalem et al. (1994), two factors, input/output (IO) operations and data transfer, are the most important for the performance of the applications in distributed database systems. As the goal of partitioning of the classes is to obtain the minimum cost for processing a set of queries, we develop an algorithm based on a cost-driven approach for executing a set of queries that respects the 80/20 rules. In Bellatreche, Karlapalem and Basak (1998) and Bellatreche, Karlapalem and Li,(1998)., we have proposed an algorithm for the horizontal partitioning in the object model based on a cost model, but it can be applied to the relational model. The basic idea of this algorithm is that it starts with a set of the most frequently asked queries, and other physical factors (like predicate selectivity, class size, page size, instance length, etc.).

Let C be the class to be horizontally partitioned, and let $P = \{p_1, p_2, \ldots, p_N\}$ be the set of simple predicates defined on this class using a set of queries. From these simple predicates, we generate all minterm predicates (Ceri, Negri adn Pelagatti, 1982) $\{m_1, m_2, \ldots, m_z\}$. After that, we exhaustively enumerate all possible schemes. A scheme can be represented by a minterm or a combination of several minterms using the logical connector OR. For each scheme, we calculate the cost of executing all these queries. The objective of this cost model is to calculate the cost of executing these queries, each of which accesses a set of objects. The cost of a query is directly proportional to the number of pages it accesses. The total cost is estimated in terms of disk page accesses. Finally, the scheme with minimal cost gives the best HP of the class C.

We note that this algorithm needs an exhaustive enumeration strategy to generate all schemes. For small values of minterms, this procedure is not computationally expensive. However, for large values of number of minterms, the computation is very expensive, for example, for 15 minterms, the number of schemes is 1,382,958,545. For further details about the complexity of enumerating all schemes, see Bellatreche, Karlapalem and Basak (1998).

To reduce the complexity of the cost-driven algorithm, we propose another algorithm called *approximate algorithm*, which is based on a hill-climbing technique (Jain, 1991). The approximate algorithm starts with the set of fragments generated by an algorithm that has a lower complexity (Bellatreche, Karlapalem and Simonet, 1997; Navathe and Ra, 1989). This algorithm gives rise to a set of fragments. Based on the queries accessing these fragments, the approximate algorithm tries to shrink or expand some fragments *in order to reduce the* query *processing cost*.

Data-driven algorithms

This kind of HP was studied in parallel databases and formulated as follows: suppose that we have *N* disks available, for any given row of a relation *R*, we must decide on which of the *N* disks it has to reside (Morse and Isaac, 1998). Three standard approaches are developed: range partitioning, round robin and hashing. With the range partitioning each of the *N* disks is associated with a range of key values. The main advantage of the range partitioning technique is that it acts as a kind of built-in index if tuples are retrieved based on the key values. But its main disadvantage is the data skew. In the second technique, the tuples are partitioned in a round-robin fashion. This strategy is used as the default strategy in Gamma machine (Dewitt et al., 1986). This technique avoids the load imbalance. Finally, the hash partitioning is performed using a hash function, where identical key values will be hashed to the same disk. It also avoids data skew.

Partitioning Issues in Data Warehouses

All work done on vertical partitioning in the data warehouse context has been applied on the physical design level (index selection problem). The vertical partitioning has been introduced in the definition of projection index proposed by O'Neil et al. (1997). Chaudhuri et al. (1999) developed a technique called index merging to reduce storage and maintenance of an index. Their method is somehow an extension of the vertical partitioning. Recently, Datta et al. (19990 developed a new indexing technique called Curio in data Warehouses, modeled by a star schema. This index speeds up the query processing and it does not require a lot of storage space.

Concerning the HP, a little work has been done. Noaman et al. (1999) proposed architecture for a distributed data warehouse. It is based on the ANSI/SPARC architecture (Tsichritzis and Klug, 1978) that has three levels of schemas: internal, conceptual and external. The distributed data warehouse design proposed by these authors is based on the top-down approach. There are two fundamental issues in this approach: fragmentation and allocation of the fragments to various sites. The authors proposed a horizontal fragmentation algorithm for a fact table of a data warehouse. This algorithm is an adaptation of the work done by Özsu and Valduriez (1991).

In this chapter, we present a methodology for partitioning a data warehouse modeled by a star schema, and we will show the issues and problems related to this problem.

Problems

Partitioning in data warehouses is more challenging compared to that in relational and object databases. This challenge is due to the several choices of partitioning schema of a star or snowflake schema:

1. Partition *only* the dimension tables using the primary partitioning. This scenario is not suitable for OLAP queries, because the sizes of dimension tables are generally small compared to the fact table. Most OLAP queries access the fact table, which is huge. Therefore, any partitioning that does not take into account the fact table is discarded.
2. Partition *only* the fact table using the primary partitioning. In a data warehouse modeled by a star schema, most OLAP queries access dimension tables first, and after that the fact table.
3. Partition *both* fact and dimension tables, but independently. This means that we use the primary partitioning to partition the fact and dimension tables without taking into account the relationship between these tables. Based on the previous choices, this partitioning does not benefit OLAP queries.
4. Partition *some/all* dimension tables using the primary partitioning, and use them to derive a partitioned fact table. This approach is best in applying partitioning in data warehouses, because it takes into consideration the queries requirements and the relationship between the fact table and dimension tables. In our study, we opt for last solution.

Partitioning Algorithm for a Star Schema

In Bellatreche, Karlapalem and Mohania (2000), we have proposed a methodology for fragmenting a star schema with dimension tables $\{D_1, D_2, ..., D_d\}$ and one fact table F. This methodology can be easily adapted to snowflake schemas. In this section, we will review the basic ideas of this approach.

Note that any fragmentation algorithm needs application information defined on the tables that have to be partitioned. The information is divided into two categories (Özsu and Valduriez, 1991): quantitative and qualitative. Quantitative information gives the selectivity factors of selection predicates and the frequencies of queries accessing these tables. Qualitative information gives the selection predicates defined on dimension tables.

A simple predicate p is defined by:

$$p : A_i, \theta \text{ Value}$$

where A_i is an attribute, $\theta \in \{=, <, \leq, >, \geq, \neq\}$, Value $\in Dom(A_i)$.

The algorithm we proposed in Bellatreche, Karlapalem and Mohania (2000) has as input a set of most frequently asked OLAP queries $Q = \{ Q_1, Q_2, ..., Q_N \}$ with their frequencies. The main steps of this algorithm are:

1. Enumeration of all simple predicates used by the n queries.
2. Attribution to each dimension table D_i ($1 \leq i \leq d$), its set of simple predicates (SSP^{Di}).

3. Each dimension table D_i having $SSP^{Di} = \phi$ cannot be fragmented. Let $D_{canditate}$ be the set of all dimension tables having a non-empty SSP^{Di}. Let g be the cardinality of $D_{canditate}$.

4. Application of COM_MIN algorithm (Özsu and Valduriez, 1991) to each dimension table D_i of $D_{canditate}$. This algorithm takes a set of simple predicates and then generates a set of complete and minimal.

5. For fragmenting a dimension table D_i, it is possible to use one of the algorithms proposed by Ceri, Negri and Pelagatti (1982) and Özsu and Valduriez (1991) in the relational model. These algorithms generate a set of disjointed fragments, but their complexities are exponential of the number of simple predicates used. As result, we use the algorithm proposed in the object model, which has a polynomial complexity (Bellatreche et al., 2000).

   Each dimension table D_i has m_i fragments $\{D_{i1}, D_{i2}..., D_{imi}\}$, where each fragment D_i is defined as follows:
   $D_{ij} = \sigma_{cl\,j}^{i}(D_i)$ where $\sigma_{cl\,j}^{i}(1 \leq i \leq g, 1 \leq j \leq m_i)$ represents a clause of simple predicates.

6. Partition the fact table using the fragmentation schema of the dimension tables.

The number of fragments of the fact table (N) is equal to: $N = \prod_{i=1}^{g} m_i$ (for more   details see Bellatreche et al. (2000)).

Therefore, the star schema S is decomposed into N sub-schemas $\{S_1, S_2,..., S_N\}$, where each one satisfies a clause of predicates.

Example 2: *To show how this algorithm works, let us consider the star schema in Figure 3 and the six OLAP queries obtained from Bellatreche, Karlapalem and Mohania (2000). From these queries, we enumerate all selection predicates:*

p_1 : C.Gender = 'M' , p_2 : C.Gender = "F" , p_3 : P.Packagetype = "Box" , p_4 : P.Packagetype = "Paper" , p_5 : T.Season = "Summer" and p_6 : T.Season = "Winter."

The set of simple predicates for each table are (Step 2): $SSP^{CUSTOMER} = \{p_1, p_2\}$, $SSP^{PRODUCT} = \{p_3, p_4\}$ and $SSP^{TIME} = \{p_5, p_6\}$.
For each set, we generate the set of complete and minimal simple predicates (Step 4). We obtain the following:

- *$SSP^{CUSTOMER}_{Min-Com} = \{p_1, p_2\}$,*
- *$SSP^{PRODUCT}_{Min-Com} = \{p_3, p_4\}$ and*
- *$SSP^{TIME}_{Min-Com} = \{p_5, p_6\}$*

By applying the fragmentation algorithm (Bellatreche, Karlapalem and Simonet, 2000) for each dimension table, we obtain the following fragments:

- *CUSTOMER : Cust_1 = $s_{Gender = 'M'}$ (CUSTOMER) and Cust_2 = $s_{Gender = 'F'}$*

(CUSTOMER),

- *PRODUCT : Prod_1 = $s_{Package\_type = 'Box'}$ (PRODUCT) and Prod_2 = $s_{Package\_type = 'Paper'}$ (PRODUCT),*
- *TIME : Time_1 = $s_{Saison = 'Winter'}$ (TIME) and Time_2 = $s_{Saison = 'Summer'}$ (PRODUCT),*

Finally, the fact table can be horizontally partitioned into eight (N = 2 x 2 x 2) fragments.

Our algorithm generates a large number of fragments of the fact table. For example, suppose that the dimension tables are fragmented as follows:

- *CUSTOMER* into 50 fragments using the State attribute case of 50 states in the USA.
- TIME into 12 fragments using the Month attribute.
- PRODUCT into two fragments using the Package_type.

Therefore, the fact table is fragmented into 1,200 (**50** x **12** x **2**) fragments.

Consequently, it will be very hard for the data warehouse administrator (DWA) to maintain these fragments. Therefore, it is important to reduce the number of fragments of the fact table. We focus on this problem in the next sections.

Horizontal partitioning and OLAP queries

When the derived HP is used to fragment a relation R based on the fragmentation schema of a relation S, two potential cases of join exist: simple join and partitioned join.

In the data warehouse context, when the fact table is horizontally partitioned based on the dimension tables, we will never have a partitioned join (i.e., the case wherein a horizontal fragment of the fact table has to be joined with more than one fragment of the dimension table will not occur). As a result, we will have only simple joins as given by the following theorem:

Theorem 1: *Let F and D_i be a fact table and a dimension table of a given star schema, respectively. If the dimension table D_i is horizontally partitioned into set of disjointed horizontal fragments, let say {D_{i1}, $D_{i2},...,$ D_{im}}, where each fragment is defined by clause predicate, and the fact table F is derived partitioned based on the HFs of D_i, then, the distributed join between F and D_i is always represented only by a simple join graph.*

Proof 1: *We prove it by contradiction. Let F_p be a fragment of the fact table F defined by: $F_p = F \chi D_{ij}$. Suppose that F_p can be joined with two fragments $D_{ij,}$ and D_{il} (l ≠ j) of the dimension table D_i. Consequently, we will have:*

$$F \chi D_{ij} \neq 0 \qquad\qquad (1)$$
$$F \chi D_{il} \neq 0 \qquad\qquad (2)$$

Note that the fragments of D_i are disjointed, and the fragment F_p is obtained using the semi-join operation between the fact table F and a fragment of dimension table D_i. Note that the join attributes are the foreign key of F and the primary key of D_i. Therefore, one semi-join condition among the two above defined in (1) and (2) is satisfied. In this case, $D_{ij} = D_{il}$. Since F_p can be any fragment of, and it is joinable with exactly one fragment of D_i, we conclude that the join graph between F and D_i is always simple. The theorem is true when we have a distributed join between the fact table and several dimension tables.

In a data warehouse modeled by a star schema, any fact table F that is derived from a horizontally partitioned based on HP schema of dimension tables $\{D_1, D_2, ..., D_d\}$ will result in simple distributed join graph. This has two advantages:

- It avoids costly total distributed join (i.e., every HF F_p ($1 \leq p \leq N$) of the fact table F joins with each and every HF D_{ik} of each and every dimension table D_i($1 \leq i \leq d$ and $1 \leq k \leq m_i$)).
- It facilitates parallel processing of multiple simple distributed joins.

The Correctness Rules of Our Proposed Algorithm

Any fragmentation algorithm must guarantee the correctness rules of fragmentation: completeness, reconstruction and disjointness.

- The completeness ensures that all tuples of a relation are mapped into at least one fragment without any loss. The completeness of the dimension tables is guaranteed by the use of the COM_MIN algorithm (Özsu and Valduriez, 1991; Ceri et al., 1982). The completeness of the derived horizontal fragmentation of the fact table is guaranteed as long as the referential integrity rule is satisfied among the dimension tables and the fact table.
- The reconstruction ensures that the fragmented relation can be reconstructed from its fragments (Özsu and Valduriez, 1991). In our case, the reconstruction of the fact and the dimension tables are obtained by union operation, i.e., $F = \cup^N_{i=1} F_i$ and $D_i = \cup^{mi}_{j=1} D_{ij}$.
- The disjointness ensures that the fragments of a relation are non-overlapping. This rule is satisfied for the dimension table since we used an no-overlap algorithm (Bellatreche et al., 2000). For the fragments of the fact table, the disjointness rule is guaranteed by the theorem 1.

Dimension Table Selection Problem

As we have seen in the previous section, the number of fragments of the fact table can be very large. This is due to the number of dimension tables used in fragmenting the fact table. In this section, we will give some issues on selecting dimension tables that reduce the number of fact table fragments. Any selection algorithm should satisfy the following constraints:

- avoids the explosion of the number of fragments of the fact table, and
- guarantees a good performance for executing a set of OLAP queries.

To reach the first objective, we give the DWA the possibility of choosing the number of fragments (W) that he/she considers is sufficient to maintain. To satisfy the second objective, we need to have the possibility of augmenting the number of fragments of the fact table until the performance is guaranteed. The problem is to find a compromise between the maintenance cost and query processing cost as shown in Figure 6.

To solve this problem, we developed a greedy algorithm (Bellatreche et al., 2000). From the number of fragments W that the DWA chooses, this algorithm starts by selecting one dimension table randomly. Once the selection is done, we partition the fact table based on the fragmentation schema of the dimension table. We compute the number of fragments of the fact table (N) and then the cost of executing a set of OLAP queries. We suppose we have a cost model for executing a set of queries. If the number of fragments N is less than W and there is an improvement of query processing cost, our algorithm selects another dimension and then it repeats the same process until the two conditions are satisfied. The main steps of this algorithm are shown in Figure 7. At the end of this algorithm, we obtain a partitioned data warehouse ensuring a good query processing cost and a maintenance cost.

Query Execution Strategy in Partitioned Star Schema

Since the dimension tables and fact table are horizontally partitioned, we need to ensure the data access transparency. That is, the user of the data

Figure 6: Cost Evolution

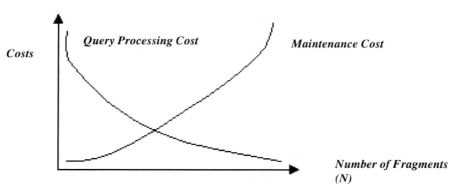

Figure 7. The steps of greedy algorithm

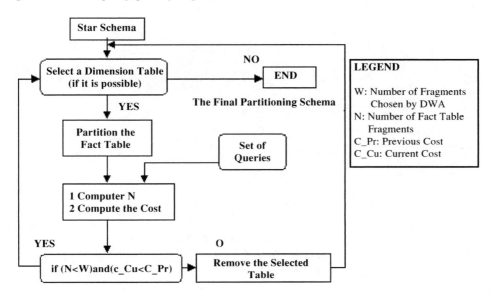

warehouse is purposefully unaware of the distribution of the data. Our goal is to provide to the data warehouse users the unpartitioned star schema, and the query optimizer task is to translate the OLAP queries on the unpartitioned star schema to partitioned star schemas. Before executing a query on a partitioned data warehouse, we need first to identify the sub-schemas satisfying this query as shown in Figure 8.

Definition 1: (**Relevant Predicate Attribute (RPA)** is an attribute that participates in a predicate that defines an HP. Any attribute that does not participate in defining a predicate that defines an HP is called an irrelevant predicate attribute.

Definition 2: (**Partitioning Specification Table**) Suppose we have an initial star schema S horizontally partitioned into sub-schemas $\{S_1, S_2,..., S_N\}$. The partitioning conditions for each partitioned table can be represented by a table called partitioning specification table of S. This table has three columns: the first one contains the table names, the second provides the fragments of its corresponding table and the last one reports the partitioning condition for each fragment.

Example 3: Suppose the dimension table CUSTOMER is partitioned into two fragments: Cust_1 and Cust_2, and the fact table is fragmented using these two fragments into Sales1 and Sales2. The corresponding partitioning specification table for this example is illustrated in Table 1.

From the partitioning specification table, we can conclude that : each

Figure 8. Sub-schemas identification

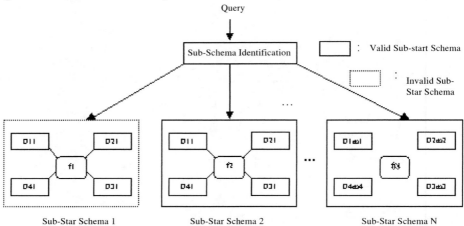

Table 1. Partitioning specification table

Table	Fragments	Fragmentation Condition
CUSTOMER	Cust_1	Gender = 'M'
	Cust_2	Gender = 'F'
SALES	Sales_1	SALES χ Cuct_1
	Sales_2	SALES χ Cust_2

attribute belonging to the partitioning specification table is a RPA. In our example, "Gender'" is the single RPA.

Fragment identification

Let Q be a query with p selection predicates defined on a partitioned star schema $S = \{S_1, S_2,..., S_N\}$. Our aim is to identify the sub-schema(s) that participate in executing Q. Let $SRPA$ be the set of RPA. Based on the selection predicates of the query Q and partitioning specification table, we proceed as follows:

- For each selection predicate SP_i $(1 \leq i \leq p)$, we define the function attr(SP_i), which gives us the name of the attribute used by SP_i. The union of attr(SP_i) gives us the names of all attributes used by Q. We call this set Query Predicate Attributes. Let $SPA(Q)$ be the set of all predicate attributes used by the query Q.
- Using $SPA(Q)$ and $SRPA(S)$, four scenarios are possible:
  1. $SPA(Q) = 0$, (the query does not contain any selection predicate). In this situation, two approaches are possible to execute Q:

a) Perform the union operations of all sub-schemas and then perform the join operations as in unpartitioned star schema.

b) Perform the join operations for each sub-schema and then assemble the result using the union operation.

2. $(SPA(Q) \neq 0)$ and $(SPA(Q) \cap SRPA(S) = 0)$ (the query has some selection predicates on non-partitioned dimension tables, or the predicate attribute of Q does not match the relevant predicate attribute). To execute this kind of query, we use the two approaches presented above.

3. $(SPA(Q) \cap SRPA(S) \neq \phi)$ means that some predicate attributes of the query Q match with certain RPA. In this case, we can easily determine the names of dimension tables and the fragments that participate in executing the query Q.

Results

In Bellatreche et al. (2000), we have developed two cost models to evaluate the utility of the HP. The first one is for unpartitioned star schema, and the second one is for partitioned star schema. These cost models are used for executing a set of frequently asked queries in the data warehouse. The objective of these cost models is to calculate the cost of executing these queries in terms of disk page accesses (IO cost) during the selection and join operations (which are the most used and most expensive operations in data warehouses (Lei and Ross, 1998). To characterize the improvement of performance using the horizontal fragmentation technique, we defined a normalized IO metric as follows:

$$Normalized\ IO = \frac{\#\ of\ IOs\ for\ a\ Horizontally\ Partitioned\ Star\ Schema}{\#\ of\ IOs\ for\ a\ Unpartitioned\ Star\ Schema}$$

We note that if the value of normalized IO is less than 1.0, then it implies that HP is beneficial. The main observations are:

- Horizontal fragmentation gives good performance compared to the unpartitioned case.
- Horizontal fragmentation may deteriorate the execution performance of certain queries, for example, the queries that do not have any selection predicates. To evaluate these two queries, we need to access all sub-star schemas.
- The number of partitioned dimension tables has a great impact on reducing the query processing cost. As the number of fragmented dimension tables increases, the performance increases too.

MATERIALIZED VIEWS

One of the techniques employed in data warehouses to improve performance is the creation of sets of materialized views. They are used to pre-compute and store aggregated data such as sum of sales. They can also be used to pre-compute joins with or without aggregations. So materialized views are used to reduce the overhead associated with expensive joins or aggregations for a large or an important class of queries (Oracle Corp., 1989). The data warehouse at the Mervyn's department-store chain, for instance, has a total of 2,400 pre-computed tables to improve query processing (Gupta, 1989). Materialized views can be used in several areas: *distributed computing* and *mobile computing*.

- In distributed environments, they are used to replicate data at distributed sites and synchronize updates done at several sites with conflict-resolution methods.
- In mobile computing, they are used to download a subset of data from central servers to mobile clients, with periodic refreshment from the central servers and propagation of updates by clients back to the central servers.

A materialized view definition can include any number of aggregates, as well as any number of joins. In several ways, a materialized view behaves like an index (Oracle Corp., 1999):

- The purpose of a materialized view is to increase request execution performance.
- The existence of a materialized view is transparent to applications (e.g., SQL applications), so a DWA can create or drop materialized views at any time without affecting the validity of applications.
- A materialized view consumes storage space.
- The contents of the materialized view must be maintained when the underlying tables are updated (modified).

All data warehousing products support materialized views (Oracle Corp., 1999; Sanjay et al., 2000).

Two major problems related to materialized views are: (1) the view selection problem and (2) the view maintenance problem.

View Selection

We initiated a discussion in the beginning of the chapter as to which views should be materialized at the data warehouse. To aid answering the queries efficiently, we materialize a set of views that are closely related to the queries at the data warehouse. We cannot materialize all possible views, as we are constrained by some resources like disk space, computation time or maintenance cost (Gupta, 1999). Hence, we need to select an appropriate set of views to materialize under some resource constraints. The view selection problem (VSP) is defined as: selection of views to materialize minimizes the query response time under some resource constraint. All studies showed that this problem is an NP-hard. The proposed solutions for the VSP can be divided into two categories: the static VSP and the dynamic VSP.

Static VSP: This problem starts with a set of frequently asked queries (apriori known), and then selects a set of materialized views that minimizes the query response time and under some constraint. The selected materialized views will be a benefit only for a query belonging to the set of a priori known queries.

Dynamic VSP: The static selection of views contradicts the dynamic nature of decision support analysis. Especially for ad-hoc queries where the expert user is looking for interesting trends in the data repository, the query pattern is difficult to predict (Kotidis and Roussopoulos, 1999). In addition, as the data and these trends are changing overtime, a static selection of views might very quickly become outdated. This means that the DWA should monitor the query pattern and periodically re-calibrate the materialized views by running theses algorithms. Kotidis and Roussopoulos (1999) present a system called DynaMat that dynamically materializes information at multiple levels of granularity in order to match the demand (workload), but also takes into account the maintenance restrictions for the warehouse, such as down time to update the views and space availability. This system unifies the view selection and view maintenance problems under a single problem. DynaMat constantly monitors incoming queries and materializes the best set of views subject to the space constraint. During updates, DynaMat reconciles the current selected materialized views and refreshes the most beneficial subset of it.

Algorithms for VSP

We have proposed several algorithms for VSP to find the optimal or near-optimal solutions for it. These algorithms can be classified into three categories based on the type of resource: (1) algorithms without resources (Baralis et al., 1997; Yang et al., 1997), (2) algorithms driven by the space constraint (Gupta, 1999) and (3) algorithms driven by maintenance cost (Gupta, 1999).

Algorithms without resource

We now discuss a heuristic (Baralis et al., 1997) in detail which uses the data cube technology and the lattice model. The lattice model feeds on the attribute hierarchy defined earlier. The nodes in the lattice diagram represent views (aggregated on certain dimensions) to be materialized at the data warehouse. If the dimensions of two views *a* and *b* exhibit attribute hierarchy such that *dim(a)* → *dim(b)*, then there is an edge from node *a* to node *b*. Node *a* is called the *ancestor* node and node *b* is called the *dependent* or *descendant* node. The lattice diagram allows us to establish relationships between views that need to be materialized. Some queries can be answered by using the already materialized views at the data warehouse. For answering such queries, we need not go to the raw data. The lattice diagram depicts dependencies between the views and a good view selection heuristic exploits this dependency. The view selection algorithm tries to minimize the average time required to evaluate a view and also keeps a constraint on the space requirements. The space requirements that can be expressed as the number of views to be materialized translates this into an optimization problem that is NP-complete. An approximate and acceptable solution for this problem is the *greedy* heuristic. The greedy algorithm selects a view from a set of views depending upon the benefit yielded on selecting that view. A view *a* that is materialized from view *b* incurs a materializing cost that is equal to the number of rows in view *b*. If there is a view *c* (materialized on *b*; number of rows in *c* £ number of rows in *b*) such that the view can be derived from *c*, the cost of materializing *a* reduces to the number of rows in *c*. Thus the benefit of materializing view *c* includes the benefit incurred by view *a* in the form of reduction in its materializing cost (number of rows in *b* - number of rows in *c*). The greedy heuristic selects a view that maximizes the benefit that will be yielded on materializing that view. The benefit of materializing each *dependent* view (a node in the lattice diagram) will change with the selection of an *ancestor* view in the data warehouse. After each selection is made, the benefit at each *dependent* node in the lattice is recalculated and a view with maximum benefit is selected. It has been shown that the greedy algorithm is at least 3/4 of optimal. The greedy algorithm can be extended to restrict on actual space requirements rather than the number of views to be materialized. The frequency with which the views are accessed can be incorporated in this algorithm. Different schema design methods will give a different set of tables at the data warehouse.

Yang et al. (1997) presented a framework to highlight issues of materialized view design. The basic concept the authors used to develop the view selection algorithm is a graph called "multiple view processing plan". This graph specifies the views that the data warehouse will maintain (either materialized or virtual). The MVPP is a directed acyclic graph that represents a query processing strategy of data warehouse views. The leaf nodes correspond to the base relations, and the root nodes represent the queries. We call the layer between root nodes and leaf nodes the potential view layer (PVL). This layer contains all potential materialized views. Each node in the PVL is assigned with two costs: the query processing cost and the maintenance cost (Yang et al., 1997) . Note that there can be more than one MVPP for the same set of queries depending upon the access characteristics of the application and the physical data warehouse parameters. If we have n-intermediate nodes, then we need to try 2^n combinations of nodes. Therefore, the authors formulate the VSP as an integer-programming problem.

Algorithms driven by space constraint

In Gupta (1999), the authors present competitive polynomial-time heuristics for selection of views to optimize total query response time, for some important special cases of the general data warehouse scenarios: (i) an OR view graph, in which any view can be computed from any one of its related views, e.g., data cubes; and (ii) an AND view graph, where each query has a unique evaluation. They extend their heuristic to the most general case of AND-OR view graphs.

Algorithms driven by maintenance cost

In Gupta (1999), the authors considered the maintenance-cost-view-selection problem in which it is required to select a set of views to be materialized in order to maximize the query response time under a constraint of maintenance time. This problem is NP-hard. The authors developed a couple of algorithms to solve this problem. For OR view graph, they present a greedy algorithm that selects a set of views. They also present an A^* heuristic for the general case of AND-OR view graphs.

View Maintenance

A *data warehouse* stores integrated information from multiple data sources in *materialized views (MV)* over the source data. The data sources (DS) may be heterogeneous, distributed and autonomous. When the data in any source (base data) changes, the MVs at the data warehouse need to be updated accordingly. The process of updating a materialized view in response to the changes in the underlying source data is called view maintenance. The view maintenance problem has evoked great interest in the past few years. This view maintenance in such a distributed environment gives rise to inconsistencies since there is a finite unpredictable amount of time required for (a) propagating changes from the DS to the data warehouse and (b) computing view updates in response to these changes. Data consistency can be maintained at the data warehouse by performing the following steps:

- propagate changes from the data sources (ST_1 - current state of the data sources at the time of propagation of these changes) to the data warehouse to ensure that each view reflects a consistent state of the base data;
- compute view updates in response to these changes using the state ST_1 of the data sources;
- install the view updates at the data warehouse in the same order as the changes have occurred at the data sources.

The inconsistencies at the data warehouse occur since the changes that take place at the data sources are random and dynamic. Before the data warehouse is able to compute the view update for the old changes, the new changes change the state of the data sources from ST_1 to ST_2. This violates the consistency criterion that we have listed. Making the MVs at the data warehouse self-maintainable decimates the problem of inconsistencies by eliminating the finite unpredictable time required to query the data source for computing the view updates. In the next subsection, we describe self-maintenance of materialized views at the data warehouse.

Self-maintenance

Consider a materialized view *MV* at the data warehouse defined over a set of base relations $R = \{ R_1, R_2,..., R_d \}$. *MV* stores a preprocessed query at the data warehouse. The set of base relations R may reside in one data source or in multiple, heterogeneous data sources. A change ΔR_i made to the relation R might affect *MV*. *MV* is defined to be self-maintainable if a change ΔMV in *MV*, in response to the change ΔR_i, can be computed using only the MV and the update ΔR_i. But the data warehouse might need some additional information from other relations in the set R residing in one or more data sources to compute the view update ΔMV. Since the underlying data sources are decoupled from the data warehouse, this requires a finite computation time. Also the random changes at the data sources can give rise to inconsistencies at the data warehouse. Some data sources may not support full database functionalities, and querying such sources to compute the view updates might be a cumbersome, even an impossible task. Because of these problems, the reprocessed query that is materialized at the warehouse needs to be maintained without access to the base relations.

One of the approaches is to replicate all base data in its entirety at the data warehouse so that maintenance of the *MV* becomes local to the data warehouse (Gupta and Mumick, 1995; Gupta et al., 1993). Although this approach guarantees self-maintainability at the warehouse, it creates new problems. As more and more data is added to the warehouse, it increases the space complexity and gives rise to information redundancy which might lead to inconsistencies. This approach also overlooks the point that the base tuples might be present in the view itself, so the view instance, the base update and a subset of the base relations might be sufficient to achieve self-maintainability in the case of SPJ (Select-Project-Join) views (Huyn, 1997). But how can the subset of the base relations that is needed to compute the view updates be stored at data warehouse? This question was addressed in Quass et al. (1996), which defines a set of minimal auxiliary views (AVs) to materialize that are sufficient to make a view self-maintainable. Although materializing auxiliary views at the Data Warehouse was a novel concept, the minimality of auxiliary views defined was still questionable since the MV instance was never exploited for self-maintenance. Most of the current approaches maintain the MV separately from each other using a separate view manager for each view and such approaches fail to recognize that these views can be maintained together by identifying the set of related materialized views. This issue of multiple-view self-maintenance was addressed for the first time in Huyn, 1997).

In some approaches to multiple-view self-maintenance, a set of auxiliary views (AV) are stored at the data warehouse along with the set of materialized views (MV) such that together MV ∪ AV is self-maintainable. The research challenge lies in finding the most economical AV s in terms of space complexity and computational costs. The view self-maintenance is still an active research problem. It is not always feasible to provide self-maintainability of the views at the data warehouse. When the cost of providing self-maintainability exceeds the cost of querying data sources for computing view updates, it is profitable to allow querying of data sources instead.

Consistency maintenance

Current research has also concentrated on ensuring consistency of the data warehouse when the MV s are not self-maintainable since it is not always possible to provide for complete self-maintainability at the data warehouse. The ECA family of algorithms (Zhuge et al., 1995) introduces the problem and solves it partially. The strobe algorithm (Zhuge et al., 1996) introduces the concept of queuing the view updates in the action-list at the data warehouse and installing the updates only when the unanswered query set (UQS) is empty. The algorithm solves the consistency problem but is subject to the potential threat of infinite waiting. There are other mechanisms that are based on time stamping the view updates (Baralis et al., 1996). These methods do not address the consistency problems in their entirety and also assume the notion of global time.

We propose that the self-maintainability of views at the data warehouse should be a dynamic property. We should continuously monitor the cost of providing self-maintainability, and when this cost increases beyond a certain threshold, the maintenance mechanism should be shifted to querying data sources to compute the view updates. This threshold can be computed depending on the cost of querying data sources. An effective algorithm that provides this dynamism and efficient garbage collection is the need of the hour.

Update filtering

The changes that take place in the source data need to be reflected at the data warehouse. Some changes may create view updates that need to be installed at the data warehouse; some changes leave the views at the data warehouse unchanged. If we are able to detect at the data sources that certain changes are guaranteed to leave the views unchanged, we need not propagate these changes to the data warehouse. This would require checking of distributed integrity constraints at a single site. As many changes as possible can be filtered at the sources, and only the changes that result in view updates may be propagated to the warehouse. The update filtering will reduce the size of the maintenance transactions at the data warehouse, thus minimizing the time required to make the data warehouse consistent with the data sources. The side effect of update filtering is that we need to make our data sources (and the wrapper/monitor) components more intelligent. They need to know about their participation in the data warehouse and the data warehouse configuration so that the updates can be checked against the constraint set before propagating them. To be able to realize this, the data sources cannot be decoupled from the data warehouse anymore. This would give rise to new problems like configuration management, i.e., if there is a change in the schema at any data source or at the data warehouse, all the participating entities need to be informed of this change so that they can modify the constraint set to reflect this change. The view maintenance strategies would now be based on the constraint set, and any change to the constraint set would warrant a change in the existing view maintenance transaction.

On-line view maintenance

Warehouse view maintenance can be done either incrementally or by queuing a large number of updates at the data sources to be propagated as a batch update from the data sources to the data warehouse. In current commercial systems, a batch update is periodically sent to the data warehouse, and view updates are computed and installed. This transaction is called the maintenance transaction. A user typically issues read-only queries at the data warehouse and a long-running sequence of user queries is called a reader session. The batch maintenance transaction is typically large and blocks the reader sessions. This makes the data warehouse offline for the duration of the maintenance transaction. The maintenance transaction typically runs at night. With the advent of the Internet and global users, this scheme will have to give way. The 24-hour shop concept is what most companies are striving for, and the data warehouse to be on-line for 24 hours allows the company to be competitive in its strategies. Incremental view maintenance, which updates the data warehouse instantaneously in response to every change at the data source, is expensive and gives rise to inconsistent results during the same reader session. An update from the data source will change the results a user might see over a sequence of queries. We need to get around these problems. Quass and Widom, 1997 discuss a possible approach to this problem by maintaining two versions of each tuple at the data warehouse simultaneously so that the reader sessions and the maintenance transactions do not block each other. A possible solution may need the integration with self-maintenance techniques, where auxiliary views can be used to answer queries during maintenance transactions.

INDEXING IN DATA WAREHOUSES

Indexing has been at the foundation of performance tuning for databases for many years. It is the creation of access structures that provide faster access to the base data relevant to the restriction criteria of queries (Datta et al., 1999). The size of the index structure should be manageable so that benefits can be accrued by traversing such a structure. The traditional indexing strategies used in database systems do not work well in data warehousing environments. Most OLTP transactions typically access a small number of rows; most OLTP queries are point queries. B trees, which are used in most common relational database systems, are geared towards such point queries. They are well suited for accessing a small number of rows. An OLAP query typically accesses a large number of records for summarizing information. For example, an OLTP transaction would typically query for a customer who booked a flight on TWA1234 on say April 25; on the other hand an OLAP query would be more like "Give me the number of customers who booked a flight on TWA1234 in say one month." The second query would access more records and these are typically range queries. B tree indexing scheme which is so apt for OLTP transactions is not the best suited to answer OLAP queries.

An index can be single-column or multi-columns of a table (or a view). An index can be either clustered or non-clustered. An index can be defined on one table (or view) or many tables using a join index (Valduriez, 1987). In data warehouse context, when we talk about index, we refer to two different things: (1) indexing techniques and (2) index selection problem.

Indexing Techniques

A number of indexing strategies have been suggested for data warehouses: Value-List Index, Projection Index (O'Neil and Quass, 1997), Bitmap Index (O'Neil and Quass, 1997), Bit-Sliced Index (O'Neil and Quass, 1997), Data Index (O'Neil and Quass, 1997), Join Index (Valduriez, 1987) and Star Join Index (Red Brick Systems, 1997).

Value-list index

The value-list index consists of two parts. The first part is a balanced tree structure and the second part is a mapping scheme. The mapping scheme is attached to the leaf nodes of the tree structure and points to the tuples in the table being indexed. The tree is generally a B tree with varying percentages of utilization. Oracle provides a B* tree with 100 utilization. Two different types of mapping schemes are in use. First, one consists of a Row ID list, which is associated with each unique search-key value. This list is partitioned into a number of disk blocks chained together. The second scheme uses bitmaps. A bitmap is a vector of bits that store either a 0 or a 1 depending upon the value of a predicate. A bitmap B lists all rows with a given predicate P, such that for each row r with ordinal number j that satisfies the predicate P,

Figure 9 : Example of a Bitmap index on gender

CUSTOMER Table				BM1	BM2
Name	**Age**	**...**	**Gender**	**M**	**F**
				1	0
Dupond	20		M	0	1
Lee	42		F	1	0
Jones	21		M	1	0
Martin	52		M	0	1
Ali	18		F	0	1
Qing	17		F	1	0
Hung	36		M		

Figure 10: Examples of a Projection Index

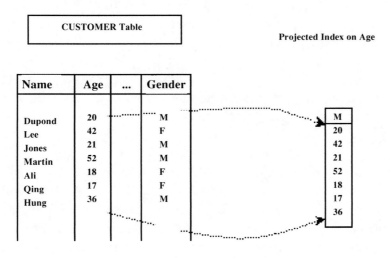

the jth bit in B is set. Bitmaps efficiently represent low-cardinality data, however to make this indexing scheme practical for high-cardinality data, compression techniques must be used. Value-list indexes have been shown in O'Neil and Quass (1997) to outperform other access method in queries involving the MIN or MAX aggregate functions, as well as queries that compute percentile values of a given column. Bitmap indexes can substantially improve performance of queries with the following characteristics (Oracle Corporation, 1999):

- The WHERE clause contains multiple predicates on low-or-medium-cardinality columns (e.g., a predicate on gender that has two possible values: female or male as shown in Figure 9).
- Bitmap indexes have been created on some or all of these low-or-medium-cardinality columns.
- Tables being queried contain many rows.

Projection index

A projection index is equivalent to the column being indexed. If C is the column being indexed, then the projection index on C consists of a stored sequence of column values from C in the same order as the ordinal row number in the table from where the values are extracted (see Figure 10). It has been shown in O'Neil and Quass (1997) that projection indexes outperform other indexing schemes for performing queries that involve computation on two or more column values and appear to perform acceptably well in GROUP-BY like queries.

Bit-sliced index

A bit-sliced index represents the key values of the column to be indexed as binary numbers and projects a set of bitmap slices, which are orthogonal to the data, held in the projection index. This index has been shown in O'Neil and Quass (1997) to particularly perform well for computing sums and averages. Also, it outperforms other indexing approaches for percentile queries if the underlying data are clustered, and for range queries whose range is large.

Join index and bitmap join index

A join index (Valduriez, 1987) is the result of joining two tables on a join attribute and projecting the keys (or tuple IDs) of the two tables. To join the two tables, we can use the join index to fetch the tuples from the tables followed by a join. In relational data warehouse systems, it is of interest to perform a multiple join (a Star Join) on the fact tables and their dimension tables. Therefore, it will be helpful to build join indexes between the keys and the dimension tables, and the corresponding foreign keys of the fact table. If the join indexes are represented in bitmap matrices, a multiple join could be replaced by a sequence of bitwise operations, followed by a relatively small number of fetch and join operations (Wu and Buchmann, 1997).

Data index

A data index, like the projection index, exploits the positional indexing strategy (Datta et al., 1998). The data index avoids duplication of data by storing only the index and not the column being indexed. The data index can be of two specific types: basic data index and join data index (for more information, see Datta et al. (1998).

Index Selection Problem

The index selection problem (ISP) has been studied since the early '70s, and the importance of this problem is well recognized. Like VSP, ISP consists of picking a set of indexes for a given set of OLAP queries under some resources constraints. Most of proposed studies show that ISP is an NP-complete problem. Recently, Microsoft (Chaudhuri and Narasaya, 1999; 1999) developed an index selection tool called AutoAdmin. The goal of our research in the AutoAdmin tool is to make database systems self-tuning and self-administering. This goal is achieved by enabling databases to track the usage of their systems and to gracefully adapt to application requirements. Thus, instead of applications having to track and tune databases, databases actively auto-tune themeselves itself to be responsive to application needs.

Note that indexes require a very huge amount of space. Chaudhuri et al. (1999) (from Microsoft) addressed a problem, called Storage-minimal index merging problem, that takes an existing set of indices, and produces a new set of indices with significantly lower storage and maintenance cost. This is a strong reason to motivate researchers to find novel techniques for better use of storage capacity available for a data warehouse. The merging technique is similar to the reconstruction of vertical fragments of a relation.

Labio et al. (1997) combined the problems of selecting views and indexes into one problem, called the view-index selection problem (VISP). This problem starts with a set of materialized views (primary views) and tries to add a set of supporting views to these primary views. The objective is to minimize total maintenance cost for the data warehouse, but not distribute storage space between materialized views and indices. For that, the authors proposed an algorithm based on A* to find the optimal solution. This algorithm takes as input the set of all possible supporting views and indices to materialize. The space allocation is not taken into consideration by this algorithm, because it supposes that the primary views are already selected (their storage capacity is already assigned). This algorithm is in fact not practical because the number of possible supporting views and indices can be very huge. Heuristic rules (concerning the benefit and cost of supporting views and indices) to reduce the complexity of A* are suggested.

INTERACTION BETWEEN INDEXES AND VIEWS

Conceptually, both materialized views and indices are physical structures that can significantly accelerate performance (Sanjay et al., 2000). An effective physical database design tool must therefore take into account the interaction between indices and materialized views by considering them together to optimize the physical design for the queries on the system (Bellatreche et al., 2000; Sanjay et al., 2000). An effective physical database design tool must therefore take into account the interaction between indices and materialized views by considering them together to optimize the physical design for the workload on the system. Ignoring this interaction can significantly compromise the quality of the solutions obtained by the physical database design tool.

This interaction gets the great attention of researchers (Bellatreche et al., 2000) and industrials (Sanjay et al., 2000). Recently, architecture and algorithms for selecting views and indexes are presented by Microsoft SQL Server 2000.

Most of the previous work in physical database design has considered the problems of index selection and materialized view selection in isolation. However, both indexes and views are fundamentally similar-both are redundant structures that speed up query execution, compete for the same resource (storage) and incur maintenance overhead in the presence of updates (Sanjay et al., 2000).

When the VSP and ISP are treated independently (i.e., the views and indices are selected in sequential manner), to select them, the DWA does the following tasks:

- The DWA has to run an algorithm to select views to be materialized according to the storage space reserved for views.
- After that, the DWA runs another algorithm to select indices over base relations and materialized views according to storage space reserved for indices.

The combination of VSP and ISP gives rise to two problems that are not addressed by the data warehouse community. The first problem is selecting join index in the presence of materialized views, and the second one is storage space distribution among materialized views and indices.

Join Index Selection with Materialized Views: Once materialized views are selected, all OLAP queries will be rewritten using these materialized views (this process is known as query rewriting (Srivastava et al., 1996). A rewriting of a query Q using views is a query expression Q¢ that refers to these views. In SQL, after the rewriting process of OLAP queries, we can find in the FROM clause a set of materialized views, dimension tables and the fact table. These views can be joined with each other or with other tables. Indexing a single materialized view can be done by using the same indexing techniques for a table (B^+-tree). The star join index (SJI) (Red Brick Systems, 1997; O'Neil and Qass, 1997) has been used in data warehouses modeled by a star schema. It denotes a join index between a fact table and multiple dimension tables. The SJI has proven to be an index structure for speeding up joins defined on fact and dimension tables in data warehouses (Red Brick Systems, 1997; O'Neil and Qass, 1997). However, there has not been much research reported in enhancing star join algorithms for efficiently selecting and performing join indices with materialized views.

Space Distribution Between Views & Indices: Since the VSP and ISP are combined, the space distribution becomes a crucial issue. The task of distributing storage space among materialized views and indices in order to improve performance is very difficult for the DWA. This difficulty is due to several factors: (1) metrics are needed to decide on the distribution of the storage space among materialized views and indices, (2) the mutual interdependencies between views and indices need to be considered for an optimal solution and (3) the problem of redistribution of storage space among materialized views and indices after update operations (deletions and insertions), or changes in query sets, needs to be addressed.

Further, when updates are performed over the underlying data warehouse, the corresponding changes should be applied to materialized views and indices (Hurtado, Mendelzon and Vaisman, 1999). Thus, their sizes can increase or decrease. Therefore, it is necessary to re-distribute the storage space among views and indices. Finally, the problem that must be addressed is: how to automatically distribute storage space between materialized views and indices to efficiently execute a set of queries?

In the next sections, we describe the graph join index concept and space distribution among materialized views and indexes.

Graph Join Indexes

The index selection phase is aimed at determining the best set of indices for a given set of OLAP queries. The objective of index selection is to pick a set of indices that is optimal or as close to optimal as possible (Chaudhuri & Narasayya, 1999; Gupta, Harinarayan, Rajaraman & Ullman, 1997; Valduriez, 1987; Lei & Ross, 1998). Like the materialized views, indices require a certain amount of disk space, and only a limited number of indices can be selected for a given set of OLAP queries. Indices can be defined on one table (dimension table, fact table or view) using for example a B^+-tree. They can also be defined on more than two tables to speed up operations such as joins.

In this section, we suggest a new type of join index called a graph join index (GJI), which is used to speed up queries defined on materialized views and on tables (dimension or fact).

Motivating example

Assume that the sales company is interested in determining the total sales for male customers purchasing product of type package "box." The following SQL query Q_1 may be used for this purpose:

SELECT	SUM(S.dollar_sales)
FROM	CUSTOMER C, PRODUCT P, SALES S,
WHERE	C.Cid = S.Cid
AND	P.Pid = S.Pid
AND	C.Gender = 'M'
AND	P.Package_type = "Box"
GROUP BY PID	

We also assume that the company maintains the following view consisting of finding the total sales for each product having "box" as type of package. This view is defined as follows:

```
CREATE          VIEW V_2
SELECT          *
FROM            PRODUCT P, SALES S,
WHERE           P.Pid = S.Pid
AND             C.Package_type = "Box"
GROUP BY PID
```

The materialized view V_2 can be used to evaluate the query Q_1 by joining V_2 with the dimension table CUSTOMER. The rewritten query $Q_1\phi$ that uses V_2 is:

```
SELECT          SUM(S.dollar_sales)
FROM            CUSTOMER C, V_2
WHERE           V_2.Cid = C.Cid
AND             C.Gender = 'M'
GROUP BY PID
```

Note that the fact table SALES is huge, and the materialized view V_2 is likely to be orders of magnitude smaller than SALES table. Hence, evaluating $Q_1\phi$ will be much faster than evaluating the query Q_1, because, Q_1 needs two join operations, and $Q_1\phi$ needs only one. There is a solution, to reduce the number of join operations of the query Q_1 which is the SJI (Red Brick Systems, 1997). The suitable SJI for Q_1 is (CUSTOMER, SALES, PROD-UCT), but it requires a very high storage capacity (Datta et al., 1999) that can slow down the execution of the query Q_1. We can define a join index between the view V_2 and the dimension table CUSTOMER (V_2, CUSTOMER). This index speeds up the execution of the query Q_1, and its size is much smaller than the SJI (CUSTOMER, SALES, PRODUCT).

Note that the complete SJI (CUSTOMER, SALES, PRODUCT, TIME) would be sufficient to process any query against our star schema in Figure 3. However, without the fact table in its element, this index does not guarantee any performance (Informix corporaiton, 1997). In the presence of material-ized views, a join index can be defined on several views; therefore, by removing one view, the join index may still guarantee the performance of some queries. This is because most of materialized views are obtained from joining the fact table with other dimension tables.

Notations definitions
Assume that the OLAP queries are based on the star join: each query is a join between the fact table and dimension tables, filtered by some selection

operations and followed by an aggregation. This type of query has the following syntax:

SELECT	*<Projection List> <Aggregation List>*
FROM	<Fact Table> <Dimension Tables>
WHERE	<Selection Predicates Join Predicates>
GROUP BY	<Dimension Table Attributes>

Note that in the syntax of queries without materialized views, the FROM clause contains the fact table and dimension tables. When we consider the materialized views, our queries should be rewritten using these views (Srivastava et al., 1996). Therefore, the FROM clause can contain: fact table, materialized views and dimension tables.

Definition 3: (Database Schema Graph (DBSG) is a connected graph where each node is a relation and an edge between two nodes R_i and R_j implies a possibility of join between relations R_i and R_j.

Definition 4: (Join Graph (JG) is a database schema graph such that there exists exactly one join condition between two relations.

For a given database schema, we can have more than one edge (join) between two nodes as shown in Figure 11, where we have two join operations between tables Employee and Department. One join condition relates employee to the department he/she is working in, and another join condition relates an employee to the department he/she is managing. In this case, we decompose the database schema graph into two join graphs as shown in Figure 11, and then we consider GJIs for each join graph, separately.

Since we are focusing on data warehouse schemas (e.g., star, snowflake), a join graph has only single join condition between tables. Further study on the complexity of GJIs derived from database schema graph with multiple independent join conditions is beyond the scope of this chapter. Therefore, a JG is the same as DBSG.

Claim 1: A JG in a data warehouse with only dimension tables and fact

Figure 11. Database schema graph and join graphs

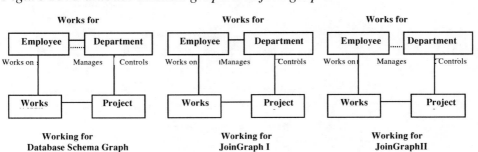

table is always connected. In this case, a JG is called total join graph.

Claim 2: In a data warehouse context with dimension tables, fact table and materialized views, a JG can be disconnected, i.e., it contains more than one subgraph. In this case, it is called partitioned join graph.

The partitioned join graph occurs when:

1. Views do not have common join attributes. For example, a view defined on CUSTOMER and another in PRODUCT.
2. Views have common join attributes, but they can never be joined. For example, suppose we have two views V_1 and V_2 defining the sales activities of female customers and male customers, respectively. The result of joining these two views is always empty.

Definition 5: **(Graph Join Index (GJI)** A GJI is a subset of nodes of a join graph.

In case of distributed join graph, a GJI is a subset of nodes of each subgraph.

Claim 3: *A SJI is a particular case of GJI.*

A data warehouse schema consists of a star schema (a set of dimension tables and a fact table) with a set of materialized views. Each table T_i being either a dimension table, or a view, or a fact table has a key K_{Ti}. A GJI on m tables is a table having m attributes $(K_{T1,} K_{T2,...,} K_{Tm})$, and which is denoted as: $(T_1 \sim T_{2,} \sim ... \sim T_m)$.

Since the star schema is connected, there is a path connecting the tables $(T_{1,} T_{2,...,} T_m)$ by including additional tables, if necessary. The GJI supplies the keys of the relations that form the result of joining all the tables along the path. In case there are multiple paths that connect tables $(T_{1,} T_{2,...,} T_m)$, then there can be multiple GJIs, each catering to a different query. A GJI with all tables of a join graph is known as a complete GJI. A GJI with a subset of nodes of a join

Figure 12. Join graph and graph join indices

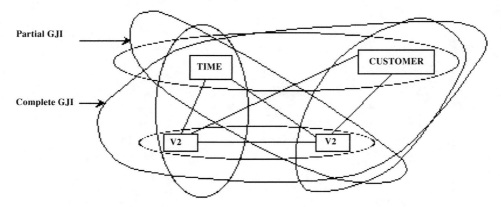

graph refers to a partial GJI (see Figure 12).

A similar indexing technique to GJI was proposed by Segev et al. (1996) called join pattern index in expert systems. This index exists on all attributes involved in selection and join conditions. It refers to an array of variables that represent the key and join attributes of the data associated with the join.

Note that for a star schema with n tables, the number of possible GJIs grows exponentially, and is given by:

$$\binom{2^n - n - 1}{0} + \binom{2^n - n - 1}{2} + \ldots + \binom{2^n - n - 1}{2^n - n - 1} = 2^{(2-n-1)}$$

As GJI has at least two nodes, the total number of GJIs possible is $2^n - n - 1$. Therefore, the above equation gives us the total number of ways a set of GJIs can be generated. However, if we want to find only one GJI, the number of GJI possibilities are $2^n - n - 1$. Therefore, the problem of efficiently finding the set of GJIs that provides the minimum total query processing cost while satisfying a storage constraint is very challenging to solve.

GJI Selection (GJI-S) Problem Formulation

All the index selection algorithms select indices to optimize the objective function employed, subject to the constraint that the indices included cannot consume more than the specified amount of storage.

The inputs of the GJI-S problem are as follows:

1. A star schema with the fact table F and dimension tables $\{D_1, D_2, \ldots, D_d\}$.
2. A set of most frequently asked queries $Q = \{Q_1, Q_2, \ldots, Q_s\}$ with their frequencies $\{f_1, f_2, \ldots, f_s\}$. Each query Q_i $(1 \leq i \leq s)$ is represented by a query graph QG_i.
3. A set of materialized views $V = \{V_1, V_2, \ldots, V_m\}$ selected to support the execution of queries in Q.
4. A storage constraint S.

The GJI-S problem selects a set of GJIs G' among all possible GJIs (G), that minimizes the total cost for executing a set of OLAP queries, under the constraint that the total space occupied by the GJIs in (denoted by $S_{G'}$ is less than S).

More formally, let $C_g(Q_i)$ denote the cost of answering a query Q_i using a GJI g $(g \in G')$. The problem is to select a set of GJIs G' $(G' \subseteq G)$ that minimizes the total query processing cost ($TQPC$) such as:

$$TQPC = \sum_{i=1}^{s} f_i \times \{min_{\forall g \in G} C_g(Qi)\} \tag{3}$$

under the constraint that: $S_{G'} \leq S$.

GJI-S Algorithms

In Bellatreche, et al. (2000), we have proposed three algorithms to select an optimal or near-optimal GJI for a set of queries: a naive algorithm, a greedy algorithm for selecting one GJI and a greedy algorithm for selecting more than one GJI. These three algorithms are guided by an objective function that calculates the cost of executing a set of queries.

1. The naive algorithm (NA) is used for a comparison purpose. NA enumerates all possible GJIs, and calculates the contribution of each GJI in executing a set of queries. Finally, it picks the GJI having the minimum cost while satisfying the storage constraint.

2. The greedy algorithm for selecting one GJI (GA1) starts with a storage constraint (SC) *S*, and then selects a GJI with two nodes that corresponds to most frequently executed join among all the queries, and tries to expand it by adding more nodes while checking whether the total processing cost decreases. When no more expand operations can be applied, the algorithm tries to shrink it to check if a better GJI can be derived. When no more expand or shrink operations can be applied, the algorithm ends, generating the best possible GJI. The details of the algorithm are presented in Bellatreche et al. (2000).

3. Note that as a single GJI generated by GA1 can only efficiently execute some but not all of the queries, we need more than one GJI to efficiently execute all the queries. Therefore, we develop a greedy algorithm for selecting more than one GJI (GAK). The GAK starts with the initial solution provided by GA1 as the first index. After that it selects the edge from weight graph that has the highest query access frequency and which is not a GJI generated by GA1. Then it tries to expand (one or more times) and shrink (one or more times) until no further reduction in total cost can be achieved and the storage constraint is satisfied. This generates the second GJI, and it keeps repeating this procedure until the storage constraint is violated.

Space Distribution Among Views and Indices

The problem of space distribution among views and indices should be treated in two cases: static and dynamic. In the static case, all data warehouse parameters are considered fixed. In the dynamic case, we assume that the tables in the data warehouse are updated.

Static space distribution between materialized views and indexes can be formulated as follows:

Given a set of frequently asked retrieval queries $Q = \{Q_1, Q_2, ..., Q_s\}$, a set of frequently asked update queries $U = \{U_1, U_2, ..., U_s \phi\}$ and their frequencies, and a storage space S to store materialized views V and indices I to support the above queries, distribute S among materialized views and indices so as to minimize the global cost. As output, we obtain:

1) the space distribution between materialized views (S^V) and indices (S^I), and

2) a set of materialized views and indices corresponding to (S^V) and indices (S^I).

Static algorithm

In Bellatreche et al. (2000), we developed a methodology that distributes the storage space among views and indices in an iterative manner, so as to minimize the total query processing cost. First, we developed a cost model that calculates the cost of processing a set of OLAP queries with materialized views and indices. Assume that the DWA initially reserves a space (S^V) and (S^I) for materialized views and indices ($S = S^V + S^I$), respectively. First, we apply an algorithm for selecting a set of materialized views to support the set of queries. The selection of views is constrained by the space quota reserved to them, i.e., S^V. After that, indices are built on base relations and materialized views using the storage space S^I.

The basic idea of this approach is to have two greedy algorithms, namely, index spy and view spy, fight for the same resource (that is, storage space). These two spies work as follows:

- An index spy keeps on stealing space used by materialized views to add/change the set of indices as long as it reduces the total query processing cost. The index spy should have some policies to select materialized views that can be stolen. We define two policies: Least Frequently Used View (LFUV), where the index spy selects the view that has the lowest frequency, and Smallest View First (SVF), where the index spy selects the smallest view.

- After that, a view spy keeps on stealing space from indices to add/change the set of materialized views as long as it reduces the total cost. Similarly, the view spy should have some policies to select indexes that can be stolen. Two policies are defined: Least Frequently Used Index (LFUI) and Largest Index First (LIF).

The algorithm ends when neither the index spy nor the view spy can reduce the total query processing cost. The winner is the spy who accumulated the most storage space from the other spy. The main strategy of this approach is to have two greedy algorithms, namely, index spy and view spy, fight for the same resource (that is, storage space), while trying to reduce the total cost of processing a given set of queries, and maintaining the set of materialized views and indices. The algorithm terminates when the total cost cannot be reduced any more.

This approach gives two results: (1) a set of materialized views and a set of indices with the lowest total cost, and (2) new *storage space allocation* for materialized views and indices $S^V\phi$ and $S^I\phi$ that may differ from the initial space quotas S^V and S^I.

Example 4: To illustrate our approach, we consider the following example. We consider the star schema of a data warehouse (Figure 3, in Section 2). This schema contains a fact table SALES and three dimension tables CUSTOMER, TIME and PRODUCT. Assume the five most frequently asked OLAP queries given in Bellateche et al. (2000). We assume that the DWA has an initial allocation of 600 megabytes for materialized views and 200 megabytes for indices.

Our algorithm starts by selecting an initial solution for VSP and ISP. First, we execute the View Select algorithm (Yang, et al., 1997) to select materialized views using the 600 megabytes storage constraint. The views selected are V_1, V_2 and V_3 as shown in Table 2. Using these three materialized views, we get 4054825 disk block accesses as the total cost of processing all queries.

After that, we build indices to speed up the above queries by selecting indices using the 200 megabytes storage constraint. By using the GJI selection algorithms, (section 6) we select a join index between the view V_2 and the dimension table CUSTOMER, called ($V_2 \sim$ CUSTOMER). The storage required for the selected index is 181821440 bytes. This index reduces the query processing cost from 4054825 to 3263405. Now, the index spy tries to steal storage space from materialized views to add one or more indices. Since the view V_3 is small and less used compared to views V_1 and V_2, the index spy steals 89047040 bytes (size of view V_3), and the storage space that can be allocated for indices is now 289047040 bytes. Note that after deleting the view V_3, we will have only two views V_1 and V_2 and two base relations CUSTOMER and TIME to execute all five queries. Now the index

Table 2. Selected materialized views and their sizes

View Name	View Definition	View Size
V_1	$SALES\chi\sigma_{State = 'IL'}$ CUSTOMER	178 094 08
V_2	$SALES\chi\sigma_{Package = 'Box'}$ PRODUCT	324 435 968
V_3	$\sigma_{Gender = 'M'}$ CUSTOMER	089 047 040
Total		591 577 088

Table 3. Cost reduction due to index spy

Without View & Indices	With Views	With View and Indices	Index Spy	View Spy
68514928	*4054825*	*3263405*	*1955305*	*68514928*

spy runs the index selection algorithm (Bellatreche et al., 2000) to find new indices. The new index is ($V_1 \sim V_2 \sim$ TIME $\sim$ CUSTOMER). It reduces the total query processing cost from **3263405** to **1955305** disk block accesses. *No further reduction in query processing cost is possible by executing the index spy or the view spy. Therefore, by allocating 500 megabytes for materialized views and 300 megabytes for indices results in a total query processing cost of 1955305 disk block accesses as shown in Table 3.*

The solution we propose for distributing space can reuse existing algorithms for views selection and index selection. Thus, the best available algorithms can be selected. Further, our methodology is flexible enough for the DWA to use only index spy or only view spy for data warehouse design. In this way, the DWA can either allocate more storage space to indices or to materialized views.

Issues for Dynamic Space Distribution

The data warehouse environments are known by their dynamic changes over the underlying warehouse database. Whenever the base relations are updated at more or less regular intervals, the materialized views and indexes should also be updated. Following these updates, it is necessary to readjust/redefine the views and the indices.

Several methods have been proposed for fast rebuild of materialized views (Mohania and Kambayashi, 2000). A view after this maintenance can indeed occupy more or less space than before the maintenance. The same observation is also valid for the indices. So, the space constraint may not longer be respected. If the total space occupied by the views and the indices is higher (respectively lower) than the required space, it is necessary to determine which views and/or indices must be removed (respectively added). The iterative algorithm for the static case can be easily adapted to handle this problem.

Let S^V_i and S^I_i be the spaces occupied by the views and indices before the updates. These two values are the new space constraints to respect. After updates, the algorithm of the dynamic case goes through following steps:

- First, we compute the new spaces occupied by the views (S^V_c) and the indices (S^I_i).

- In case of deletions, the total space S_c ($S^V_c + S^I_c$) may decrease. Therefore, unused spaces for both materialized views and indices are available. We fill the unused space for materialized views by selecting a new view. Similarly, the unused space for indices is filled incrementally, using the greedy algorithm GAK. It considers each index of the set of selected indices as an initial solution and then generates a new index (not belonging to the current set of indices).
- When insertions occur, the current total space (S_c) occupied by the views and indices may be higher than their initial space (S_i). This augmentation can affect view space, index space or both.

  1. Only the space occupied by the views is higher than their required space.   Intuitively, we need to remove view(s) to satisfy the storage constraint. But   before removing view(s), we check out if the view-spy can steal index space to keep these views. If it cannot steal space, we remove view(s) using one of the view policies (LFUV or SVF).

  2. Only the space occupied by the indices is higher than their required space. As in the previous situation, we need to remove index(es) to satisfy the storage constraint. But before removing these index(es), we check out if the index-spy can steal view space to keep these indices. If it cannot steal space, we remove index(es) using one of the index policies (LFUI or LIF).

  3. Both spaces are higher than their required spaces. In this case, we remove views and indices using the policies for views and indices till their storage constraints are satisfied. We then apply our static algorithm to verify if the global cost can be reduced.

Discussion

Our evaluation of the iterative algorithm for the VISP problem shows that there is a balance between amount of space allocated to materialized views vis-à-vis indices in data warehousing environments. Blindly allocating space to either materialized views or indices will not guarantee faster execution of queries. This level of interaction can be easily supported in any data warehouse design tool, and can facilitate efficient query processing in data warehouses. As the approach we developed is essentially a greedy algorithm, one cannot guarantee an optimal distribution of space between materialized views and indices. But, as our illustrative examples show, there is a tremendous reduction in query processing cost, which supports the utility of this approach.

DISCUSSION OF PRACTICAL ASPECTS OF THIS CHAPTER

In this chapter, we have treated two major problems in data warehousing environments: (i) the data partitioning, and (ii) the interaction between indexes and materialized views. Each problem gets an important place in data warehouse trends.

Data Partitioning: Oracle8i incorporates the horizontal partitioning to support very large tables, materialized views and indexes by decomposing them into smaller and manageable pieces called partitions. Oracle 8i defines some partitioning methods: the *range partitioning*, the *hash partitioning*, the *composite partitioning* and the *partition-wise joins*.

In the range partitioning, the data in a table (a view or an index) is partitioned according to a range of values. In the hash partitioning, the data is partitioned according to a hash function. In the composite partitioning, data is partitioned by range and further subdivided using a hash function. Finally, in partition-wise joins, a large join operation is broken into smaller joins that are performed sequentially or in parallel. In order to use this partitioning, both tables must be equi-partitioned.

Indexing Materialized Views: Oracle8i provides a new query-rewrite capability, which transforms an SQL statement so that it accesses materialized views that are defined on the detail tables. Coupled with materialized views, Oracle8i's query-rewrite capability can significantly reduce the response time of queries that summarize or join data in the tables of a data warehouse. When a query targets one or more detail tables to calculate a summary or an aggregate (or perform a join) and an available materialized view contains the requested data, Oracle8i optimizer can transparently rewrite the query to target the precomputed results in the materialized view, which returns the results more quickly.

But when a query targets one or more detail tables to calculate a summary or an aggregate (or perform a join) and *more than one materialized view* contains the requested data (for example, joining these materialized views), Oracle8i's should define a join index covering these tables to optimize this query. We are not sure if these kinds of join indexes are defined by industrials.

The Interaction Between Indexes and Views: This problem gets great attention from the industrials and practitioners. Recently, the Data Management, Exploration Mining group at Microsoft Research considered the interaction between indexes and views. The researchers at this group (Sanjay et al., 2000) presented solutions for automatically selecting an appropriate set of materialized views and indexes for SQL databases.

Business Perspective: Data warehousing has become a standard tool used to evaluate the health of a company and it competitiveness in the marketplace. Therefore, a large amount of decision analysis and processing is performed on data warehousing systems. The tools and techniques proposed in this chapter form the core of techniques that can be applied by the data warehouse administrator in not only designing a data warehouse for the organization, but also fine tuning it by taking in to account the changes in user query processing. A well-designed data warehouse will process user queries faster while maintaining the currency of the data. This enhances competitiveness of the company and makes it agile to address changes in their customer behavior or changes in the environment where the company operates. Finally, a data warehouse developer can build a data warehouse design tool that is based on techniques presented in this chapter.

CONCLUSIONS AND FUTURE WORK

Data warehousing design facilitates efficient query processing and maintenance of materialized views. There are few trade-offs that were introduced in data warehousing design. The first trade-off is whether to materialize a view or not. The view selection problem minimizes the total cost of query processing and maintaining materialized views for a given set of queries. There has been lot of work on selecting materialized views for static environments (such as Yang et al., 1997), and under dynamic environments (such as, Kotidis and Roussopoulos, 1999). The second trade-off is whether to partition a data warehouse or not. In our study (Bellatreche et al., 2000; Gopalkrishnan et al., 2000; Gopalkrishnan et al., 2000; Gopalkrishnan et al., 1999) we found that partitioning helps in reducing irrelevant data access and eliminating (some of the) costly joins. Further, too much partitioning can increase the cost for queries that access entire data warehouses. The third trade-off is index selection to efficiently execute queries. We found that judicious index selection does reduce the cost of query processing, but also showed that indices on materialized views improve the performance of queries even more (Bellatreche et al., 2000) . Since indices require storage space, and so do materialized views, the final trade-off presented was the storage distribution among materialized views and indices. We found that it is possible to apply heuristics to distribute the storage space among materialized views and indices so as to efficiently execute queries and maintain materialized views.

Data warehousing design under dynamic environments is still a very open issue of research. The ability to adapt a given set of materialized views and partitions to dynamically changing queries executed over time by users is required to facilitate optimal performance from a data warehousing system. This problem could be addressed by treating materialized views and partitions to be composed of grid cells (Navathe, et al., 1995) and dynamically changing the materialized views and partitions by changing the composition.

Such a methodology is amenable to heuristics based on composition algebra, and efficient hill-climbing algorithms can be designed. The notion of atomic grid cells can facilitate parallel processing of costly OLAP queries on a shared-nothing parallel processing system. Even though a lot of work has been done on view maintenance algorithms and view adaptation algorithms, there is explicit tie-up between these and data warehousing design. In particular, given a particular view maintenance strategy, what kind of data warehousing design strategy has to be employed and vice-versa? Data warehousing design is application specific; for report generation a specific data warehousing design might be needed, where as for data mining a different data warehousing design might be needed. Hence a design methodology that can support multiple data warehouse designs for different types of applications needs to be developed.

REFERENCES

Agrawal, Gupta, A. and Sarawagi, S. (1997). Modeling multidimensional databases. *Technical Report Research*, IBM.

Baralis,E., S. Ceri, and Paraboschi, S. (1996). Conservative timestamp revisited for materialized view maintenance in a data warehouse. In *Proceeding of the Workshop on Materialized Views: Techniques and Applications (VIEW'1996)*, June, 1-9.

Baralis, E., S. Paraboschi, and Teniente, E. (1997). Materialized view selection in a multidimensional database. *Proceedings of the International Conference on Very Large Databases*, August, 156-165.

Bauer, L. and Lehner, W. (1997). The cube-query-languages (CQL) for multidimensional statistical and scientific database systems. In *Proceedings of the Fifth International Conference on Database Systems for Advanced Applications(DASFAA'97)*, April, 263-272.

Bellatreche, L., Karlapalem, K. and Simonet A. (2000). Algorithms and support for horizontal class partitioning. In *Object-Oriented Databases in the Distributed and Parallel Databases Journal*, April, 8(2), 155-179.

Bellatreche, L., Karlapalem, K. and Basak, G. B. (1998). Query-driven horizontal class partitioning. In *Object-Oriented Databases In 9th*

International Conference on Database and Expert Systems Applications (DEXA'98), Lecture Notes in Computer Science 1460, August, 692-701.

Bellatreche, L., Karlapalem, K. and Li, Q. (1998). Derived horizontal class partitioning in oodbss: Design strategy, analytical model and evaluation. In *The 17th International Conference on the Entity Relationship Approach (ER'98)*, November, 465-479.

Bellatreche, L., Karlapalem, K. and Li, Q. (1999). Algorithms for graph join index problem in data warehousing environments. *Technical Report HKUST-CS99-07*, Hong Kong University of Science & Technology, March.

Bellatreche, L., Karlapalem, K. and Li, Q. (2000). Evaluation of indexing materialized views in data warehousing environments. *Proceedings of the International Conference on Data Warehousing and Knowledge Discovery (DAWAK'2000)*, September, 57-66.

Bellatreche, L., Karlapalem, K. and M. Mohania, M. (2000). What can partitioning do for your data warehouses and data marts. *Proceedings of the International Database Engineering and Application Symposium (IDEAS'2000)*, September, 437-445.

Bellatreche, L., Karlapalem, K. and Schneider, M. (2000). Interaction between index and view selection in data warehousing environments. *Information Systems Journal*.

Bellatreche, L., Karlapalem, K. and Schneider, M. (2000). On efficient storage space distribution among materialized views and indices in data warehousing environments. In *The International Conference on Information and Knowledge Management (CIKM'2000)*, November.

Bellatreche, L., Karlapalem, K. and Simonet, A. (1997). Horizontal class partitioning. In *Object-Oriented Databases In 8th International Conference on Database and Expert Systems Applications (DEXA'97), Toulouse, Lecture Notes in Computer Science 1308*, September, 58-67.

Ceri, S., Negri, M. and Pelagatti, G. (1982). Horizontal data partitioning in database design. *Proceedings of the ACM SIGMOD International Conference on Management of Data. SIGPLAN Notices*, 128-136.

Ceri, S. and Pelagatti, G. (1984). *Distributed Databases: Principles & Systems*. McGraw-Hill International Editions.

Chaudhuri, S. and Narasayya, V. (1997). An efficient cost-driven index selection tool for microsoft sql server. *Proceedings of the International Conference on Very Large Databases*, August, 146-155.

Chaudhuri, S. and Narasayya, V. (1998). Autoadmin 'what-if' index analysis utility. *Proceedings of the ACM SIGMOD International Conference on Management of Data*, June, 367-378.

Chaudhuri, S. and Narasayya, V. (1999). Index merging. *Proceedings of the International Conference on Data Engineering (ICDE),* March, 296-303.

Datta, A., Moon, B., Ramamritham, K., Thomas, H. and Viguier, I. (1998). Have your data and index it, too: Efficient storage and indexing for datawarehouses. *Techreport Technical Report 98-7, Department of Computer Science, The University of Arizona.*

Datta, A., Ramamritham, K. and Thomas, H. (1999). Curio: A novel solution for efficient storage and indexing in data warehouses. *Proceedings of the International Conference on Very Large Databases,* September, 730-733.

Dewitt, D., Gerber, R. H., Graefe, G., Heytens, M. L., Kumar, K. B. and Muralikrishna, M. (1986). Gamma-A high performance dataflow database machine. *(VLDB},* 10, 228-237.

Ezeife, C. I. and Barker, K. (1995). A comprehensive approach to horizontal class fragmentation in distributed object based system. *International Journal of Distributed and Parallel Databases,* 3(3), 247-272.

Firestone, J. M. (1997). Data warehouses and data marts: A dynamic view. *White Paper~3, Executive Information Systems, Inc.,* March.

Gopalkrishnan, V., Li, Q. and Karlapalem, K. (1999). Star/snow-flake schema driven object-relational data warehouse-design and query processing strategies. In *Proceedings of the First International Conference on Data Warehousing and Knowledge Discovery,* 11-22.

Gopalkrishnan, V., Li, Q. and Karlapalem, K. (2000). Efficient query processing with associated horizontal class partitioning in an object relational data warehousing environment. In *Proceedings of 2nd International Workshop on Design and Management of Data Warehouses,* June, 1-9.

Gopalkrishnan, V., Li, Q. and Karlapalem, K (2000). Efficient query processing with structural join indexing in an object-relational data warehousing environment. In *Information Resources Management Association International Conference,* 976-979.

Gupta, A. and Mumick, I. S. (1995). Maintenance of materialized views: Problems, techniques and applications. *Data Engineering Bulletin,* June, 18(2), 3-18.

Gupta, A., Mumick, I. S. and Subrahmanian, V. S. (1993). Maintaining views incrementally. *Proceedings of the ACM SIGMOD International Conference on Management of Data,* June, 157-166.

Gupta, H. (1999) Selection and maintenance of views in a data warehouse. *PhD Thesis, Stanford University,* September.

Gupta, H., Harinarayan, V., Rajaraman, A. and Ullman, J. (1997). Index selection for OLAP. *Proceedings of the International Conference on Data Engineering (ICDE)*, April, 208-219.

Hevner, A.R. and Rao, A. (1988). Distributed data allocation strategies. *Advances In Computers*, 12, 121-155.

Hull, R. and Zhou, G. (1996). A framework for supporting data integration using materialized and virtual approaches. *Proceedings of the ACM SIGMOD International Conference on Management of Data*, 481-492.

Hurtado, C.A., Mendelzon, O. A. and Vaisman A. A. (1999). Maintaining data cubes under dimension updates. *Proceedings of the International Conference on Data Engineering (ICDE)*, March, 346-355.

Huyn. N. (1997). Multiple-view self-maintenance in data warehousing environments. *Proceedings of the International Conference on Very Large Databases*, August, 26-35.

Hyperion. *Hyperion Essbase* OLAP Server. http://www.hyperion.com/.

Informix Corporation. (1997). Informix-on-line extended parallel server and informix-universal server: A new generation of decision-support indexing for enterprise data warehouses. *White Paper*.

Informix Inc. (1997). *The Informix-MetaCube Product Suite*. http://www.informix.com.

Inmon, W.H. (1992). *Building the Data Warehouse*. John Wiley.

Jain, R. (1991). *The Art of Computer Systems Performance Analysis*. Wiley Professional Computing.

Karlapalem, K., Navathe, S. B. and Morsi, M. M. A. (1994). Issues in distributed design of object-oriented databases. In *Distributed Object Management*, Morgan Kaufman Publishers Inc., 148-165.

Kimball, R. (1996). *The Data Warehouse Toolkit*. John Wiley & Sons.

Kotidis, Y. and Roussopoulos, N. (1999). Dynamat: A dynamic view management system for data warehouses. *Proceedings of the ACM SIGMOD International Conference on Management of Data*, June, 371-382.

Labio, W., Quass, D. and Adelberg, B. (1997). Physical database design for data warehouses. *Proceedings of the International Conference on Data Engineering (ICDE)*.

Lehner, W., Ruf, T. and Teschke, M. (1996). Cross-db: A feature-extended multidimensional data model for statistical and scientific databases. In *The 5th International Conference on Information and Knowledge Management (CIKM'96)*, 253-260.

Lei, H. and Ross, K. A. (1998). Faster joins, self-joins and multi-way joins using join indices. *Data and Knowledge Engineering*, November, 28(3), 277-298.

Li, C. and W. S. Wang. (1996). A data model for supporting on-line analytical processing. In *The 5th International Conference on Information and Knowledge Management (CIKM' 96)*, 81-88.

Mohania, M. and Kambayashi, Y. (2000). Making aggregate views self-maintainable. *Data and Knowledge Engineering*, January, 32(1), 87-109.

Mohania, M., Samtani, S., Roddick, J. F. and Kambayashi, Y. Advances and research directions in data warehousing technology. In *The Australian Journal of Information Systems*.

Morse, S. and Isaac, D. (1984) Parallel Systems in the Data Warehouse. Prentice Hall PTR.

Navathe, S. B., Ceri, S., Wiederhold, G. and Dou J. (1984). Vertical partitioning algorithms for database design. *ACM Transaction on Database Systems*, December, 9(4), 681-710.

Navathe, S. B., Karlapalem, K. and Ra, M. (1995). A mixed partitioning methodology for distributed database design. *Journal of Computer and Software Engineering*, 3(4) 395-426.

Navathe, S. B. and Ra, M. (1989). Vertical partitioning for database design : A graphical algorithm. *ACM SIGMOD*, 440-450.

Noaman, A.Y. and Barker, K. (1999). A horizontal fragmentation algorithm for the fact relation in a distributed data warehouse. In *the 8th International Conference on Information and Knowledge Management (CIKM' 99)*, November, 154-161.

O'Neil, P. and Quass, D. (1997). Improved query performance with variant indexes. *Proceedings of the ACM SIGMOD International Conference on Management of Data*, May, 38-49.

Oracle Corporation. (1992). *Oracle 7 Server Concepts Manual*. Redwood City, CA.

Oracle Corporation (1999). Oracle8i enterprise edition partitioning option. *Technical report, Oracle Corporation*, February.

Oracle Corporation. (1999). *Oracle8i Concepts*. Release 8.1.5.

Özsu, M.T. and Valduriez, P. (1991). *Principles of Distributed Database Systems*. Prentice Hall.

Quass, D., Gupta, A., Mumick, I. S. and Widom, J. (1996). Making views self-maintainable for data warehousing. In *Proceedings of the Fourth International Conference on Parallel and Distributed Information Systems*, December, 158-169.

Quass, D. and Widom, J. (1997). On-line warehouse view maintenance for batch updates. *Proceedings of the ACM SIGMOD International Conference on Management of Data*, May, 393-404.

Red Brick Systems. (1997). Star schema processing for complex queries. *White Paper*, July.

Sanjay, A., Surajit, C. and Narasayya, V. R. (2000). Automated selection of materialized views and indexes in Microsoft SQL server. In *VLDB'2000*, September.

Segev, A. and Zhao, J. L. (1995). A framework for join pattern indexing in intelligent database systems. *IEEE Transactions on Knowledge and Data Engineering*, December, 7(6), 941-947.

Simpson, D. (1996). Build your warehouse on mpp. Available at *http://www.datamation.com/servr/12mpp.html*, December.

Srivastava, D., Dar, S., Jagadish, H. and Levy, A. Y. (1996). Answering queries with aggregation using views. *Proceedings of the International Conference on Very Large Databases*, 318-329.

TPC Home Page. TPC Benchmark™ (decision support). http://www.tpc.org.

Tsichritzis, D. and Klug, A. (1978) *The Ansi/X3/Sparc Framework*. AFIPS Press, Montvale, N.J.

Valduriez, P. (1987). Join indices. *ACM Transactions on Database Systems*, June, 12(2), 218-246.

Vassiliadis, P. and Sellis, T. (1999). A survey of logical models for olap databases. *SIGMOD Record*, December, 28(4), 64-69.

Widom, J. (1995). Newblock research problems in data warehousing. In *The 4th International Conference on Information and Knowledge Management (CIKM'95)*, 25-30.

Wu, M. C. and Buchmann, A. (1997). Research issues in data warehousing. In *Datenbanksysteme In Büro, Technik und Wissenschaft(BTW'97)*, March, 61-82.

Yang, J., Karlapalem, K. and Q. Li, Q. (1997). Algorithms for materialized view design in data warehousing environment. *Proceedings of the International Conference on Very Large Databases*, August, 136-145.

Zhuge, Y., Garcia-Molina, H., Hammer, J. and Widom, J. (1995). View maintenance in a warehousing environment. *Proceedings of the ACM SIGMOD International Conference on Management of Data*, 316-327.

Zhuge,Y., Garcia-Molina, H. and Widom, J. (1996). The strobe algorithms for multi-source warehousing consistency. In *Proceeding of the Fourth International Conference on Parallel and Distributed Information Systems*, December, 146-157.

Chapter 3

Benchmarking
Data Mining Algorithms

Balaji Rajagopalan
Oakland University, USA

Ravi Krovi
University of Akron, USA

Data mining is the process of sifting through the mass of organizational (internal and external) data to identify patterns critical for decision support. Successful implementation of the data mining effort requires a careful assessment of the various tools and algorithms available. The basic premise of this study is that machine-learning algorithms, which are assumption free, should outperform their traditional counterparts when mining business databases. The objective of this study is to test this proposition by investigating the performance of the algorithms for several scenarios. The scenarios are based on simulations designed to reflect the extent to which typical statistical assumptions are violated in the business domain. The results of the computational experiments support the proposition that machine learning algorithms generally outperform their statistical counterparts under certain conditions. These can be used as prescriptive guidelines for the applicability of data mining techniques.

INTRODUCTION

The amount of data collected by businesses today is increasing at a phenomenal rate. Businesses face the challenge of integrating and correlating data related to online sales, offline sales, customer satisfaction surveys, and server log files. Data mining is the process of sifting through the mass of organizational (internal and external) data to identify patterns critical for decision support. Data mining techniques have been successfully employed in applications like fraud detection and

Previously Published in the *Journal of Database Management, vol.12, no.1,* Copyright © 2002, Idea Group Publishing.

bankruptcy prediction (Tam and Kiang, 1992; Lee, Han, and Kwon, 1996; Kumar, Krovi and Rajagopalan, 1997), strategic decision-making (Nazem and Shin, 1999) and database marketing (Brachman, 1996). Today, businesses have the unique opportunity for using such techniques for target marketing and customer retention. The analysis of this data is critical as more and more businesses use this information to analyze their competition, product or market. Intelligent tools which are based on rules derived from web mining can also play an important role in personalization related to site content and presentation. Recently, there has been considerable interest on how to integrate and mine such data (Mulvenna, Anand, & Buchner, 2000, Brachman, Khabaza, Kloesgen, Piatetsky-Shapiro, and Simoudis, 1996).

Business databases in general pose a unique problem for pattern extraction because of their complex nature. This complexity arises from anomalies such as discontinuity, noise, ambiguity, and incompleteness (Fayyad, Piatetsky-Shapiro, and Smyth, 1996). Analyzing such data is a key requirement for effective decision making. Decision support tools, however, vary in their ability to provide this degree of analytical processing. This is illustrated in Figure 1. Historically, decision makers had to manually deduce patterns using information generated by query reporting systems. One level of analytical sophistication above this was the ability to look at the data and perform analyses such as What-If and goal seeking. More recently, online analytical processing (OLAP) systems have shown promise in providing drill down capabilities. However, knowledge discovery of non-intuitive patterns is possible only by using data mining. These approaches can extend the power of decision support tools for more unstructured tasks.

Figure 1: A Framework for Analytical Processing

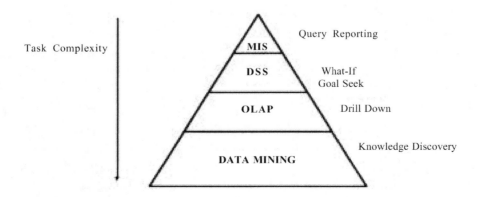

Data mining approaches are mainly comprised of statistical and machine learning algorithms. Traditional statistical techniques are more limited in their mining ability because their effectiveness depends on underlying assumptions such as data normality (Hudson, Leuthold, & Sarassoro, 1986; Hsieh, 1988; Fayyad et al., 1996; Lucas and Klassen, 1998). Given this, the challenge lies not only in the design of new techniques but also in developing criteria for using these techniques in specific problem domains. While several techniques ranging from statistical to machine learning methods have been deployed in various applications, little progress has been made toward the development of a theory regarding the correspondence between techniques and the specific problem domain to which they apply. Questions regarding the relative performance of data mining algorithms remain largely unresolved. With a myriad of algorithms and problem sets to which they are applied, a systematic investigation of their performance is critical to guide the selection of a data mining algorithm for a specific case. This research aims to develop a detailed benchmarking of five different types of data mining algorithms. These techniques are drawn from statistical algorithms and machine learning techniques such as neural networks and genetic algorithms. The basic premise of this study is that machine-learning algorithms, which are assumption free, should outperform their traditional counterparts when mining business databases. The objective of this study is to test this proposition by investigating the performance of the algorithms for several scenarios. The scenarios are based on simulation designed to reflect the extent to which typical statistical assumptions are violated in the business domain. The results of the computational experiments can be used to develop prescriptive guidelines regarding the applicability of the data mining techniques.

The rest of the chapter is organized as follows. In the next section, we present taxonomy of data mining approaches and provide an overview of the algorithms used in this study. Then we discuss the need for a systematic approach to the data mining problem and present a framework for an experimental test bed. Methodology used in the study, including the details on data simulation and algorithm testing is given and the results of the study are presented and discussed. Finally, concluding remarks and directions for future work are set forth.

DATA MINING ALGORITHMS: AN OVERVIEW

At the core of the data mining process is the algorithm that aids the generation of a decision support model. Building a decision support model is the key to fostering an understanding of and eventually a resolution of the problem. Parametric models based on traditional statistical algorithms attempt to fit a mathematical model defined a priori to describe the relationship between input and output variables. Typically they assume that the domain has an underlying data structure. In cases when there is little knowledge of the underlying distribution, the success of these models is limited or at least unknown. Non-parametric models on the other hand do not use domain specific knowledge but instead rely heavily on the data to derive the relationship. Data mining algorithms generally belong somewhere along a continuum between these two categories of parametric and non-parametric models. In some cases, several algorithms can be combined to create hybrid ones. Figure 2 shows several representative examples under both types of models. An excellent description of these algorithms can be found in Kennedy, Lee, Roy, Reed, and Lippman (1997). Certain algorithms are more applicable to some problem domains than others. For example, linear regressions are well-suited for linear systems where as binary decision trees are well suited for problems where clear boundaries can be drawn between categories. These algorithms also vary in terms of the amount of memory requirements to store the variables and their relationships. Typically, non-parametric algorithms are more memory intensive.

Before reviewing the algorithms benchmarked in this study, it is necessary to discuss the classification problem. Classification models predict the group membership of entity instances based on a set of attributes. An interest in the classification problem permeates many business applications. Problems that require the use of such models in the business domain include categorizing investments as high, medium or low risk based on financial attributes, prediction of viability of a firm (viable or bankrupt) and consumer credit approval (approve or

Figure 2: Taxonomy of Models

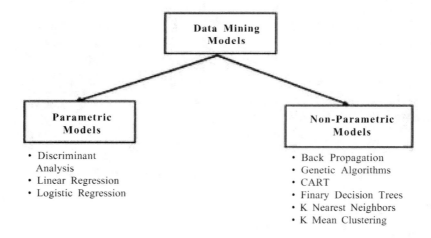

reject). Statistical algorithms such as the Fisher's linear discriminant analysis and quadratic discriminant analysis have been applied to classification problems with some success in a variety of situations. For example, Pastena and Ruland (1986) applied the statistical algorithms to predict the group membership of financially distressed firms. The two groups under consideration in this case were merger and bankruptcy. Despite the success of the models in some situations it is well known that these algorithms have been designed based on the assumptions about the nature of the population distribution from which the data is drawn. Specifically, the underlying population distribution is assumed to be multivariate normal with a homogenous variance-covariance structure. However, evidence from prior work clearly shows that business data in general and financial data in particular violate the stated assumptions (Hudson et al., 1987; Peters, 1991, Brock, Hsieh, and LeBaron, 1991; Hsieh, 1988). Machine learning paradigms do not make any assumption a priori about the population distribution nor are they designed for specific conditions such as the homogeneity of the variance-covariance structure.

Below, we provide an overview of the algorithms used in this study as they apply to the classification problem. For an extensive review of classical statistical algorithms for classification see Johnson and Wicheren (1998) and for an exhaustive review of machine learning algorithms see Kennedy et al. (1997).

Statistical Algorithms

Fisher's Linear Discriminant Model (FLDM)

Fisher's classification rule has been widely applied in the business domain and works well where the groups are linearly separable. The idea is to transform the multivariate observations **x** to univariate observations y in such a way that the y's derived from groups g_1 and g_2 are separated as much as possible. Multivariate normality of the underlying distributions and homogeneity of variance-covariance structure are the underpinning assumptions of Fisher's function. Fisher's classification rule for classifying an observation $\mathbf{x_0}$ into one of two groups, (g_1) or (g_2), is: classify $\mathbf{x_0}$ into (g_1) if:

$$v = (x^{(1)} - x^{(2)})' S^{-1}(x - (1/2)) (x^{(1)} + x^{(2)}) > c \text{ otherwise, classify into } (g_2).$$

Here $x^{(1)}$ and $x^{(2)}$ denote the vector means of two independent samples (the training samples) of sizes n_1 and n_2, respectively, and S denotes the pooled sample covariance matrix.

Quadratic Discriminant Model

The quadratic function is applicable to classify entities when the underlying population has unequal variance-covariance structures. The quadratic rule does assume that populations are multivariate normal. In fact, according to Johnson and Wicheren (1998), the drawback of the quadratic rule is that it is sensitive to departures from this assumption of multivariate normality. Quadratic classification rule for classifying an observation $\mathbf{x_0}$ into one of two groups, (g_1) or (g_2), is: classify $\mathbf{x_0}$ into (g_1) if:

$$-\frac{1}{2}x_0(s_1^{-1} - S_2^{-1})x_0 + (x_1 S_1^{-1} - x_2 S_2^{-1})x_0 - k > \ln\left[\left(\frac{c(1|2)}{c(2|1)}\right)\left(\frac{(p_2)}{(p_1)}\right)\right]$$

otherwise, classify into g_2

where S_1 and S_2 denote the covariance structure of the two populations under consideration.

Logit Model

Logit models extend the principles of generalized linear models (e.g., regression) to address the case of dichotomous dependent variables (Coskunoglu et al., 1985). They differ from standard regression in substituting maximum likelihood estimation of a link function of the dependent for regression's use of least squares estimation of the dependent itself. The function used in logit is the natural log of the odds ratio. Logit extends the log-linear model to allow a mixture of categorical and continuous independent variables with respect to a categorical dependent variable.

Machine Learning Algorithms

Neural Network Classifier

Neural network models have been widely applied recently, ranging from assessing management fraud (Green and Choi, 1997) and portfolio management to customer retention (Mena, 2000). The models, being assumption free, are very appropriate for applications in the business domain where violations of multivariate normality and unequal variance-covariance structures are not uncommon.

Neural networks or multi-layer perceptrons are composed of highly interconnected neurons or processing elements organized in layers. The simplest form of such a network to capture non-linearity has three layers: input, hidden and output. A feedforward neural network is characterized by flow of signals in one direction – the input to the output layer. Connections between the neurons have a numerical weight associated with them. The numerical weight explains the influence of input units on the output units. These weights emerge as a result of the training of the network. Figure 3 depicts a typical architecture of a feed-forward neural network with four inputs, two hidden nodes and one output node.

For a two-group classification problem under consideration in this research with p ($p \bullet 1$) discriminating variables, we consider a feedforward network with p nodes ($p=5$ in this study), in the input layer (one node for each variable), one output node and one hidden layer. Prior research has shown that for most classification problems a feedforward network with one hidden layer is sufficient (Salchenberger,

Figure 3: A feedforward neural network

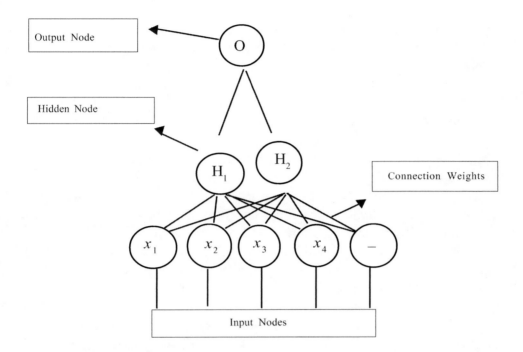

Cinar, and Lash, 1992, Dutta and Shekhar, 1988, Collins, Ghosh, and Scofield, 1988). There are no established methods for deciding on the number of nodes in a hidden layer. However, for a two-group classification problem, the suggested number of nodes in the hidden layer ranges from 0.75p (Salchenberger et al., 1992) to 2p+1 (Patuwo et al., 1993), where p is the number of input variables. The sigmoidal transfer function $\frac{1}{(1+e^{-1})}$ is applied to the hidden and output layers. The efficiency of feed forward training strategies can be improved by varying the direction of search and step length (Denton and Hung, 1996). Since our focus was not so much on computational complexity, the widely used back propagation (BP) technique was employed. The BP is based on gradient descent minimizing the mean squared error of the system by moving down the gradient on the error surface. The error surface is multi-dimensional with several local minima. The objective of training the network is to find a set of connection weights based on the global minimum (or as close to it as possible). Once the connection weights stabilize, the network can be applied to the test set. There are several ways in which the network training can be achieved. The network can be trained for a set number of iterations, or a specific error rate can be set and training stopped when that is achieved. The latter approach is most commonly applied and in the present case the root mean square error (RMSE) was set at 0.01 as the condition to stop training. Further, to prevent over-training of the network twenty percent of the training data set was used as a validation set.

Hybrid Genetic Classifier

A Genetic Algorithm (GA) is a procedure that operates on the principles of heuristic search. The search mechanism itself is based on the principles of adaptation and evolution – i.e. species constantly search for beneficial adaptations in order to survive in a complex and changing environment. The stronger characteristics survive while the weaker ones are rejected. While the initial concepts were developed by John Holland (1975), these algorithms have since been applied in diverse applications ranging from document clustering to pipeline optimization (Goldberg, 1989, 1994). More recently we have seen implementations in optimal pricing strategies (Wu,1999), trading (Allen and Karjaleinen, 1999), network design (Premkumar, Chu, & Chou, 2000), and production scheduling (ElMaraghy, Patel, and Abdallah, 2000).

The common theme underlying these applications is that they are all "hard" domains – i.e., domains that are characterized by very large search spaces. The GA is particularly useful in these domains also because there is a lot of discontinuity and noise. Traditional search procedures that are primarily based on hill climbing tend to converge to local optima based solutions. The GA is able to avoid this by considering several solution points and developing the ones that appear to be promising based on a defined criterion. A typical sequence in a GA consists of the following steps:

1. Initialize a population of chromosomes (possible solutions).
2. Evaluate each chromosome in the population based on domain specific evaluation function.
3. Create more chromosomes by applying the crossover and mutation.
4. Delete members of the population to make room for the new chromosomes.
5. Repeat steps (3-5) until a specific evaluation criterion is reached.

Given the above sequence, it is important to note that studies typically differ in two aspects. First, most real world applications have to make use of domain specific knowledge in the form of heuristics to improve the algorithm (El Maraghy et al., 2000). Second, studies differ in what operators to apply and further how exactly to apply these operators or parameter settings (Yao, 1993; Reid, 1997). While the standard GA uses the mutation and crossover operators to generate more chromosomes, some studies have used different operators to enhance the search process (Whitley, Starkweather and Shaner, 1991). The second issue of how exactly to apply these operators is tricky and influences the speed and quality of solution. The key is to select a set of parameters that will result in rapid convergence towards promising parts of the search space. The problem here is that what works well for one problem might not result in a good solution for another problem. A few attempts (Dejong, 1980; Yao, 1993; Reid, 1997) have been made to parameterize the GA or at least identify the conditions, which augment performance. Broadly speaking, it appears that good performance requires moderate selections in population size, high crossover rate, and a low mutation rate. In our study, we used the standard genetic operators with the following parametric values:

Population size = 50, Crossover rate = 0.75,
Mutation Rate = 0.02, Number of trials = 300.

The hybrid GA used in this study is modeled after the approach used in prior studies (Kumar, et al., 1997; Kelly and Davis, 1991). This hybrid procedure combines the search efficiency of the GA with the simplicity of yet another classification technique; the k-nearest neighbors algorithm. In the k-nearest neighbors algorithm, a new instance is assigned to the same class as the majority of its nearest neighbors. The k-nearest algorithm itself is not very effective for mining business databases, especially when the attributes vary in terms of the degree of importance. The GA enhances the k-nearest neighbor algorithm by attempting to learn the weights or coefficients associated with the variables in the training set. The specific implementation details of the hybrid genetic classifier are presented below in three parts. They include: the class assignment procedure as performed in the k-nearest neighbor algorithm, the problem representation in the GA, and the evaluation function used in the GA to evaluate candidate solutions.

Class Assignment:
1) Compute the distance between two points, i and j, given n variables, m instances and k neighbors.

$d_{ij} = \Sigma w_y (X_{iy} - X_{jy})$, where
X_{iy} = value of the yth attribute for the ith member of the data set
w_y = weight associated with the yth attribute; $y = 1$ to n; $i = 1$ to m; $i = j$.
2) Identify the k nearest neighbors based on the distances.
3) Compute vote for each class.
V_0 = Vote for class 0;
= sum of the votes of neighbors belonging to class 0.
V_1 = Vote for class 1;
= sum of the votes of neighbors belonging to class 1.
(4) Assign an instance based on the class with the largest vote.

Problem representation
The GA considers each chromosome as a candidate solution. Each chromosome was represented as a real valued string of 5 (variables) plus 9 (votes of the k closest neighbors). Each variable weight ranged from 0 to 1. The actual

representation in the GA is eventually in the form of a bit string. The GA searches for the configuration that best fits the evaluation criteria. For example, in the following string, the first five values are the weight coefficients for variables followed by the vote for the closest neighbor (0.74), followed by the vote for the second closest neighbor (0.06), and so on.

0.02 0.12 0.09 0.056 0.23 0.74 0.06
0.43 0.07 0.23 0.56 0.04

Evaluation function

A candidate solution was evaluated in the following manner. Each instance in the data set A chromosome was evaluated by going through the training data set and classifying each instance by computing its distance from the data set, finding the k nearest neighbors, and then adding up the individual voting strengths for each class to make the assignment. The hit rate (percent of correct classifications) was computed for each chromosome. To differentiate between chromosomes, which had the same hit rates, we used the following decision rules to break a tie.

Chromosome X was ranked higher than Y ($H_x > H_y$) if:

$H_x = H_y$ and $C_x > C_y$

or

$H_x = H_y$ and $C_x = C_y$ and $D_x > D_y$

where H is the hit rate for a chromosome on the training set, C is the hit rate for a chromosome on a cross-validation set, D is the average distance of dissimilar neighbors from that instance.

EXPERIMENTATION AND PERFORMANCE ISSUES

Given the varied nature of the algorithms, their requirements and applicability to a domain, it will be invaluable to have guidelines based on their performance. With regard to experimentation, there are two fundamental issues that need to be addressed. The first issue pertains to the use of real world versus simulated data sets. The second issue pertains to a focus on variables that affect performance.

As stated earlier, there are two fundamental approaches to data mining research. One approach would be to apply the algorithms to real world data sets and gauge their performance (Tam and Kiang, 1992; Salchenberger et al., 1992; Kumar et al., 1997). Then, when there is a critical mass of such comparative studies, a meta-analysis can draw inferences about the performance of algorithms on a variety of problem sets. Indeed, some problems with this approach include not enough studies to draw inference from, the use of different algorithms with subtle differences rending parity of them impossible to achieve, and the myriad of problem types to which they have been applied without enough a sample size of each problem type to draw conclusions from. One way that these problems are being addressed is by encouraging researchers to use a common test data set when testing algorithms. Well known resources for test data sets include the Web site Kdnuggets.com, and the University of California, Irvine repository where researchers share data sets and information about data mining algorithms. Another approach to gauge the performance of algorithms for a specific problem type is to test several algorithms on multiple data sets. This approach is not free from bottlenecks, either; the most important of them being having access to multiple real world data sets to test the algorithms. One of the ways to overcome this is by simulating specific conditions to reflect the domain of interest and generating data sets for a given problem type based on it. Then, the comparative investigation can be carried out based on the performance of the algorithms on simulated data sets.

Data mining algorithm complexity and subsequently performance is affected by several variables. Hence, it is necessary to have a framework that serves as an integrative test bed for future research. In Figure 4, we present a three dimensional framework to represent all the variables which affect decision making performance. Typically, performance metrics for data mining algorithms include solution quality and solution time. The former refers to the degree of deviation from an optimal solution. The latter could refer to the amount of time required for model convergence. The essence of the above framework is that performance really should be measured on three key indices. These are Data Structure, Noise, and Incompleteness.

The *Data Structure* dimension refers to how well the algorithm can handle variations in the underlying data distribution. This may be reflected, for example, by deviations from normality or unequal variance-covariance structure. The *Incompleteness* dimension is a factor when there are fewer data elements to extract

Figure 4: Experimental Test Bed

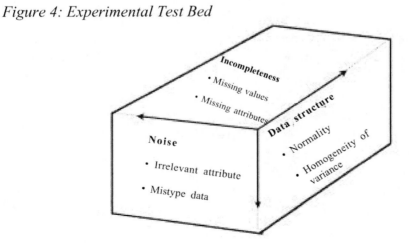

useful patterns. This could be in the form of missing values or missing relevant variables. Missing values can have a subtle impact on performance. This is because analysts have to reject the entire tuple or record that has a missing value. The consequent decrease in tuples or observations reduces the predictive ability of the mining algorithm. Unless steps are taken to estimate the missing values, this could pose a serious problem. Performance may also be affected because there may be several attributes that may be relevant to the problem for which either there is no data or for which data cannot be collected. The predictive ability of the data mining algorithm decreases as the number of such missing attributes increases. The *Noise* dimension refers to algorithm performance in the presence of useless or distracting data elements. Noise usually manifests through irrelevant attributes or mistyped data. Irrelevant attributes are usually a result of insufficient development in domain theory. As a result, analysts often include many variables that are irrelevant to the problem. Most data mining algorithms are able to separate the effects of such irrelevant attributes in determining the actual pattern. However, the predictive power of the mining algorithm may decrease as the number of such attributes increases. There may be instances where attribute value pairs have data inaccuracies. This indicates the degree of random noise in the database, and as such directly affects the predictive power of the algorithm. Mistyped data is a serious problem and is hard to detect and control. Such a quality issue needs to be resolved at the pre-processing stage by building in data integrity checks and other validation controls. A subset of this problem is when there is high dimensionality (number of fields) or data volume (number of records). In these cases, the algorithm performance depends on how well it is scalable.

This study uses simulated data sets for benchmarking data mining algorithms. The problem type chosen for examining the performance is the classification problem, one that has wide application in the business domain. The algorithms being examined for the classification problem in this study are Fisher's linear discriminant model (FLDM), Quadratic discriminant model (QDM), Logit, neural network and hybrid genetic algorithm. Our specific focus is on the Data Structure dimension and we seek to study the relative performance under deviations of the above dimension.

RESEARCH METHOD

This study tests the effectiveness of popular statistical techniques vis-à-vis machine learning techniques for a specific data mining task: the classification problem. The focus of this study is on the data structure dimension of the experimental test bed. To accomplish a comparative analysis of algorithms across the data structure dimension, there is a need for data sets conforming to specific characteristics along multivariate normality and covariance structure. To generate the data sets for these conditions we use a Monte Carlo simulation to generate the population distribution.

Monte Carlo Simulation

The simulation is based on the Fleishman (1978) power method. The procedure uses a polynomial transformation to produce non-normal data. It proceeds by taking the sum of a linear combination of a standard random normal variable, its square and its cube. For a detailed description of the method see Fleishman (1978), and for a discussion of alternate ways of generating distributions, see Tadikamalla (1980), Vale and Maurelli (1983), and Headrick and Sawilowsky (1999). The Fleishman approach has been by far the most widely studied and applied. For example, Tadikamalla (1980) suggests the use of Fleishman method "If what is needed is a method to generate different distributions with the least amount of difficulty and as efficiently as possible" (p. 278).

Using the Monte Carlo simulation approach of Fleishman's power method, we generate two distributions each (corresponding to the two-group classification problem) with five variables for three levels of normality and two levels of covariance structure. $U_1 = \{0,0,0,0,0\}$ and $U_2 = \{1,1,1,1,1\}$ represent the means for the five input variables for groups g_1 and g_2 respectively across all conditions of normality and variance-covariance structures. Along the normality dimension, two levels correspond to specific non-normal distributions: leptokurtic (skewness = 0.25, kurtosis = 3) and platokurtic (skewness = 0, kurtosis = -1). These distributions were chosen, as they are representative of multivariate distributions in the business domain. The third is a normal distribution for benchmarking the

Table 1: Design Overview

	Equal Variances	Unequal Variances
Normal Distribution (Gaussian)	XXXXXXX XXXXXXX XXXXXXX	XXXXXXX XXXXXXX XXXXXXX
Non-Normal Distribution 1 (Leptokurtic)	XXXXXXX XXXXXXX XXXXXXX	XXXXXXX XXXXXXX XXXXXXX
Non-Normal Distribution 2 (Platokurtic)	XXXXXXX XXXXXXX XXXXXXX	XXXXXXX XXXXXXX XXXXXXX

algorithms. The two levels along the covariance structure correspond to the two distributions having identical, $COV_1 = COV_2 = I$, and dissimilar variance-covariance structures, $COV_1 = I \; COV_2 = 2I$. COV_1 and COV2 represent the covariance structures for the two groups under consideration and "I" represents the identity matrix. The experimental framework depicted as a 3x2 matrix along the two dimensions is shown in Table 1. Five data sets per cell are generated. This will result in a total of 5x3x2 = 30 data sets.

For each data set, the probability that an observation will belong to a group is 0.5. Each data set is divided into a training sample (200, 100 in each group) and a testing sample (200). To benchmark the performance of algorithms, they will be run against 5 data sets per cell (see Table 1). As discussed in the previous section, the statistical algorithms under consideration are the Fisher's linear discriminant model, Quadratic discriminant model, and Logit. Machine learning algorithms included in this study are the feedforward neural network based on backpropogation algorithm and hybrid genetic classifier based on the genetic algorithm. The performance of each classification technique will be measured by the average classification or hit rate (i.e., the percentage of accurate predictions) on the test data sets.

RESULTS AND DISCUSSION

The effectiveness of traditional statistical procedures such as FLDM rests on the robustness to withstand the violations of their underlying assumptions. Our expectation therefore was that there would be appreciable drops in hit rates for FLDM under conditions of severe violations in assumptions. Hence, we expected to see drops in FLDM hit rates across the assumption of unequal variances and for non-normal distributions. Tables 2 and 3 present the average hit rates for the five algorithms across the conditions of variance equality and distribution type. Table 4 provides a consolidated overview.

Figures 5 and 6 illustrate the pattern of algorithm performance by algorithm and the underlying population distribution for equal variance-covariance structures. Figures 7 and 8 present the pattern of algorithm performance by algorithm and the underlying population distribution for unequal variance-covariance structures.

There are some patterns that are immediately discernible. For example, QDM appears to be the most robust method. Except for a slight drop under Leptokurtic distribution and Unequal Variances, it is fairly consistent with hit rate performances in the eighties. There appear to be no differences in hit rates for the condition of equal variance structures. However, most of the differences are accentuated under the unequal variances condition. There appear to be large differences by algorithms (for example, QDM and GA are better than FLDM).

Table 2: Algorithm performance for equal variance-covariance structures

	Guassian	Leptokurtic	Platokurtic	Average
FLDM	87.50	87.40	86.20	**87.03**
QDM	87.20	87.20	85.10	**86.50**
Logit	85.00	89.50	84.50	**86.33**
NN	85.00	89.00	84.00	**86.00**
Hybrid GA	82.20	91.50	91.40	**88.37**
Average	**85.38**	**88.92**	**86.24**	

Table 3: Algorithm performance for unequal variance-covariance structures

	Guassian	Leptokurtic	Platokurtic	Average
FLDM	76.10	78.40	78.30	**77.60**
QDM	88.00	83.30	93.20	**88.17**
Logit	72.00	82.00	75.00	**76.33**
NN	78.00	86.00	92.00	**85.33**
Hybrid GA	78.00	92.30	91.00	**87.10**
Average	**78.42**	**84.40**	**85.90**	

Table 4: Descriptive Statistics for Algorithm Performance by Underlying Distribution

	FLDM	QDM	Logit	NN	Hybrid GA
Gaussian					
Average	81.80	87.60	79.65	81.60	80.10
Variance	39.11	7.19	34.60	12.84	4.79
Leptokurtic					
Average	82.90	85.30	85.90	87.40	91.90
Variance	24.69	9.33	21.55	8.76	16.32
Platokurtic					
Average	82.25	89.15	80.25	87.15	91.20
Variance	18.21	18.00	21.26	7.40	0.61

Figure 5: Performance by algorithm (Equal Variance-Covariance Structure)

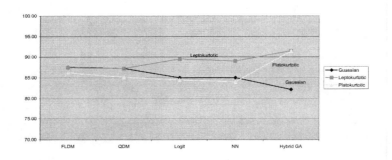

Figure 6: Algorithm Performance by Underlying Population Distribution (Equal Variance-Covariance Structure)

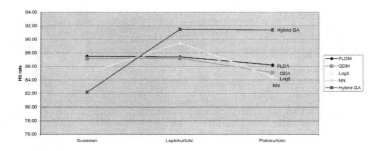

Figure 7: Performance by algorithm (Unequal Variance-Covariance Structure)

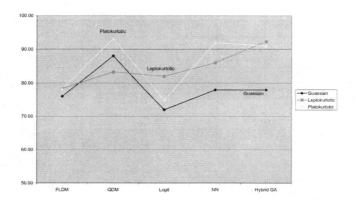

Figure 8: Algorithm Performance by Underlying Population Distribution (Unequal Variance-Covariance Structure)

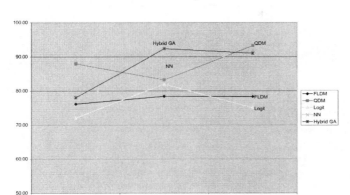

There also appear to be large differences by distribution (for example, hit rates under platokurtic distribution are better than those under Gaussian distribution). Also a comparison across the equal variance assumption reveals that FLDM and Logit are the most severely affected with appreciable drops. There are also some patterns that are consistent across the equality of variance assumptions. For example, the pattern of hit rate performance across (equal variance) assumptions is the same for both GA and Logit.

The graphs also reveal some anomalies. For example, GA always performs poorly under Gaussian distribution. This performance decreases further under the condition of unequal variances. It is not clear what exactly is it about Heterogeneity and Gaussian that makes the GA perform very poorly. The above discussion leads us to believe that there is the possibility of a significant interaction effect.

To test for such a possibility we conducted a three way analysis of variance. Table 5 presents the ANOVA table. As can be seen there are significant main and interaction effects. This means that performance does vary across conditions.

Table 5: ANOVA
TABLE 5a: Analysis of Variance Procedure Class Level Information

Class	Levels	Values
VARCOV	2	1 2
DISTRIB	3	1 2 3
ALGORIT	5	1 2 3 4 5

Number of observations in data set = 150

TABLE 5b: Analysis of Variance Procedure (Dependent Variable: HITRATE)

Source	DF	Sum of Squares	Mean Square	F Value	Pr > F	R-Square	CV	Root MSE	HITRATE Mean
Model	29	4097.56	141.29	55.28	0.0001	0.930363	1.882075	1.59	84.94
Error	120	306.70	2.55						
Corrected Total	149	4404.26							
VARCOV	1	574.28	574.28	224.69	0.0001				
DISTRIB	2	596.76	298.38	116.75	0.0001				
ALGORIT	4	891.87	222.96	87.24	0.0001				
VARCOV*DISTRIB	2	219.56	109.78	42.95	0.0001				
VARCOV*ALGORIT	4	760.24	190.06	74.36	0.0001				
DISTRIB*ALGORIT	8	813.70	101.71	39.80	0.0001				
VARCOV*DISTRI*ALGORI	8	241.13	30.14	11.79	0.0001				

Table 6: Pairwise comparisons of algorithms

Factor	Minimum Significant Difference	Critical value	Grouping	Significance
Variance Covariance Structures	0.5169	2.800	Equal Variance v. Unequal Variance	Yes
Algorithm	1.1433	3.917	FLDM v. Logit	No
			FLDM v. QDM	Yes
			FLDM v. NN	Yes
			FLDM v. GA	Yes
			QDM v. GA	No
			QDM v. NN	Yes
			QDM v. Logit	Yes
			Logit v. NN	Yes
			Logit v. GA	Yes
			NN v. GA	Yes
Distribution	0.7588	3.356	Leptokurtic v. Platokurtic	No
			Leptokurtic v. Gaussian	Yes
			Platokurtic v. Gaussian	Yes

To find what exactly causes these differences, we conducted post hoc tests. Since we had not planned any comparisons a priori and also since mainly pairwise comparisons were desired we employed the Tukey procedure. The results are presented in Table 6 show the various pairwise comparisons.

Another interesting comparison is the average performance of machine learning algorithms vis-à-vis statistical algorithms. To do this, we want to contrast the means of three groups (three statistical algorithms - FLDM, QDM, and Logit) with the means of two other groups (two machine learning algorithms - NN, GA). Such a compound comparison or contrast can be summarized as:

$$(\mu_1 + \mu_2 + \mu_3) / 3 = (\mu_4 + \mu_5)/2$$

The means and deviations for the five groups are summarized in Table 7.

The Dunn post hoc procedure was employed to make the above compound comparison. Since the t-statistic, $t = 10.07$, is larger than the critical value of 2.24, the average of the combined machine learning algorithms significantly exceeds the combined average of the statistical algorithms.

Yet another compound comparison which is useful to consider is the average performance under the normal distribution vis-a-vis the combined performance under deviations from gaussian distribution. Here, the compound comparison of interest is:

$$\mu_1 = (\mu_2 + \mu_3)/2$$

The means and deviations for the three groups are summarized in Table 8. The Dunn post hoc procedure was employed again to make the above compound

Table 7: Means and Deviations of the five algorithms

	FLDM	QDM	Logit	NN	Hybrid GA
Mean	82.32	87.35	81.93	85.38	87.73
Deviation	5.38	3.74	5.59	3.90	5.67
Sample size	30	30	30	30	30

Table 8: Means and Deviations of the Three Distributions

	Guassian	Leptokurtic	Platokurtic
Mean	82.15	86.68	86.00
Deviation	5.32	4.30	5.54
Sample size	50	50	50

comparison. Since, the t-statistic, $t = 15.13$, is larger than the critical value of 2.24, the average of the combined performance under non-gaussian distributions significantly exceeds that of performance under gaussian distribution.

CONCLUSIONS

This contribution of this research is twofold. First, it provides a critical examination of issues to be considered when making comparative analyses of data mining algorithms. In this vein, the paper proposes an experimental test bed that future studies can use in their investigations. Second, the study addresses two important dimensions, multivariate normality and variance-covariance structure, along which the performance of data mining algorithms is compared. This can form the basis for generating guidelines to apply the algorithms. For example, it is clear that in the case of severe violations of multivariate normality and equality of variance-covariance structure, the machine learning algorithms are to be preferred over the statistical algorithms. However, it is to be noted that several other issues also influence the choice and successful application of data mining algorithms.

Ultimately, successful implementation of data mining algorithms may require creative approaches. For example, problem size increases may be manifested by very large databases (such as Census) that may have data in the range of terabytes and gigabytes. In such cases, it may be necessary to create separate work areas by offloading to a separate temporary folder. In some cases this can also be creatively achieved by data partitioning. For example, a credit card company can analyze data separately either by region or by expense category etc. To make algorithms scalable also requires using more computational power - i.e., faster CPUs. In some cases this may be enhanced by multiple CPUs; however, the algorithms then need to be redesigned to take advantage of the explicit parallelism in hardware (Galal, Cook, and Holder, 1999). Consideration of which algorithm to be used might also depend on the specific variables that are employed. For example a variable such as State that has 51 levels might result in a larger model as opposed to Student Classification which has 4 levels. Future studies can examine the impact of one or more these factors in the choice of an algorithm.

Another area that needs attention is theory building. Despite several studies examining the performance of data mining algorithms for specific tasks in a specific domain, there is a lack of studies that integrate these findings to offer more useful insights that can lay the foundations for theory building. There is a strong need for research that can provide such an integrative focus. One of the ways that this can be achieved is by conducting a meta-analysis. Another avenue for research would be to adopt the approach taken by this study to examine the performance issues along one or more dimensions of noise, incomplete information, etc.... using simulated data sets. Finally, it would be very useful for studies focusing on implementations of one or more data mining algorithms to be able to integrate their investigation with prior work in a way to offer prescriptive insights.

REFERENCES

Allen, F. & Karjalainen, R. (1999). Using genetic algorithms to find technical trading rules. *Journal of Financial Economics*, 51(2), 245-271.

Brachman, R.J. Khabaza, T. Kloesgen, W. Piatetsky-Shapiro, G. & Simoudis, E. (1996). Mining business databases. *Communications of the ACM*, 39(11), 42-48.

Brock, W.A., Hsieh, D.A., & LeBaron, B. (1991). *Nonlinear dynamics, chaos, and instability: Statistical theory and economic evidence*. Cambridge, MA: The MIT press.

Collins, E. Ghosh, S. & Scofield, C. (1988). An application of a multiple neural network learning system to emulation of mortgage underwriting judgements. *Proceedings of the IEEE conference on Neural Networks*, 2, 459-466.

Coskunoglu, O. Hansotia, B. & Muzaffar, S. (1985). A New Logit model for decision making and its application. *The Journal of the Operational Research Society*, 36(1), 35-41.

DeJong, K.A. (1980). Adaptive systems design: A genetic approach. *IEEE transactions on systems, man and cybernetics*, 10(9), 566-574.

Denton, J. W. & Hung, M. S. (1996). A Comparison of nonlinear optimization methods for supervised learning in multilayer feedforward neural networks. *European Journal of Operational Research*, 93, 358-368.

ElMaraghy, H. Patel, V. & Abdallah, I. B. (2000). Scheduling of manufacturing systems under dual resource constraints using genetic algorithms, *Journal of Manufacturing Systems*, 19(3), 186-201.

Fayyad, U. Piatetsky-Shapiro, G. & Smyth, P. (1996). From data mining to knowledge discovery in databases, *AI magazine*, 17(3), 37-54.

Fleishman, A.I. 1978. A method for generating non-normal distributions. *Psychometrika*, 43,521-532.

Galal, G. M. Cook, D. J. & Holder, L. B. (1999). Exploiting Parallelism in a Structural Scientific Discovery System to Improve Scalability. *Journal of the American Society for Information Science*, 50(1), 65-73.

Goldberg, D. E. (1994). Genetic and evolutionary algorithms come of age. *Communications of the ACM*, 37(3), 113-119.

Goldberg, D.A. (1989). Genetic algorithms in search, optimization, and machine learning. MA:Addison-Wesley.

Green, B.P. & Choi, J.H. (1997). Assessing the risk of management fraud through neural network technology. *Auditing: A journal of practice and theory*, 16(1), 14-27.

Headrick, T. C. & Sawilowsky, S. S. (1999). Simulating correlated multivariate nonnormal distributions: extending the Fleishman power method. *Psychometrika*, 64(1), 25-35.

Hsieh, D. A. (1984). The statistical properties of daily foreign exchange rates: 1974-1983. *Journal of International Economics*, 24, 129-145.

Hudson, M. A. Leuthold, R. M. & Sarassoro, G. F. (1986). Commodity futures price changes: Recent evidence for wheat, soybean, and live cattle. *The Journal of Futures Markets*, 7, 287-301.

Johnson, R. & Wicheren, D.W. (1998). *Applied Multivariate Statistical Analysis*. Prentice Hall.

Kelly, J.D. & Davis, L. (1991). A hybrid genetic algorithm for classification. *Proceedings of the twelfth international conference on artificial intelligence*. Darling harbor, Sydney, 645-650.

Kennedy, R. L. Lee, Y. Roy, B. V. Reed, C. D. & Lippman, R. P. (1997). *Solving Data Mining Problems Through Pattern Recognition*. New Jersey: Prentice Hall Professional Technical Reference.

Kumar, N. Krovi, R. & Rajagopalan, B. (1997). Financial decision support with hybrid genetic and neural based modeling tools. *European Journal of Operational Research*, 103(2), 339-349.

Lee, K.C. Han, I. & Kwon, Y. (1996). Hybrid neural network models for bankruptcy predictions. *Decision Support Systems*, 18(1), 63-73.

Lucas, A. & Klaasen, P. (1998). Extreme returns, downside Risk, and optimal asset allocation. *Journal of Portfolio Management*, 25(1), 71-79.

Mena, J. (2000). Bringing them back. *Intelligent Enterprise*, 3(12).

Mulvenna, M. D. Anand, S. S. & Buchner, A. G. (2000). Personalization on the net using web mining. *Communications of the ACM*, 43(8), 123-125.

Nazem, S. & Shin, B. (1999). Data mining: New arsenal for strategic decision making. *Journal of Database Management*. 10(1), 39-42.

Pastena, V., & Ruland, W. (1986). The merger/bankruptcy alternative. *The Accounting Review* 61(2), 288-302.

Patuwo, E., Hu, M.Y., & Hung, M.S. (1993). Two-group classification using neural networks. *Decision Sciences*, 24(4), 825-845.

Peters, E.E. (1991). *Chaos and order in the capital markets : A new view of cycles, process and market volatility*, New York :John Wiley.

Premkumar, G. Chu, C. & Chou, H. (2000). Telecommunications network design – comparison of alternative approaches. *Decision Sciences*, 31(2), 483-506.

Reid, D. J. (1997). Enhanced genetic operators for the resolution of discrete constrained optimization problems. *Computers and Operations Research*, 24(5), 399-411.

Salchenberger, L.M. Cinar, M.E. & Lash, N.A. (1992). Neural networks: A new tool for predicting thrift failures. *Decision Sciences*, 23, 899-916.

Tadikamalla, P.R. (1980). On simulating non-normal distributions, *Psychometrika*, 45(2), 273-279.

Tam, K.Y. & Kiang, M.Y. (1992). Managerial applications of Neural networks : The case of bank failure predictions. *Decision Sciences*, 38(7), 926-948.

Vale, D.C. & Maurelli, V.A.(1983). Simulating multivariate nonnormal distributions. *Psychometrika*, 48(3), 465-471.

Whitley, D. Starkweather, T., & Shaner, D. (1991). The traveling salesman and sequence scheduling:Quality solutions using genetic edge recombination. In:Davis, L.(Ed.), *Handbook of Genetic Algorithms*. New York: Van Nostrand Reinhold.

Wu, D. J. (1999). Discovering near-optimal pricing strategies for the deregulated electric power marketplace using genetic algorithms, *Decision Support Systems*, 27(2), 25-45.

Yao, X. (1993). An empirical study of genetic operators in genetic algorithms. *Microprocessing and Microprogramming*, 38(1-5), 707-714.

Chapter 4

Justifying
Data Warehousing Investments

Ram L. Kumar
University of North Carolina-Charlotte, USA

Organizations are increasingly recognizing the importance of information technology. Many large IT projects in the area of data warehousing and data mining have been taken up in the last few years. While many data warehousing and data mining projects have resulted in interesting business benefits, there are also many examples of cost and schedule overruns and dissatisfaction regarding the results from these projects. A recent issue of Information Week *(May 24, 1999) reported that organizations are carefully scrutinizing the returns from large data warehousing projects. This makes it increasingly important for information systems professionals to understand the payoff from data warehousing investments. It is also extremely important for information systems professionals to articulate the business benefits of data warehousing and other big ticket information technology projects in terms that senior managers in general and finance executives in particular can relate to. This article outlines an approach to justifying data warehousing investments that is based on the concept of options in finance. This approach to justifying investments is being increasingly recognized as being superior to traditional methods by finance professionals (*Business Week, *June 7, 1999).*

Previously Published in the *Journal of Database Management, vol.11, no.3,* Copyright © 2000, Idea Group Publishing.

OPTIONS

This section briefly describes a financial call option, which is one type of a financial option. A financial call option is a right, but not an obligation to buy a financial asset (such as a share). For example, one could acquire an option to buy 1,000 shares of AMAZON.COM stock at $150 on 3/1/2000 by paying a certain amount of money (say $10,000) since financial options are traded. The value of this option depends on the expected price of AMAZON.COM on 3/1/2000. Some people might be willing to pay $10,000 for this option if they expect the price of AMAZON.COM on 3/1/2000 to be high enough (higher than $160). They can then buy 1,000 shares of AMAZON.COM at $150 per share, sell them at a price higher than $160 and still make a profit that exceeds their initial payment of $10,000. It is important to realize that if on 3/1/2000 AMAZON.COM shares trade at less than $150, then the person who bought the option (the option holder) need not buy the 1000 shares of AMAZON.COM. The option holder would then lose $10,000 (the amount originally paid to acquire the option). Thus the person who buys the option stands to gain an indeterminate (potentially large) amount of money if the value of the underlying asset (AMAZON.COM stock) increases. However, losses are limited to $10,000 even if the value of the underlying asset drops significantly.

Techniques for valuing financial call options exist. The value of a financial call option thus depends on the expected value of the asset (stock) at the time of exercising the option. In addition, the value of call option is greater when there is more uncertainty surrounding the future value of the stock.

It is being increasingly recognized that the logic and techniques of financial option pricing are increasingly relevant to "real" investment projects or investment in non-financial assets such as information technology projects. The next section discusses the similarity between data warehousing investments and financial options.

THE DATA WAREHOUSING PROJECT AS AN OPTION

Investment in data warehousing projects can be considered similar to buying financial call options. The cost of the project is analogous to the cost of buying the option or the value of the option. In other words, an organization acquires an option by investing in a data warehousing project. This investment results in the option to get the business benefits of data warehousing on the date of completion of the project by using sophisticated OLAP and /or data mining techniques. The value of this option can be calculated (approximately) using techniques based on financial option pricing. This method of valuing investment projects usually results in a higher value than traditional financial techniques such as net present value (NPV). Also, using the option pricing methodology recognizes that investments can be more valuable when there is a high degree of uncertainty.

For example, consider a data warehouse for an organization engaged in marketing products over the Web. Investment in a data warehouse allows the organization to run sophisticated queries and data mining algorithms, and thus uncover changing consumer preferences. This scenario can be visualized as buying an option (by investing in a data warehouse) to run sophisticated queries and data mining algorithms. Running these queries in turn could result in the option to modify prices (in response to customer preferences), or the option to *quickly* change the product mix in response to market shifts. Investments in data warehouses could create new options (for decision making) that were not envisaged earlier because the technology makes it possible to run OLAP queries that were infeasible earlier. These options are more valuable when there is a high degree of uncertainty or when market conditions change more frequently. Frequent market changes mean that OLAP-based queries are more frequently required in order to understand consumer behavior and take appropriate action. In other words, investing in a data warehouse provides a variety of options such as the option to *quickly* change pricing in response to customer preferences, or the option to *quickly* change the product mix in response to market shifts. The data warehouse technology adds value by facilitating quick response to changing conditions. Option pricing theory allows the (approximate) calculation of the value of quicker decision making.

CONCLUSION

It is important for database administrators and information technology managers to look beyond traditional financial evaluation methods such as net present value (NPV) and return on investment (ROI) in justifying sophisticated IT investments such as data warehouses. Finance managers are increasingly becoming aware of option-based arguments for justifying investments. These arguments can be used to build a stronger case for information technology investments.

Chapter 5

Data Mining: New Arsenal for Strategic Decision-making

Sufi M. Nazem and Bongsik Shin
University of Nebraska – Omaha

During the early years of database management the contemporary wisdom was to store only 'useful data.' In large part, this philosophy was encouraged because of the then-limited storage capacity offered by the prevailing technology. Then along came the microprocessor revolution, enormously expanding the scope of data storage. Subsequent advancement in information technology and recognition of potential business opportunities thereof, resulted in enormous expansion of data storage. Although the future is unknown and unpredictable, it often provides new business opportunities. Thus, new management strategies emerged which encouraged the massive accumulation of data and thus the advent of data warehousing. These massive data depositories are now providing both challenges and opportunities for strategic decision-making concerned with improving existing businesses and exploring new business opportunities. Data mining is an essential part of the process involved in locating relevant information from data warehouses for use in making such strategic decisions. Naturally, business leaders everywhere are willing to make investments in corporate data warehouses to enhance their access to information. The return on such investment is by no means guaranteed but all business activities include a certain amount of risk.

The value of information is created through mining of database in two different ways. First, this is achieved through careful exploitation of the intrinsic value of information. In such a situation, the information itself becomes the source of income through a process of conversion to a valuable

Previously Published in the *Journal of Database Management, vol.10, no.1,* Copyright © 1999, Idea Group Publishing.

commodity, leading to new businesses. Secondly, information often becomes an effective instigator for improved organizational performance. In this case, information acts as a vehicle for effective organizational reengineering that achieves better customer service, permits more flexible business approaches, integrates value chains, speeds up decision processes and expedites responses to customer needs. In the business environment where "time" is becoming a key success factor, maintenance of efficient systems for information processing and organizational learning is critical. As the volume of database itself grows at an exponential pace, technological innovation is becoming especially instrumental in offering a golden opportunity for organizations to arm themselves with more business intelligence and knowledge-making capabilities.

In this paper we intend to provide an overview of this emerging technology and related trends in the application of data mining. Given the confidential and highly proprietary nature of data mining activities critical organizational issues have rarely enjoyed an open discussion. The paper addresses issues of data mining from the organizational strategy perspective.

OVERVIEW OF DATA MINING

Data mining requires the understanding of types of knowledge and search algorithms used to explore them, each of these has two aspects been expanded in this section.

Type of Knowledge

Data-mining makes possible the intelligent discovery and application of various types of knowledge from large-scale databases. Such advanced knowledge is difficult to recover from conventional query processing or on-line analytical processing (OLAP). It is also different from traditional forms of data analysis in that the process itself is dealing with a massive amount of data and more innovative intelligence is incorporated in the knowledge discovery process. Data-mining enables the discovery of various types of knowledge, including, but not limited to:

- Dependency and association relationships among attributes
- Deviation (or anomaly) detection
- Sequential and temporal patterns among inter-transactions.
- Classification of knowledge
- Clustering of records that have similar characteristics
- Summarization of data.

The discovery can be initiated by end-users or by the data-mining system. With the user initiative, knowledge seekers have to develop data-mining questions, then the data-mining system searches for relevant knowledge based on the search directions. The shortcoming of this user initiative approach is that it takes a verification or confirmative modeling approach for the understanding of relationships among variables. The effectiveness of this approach might be limited depending on the level of training and knowledge end-users have on the task domain. It is almost certain that knowledge-miners will never be able to devise all relevant questions and much of the hidden information will go unnoticed.

On the other hand, when a data-mining system has an initiative for a knowledge search, it looks for interesting and significant patterns with no hypotheses posed by the user (exploratory model). In fact, if data-mining is the "discovery of information without a previously formulated hypothesis," (Cabena et al., 1997) only the system initiative approach could be labeled as true data-mining. Despite its potential, exclusive dependence on system initiation is not attracting much attention either from academia or practitioners due to a lack of established methodology. Algorithmic complexity and enormous resource requirements as well as expected inefficiencies in the discovery process are some of the major pitfalls. It is our suggestion that the balanced use of exploratory and confirmatory searches would truly take advantage of the potential that data mining technology offers.

Search Algorithms

A number of scientific and intuitive search algorithms are available for the discovery of knowledge. In general, artificial intelligence (AI) and statistics are the favored scientific and theory-driven approaches. Neural networks, decision trees, memory-based reasoning (MBR), and genetics algorithms are popular AI techniques utilized for data-mining. Statistics are different from AI in several aspects of computing.

Statistics offer numerous techniques that are easily applicable to different circumstances and bear rich information. Most statistical models take a parametric approach that requires certain assumptions for the analysis of data. If the assumptions are not satisfied, however, the validity of the discovered knowledge is subject to question. Statistics use sample data for knowledge discovery. Depending on the types of knowledge, types of application and characteristics of data, certain data-mining will be more effective and efficient with the use of samples. Also, initial analysis of data based on a sample could offer insights that trigger a more iterative and extensive search using the whole data set. Using samples for statistical analysis, however, is not always justified. Knowledge discovered through samples, in many cases, may not be representative of population characteristics. Selecting samples may not be appropriate when the relationships among a number of attributes are dynamically searched. Analysis that requires segmentation of a database or transformation of attributes thorough partitioning, category collapsing or user-defined predicators may be better off when the whole data set is mobilized.

Compared to statistical analysis, most AI techniques take a non-parametric approach. AI can easily be applied to large databases such as data warehouse and offers an easy interpretation. Nevertheless, there are limitations, too. First, AI is limited in the types of knowledge it can recover from databases. Two of the most popular AI techniques, neural networks and decision trees are mostly applied to the task of classification and predictive modeling. Besides, although the neural network is appropriate for tasks of classification and value prediction, its discovery process is not transparent to knowledge workers. Also, AI, because of its structure and non-parametric nature, does not produce as rich a store of knowledge as statistics do.

In addition to statistics and AI, algorithms that are rather intuitive as well as others based on theories are also available. These may be referred to in Agrawal et. al (1993); Dhar and Tuzhilin (1993); Han et al (1993). Smyth and Goodman (1991) used information theory for the induction of classification rules. So far, these methods have stayed at the level of academic research due to the lack of flexibility in information searches and of proven stability in knowledge mining processes. Besides, effective incorporation of conventional query processing and multi-dimensional analysis provides important flexibility in the process of data-mining through the redefinition of search space. Geographical information systems (GIS) are also beginning to be adopted for data-mining systems. Lastly, inspection of data through graphical visualization is already regarded as an integral process of data mining.

ORGANIZATIONAL ISSUES IN DATA MINING

Organizational issues that have to be addressed for effective data mining are discussed in this section. Two primary organizational issues are: (i) objectives of data mining, and (ii) information management and data warehouse, each of which is discussed below.

Objectives of Data Mining

Potential applications of data mining are numerous. In fact, any business that relies heavily on information can benefit from data mining. Organizations that intend to introduce data-mining should identify organizational problems or opportunities to be addressed by data-mining. Identification of appropriate data mining goals that justify the substantial investment is one of the critical success factors of data-mining. As Daft's dual-core model (1978) suggested, identification of opportunities for data mining is possible through either a top-down or bottom-up initiation.

In the top-down mode, management defines strategic applications through which data mining increases the effectiveness of organizational processes. Currently, many data-mining exercises are targeted for marketing strategy and finance. Some of these popular applications are customer segmentation, target marketing, market basket analysis, price analysis, fraud detection, credit quality and risk management. Because of the focused nature of current data-mining tasks, several vendors have developed mining systems specifically targeted for specialized markets providing solution frameworks that are specific to business applications. Naturally, finance and retail industries are forerunners in adopting data-mining technologies.

There are, however, other applications in which data-mining can increase the effectiveness of organizational performance. Effectiveness is a multi-dimensional concept. For instance, the competing values framework introduced by Cooper and Quinn (1993), suggests four primary dimensions of organizational effectiveness. Most existing data-mining applications attempt to benefit organizations through the achievement of *rational goals* where the effectiveness is defined by economic measures such as profit maximization, productivity and cost reduction. However, data-mining can also benefit organizations in several different ways. For instance, it can be a useful tool for human resource management, organizational adaptation to environment, various types of predictive modeling and data quality management. Insightful management should be able to foresee the hidden value of data mining in these applications.

Organizations that do not have a specific focus on data-mining but are interested in taking advantage of the technology can take the bottom-up approach of innovation adoption. In this case, objectives of data-mining must be identified through the process of data collection and evaluation. This requires a clear understanding of how existing databases are used and of the information needs of knowledge seekers. Gathering such information is possible through traditional methods of data collection, such as usage surveys of existing data warehouses. Through research, information can be gathered regarding the organizational goals of the data warehouse and how well the current system serves these goals as well as the problems and opportunities for data mining. In addition, information on the system environment such as data quality, locatability of information, authorization, consistency of data, user satisfaction, ease of use and need of user training, should be collected for effective planning of a data-mining system. The sponsorship of top management and the active role of the chief information officer is critical for the success of the project.

Information Management and Data Warehouse

Effective management of information is critical for successful dat mining. Creation of a data warehouse that incorporates a variety of data sources could provide an ideal environment that is integrated, subject-oriented, time-variant, and non-volatile (Inman, 1992). It also offers additional advantages in improved data quality, consistency, intelligence, control and performance. However, the data warehouse is, in many cases, the product of a compromise that reflects the interests of each functional department and accordingly the existing data structure may not be optimized to serve the enterprise goals of data-mining. This is especially true when the development of a data warehouse was not initially intended for specialized decision-making support.

When a data warehouse is structured for traditional query processing or OLAP rather than for specialized and intelligent data mining, certain key attributes may be excluded from the system design and/or data structures may not support the rich abstraction of information that mobilizes cross-functional and external information. The potential limitations of data warehouses led to recommendations for database designs that better facilitate information management. More specialized forms of the database such as data-mart or data-mine that are more subject-specific and uncompromising may provide better information sources for data mining.

If an organization chooses to undertake data-mining based on its existing data warehouse, measures should be taken to extract more intelligence out of the available data. This is especially necessary when the data warehouse is the result of data "dumping" from existing operational databases. First, intensive efforts in detecting, filtering, correcting and cleansing of noisy and missing data are necessary, as least for the data subject to certain data-mining tasks. Second, relations should be reorganized to reflect current usage of the data warehouse and to improve the productivity of users and the system. For instance, relations that are frequently joined by end users should be merged into a single table to reduce the complexity of queries or data-mining processing. When knowledge workers have to issue a number of queries in order to retrieve one piece of information, the procedural complexity could substantially affect their productivity, as well as decrease the accuracy of information acquired and deteriorate systems performance. Finally, relations to be used for data mining need to be redefined in their data structures. This entails structural enrichment of tables through the incorporation of various data abstractions, of intelligent meta-data, and of external data. Existing guidelines of data warehouse implementation such as the sandwich paradigm (Parsaye, 1995) could render a robust design methodology.

Other organizational issues regarding data management must be cleared. For instance, policies on the ownership of data should be established to facilitate the use of the data warehouse and to maintain data integrity. In this case, issues regarding who owns the data belonging to certain tables, who owns cross-functional data and how it is managed, who authorizes access to or changes in data must be resolved. In addition, decisions on what data should be warehoused, and what corporate or departmental procedures exist for the control of warehoused data have to be addressed in ways that enable effective data mining.

METHODOLOGICAL ISSUES IN DATA MINING

Besides the organizational issues discussed above several methodological issues also need to be resolved for effective data-mining. Needless to say, the source of data-mining, in general, is large-scale databases and this makes the process of data-mining fundamentally different from traditional forms of discovering knowledge. Therefore, a balanced research approach which pays attention to a variety of issues including the selection of methodology and appropriate search tools is important for effective data mining and knowledge discovery. Existing literature in the area tends to emphasize the development of search algorithms. In fact, there are already a number of information discovery algorithms that are both linear and non-linear and are flexible, scaleable, stable and robust theory-based. In that sense, more attention should be paid to the non-algorithm aspects of data-mining such as design of data warehouses and data marts, integration of data mining with DSS or EIS, rule-base management, methodologies for knowledge search and evaluation of return-on-investment.

Among these, the foremost importance goes to developing effective search methodologies or solution frameworks to guide data mining. There are a few frameworks suggested in academia and in industry. SEMMA, the framework from SAS institutes, defines the data-mining stages as "sample, explore, manipulate, model, and assess." Fayyad et al. (1996) and Cabena et al. (1997) suggest a data-mining methodology based on "selection, preprocessing, transformation, and interpretation and assimilation".

In the selection stage, internal and external sources of data appropriate for an application domain are identified and data are organized based on sampling, aggregation, projection, and grouping. Data quality is addressed through pre-processing, in which data integrity and reliability are improved by cleansing missing and noisy data. Several statistical and non-statistical (i.e., visualization) methods are available for the cleansing efforts (Cabena et. al., 1997). Pre-processed data are transformed to fit into the analytical format of data-mining at the data transformation stage. A variety of transformations can be undertaken for data-mining including data re-coding, format conversion, dimension reduction and aggregation of observations.

SYSTEM-RELATED ISSUES OF DATA-MINING

Important system-related issues in data-mining are briefly discussed in this section. First, graphical user interface (GUI) is an important factor because of several reasons. GUI in user-inputs and output presentations enables "ease of use" that critically influences data-mining adoption by prospective users as well as facilitate the process of effective data mining. Knowledge seekers spend most of their time in data preparation such as pre-processing and data transformation (Cabena et al., 1997) and easy manipulation of data through GUI could substantially curtail the overhead of data mining. Data-mining in many cases requires dynamic, iterative, and progressive interactions between systems and knowledge seekers. Software that uses none-GUI interfaces is more interruptive in nature and thus may lack the flexibility in supporting interactive and progressive searches of databases in real-time basis.

Intelligent search of large-scale data warehouses or logical databases requires an efficient computing environment such as client/server computing and scalability through MPP or SMP parallel processing. An effective data-mining system should carry a high-degree of functional flexibility in facilitating the data mining process. Support for both sampling and no-sample processes is important. A data-mining system should enable the knowledge search at multiple abstraction levels and with different data types to be handled in a uniform manner. It should provide explanations as to how and why it discovered various knowledge and offer quality measurements of the discovered information. It should provide a seamless integration between the data-mining processes and rule-bases or model-bases management. For the search of rich information, it should offer a variety of pre-processing capabilities, and handle noise and exceptional data. For an effective search, the running time of a data mining algorithm must be acceptable in large databases.

A FEW CONCLUDING REMARKS

The complexity of the data mining procedure offers a non-trivial challenge to knowledge workers in the definition of search space, in the choice of appropriate methodology and in the mix of data mining techniques. While established methodology on the use of search methods and on the knowledge discovery process is deemed prudent it is also important to recognize that this is a relatively new area and related techniques and methodologies are still evolving. Another issue is the confidential nature of the work, corporate experiences often remained undisclosed to the outside world. Business organizations are unlikely to share their experiences from data mining exercises with other competitors except maybe in very general terms, thus prohibiting the free flow of knowledge. The process in turn slows down innovations in data mining.

For effective data mining, users must have a thorough domain knowledge including the nature of the task, type of databases, and possible usage of outcomes from the exercise. Essentially, the process generally will lead to a team approach including individuals contributing their specialized knowledge in areas of methodology, techniques, and business. We view current activities in data mining as being in the developing stage and for most organizations the technique is somewhat experimental. As we move through the twilight years of the twentieth century and enter the new millennium data mining is certain to emerge as a routine operation providing a new arsenal for businesses to stay efficient and competitive.

REFERENCES

Agrawal, R., Imielinski, T., and Swami, A., "Database Mining: A Performance Perspective," *IEEE Transactions on Knowledge and Data Engineering*, 5, 6, 1993, 914-925.

Azuma, M., "Software products evaluation system: quality models, metrics and processes - International Standards and Japanese Practice," *Information and Software Technology*, 38, 1996, 145-154.

Cabena, P., Hadjinian, P., Stadler, R., Verhees, J., and Zanasi, A., *Discovering Data Mining, From Concept to Implementation*, Prentice Hall, 1997.

Cooper, R. B., & Quinn, R. E., "Implications of the Competing Values Framework for Management Information Systems," *Human Resource Management*, 32, 1993, 175-201.

Daft, R. L., "A Dual-Core Model of Organizational Innovation," *Academy of Management Journal*, 21, 2, 1978, 193-210.

Dhar, V. and Tuzhilin, A., "Abstract-Driven Pattern Discovery in Databases," *IEEE Transactions on Knowledge and Data Engineering*, 5, 6, 1993, 926-938.

Fayyad, U., Shapiro. G. P., and Smyth, P., "Knowledge Discovery and Data Mining: Towards a Unifying Framework," *KDD-96*, 1996, 82-88.

Han, J., Cai, Y., and Cercone, N., "Data-Driven Discovery of Quantitative Rules in Relational Databases," *IEEE Transactions on Knowledge and Data Engineering*, 5, 1, 1993, 29-40.

Inman, W. H., *Building the Data Warehouse*, Wellesley, MA: QED Technical Publishing Group, 1992.

Parsaye, K., "The Sandwich Paradigm," *Database Programming & Design*, April 1995, 50-55.

Smyth, P. and Goodman, R. M., "Rule Induction Using Information Theory," In Knowledge Discovery in Databases, G. Piatetsky-Shapiro and W. Frawley (Eds.) AAAI/MIT Press, 1991.

Chapter 6

What's in a Name?
Exploring the Metaphysical
Implications of Data Warehousing
in Concept and Practice

Elizabeth J. Davidson
University of Hawaii, Manoa

Data warehousing is an information technology (IT) innovation based on an evocative metaphor for physical materials management. This metaphor has implications not only for the design of corporate-wide databases but also for the meaning and utility of data used in business analysis and for relationships between IS staff and end-users. While acknowledging that data warehousing offers many benefits, this paper argues that the data warehousing approach has been applied without critical reflection on the cognitive mappings implied by the underlying metaphor and that possible consequences of its use as a guide for organizing IT practices have not been fully explored. The paper examines the metaphorical implications of data warehousing in concept and presents findings of an empirical study of a data warehousing project that illustrated limitations of metaphor in practice. Drawn from these conceptual and empirical analyses, a critique of the metaphor highlights inherent limitations in the data warehousing concept for conceptualizing key aspects of the organizational data management problem. Implications for theory and practice are considered.

Previously Published in the *Journal of End User Computing, vol.11, no.4,* Copyright © 1999, Idea Group Publishing.

INTRODUCTION AND MOTIVATION

Data warehousing is a label used to describe the application of information technologies such as multidimensional and relational data bases and online analytic processing software for cross-organizational business analysis. Design concepts for data warehousing and experiential reports on their use have received considerable attention in the business press (Sakaguchi and Frolick 1997). Data warehousing has in recent years become the subject of academic research, where research has focused primarily on technical design and development issues. Yet this information technology (IT) innovation is based on an evocative metaphor that has implications not only for the design of corporate-wide databases, but also for the meaning and utility of data used in business analysis and the relationships between IS staff and end-users involved in these endeavors. These implications have not been fully explicated and debated. As more companies commit to a data warehousing strategy, it becomes increasing important to consider the social and organizational aspects of data warehousing. This paper begins such a discussion by first outlining the role of metaphor in conceptualizing IT innovations and then by examining the data warehousing metaphor in concept. Consequences for practice are illustrated with findings of a field study of a data warehousing project. Limitations of the warehousing metaphor as a guide for organizing IT support of business analysis are then considered, alternative metaphors explored, and the implications of this analysis for theory and practice discussed.

THE ROLE OF METAPHOR IN CONCEPTUALIZING IT INNOVATIONS

Metaphor is a central mechanism that enables human beings to comprehend abstract concepts and reason abstractly (Lakoff and Johnson, 1980). Contemporary cognitive linguistics theory views the phenomenon of metaphor primarily as generalized, conceptual mappings between a source domain and target domain and secondly, as individual linguistic expressions that reflect these mappings (Lakoff, 1993). In a metaphor, conventional mental images conveyed by an idiomatic expression are mapped to a new domain through a pattern of ontological correspondences across the domains. Systems of metaphors, arising from root metaphors, become implicit in the vocabulary and language used to communicate thoughts and interpret events (Ortony, 1979). For example, the metaphor *love is a journey* maps cognitive structures that arise from the experience of travel to the experience of love. Aspects of this mapping are evident in idiomatic expressions such as "This is a *dead-end* relationship" or "He *bailed out* of the marriage." Such metaphors not only describe experience but may also shape interpretation and influence action. Thus, expressions like "this relationship *isn't going anywhere*" and "it's time *to move on*" reflect the expectation that love, like a journey, must progress from point to point, suggest an interpretation of a relationship (its failure to progress), and point to a course of action (ending the relationship).

In organizations, metaphors play a crucial role in communication and sensemaking and are particularly helpful when new phenomena are encountered, providing a vocabulary drawn from familiar circumstances to facilitate discourse in a new domain (Weick, 1979). Using a particular metaphor highlights some aspects of a situation while masking others (Weick, 1979; Morgan, 1986). Consider, for example, the implied differences if a project is characterized as a *runaway project* versus a *political football*. Although both metaphors suggest project control issues, interpretations of causes, effects and appropriate actions are different. The first metaphor suggests a situation in which no one is in control, progressing rapidly towards grievous damage and perhaps injury. This situation requires intervention to *put on the brakes* and *slow the project down*. Characterizing a project as a *political football* suggests key stakeholders are struggling for control and domination, moving the project back and forth towards opposing goals. The IT manager might identify *who the key players are* and determine *the rules of the game*. Using one metaphor versus the other directs attention in ways implied by the cognitive mappings of the metaphor and thus may mask other aspects of the situation.

Metaphors, self-conscious and contrived or deeply embedded and implicitly applied, have long pervaded the discourse around information technology design and use (Johnson 1994). For instance, the *computer as desktop* metaphor inspired the design and development of computer operating systems (Rechtin, 1997). Interface designers actively search for metaphors to guide their design of multi-media and Internet applications (Golovchinsky and Chignell, 1997; Rauch, Leone, and Gillinhan, 1997). Systems developers and users utilize metaphors to articulate IT application requirements (Boland and Greenburg, 1992; Davidson 1996a). In this way metaphors provide a valuable cognitive device for conceptualizing and exploring IT innovations, but their use can also raise false expectations about how an actual system will operate (Rechtin, 1997).

Metaphors for IT innovations also play an important role in conveying what Swanson and Ramiller (1997) call the *organizing vision* for the application of information technology in organizations. An organizing vision, which develops through the discourse of a community of technology producers, IS professionals, business managers, and other stakeholders, provides an interpretation of the organizational applications of an IT innovation and the rationale for its use. IT innovations in organizations typically entail new roles, responsibilities, relationships, control mechanism, work processes, and so on. The organizing vision implies ways in which the technology will be embedded and utilized in these organizational structures and processes. "Buzzwords" are labels or names that come to be identified with an organizing vision and "may serve as a potent metaphor" (Swanson and Ramiller, 1997, p. 463). The implications of metaphorical buzzwords extend beyond technology design questions to organizational issues such as suitable business applications for the innovation, new or altered roles related to its development and use, and appropriate control over IT resources. The *computer as desktop* design metaphor, for example, became part of an organizing vision for *desktop computing* which entailed a shift in organizational access to and control over computing resources.

Although metaphors are powerful conceptually, their use is often taken for granted. Their efficacy in conceptualizing IT applications, however, requires elaboration of the cognitive mappings implied by the metaphor and reflection on the possible consequences of these mappings for the ways in which information technologies will be developed and utilized in organizations. Without such examination, reliance on a metaphor may have unanticipated and undesirable effects, as Mason (1991) illustrated in his analysis of the limitations of the *IT as competitive weapon* metaphor. Explicit consideration of metaphors, on the other hand, can bring to light both their strengths and limitations (Boland and Greenberg, 1992; Mason, 1991; Morgan, 1986) and may stimulate creative thinking about IT development and use (Couger, Higgins, and McIntyre, 1993).

EXAMINING THE METAPHORICAL IMPLICATIONS OF DATA WAREHOUSING

Data warehousing maps concepts and experiences from the management of physical materials in manufacturing or distribution processes to the domain of data management for cross-organizational business analysis. *Warehousing* is the management of materials while they are in storage, including storing, dispersing, ordering, and accounting for all materials (Gaither, 1992). The *warehouse* is the physical location where items are stockpiled or stored between receipt and disbursement, and its layout is designed to accommodate the arrival and disbursement of materials. Warehousing ensures materials are available when needed by providing an inventory buffer between material suppliers and production processes, while reducing inventory costs through efficient purchasing and materials handling operations.

The implied cognitive mappings from materials warehousing to the target domain of data management for business analysis are easy to discern. In data warehousing, operational data (materials) are collected from transaction processing systems (suppliers) for storage until needed in business analysis (production). Data files from operational systems or external data sources (shipments) are received and stored in databases (warehouses). Incoming materials are inspected for compliance to quality standards and may be standardized by converting fields to a common code or format. Data may be assigned to "lots" via a timestamp and "packaged" for storage and retrieval in summarized form (Inmon, 1995; Orr, 1997). End-user analysts or management information systems carry out the information production process, transforming data requisitioned from the warehouse via queries or scheduled data "feeds" into products (analytical reports) for use by customers (managers, decisionmakers). Business practices for data warehousing also emulate activities closely related to materials warehousing efforts such as purchasing. The mission of purchasing is to develop and implement purchasing plans for each major product/service, select suppliers, negotiate contracts, and act as the interface between the company and supplier (Gaither, 1992). To establish a data warehouse, the development team assumes similar responsibilities for determining what types of data are needed for business analysis, locating acceptable suppliers among operational systems, and establishing supply channels for data.

In the discourse on materials warehousing, much attention is given to optimizing the design and layout of the physical warehouse (Gaither, 1992). Similarly, discussions of data warehousing focus on topics such as how to design and build multidimensional or relational databases to efficiently store and access data (Gray and Watson, 1998; Orr, 1997). Warehouse design and layout issues are, of course, critically important, because large volumes of data are loaded and accessed in a typical data warehouse. However, data warehousing is more that a design metaphor; it has become the buzzword for an organizing vision for this IT innovation (Swanson and Ramiller, 1997). As such, it implies ways in which IT will be embedded in organizational structures and processes, such as appropriate roles and responsibilities for users versus IT staff in business analysis. It also provides a basis for legitimizing the IT innovation in business terms. One of the primary motives for creating a data warehouse is to provide a data buffer between operational systems and business analysis activities, allowing each process to run efficiently and independently (Hathathorn, 1995; Orr 1997; Sakaguchi and Frolick, 1997). Another rationale for warehousing data — improving the quality of data used in business analysis by collecting operational data from "preferred vendors" and forcing data to conform to a single set of standards (Gray and Watson 1998; Sakaguchi and Frolick, 1997) — reflects modern materials management and warehousing strategies. Expectations that data warehousing will create "a single version of the truth" (Gray and Watson, 1998, p. 19) or a single image of business reality by integrating various data (Sakaguchi and Frolick, 1997) arise from these rationales.

The organizing vision for data warehousing is compelling. The business press is replete with reports extolling its strategic advantages and citing anecdotal evidence of successful applications. However, no metaphor can adequately represent all aspects of a complex social reality, and relying on one metaphor, particularly without critical reflection on its limitations, may mask important issues, suggest inappropriate interpretations, and limit creative thinking. With these issues in mind, the next sections review findings of a case study to explores how the data warehousing metaphor may influence practice.

DATA WAREHOUSING IN PRACTICE: AN ILLUSTRATIVE CASE ANALYSIS

The case study discussed in this paper was conducted as part of a research project which investigated the ways in which IT developers, users, and managers conceptualize technology use in organizations and how differences in conceptualization affect requirements definition processes and outcomes (Davidson, 1996b). Data were collected through interviews, observations of project events, and document analysis on two systems development projects during a longitudinal field study at one research site. Using techniques and methods for qualitative data analysis (Miles and Huberman, 1994), a framework of analytical categories was developed to categorize the assumptions, expectations and knowledge organization members used to interpret the meaning of and uses for the IT applications being implemented. Data were then coded and analyzed to identify similarities and differences between developers' and users' understanding of the IT application and to assess whether differences affected development and implementation outcomes. (See Davidson (1996b) for a detailed description of the research project, methodology, and findings).

The findings presented here are drawn from this larger project. One of the projects studied, INFOSYS, involved building a data warehouse. Data on the INFOSYS project were primarily collected in semi-structured interviews with INFOSYS developers (15), business analysts (13), and IS managers and executives (3). In these semi-structured interviews, informants were asked to describe, from their own perspective, how and why the project got started, what events or circumstances influenced understanding of the INFOSYS system, how implementation of the system would influence the research site, Group Health Inc. (GHI), and personal hopes and expectations for what would happen with the system. Interviews were audiotaped and transcribed to preserve details of language use. Observational data on user/developer interactions were collected during several requirements interviews and in training sessions. Project artifacts such as systems documentation, project proposals, training materials, memos, and meeting notes were also examined. Through these data collection methods, data on over two years' history of the project were compiled.

Table 1: Developers' and Users' Expectations for the IT Innovation Differed in Several Key Categories

Transitioning the application into use

Developers' assumptions:

Technical tasks are the major focus of transitioning the system into use; the purpose of training is to teach systems mechanics; continued implementation is the key IS responsibility.

Users' assumptions:

Training is just a first step to integrating a system; on-the-job practice is needed to learn the system; developers' assistance is needed to become familiar with the system and overcome time constraints.

Using the IT application in practice

Developers' assumptions:

The GUI interface will allow end users to generate their own reports without programmer assistance; this is the major goal of the system.

Users' assumptions:

End users and programmers will both use the system to generate reports; standard, batch reports will still be required.

Assessing information and data legitimacy

Developers' assumptions:

Though data quality ultimately depends on the quality of data in operational systems, it can be improved through "cleansing" and "scrubbing"; quality data are legitimate.

Users' assumptions:

Data quality depends on operational systems; there are many competing ways to interpret raw data; data that make sense in the total information environment are legitimate.

Adapted from Davidson (1996b)

The analysis of the influence of the data warehousing metaphor on practice presented here draws on Davidson's (1996b) findings of differences in developers' and users' expectations for the IT application in three analytic categories (see Table 1). The first two categories concern users' and developers' roles and relationship in business analysis activities. The third category relates to how these groups interpreted the meaning and validity of data used in business analysis.

These findings were extended in this analysis by reexamining data for evidence of the influence of data warehousing concepts on developers' and users' interpretations of the value and uses of the INFOSYS system and their actions and interactions in the project. Particular attention was paid to informants' use of language and metaphors. Through this analytic process, four areas in which data warehousing concepts appeared to influence users' and developers' expectations and which were sources of unresolved differences were identified and analyzed. Data in the form of quotations from study informants are presented throughout the discussion that follows to demonstrate and substantiate the author's analysis. These data are representative of comments from key informants, including most of the development team and those business analysts who had had direct experience with the INFOSYS system.

The Research Site and Project

The research site, Group Health, Inc. (GHI) is a health care insurance company in the United States. During the last decade, GHI diversified its product lines by developing and acquiring new types of products and services such as health maintenance organizations (HMOs). These product lines utilized separate systems for processing subscriber enrollments and claims for services. As a result, there were a variety of operational systems running on different hardware and software platforms, ranging from the company's IBM mainframe to various mid-sized computers. Several years before the research project began, GHI decided to outsource its operational systems to a software vendor, and IS personnel began a multi-year project to transfer all transaction processing to a single, unified set of enrollment and claims processing systems. While the move to a single transactional system was expected to reduce problems with inconsistent operational data, the new system did not directly support multi-year, multi-product line business analysis.

The INFOSYS project began in 1991 as a pilot project to develop a claims database for end-user computing. The initial purpose of the project was to install a software package (INFOSYS) to facilitate business analysis and reporting for one of GHI's largest customers. The package's major appeal was its graphical user interface (GUI), which included standardized reports, ad hoc reporting features, and programmed algorithms for summarizing or adjusting individual claims records. At the time of the research study, the INFOSYS project had been underway for three years at a cost of over three and a half million dollars. Two pilot databases were installed, a third version of the database was in final testing, and user training was underway. During this time, the INFOSYS project had evolved from the initial idea of providing an end-user computing tool to that of building a corporate-wide data warehouse. This evolution in conceptualizing the IT application provided an opportunity to examine how data warehousing concepts may have influenced developers' and users' expectations for the IT application.

Case Study Findings

The INFOSYS project began as a solution to a specific problem, that is, providing a reporting tool to end users who produced analytical reports from health insurance claims for GHI's largest customer. Key project sponsors did anticipate, however, that the INFOSYS package might serve as the basis for creating a broad, end-user programming environment. As part of this larger goal, data for other large customers were added to the database after the first pilot was completed. When the software vendor developed a new version of the system, GHI management determined that the package could be used for business analysis of new HMO product lines. Eventually, a strategy was developed to include all of GHI's claims data as developers' ideas about INFOSYS crystallized around the concept of building a corporate-wide database for business analysis.

This evolution in conceptualizing how GHI might use INFOSYS, and its transformation into a data warehousing project, occurred for several reasons. When the software vendor expanded system functionality, project sponsors recognized new business areas to apply the system. Technological changes meant a wider variety of data could be stored in the package's database. Developers came to realize that the data in the database would have to be accessed directly through batch-style programs, not only through ad hoc GUI reports. These changes shifted their attention from INFOSYS's GUI interface, which they believed would facilitate end-user programming, to the importance of the claims database they were building.

One of the most interesting aspects of this evolution was team members' adoption of the term *data warehouse* to describe INFOSYS. This term was not evident in early project documentation; instead, the system was described as an *MIS system* that would support *end-user computing*. INFOSYS project team members were later exposed to the terminology and concepts of data warehousing through their interactions with another IS group from a recently acquired HMO business. This group had built a data warehouse for the HMO and was extending its use to another of GHI's HMO product lines, in parallel with the INFOSYS project. The term data warehousing began to take root among the INFOSYS project staff. Note, for example, how the project sponsor explained the INFOSYS project, using the term *data warehouse* interchangeably with the older term *MIS system*:

> *We had been talking for years about a data warehouse, an MIS system for, probably going on a decade pretty soon.*

Other team members began to use the terminology of data warehousing to describe INFOSYS, as these systems analysts did to describe their expectations for INFOSYS:

> *I would like to see it become the center of some sort of information warehouse, some sort of data warehouse, that everyone comes to for claims data.*

> *You're going to take and see a single repository of information that will be used to meet reporting needs.*

GHI management realized that the INFOSYS system and the HMO system were redundant. When the two project teams were forced to compete for limited IS resources, the INFOSYS team, by using the term data warehouse, laid claim to the business rationales associated with warehousing as well as to the value of the GUI interface for end-user computing. The assumption that they were building a data warehouse also influenced INFOSYS developers' ideas and plans, notably the priority they gave to adding new data sources to the INFOSYS database. In adopting the warehousing goal, project sponsors and developers did not explicitly consider the implications of transforming INFOSYS from a limited, end-user programming tool into a corporate-wide data warehouse. Data collected in research interviews suggested, however, that significant differences in developers' and users' expectations and assumptions about INFOSYS threatened users' acceptance of the system. The first three issues stem from differences in developers' and users' assumptions about assessing information and data legitimacy. The fourth issue arises from differences in their expectations about transitioning the system into use and using the IS application in practice (see Table 1).

Meaning Embedded in the Operational Context of Data

An essential function of data warehousing is to extract data from operational systems and store them in the warehouse database. The need to do so and the advantages for business analysis activities were readily apparent to developers at GHI. Not only were data strewn among diverse operational systems, these systems were often inaccessible to business analysts. To secure appropriate data sources, developers had to search amid this confusion of systems, as one of the INFOSYS systems analysts explained:

From our perspective, we were looking at a set of claim payment files, to see if data was accurate, to see if data was really representative of what it was supposed to be, whether the data fields which we were directed towards satisfied needs, actually performed the function that they expected them to.

Deciding what data to stock in the INFOSYS data base was no easy task. Project files were replete with memos defining data issues and monitoring their resolution during the migration from the existing enrollment and claims processing systems to the single transaction processing system provided by the outsourcing company. Examining just a few excerpts from these memos indicated the extent to which data structure and content reflected the complexity of business processes and practices in these operational systems, for example:

How is a voided claim identified? Does a void come through looking like a zero-paid adjustment (with a positive qualifier)? Is there an identifier on the reversal (negative) record?

In some cases, the account number is the group number. However, any time an account needs to differentiate segments of its members, group numbers are assigned within the account number unit.

Business analysts relied on their familiarity with existing databases and the operational context to detect major problems with the data they used, as this analyst explained:

If I see something wrong, I'll know it's wrong. Probably just from looking at this clinical data over and over and over and getting to know what it means and seeing things.

IT developers relied on users' detailed knowledge of data sources, acquired through their exposure to operational systems, to verify data sources. A systems analyst observed:

When somebody says they need an element, the first thing we say to them, I think, is, 'Well, are there any oddities associated with this element?'

"Scrubbing" operational data and standardizing them to fit INFOSYS formats did removed some anomalies. However, extracting data for storage in the data warehouse also meant losing cues, and clues, embedded in the operational context about the meaning, validity and interpretation of data.

Commenting on this issue, one business analyst observed that to effectively use a database, he needed to know the history of the company. To illustrate his point, he cited fluctuations in the volume of claims processed several months earlier, caused by a transaction processing backlog in the operational system. Without knowledge of this operational problem, the analyst might have made the wrong assumptions about the meaning of increased transaction volumes. Although buffering business analysts from the realities of operational processes through warehousing data would lessen data access issues, they anticipated losing some of the knowledge and understanding about the idiosyncrasies, the "oddities" of data, needed to interpret them correctly.

Transforming Raw Data for Analysis

To be of value in business analysis, operational data have to be transformed into summary records, indices, and measurements that depict "real world" events and outcomes. One business manager used the example of determining "in-patient admission counts," a critical index used in many analytical reports at GHI, to illustrate the difficulties inherent in construing reality from raw data:

It's pretty easy in the real world to define it, I think. Walk in the hospital door, they put you on a bed, you stay there all night. That's admitted to a hospital. That's an in-patient admission. But you're dealing with numbers and a computer that are structured in any of a number of different ways, and you want to put all those numbers together in some way that equates to what happens in the real world. There's a lot of different ways you can do that. People don't agree on the best way to do it.

Some analysts believed that, since INFOSYS had defined algorithms and standardized reports, it would be more feasible to have agreed-up definitions. An account reporting analyst voiced his hope about INFOSYS use:

If I want the top three hundred providers, and somebody else wants the top three hundred providers, we're going to get the same report ... there's going to be a lot more standardization and I think that's a nice piece of it.

However, INFOSYS's algorithms conflicted with algorithms that had been developed over the years at GHI to summarize raw data and to interpret its meaning. These algorithms were not sanctioned standards, but their use had become institutionalized in some departments, and several business analysts resisted the change, as this analyst's comment illustrated:

'Built admissions' was different by definition, than the built admis-
sions that we had put together ... The people who were bringing
INFOSYS into the company knew that there were differences in the
definitions, and they hadn't kept the standards that the company
had.

Though INFOSYS provided a potential "standard", its use could not easily be enforced, as this business manager observed:

As long as they (analysts) have other ways of getting information
the way they choose to view it, it's going to be very hard to get them
to buy into using a tool like INFOSYS.

As the development team promoted INFOSYS's use as a corporate-wide data warehouse, such disagreements over the proper methods of interpreting data were likely, unless INFOSYS use could in fact be dictated for all business analysis.

Assessing Data Quality versus Data Legitimacy

Developers and business analysts agreed there were data quality problems in existing reporting systems. By finding reliable data suppliers, patching up data quality problems, and standardizing and integrating data in the warehouse database, INFOSYS developers assumed the INFOSYS database would be more accurate and complete. They realized some data quality problems would continue, due to problems in the underlying operational systems, and that this might cause users to question the INFOSYS database. The INFOSYS project manager noted this in an interview:

People who are using the data will not understand that this
particular record looks crazy because of something that happened
at claims processing ... That's like my big public relation kind of
thing ... I think that's going to be a big challenge.

Business analysts did understand that the quality of data in informational systems depended on the transactional systems from which data was derived. Beyond questions of data quality, business analysts had concerns about *data legitimacy*. Account reporting analysts, for example, had an existing data source from which they obtained both ad hoc reports and periodic, standard reports for customers. This system had embedded schemes for summarizing and reporting claims data that were different from those in INFOSYS. In addition, it was difficult to know whether the same sets of raw data were used in calculations in both systems. Analysts were concerned that reports produced from INFOSYS gave different results than the periodic reports and ad hoc reports produced using existing procedures, algorithms, and data files. In some cases, reports had been produced continually over a period of years to monitor trends. An analyst described her dilemma, when she used INFOSYS to produce an ad hoc report for GHI's largest customer: the customer compared the INFOSYS report to earlier reports she had provided and found discrepancies which the analyst was at a loss to explain.

Developers interpreted business analysts' concerns about inconsistent reports in terms of data quality. Assuming INFOSYS had a higher quality database, they expected business analysts to willingly switch to this source, as the INFOSYS trainer commented:

I think with the way I'm trying to promote this to users is that, you know, you have a baseline that probably wasn't a reliable one ... Make this your baseline ... make this the new standard.

Business analysts were hesitant to switch to INFOSYS, in part because they understood current data sources well and INFOSYS not at all, and in part because they needed to be able to explain differences in the reports. Team members, assuming they had done all they could to enhance data quality, didn't acknowledge that data *legitimacy* was an important issue separate from data *quality* that required action to increase users' confidence in INFOSYS. An INFOSYS project leader illustrated this dismissive attitude:

Well, most certainly it is entirely conceivable to run similar type of reports in all three of those systems [for claims reporting]. You will probably come up with different answers. Are there going to be huge differences? There shouldn't be huge differences, and, in fact, really we should be able to explain why the numbers are different.

However, when questioned in the research interview, he acknowledged that differences in the systems were not readily apparent:

There are not a whole lot of people even within this whole company that could sit down and explain the differences ... I'm not sure there is anyone that could do that.

Thus, INFOSYS's role as the single source of data for business analysis could not be taken for granted. Unless all other information sources were eliminated, a process that would take some time to complete, questions of data legitimacy, as well as arguments about who had the right numbers, were likely to persist.

Building the Warehouse Versus Supporting
End Users in Business Analysis

When the INFOSYS project began as an initiative to build an end user computing facility, the goal was to enable business analysts to produce ad hoc, analytic reports without assistance from programmers. As the project evolved into a data warehousing project, this goal remained, as the project sponsor indicated:

I think the perception is still what it was originally, and that was to be a way to access information so that the end users don't have to depend on the programmers to get at most of their data.

Calling INFOSYS a *data warehouse* not only emphasized the role of end user computing in business analysis but it also highlighted the importance of building and expanding the database rather than having technical personnel support business analysts. Developers came to view their primary responsibility as building and expanding the warehouse database, believing that their critical task was to get more data loaded as soon as possible. Through their efforts to locate data sources and design database extract and load programs, developers had acquired a deep knowledge of the "oddities" of data fields — knowledge that would have been very beneficial to business analysts struggling to understand the INFOSYS system. However, little time could be spared for training or support, as a project leader commented:

We are still in a constant implementation mode ... and we are often torn between our desire to go out and help use the product on a production basis and our need to continue to implement data so that more and more business units can use it.

Instead, a full-time trainer was hired to conduct brief, half-day sessions focused on the mechanics of logging on and off the system and moving through the menu of reports and queries, with little discussion of the meaning of data elements and none of practices for using the system.

Business analysts, on the other hand, expected that, beyond classroom training, they needed to "play with" the system, to experiment in work situations with its features and data in order to understand its limits and capabilities. To help them over this hurdle, they wanted more than documentation, demonstrations, and brief training sessions. They expected in-depth support from the development team, as this analyst commented:

Adults don't learn in the classroom. They learn by doing. When I try to use INFOSYS, I need one of the developers by my side ... If I had this for a week, I would know the system.

Given the priority developers placed on building the warehouse, it is not surprising adequate support was lacking in this analyst's opinion:

What they were doing was just leaving people in the lurch, I think, on how to practically use it.

The INFOSYS trainer's views on the situation contrasted sharply with users' perspective. Expressing the developers' assumption that business analysts could function independently as information producers and should not expect the kind of assistance they had received in the past from programmers, she commented in an interview:

> *They've all come to us asking us to do their work for them ... They want to be spoon fed ... They've asked me, basically ... 'I need to generate a report for an account. What do I do? What data do I select?' Like, 'You don't know? I mean, you need to know these things. I can't tell you these things.'*

Analysts and managers did expect eventually to do some ad hoc reporting from INFOSYS themselves, but they also realized that not all would chose to be hands-on users. They also realized that much of the reporting currently done or planned involved producing large numbers of standardized reports on a periodic basis. One analyst pointed out in an interview that it was infeasible to do such reports interactively through the INFOSYS interface:

> *I think in terms of profiling the doctors, I don't think that I will crank out 500 or 600 or 700 profiles at my local workstation and disseminate them.*

If users were to accept INFOSYS as the preferred data source and utilize it for business analysis, such issues had to be addressed. When the research project concluded, developers were waiting for users to specify standard reporting packages that IS staff would then code and operate using the INFOSYS database. However, questions about technical support for ad hoc reporting remained unacknowledged and thus unresolved.

LIMITATIONS OF THE DATA WAREHOUSING METAPHOR IN CONCEPT AND PRACTICE

Excitement about INFOSYS was high among developers and business managers in many parts of GHI, with plans in place to add all claims and enrollment data to the warehouse over the next several years. On the other hand, business analysts were actually making little use of the two pilot data bases, in part because of questions about the meaning and legitimacy of data in the warehouse and the difficulties they were having learning how to use INFOSYS. Project sponsors and developers had not acknowledged users' reluctance to adopt INFOSYS as anything more than typical resistance to change. Without positive action on their part to address analysts' questions about warehoused data and to help establish a group of knowledgeable end users, it seemed likely that INFOSYS would be underutilized for some time and might never live up to its potential. These types of problems are not unique to data warehousing projects, of course, and developers might have lessened the consequences with a stronger marketing and implementation effort. However, these findings suggested that relying on the warehousing metaphor as a guide for organizing IT support of business analysis might have inhibited recognition of problems. Findings also highlighted inherent weaknesses in the metaphor which are discussed in the next sections.

Can Data be Treated like Physical Materials?

Fundamental to the ontological mappings of the warehouse metaphor is the notion that data can be treated in much the same way that physical materials are treated, i.e., they can be collected, transported, stored, and used in production processes without losing their value. While value ultimately depends on utility, quality is a key component of value, and data warehousing is billed as a way to improve data quality. However, data quality is a multi-dimensional concept that includes factors such as believability, reputation, accuracy, relevancy, completeness, interpretability, representational consistency, and accessibility (Wang and Strong, 1996). The potential for trade-offs between quality dimensions may be intrinsic to the data warehousing concept. For instance, extracting data from operational systems and consolidating them in a warehouse can improve data accessibility. On the other hand, data interpretability may be diminished when data are abstracted from the operational context that provides cues for appropriate interpretation, or when analysts, buffered from operational systems by the warehouse, lose their understanding of complex operational realities encoded in data. Information about data formats and contents can be stored as metadata in data dictionaries or recorded in documentation, but this information cannot capture all the knowledge analysts develop through their experience with and exposure to operational processes. Similarly, standardizing data in the warehouse may improve accuracy, completeness, and representational consistency, but the relevancy of data for specific analytical purposes may be compromised as a result. "Cleansing" data may improve accuracy and completeness, but these activities will not automatically increase the believability of warehoused data. These types of issues were evident with the INFOSYS project, as business analysts struggled to understand and accept warehoused data. Although such trade-offs may be acceptable in the interest of facilitating corporate-wide analysis, it is valuable to acknowledge they may occur and to consider the consequences for data value before consigning data to a warehouse.

Is the Real Requirement Stockpiling Data or Negotiating Meaning?

The data warehousing metaphor focuses attention on the tangible task of collecting and storing data created by diverse computerized systems and stored in electronic formats. However, data have no value until they are interpreted by users in ways that reflect events, actions, or objects of interest in the real world, in other words, until they are transformed into information. Boland (1987) characterized the notion that information is the same thing as structured data a fantasy, maintaining that "information is not a resource to be stockpiled as one more factor of production. It is meaning, and can only be achieved through dialogue in a human community" (p. 377). As was evident in the INFOSYS project, there are many ways to interpret raw data to represent real world events, and individuals or groups may resist giving up their own approaches. Uniform definitions and algorithms for processing data can be implemented in a data warehouse, but forcing common definitions may decrease the relevancy or the believability of data for those groups forced to acquiesce to warehouse standards. Furthermore, in this social organization of computing, operational personnel surrender control over data from transactional systems and in doing so, accede to interpretations that emerge through analytical processing over which they may have little or no influence. Reaching consensus on the interpreted meaning of warehoused data is vital to its useful application in business analysis, but this remains a human accomplishment, not a technological feature of data warehousing.

Can Data Warehousing Ensure a "Single View of Reality" in an Organization?

Building one integrated source of data for use in diverse business analysis processes is fundamental to the concept of data warehousing. In the organizing vision for data warehousing, the rationale is to create a single source of data, and in this way, a single version of business realities (Gray and Watson, 1998). In this regard, the warehouse metaphor masks important aspects of the organizational data management problem and suggests unrealistic expectations for data warehousing outcomes. At GHI, the INFOSYS data warehouse coexisted with other information systems, and these systems produced different versions of "reality." Questions about the legitimacy of INFOSYS data arose because INFOSYS results were inconsistent with historical trends and reports and differences could not be explained. Questions would likely have diminished over time if these other data sources were eliminated and INFOSYS did in fact become established as the new baseline. GHI's experiences with INFOSYS illustrate, however, that building a warehouse does not guarantee a single source of data. Warehousing must be part of a larger plan that takes into account the whole MIS environment. At a minimum, there will be a transition time during which the data warehouse is built, other information systems are dismantled, and users are persuaded or compelled to abandon alternative data sources.

Even if all preexisting MIS systems are eradicated after a data warehouse is implemented, data legitimacy problems can reoccur in a warehousing model. Unlike physical products that can be consumed only once, the same data set can be used many times, stored in multiple locations, and processed through more than one system. The data warehouse may be the official "store," but there is little to prevent users from creating local stockpiles of data in desktop applications for later use. Furthermore, data extracted from a warehouse will be used by analysts or in information systems, which may select, process, and interpret data differently, arriving at different "versions of reality." The warehousing metaphor, which focuses attention on acquiring, storing and dispersing data shipments, offers limited insight on how to control data and data interpretation once data are shipped out of the warehouse database.

How Should IT Staff Support Business Analysis Activities?

The data warehousing metaphor suggests two primary roles for IS staff: purchasing agent who sets up data acquisition channels and warehouse operator who manages storage and movements of data shipments. Business analysts become producers of business analysis. In fact, expectations for end-user computing pervade the organizing vision for data warehousing. This intermingling of end-user computing and data warehousing concepts was evident in the INFOSYS project. When developers adopted the concept of data warehousing, they began to focus on their role as warehouse builders and operators, in the belief that end users could assume responsibility for producing analytic reports if given tools such as INFOSYS's GUI interface. Some data warehousing gurus recommend against building standard reports or regularly scheduling report production in the warehouse, but it was apparent at GHI that these forms of business analysis were still needed, and IS staff would be involved in developing and operating such information systems. More problematic at GHI was the question of whether developers should assist end users in ad hoc reporting. Developers had unique knowledge of the negotiated meanings of data in the warehouse. Supporting users, however, conflicted with their plans to continue building the warehouse. Metadata contained in data dictionaries might have sufficed to convey basic information about data fields, but it could not replicate the in-depth knowledge of warehouse developers nor eliminate the need to help business analysts develop their own knowledge through practice. The warehousing metaphor, by focusing attention on the benefits and rationales for stockpiling corporate-wide data, may mask the need to support users in business analysis as well as the need for IS to maintain its role in the production of business analysis reports.

A DATA WAREHOUSE BY ANY OTHER NAME?

Undoubtedly, gathering data from diverse operational systems, standardizing its form, and maintaining a stockpile of historical data addresses numerous, long-standing problems with corporate-wide business analysis. Data from across the organization is more accessible, more accurate, and more complete. Organizations developing and using warehouses to good advantage attest to the value of this approach. However, relying too heavily on warehousing as the metaphor to guide the social organization of IT support for business analysis also raises false expectations about what can be achieved with this approach and diverts attention from other important opportunities and needs. The INFOSYS case study suggested several areas of potential weakness with the metaphor. Comparing and contrasting the warehouse metaphor with other potential metaphors illuminates additional aspects of the problem of using IT to support business analysis. Here, two alternative metaphors are briefly considered.

The data department store: The term *warehouse* carries with it mental images of a large, cavernous building, crammed with piles of materials, located along the train tracks or at the harbor. Customers do not poke around a warehouse with a shopping list, looking for items that might be useful or interesting. Instead, they go to a retail store, where a variety of related products have been selected and arranged for easy access, convenience and appeal, and there are service people ready to help them find items and make purchases. The need for and advantages of retailing to enhance customer service are not evident in the warehousing metaphor. Instead, end users are treated as producers who are expected to find their way, with the aid of the data dictionary, through multi-dimensional or relational data bases containing terabytes of data. While some users are comfortable doing so, many might prefer a visit to a *data department store*. If IT support for business analysis were organized according to this metaphor, users might find a variety of data "brands" to select from and knowledgeable IT staff to explain differences in the features of each brand. They would probably find a broad selection of related data in the department store, with less raw data and more finished informational goods. A shift towards *data retailing* is evident to a limited extent in the use of smaller, more focused *data marts*. However, data marts tend to be merely scaled down versions of data warehouses rather than true data department stores. The metaphorical implications of *data retailing*, which emphasize information products and customer service, have not yet been fully debated.

The data library: Perhaps because data warehousing deals with structured operational data, the focus in building warehouses has been on finding and maintaining a single, best source of data, on supplying the right facts to represent organizational "truth," on once and for all settling disputes about "who has the right numbers." Knowledge, on the other hand, involves experience, interpretation, learning, opinions and diverse viewpoints, and discussions about IT support for knowledge management takes this into consideration. A metaphor that has been helpful in conceptualizing how to apply IT in knowledge management activities is that of a library. Borrowing this metaphor to think in terms of a *data library* might be a useful way to explore alternative social and technical designs for IT support of business analysis activities. In a data library, data-as-knowledge might be available at different levels of abstraction, from structured, raw data files to completed analysis. Data sources might present a variety of viewpoints on an issue, and patrons of the library would resist efforts to restrict the library's contents to one version of "the truth." For example, the library might contain not only raw operational data, but also data interpretations from operational personnel as well as corporate analysts. Librarians would select useful data for the library's collection, and reference experts would help patrons locate good sources of information, pointing out limitations in each source and suggesting alternatives.

To the data warehouse practitioner or theorist, the notion of a data department store or data library may seem abhorrent, a step backward from the gains achieved through data warehousing. However, these metaphors are not proposed as a replacement for the data warehouse metaphor, but merely as alternative perspectives that illuminate different aspects of the organizational problem of managing data for corporate-wide business analysis. The first metaphor points to the need to build information distribution channels to enhance customer support and service. The second metaphor implies that the quest to establish one source for "business reality" may be detrimental if it limits the organization's flexibility and openness to alternative interpretations of operational data. Exploring the cognitive mappings of these and other metaphors further and contrasting them with the mappings of the warehousing metaphor could stimulate creative thinking about the social organization and the technical design of IT support for business analysis.

CONCLUSIONS

Many organizations consider data warehousing to be among the most important strategic applications of information technologies. Indeed, a compelling organizing vision for this IT innovation has evolved in the last decade. While acknowledging that data warehousing offers many benefits, this paper argues that the data warehousing approach has been applied without critical reflection on the cognitive mappings implied by the underlying metaphor or the possible consequences of its use in practice. Findings of a case study of a data warehousing project illustrated how attention was diverted from users' questions about warehoused data and their expectations for IT staff support to the task of expanding the warehouse. A critique of the warehouse metaphor in concept and in practice highlighted inherent limitations of the metaphor for conceptualizing key aspects of the data management problem in business analysis.

Business managers and data warehousing practitioners may find this critique useful in several respects. Explicitly examining the conceptual mappings of the data warehousing metaphor points out where data warehousing outcomes can differ from the results achievable with materials management, and thus may indicate where expectations for the data warehouse are unrealistic. Asking users and developers to explore the metaphorical implications of data warehousing for data quality and user support may unearth areas of disagreement and latent problems with user satisfaction. Finally, exploring other metaphors to guide development and design can stimulate creative thinking about requirements for IT support of business analysis.

This paper begins a discussion of the influence of the warehousing metaphor on the social design of IT support for business analysis in an organizational context. It takes as a starting point the existence of an organizing vision for the IT innovation represented by the buzzword "data warehousing." Further research will be needed to investigate the ways in which this organizing vision has developed, and continues to develop, among a community of practitioners, hardware and software vendors, and academics, and to discern how the warehousing metaphor has shaped the discourse and influenced development of this IT innovation, including organizational practices in this area. Such research would consist of process-oriented, historical studies focused on the evolving text of practitioner conferences, exhibitions, and publications as well as developments in academic areas (Swanson and Ramiller, 1997). Studies may bring to light areas of overlap and conflict between organizing visions, such as between data warehousing and end-user computing or knowledge management. Further research into possible organizational consequences of using the warehouse metaphor as a guide for designing and structuring IT support is also needed. The case study reviewed in this paper suggested two areas of particular interest. First, investigating how different organization members, such as operational users, business analysts, or managers assess the legitimacy of warehoused data will improve understanding of the dimensions of data quality and may suggest ways to increase the utility of warehoused data. Second, examining the roles of end-users and IT staff implied by the warehousing metaphor, studying the ways in which roles are enacted in practice, and assessing whether these groups have different expectations for IT support will help to identify factors that contribute to users' acceptance of data warehousing and the types of roles and skills that IT departments will need to develop and maintain.

REFERENCES

Boland, Jr., R. (1987). The In-Formation of Information Systems. In R. Boland, Jr. and R. Hirschheim (eds.), *Critical Issues in Information Systems Research*. New York: John Wiley & Sons, Ltd., 363-379.

Boland, Jr., R. & Greenberg, R. (1992). Method and Metaphor in Organizational Analysis. *Accounting, Management and Information Technology*, *2*(2), 117-137.

Couger, J., Higgins, L., and McIntyre, S. (1993). (Un)Structured Creativity in Information Systems Organizations. *MIS Quarterly, 17*(4), 375-397.

Davidson, E. (1996a). Negotiating Requirements: A Social Cognitive Perspective on the Systems Development Process. *Proceedings of the Second Annual AIS Americas Conference on Information Systems*. Phoenix, Arizona, 422-424.

Davidson, E. (1996b). Framing Information Systems Requirements: An Investigation of Social Cognitive Processes in Information Systems Delivery, unpublished doctoral dissertation, MIT Sloan School of Management.

Gaither, N. (1992). *Production and Operations Management, Fifth Edition*. Orlando, Florida: The Dryden Press, 548-570.

Golovchinsky, G. & Chignell, M. (1997). The newspaper as an information exploration metaphor. *Information Processing and Management, 33*(5), 663-683.

Gray, P. & Watson, H. (1998). *Decision Support in the Data Warehouse*. New Jersey: Prentice Hall.

Hathathorn, R. (1995). Data Warehouse energizes your enterprise. *Datamation*, *41*(2), 38-45.

Inmon, W. (1995). Tech Topic: What is a Data Warehouse? Prism, *1*(1), located at *http://www.cait.wustl.edu/cait/papers/prism/vol1_no1/*.

Johnson, G. (1994). Of Metaphor and the Difficulty of Computer Discourse. *Communications of the ACM, 37*(12), 97-102.

Lakoff, G. (1993). The Contemporary Theory of Metaphor. In Ortony, A (ed.) *Metaphor and Thought, 2nd. ed.* New York: Cambridge University Press, 201-251.

Lakoff, G. & Johnson, M. (1980). *Metaphors We Live By*. Chicago: University of Chicago Press.

Mason, R. (1991). The Role of Metaphors in Strategic Information Systems Planning. *Journal of Management Information Systems, 8*(2), 11-30.

Miles, M. and Huberman, A. (1994). *Qualitative Data Analysis*. Thousand Oaks, CA: Sage Publications, 1994.

Morgan, G. (1986). *Images of Organization*. Newbury Park, California: Sage.

Orr, K. (1997). Data Warehousing Technology. The Ken Orr Institute, located at *http://KenOrrInst.com*.

Ortony, A. (1979). *Metaphor and Thought*. Cambridge: Cambridge University Press.

Rauch, T., Leone, P., & Gillinhan, D. (1997). Enabling the book metaphor for the World Wide Web: Disseminating on-line information as dynamic Web documents. *IEEE Transactions on Professional Communications, 40*(2), pp. 111-128.

Rechtin, E. (1997). The synthesis of complex systems. *IEEE Spectrum*, July, 51 - 55.

Sakaguchi, T. & Frolick, M. (1997). A Review of the Data Warehousing Literature. *Journal of Data Warehousing, 2*(1), 34-54.

Swanson, E. & Ramiller, N. (1997). The Organizing Vision in Information Systems Innovation. *Organization Science, 8*(5), 458-474.

Wang, R. & Strong, D. (1996). Beyond Accuracy: What Data Quality Means to Data Consumers. *Journal of Management Information Systems, 12*(4), 5-33.

Weick, K. (1979). *The Social Psychology of Organizing, 2nd Edition*. New York: Random House.

Chapter 7

Incremental Data Allocation and ReAllocation in Distributed Database Systems

Amita Goyal Chin
Virginia Commonwealth University, USA

In a distributed database system, an increase in workload typically necessitates the installation of additional database servers followed by the implementation of expensive data reorganization strategies. We present the Partial REALLOCATE and Full REALLOCATE heuristics for efficient data reallocation. Complexity is controlled and cost minimized by allowing only incremental introduction of servers into the distributed database system. Using first simple examples and then, a simulator, our framework for incremental growth and data reallocation in distributed database systems is shown to produce near optimal solutions when compared with exhaustive methods.

INTRODUCTION

Recent years have witnessed an increasing trend of the implementation of Distributed Database Management System (DDBMS) for more effective access to information. An important quality of these systems, consisting of n servers loosely connected via a communication network, is to adjust to changes in workloads. To service increases in demand, for example, additional servers may be added to the existing distributed system and new data allocations computed. Conventionally, this requires a system shutdown and an exhaustive data reallocation. Such static methods are not practical for most organizations for these methods result in high costs and in periods of data unavailability.

Previously Published in the *Journal of Database Management*, vol. 12, no. 1. Copyright © 2001, Idea Group Publishing.

We present the incremental growth framework to address incremental expansion of distributed database systems. Data is reallocated using one of two data reallocation heuristics - Partial REALLOCATE or Full REALLO-CATE. Both heuristics are greedy, hill-climbing algorithms that compute new data allocation based on the specified optimization parameter of the objective cost function. Due to their linear complexity, both heuristics can be used to solve both small and large, complex problems, based on organizational needs. The robustness of the heuristics is demonstrated first by simple, illustrative examples and then by parametric studies performed using the SimDDBMS simulator.

The REALLOCATE algorithms in conjunction with SimDDBMS can be used to answer many practical questions in distributed database systems. For example, in order to improve system response time, a database administrator (DBA) may use SimDDBMS for parametric evaluation. For example, the DBA may analyze the effect of upgrading CPU processing capability, increasing network transfer speed, or adding additional servers into the distributed database system. Furthermore, SimDDBMS may easily be modified to evaluate heterogeneous servers, with different CPU processing capabilities. A DBA may also use SimDDBMS to determine the impact and cost-benefit analysis of adding some number, $s \geq 1$, additional servers at one time.

RELATED WORK

Following the pioneering work in (Porcar, 1982) many researchers have studied the data allocation problem (Daudpota, 1998; So, Ahmad, and Karlapalem, 1998; Tamhankar and Ram, 1998; Ladjel, Karlapalem, and Li, 1998). The single data allocation problem has been shown to be intractable (Eswaran, 1974), which means that as the problem size increases, problem search space increases exponentially (Garey and Johnson, 1979). Due to the complex nature of the problem, some researchers (Cornell and Yu, 1990; Rivera-Vega, Varadarajan, and Navathe, 1990; Lee and Liu Sheng, 1992; Ghosh and Murthy, 1991; Ghosh, Murthy and Moffett, 1992) have resorted to integer programming methods in search for good solutions. Since optimal search methods can only be used for small problems, heuristic methods are often used for solving large data allocation problems (Apers, 1988; Blankinship, 1991; Ceri, Navathe, and Wiederhold, 1983; Du and Maryanski, 1988).

Researchers have studied both the static data allocation problem, in which data allocations do not change over time, and the dynamic data allocation problem (Theel and Pagnia, 1996; Wolfson, Jajodia, and Huang, 1997; Brunstrom, Leutenegger, and Simha, 1995), which may be adaptive or non-adaptive. Adaptive models (Levin, 1982; Son, 1988; Levin and Morgan,

1978) are implemented when the system senses a substantial deviation in access activities; these models determine a one-time reallocation (for a relatively short period of time) in response to surges in demand. For example, the volume of reservations for a particular airline route may increase during a specific season. Therefore, an airline reservation system may temporarily store additional copies of the files associated with the route at a local server. However, this is a short-term situation which is resolved by introducing replicated file copies. Non-adaptive models (Levin, 1982; Porcar, 1982, Segall, 1976) are employed at the initial system design stage or upon system reorganization; these models do not adjust to variations in system activities.

Most previous research on data allocation assumes a fixed number of servers in the distributed database system (Carey and Lu, 1986; Chu, 1969, Laning and Leonard, 1983; Lee and Liu Sheng, 1992; Rivera-Vega, Varadarajan, and Navathe, 1990). Experiments and simulations are designed to test DDBMS factors such as the degree of data replication, workloads per server, and different levels and classes of queries and transactions (Carey and Lu, 1986; Ciciani, Dias, and Yu, 1990). Simulation runs vary the number of servers to arbitrary values. However, these values are fixed per run and vary only between runs. Incremental system growth and subsequent data reallocation has not previously been addressed.

INCREMENTAL GROWTH FRAMEWORK

The incremental growth framework (see Figure 1) is invoked when system performance, as computed using the objective cost function, is below the acceptable threshold (specified by the DBA). To return to an acceptable state, new servers are introduced incrementally, one at a time, into the distributed database system. With the introduction of each new server, a new data reallocation for the system is computed. This process is iteratively executed until acceptable performance is achieved or the number of servers equals the number of relations in the distributed database system (the latter constraint can easily be relaxed in a distributed database system housing partitioned data).

The incremental growth framework, which can easily be adapted for one-server or multiple-server systems, can be used by small, mid-size, and large organizations, each having distributed database systems of varying size. In one-server systems, the initial data allocation locates all relations at the server. In multiple-server systems, the current data allocation is required as input into the framework.

Additional input information required for the incremental growth framework includes: the database server or servers, including the local processing

Figure 1

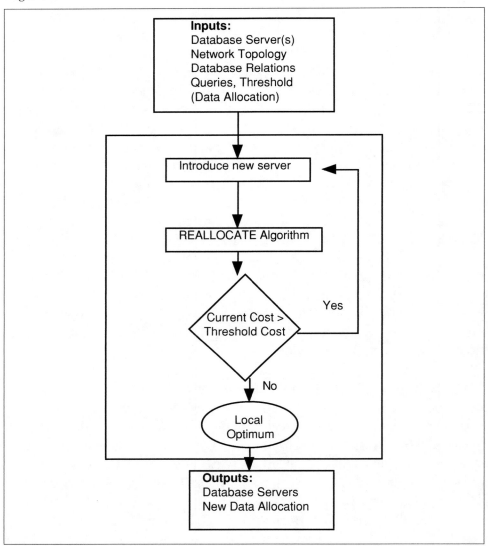

capacity; the network topology, including transmission capacity; the database relations, including relation sizes and selectivities; the query set, the optimization parameter, and the acceptable threshold for the optimization parameter.

DEFINITIONS

The relational data model is used to describe the data and query processing on the data. Only simple queries are considered. Queries are assumed to be independent and are solved independently. Queries are processed in parallel in the distributed database system. To simplify the estimation of query result sizes, the concept of selectivity (Blankinship, 1991; Chin, 1999; Date, 1991; Goyal, 1994) is utilized. Attribute values are assumed to be uniformly distributed and each attribute in a relation is assumed to be independent of all other attributes in the database. The simple query environment has been chosen because it has a manageable complexity while remaining realistic and interesting.

The parameters describing the simple query environment are (Blankinship, 1991; Chin, 1999; Goyal, 1994; Hevner and Yao, 1979):

S_i:Network Servers, i = 1, 2, ..., s, s+1

(S_{s+1} = the new server joining the system)

R_j: Relations, j = 1, 2, ..., r

For each relation R_j, j = 1, 2, ..., r:

n_j:number of tuples,

a_j: number of attributes,

β_j:size (in bytes)

For each attribute d_{jk}, k = 1, 2, ..., a_j of relation R_j:

p_{jk}: attribute density, the number of different values in the current state of the attribute divided by the number of possible attribute values. So, $0 <= p_{jk} <= 1$ (Hevner and Yao, 1979). During join operations the density is used as a selectivity coefficient.

w_{jk}: size (in bytes) of the data item in attribute d_{jk}

For local transaction processing, each server in the distributed database system maintains a queue of incoming requests. Queries are maintained in queue until they are processed using a First In, First Out (FIFO) order.

Finally, the distributed database system maintains a centralized data dictionary housing the following information (Blankinship, 1991; Goyal, 1994; Hevner and Yao, 1979):

- for each relation R_j, j = 1, 2, ..., r: n_j, a_j, β_j, and S_j (server to which relation R_j is allocated)
- for each attribute d_{jk}, k = 1, 2, ..., a_j of relation R_j: p_{jk}, w_{jk}, and b_{jk} (projected size, in bytes, of attribute d_{jk} with no duplicate values)

Optimizing query strategies is not within the scope of this research. However, since the optimal data allocation is dependent on the implemented query strategy, when computing new data allocations, Algorithm Serial (Hevner and Yao, 1979) for query processing is implemented. Any query optimization algorithm from the research literature, however, can be used in place of Algorithm Serial.

Algorithm Serial (Hevner and Yao, 1979) considers serial strategies to minimize total transmission time in the simple query environment. For each query q accessing $\hat{A}$ relations, there are $\hat{A}!$ possible combinations for processing q. The serial strategy consists of transmitting each relation, starting with R_1, to the next relation in a serial order. The strategy is represented by $R_1 \rightarrow R_2 \rightarrow ... \rightarrow R_\sigma$, where σ is the number of relations in the query (Hevner and Yao, 1979). Consider for example a query which accesses relations A, B, and C. Then, the $\hat{A}! = 6$ processing combinations for the query are: $A \rightarrow B \rightarrow C$, $A \rightarrow C \rightarrow B$, $B \rightarrow A \rightarrow C$, $B \rightarrow C \rightarrow A$, $C \rightarrow A \rightarrow B$, $C \rightarrow B \rightarrow A$. Therefore, given 4 queries, two of which access 2 relations, one of which accesses 3 relations, and one of which access 4 relations, the number of possible serial strategy combinations is $(2!)(2!)(3!)(4!) = (2)(2)(6)(24) = 576$. The serial order is computed so that $ß_1 \le ß_2 \le ... \le ß_\sigma$, where $ß_j$ is the size of relation R_j, j = 1, ..., r (Hevner and Yao, 1978).

SYSTEM COST EQUATIONS

A fully connected, reliable communication network (Liu Sheng, 1992) with all servers having equal local storage and processing capacity is assumed. A single instance of each relation is allocated to the distributed database system (Blankinship, 1991; Cornell, 1989; Goyal, 1994). (Data partitioning and data replication are not considered in this research.)

When measuring system response time, the objective cost function consists of three cost components: transmission costs, local processing costs, and queuing costs. Costs are measured in terms of the number of CPU cycles or time ticks (Goyal, 1994) needed to complete a task. The system response time is equal to the number of CPU cycles needed to process $Q = \{Q_1, ..., Q_q\}$ queries.

Transmission cost equations are identical between any two servers (Blankinship, 1991; Goyal, 1994), and costs are based on the amount of data transmitted. Local processing cost equations are also identical at any two servers, and costs are based on the amount of data processed. Queuing costs are based on the number of CPU cycles a query spends in queue at each server. Storage costs are considered negligible and are not considered in the cost analysis.

Using the additional notation:

CS_n: cumulative selectivity for Q_n n = 1, ..., q

QR_n: query result for Q_n n = 1, ..., q

QWT_{ni}: wait time in queue for Q_n at S_i n = 1, ..., q; i = 1, ..., s+1

LPT_{ni}: local processing time for

    processing Q_n at S_i n = 1, ..., q; i = 1, ..., s+1

NTT_{nii}: network transfer time for

transferring Q_n from S_i to $S_{\hat{i}}$ $\quad$ n = 1, ..., q; i, î = 1, ..., S+1; $\hat{i} \neq \hat{i}$

Θ_{ni}: transmission of Q_n to S_i $\qquad$ n = 1, ..., q; i = 1, ..., s+1

ρ: CPU rate per CPU cycle

μ: network transfer rate per CPU cycle

we state our cost equations as follows (Goyal, 1994):

$QR_n = (CS_n)(\beta_j)$ $\qquad$ n = 1, ..., q; j = 1, ..., r

$$LPT_{ni} = \frac{\beta_j + QR_n}{\rho} \text{ at } S_i \qquad n = 1, ..., q; j = 1, ..., r; i = 1, ..., s+1$$

$$NTT_{ni\hat{i}} = \frac{QR_n}{\mu} \text{ from } S_i \text{ to } S_{\hat{i}} \qquad n = 1, ..., q; i, \hat{i} = 1, ..., s+1; i \neq \hat{i}$$

$$QWT_{ni} = T_{P_{ni}} - T_{Q_{ni}} \qquad n = 1, ..., q; \ i = 1, ..., s+1$$

where,

$T_{Q_{ni}}$ = the CPU cycle S_i places Q_n into its queue

$T_{P_{ni}}$ = the CPU cycle S_i begins processing Q_n

The objective cost function when computing data allocations to minimize response time is to minimize:

$$RT = \sum_{t=1}^{T}(t) + ç$$

where,

$$C(t) = \begin{cases} 1 \ if \ (Q_n \in Q \ in \ queue \ at \ S_i \\ \quad \vee \ (Q_n \in Q \ in \ process \ at \ S_i \\ \quad \vee \ (\ Q_n \in Q \ in \ transmision \ S_i \to S_i) \\ 0 \ otherwise \end{cases}$$

and ç = system idle time while processing $Q = \{Q_1, ..., Q_q\}$.

The following example demonstrates cost computations:

Example

Given the relations $R = \{R_A, R_B, R_C\}$, with selectivities, size β, and server allocations on $S = \{S_1, S_2\}$ as follows:

Table 1: Example - Relations and Allocations

Relation	Selectivity	β	Allocation
R_A	0.2	200	S_1
R_B	0.4	400	S_1
R_C	0.6	600	S_2

and the following queries and query strategies (computed so that $ß_1 \leq ß_2 \leq ... \leq ß_\sigma$):

Table 2: Example - Queries and Query Strategies

Query ID	Query	Query Strategy
Q_1	Join A, B, & C	$R_A \rightarrow R_B \rightarrow R_C$
Q_2	Join B & C	$R_B \rightarrow R_C$

Based on the example in Table 3 (see next page), the system response time is 370 CPU cycles. The response time for query Q_1 is 221-10=211 CPU cycles and the response time for Q_2 is 370-15=355 CPU cycles.

DATA REALLOCATION HEURISTICS

We present two heuristics for data reallocation: Partial REALLOCATE and Full REALLOCATE. Both algorithms are greedy, iterative, "hill-climbing" heuristics that will not traverse the same path twice. With each iteration, they will find a lower cost solution, or they will terminate. Both algorithms require as input: the current data allocation, the relations, and the queries in the distributed database system.

We define the notation:

$S = \{S_1, ..., S_s, S_{s+1}\}$:   set of servers ($S_{s+1}$ = the new server)

$R = \{R_1, ..., R_r\}$:   set of relations allocated to S_i, i = 1, ..., s

$R' = \{R'_1, ..., R'_r\}$:   set of relations allocated to S_{s+1}

      $R \cap R' = \varnothing$

$R_j \Rightarrow S_i$:   permanent allocation of R_j to S_i, j= 1, ..., r; i = 1, ..., s

$R_j \rightarrow S_i$:   temporary allocation of R_j to S_i, j= 1, ..., r; i = 1, ..., s

$O_o = \delta(\forall R_j \in R, R_j \Rightarrow S_i)$, i = 1, ..., s

$O_{(s+1)j} = \delta(R_j \rightarrow S_{s+1})$ j= 1, ..., r

where $\delta(R_j \rightarrow S_i)$ and $\delta(R_j \Rightarrow S_i)$ is the objective cost function evaluated for $R_j \rightarrow S_i$ and $R_j \Rightarrow S_i$, respectively.

Each relation R_j must be allocated to a server and can be allocated to only one server at any given time. Therefore,

For each $R_j \in (R \cup R')$,   where $\sum_{i=1}^{S+1} x_{ij} = 1$

$$X_{ij} = \begin{cases} 1, R_j \rightarrow S_i \vee R_j \Rightarrow S_{ji} \\ 0, \text{otherwise} \end{cases}$$

Table 3: Example - Cost Computations

Assuming ρ=10 bytes per unit time and μ=20 bytes per unit time,

CPU cycle	Processing and Computations (unit = CPU cycles)
10	Θ_{11}; S_1 places Q_1 in its queue; QR_1=0; CS_1=1.0
15	Θ_{21}; S_1 places Q_2 in its queue; QR_2=0; CS_2=1.0
30	S_1 begins processing Q_1; QWT_{11}=30-10=20; $LPT_{11}=\frac{200+0}{10}=20$; QR_1=(1.0)(200)=200; CS_1=(1.0)(0.2)=0.2
50	Since R_B is also at S_1, NTT_{111}=0; S_1 begins processing Q_1 with R_B; QWT_{11}=20; $LPT_{11}=20+\frac{400+200}{10}=80$; QR_1=(0.2)(400)=80; CS_1=(0.2)(0.4)=0.08
110	Θ_{12}; $NTT_{112}=\frac{80}{20}=4$; S_1 begins processing Q_2; QWT_{21}=95; $LPT_{21}=\frac{400+0}{10}=40$; QR_2=(1.0)(400)=400; CS_2=(1.0)(0.4)=0.4
114	S_2 places Q_1 in its queue
150	Θ_{22}; $NTT_{212}=\frac{400}{20}=20$; S_2 begins processing Q_1; QWT_{12}=36; $LPT_{12}=\frac{600+80}{10}=68$; QR_1=(0.8)(600)=48; CS_1=(0.08)(0.6)=0.048
170	S_2 places Q_2 in its queue
190	S_2 begins processing Q_2; QWT_{22}=20; $LPT_{22}=\frac{600+400}{10}=100$; QR_2=(0.4)(400)=160; CS_2=(0.4)(0.6)=0.24
218	$\Theta_{1(client)}$; $NTT_{12(client)}=\frac{48}{20}=2.4$
221	Client receives result of Q_1
290	$\Theta_{2(client)}$; $NTT_{22(client)}=\frac{160}{20}=80$
370	client receives result of Q_2

Partial REALLOCATE

The steps of the Partial REALLOCATE algorithm are:

<u>Step 1</u>: Compute O_o.

<u>Step 2:</u> For each $R_j \in R$, Compute $O_{(s+1)j} = \delta(R_j \rightarrow S_{s+1})$, where for $R'' = R - R_j$, $\forall R_k$'s $\in R''$, $R_k \neq> S_{s+1}$, $1 \leq k \leq (r-1)$.

<u>Step 3</u>: Compare $O_\Delta = \underset{j}{\text{MIN}}\ O_{(s+1)j}$ to O_o. If $O_\Delta \geq O_o$, O_o is the local optimum. If $O_\Delta < O_o$, update O_o to O_Δ, $R' = R' + R_j$, $R = R - R_j$, $R_j \Rightarrow S_{s+1}$.

Consider for example the relations and server allocations in Table 1. Assume $S_{s+1} = S_3$ is the new server joining the distributed system. Then, in Step 1, Partial REALLOCATE computes the value of the objective function given the current allocation. Assume $O_o = 115$. In Step 2, Partial REALLO-CATE computes the value of the objective function when independently moving each relation to S_{s+1}:

* Move only R_A to S_3: Compute $O_{(s+1)A} = \delta(R_A \rightarrow S_3)$; $R'' = \{R_B, R_C\}$
* Move only R_B to S_3: Compute $O_{(s+1)B} = \delta(R_B \rightarrow S_3)$; $R'' = \{R_A, R_C\}$
* Move only R_C to S_3: Compute $O_{(s+1)C} = \delta(R_C \rightarrow S_3)$; $R'' = \{R_A, R_B\}$

Assume $O_{(s+1)A} = 100$, $O_{(s+1)B} = 75$, and $O_{(s+1)C} = 125$. Then, in Step 3, Partial REALLOCATE selects the move resulting in the minimum cost, $O_\Delta = O_{(s+1)B} = 75$. Since $O_\Delta < O_o$, a lower cost solution has been found; R_B is relocated from S_1 to S_3.

Partial REALLOCATE minimizes the number of $\delta(R_j \rightarrow S_{s+1})$ evaluations while searching for a better solution. The number of Partial REALLO-CATE tests per additional server is bounded by R, the number of relations in the distributed database system. Partial REALLOCATE is not guaranteed to find the optimum solution (as determined using Exhaustive Search). However, if evaluating $\delta(R_j \rightarrow S_{s+1})$ is expensive and/or if Partial REALLOCATE's percentage deviation from the optimal solution is acceptable, Partial REAL-LOCATE is more cost-effective than either Full REALLOCATE or Exhaustive Search.

Full REALLOCATE

The steps of the Full REALLOCATE algorithm are:

<u>Step 1 & Step 2:</u> Same as in Partial REALLOCATE.

<u>Step 3</u>: Holding the R_j yielding $O_{1\Delta} = \overset{MIN}{j} O_{(s+1)j}$ at S_{s+1}, $R_j \Rightarrow S_{s+1}$, $R' = R' + R_j$, $R = R - R_j$, Full REALLOCATE reiterates with a new $R_j \in R$ until either $O_{x\Delta} \geq O_{(x-1)\Delta}$ or $R = \emptyset$.

<u>Step 4</u>: Compare $O_{y\Delta} = \overset{MIN}{j} O_{(s+1)j}$ from the yth iteration, $y = x$ yielding MIN$(O_{x\Delta}, O_{(x-1)\Delta})$, to O_o. If $O_{y\Delta} \geq O_o$, O_o is the local optimum. If $O_{y\Delta} < O_o$, update O_o to $O_{y\Delta}$, $R' = R' + R_j$, $R = R - R_j$, $R_j \Rightarrow S_{s+1}$.

As in Partial REALLOCATE, Full REALLOCATE begins by computing $\delta(R_j \rightarrow S_{s+1})$ for each $R_j \in R$. Rather than outputting the MIN $\delta(R_j \rightarrow S_{s+1})$, Full REALLOCATE holds the R_j yielding $O_{1\Delta}$ at S_{s+1}, so $R_j \Rightarrow S_{s+1}$, $R' = R' + R_j$, $R = R - R_j$. Full REALLOCATE then reiterates with a new $R_j \in R$ until either $O_{x\Delta} \geq O_{(x-1)\Delta}$ or $R = \emptyset$. The number of Full REALLOCATE tests per additional server is bounded by $\sum_{r=1}^{R} r$.

Full REALLOCATE iterates a greater number of times than Partial REAL-LOCATE before choosing from the yth iteration of the algorithm.

EXAMPLE - COMPARISON OF PARTIAL, FULL REALLOCATE, EXHAUSTIVE SEARCH

We provide an illustrative example to demonstrate the benefits of implementing the REALLOCATE algorithms over Exhaustive Search. We solve the same problem using each of the three data reallocation algorithm — first using Exhaustive Search, then using Partial REALLOCATE, and finally using Full REALLOCATE. Response times have been computed by the SimDDBMS simulator. The serial query strategy (Hevner and Yao, 1979) has been implemented and query results are computed as described in (Blankinship, 1991; Goyal, 1994, Hevner and Yao, 1979). Assume the system parameters in Table 4, the relations in Table 5, and the queries in Table 6.

Base Case

The base case assumes there is only one server, $S = \{S_1\}$, in the system and $\forall R_j$'s $\in R$, $R_j \Rightarrow S_1$. Therefore, the initial allocation is $R_A \Rightarrow S_1$, $R_B \Rightarrow S_1$, $R_C \Rightarrow S_1$, and $R_D \Rightarrow S_1$. Using a poisson arrival rate for queries, SimDDBMS has computed a total response time of 307 CPU cycles. Since 307 is greater than the specified threshold of 200, a new server is added to the distributed database system.

Exhaustive Search

$S = \{S_1, S_2\}$: (incremental growth from s=1 to s+1=2 servers)

There are 16 possible allocations of 4 relations to 2 servers (see Table 7). The Exhaustive Search method finds the lowest response time of 216, with the allocations $(R_A \rightarrow S_1)$, $(R_B \rightarrow S_2)$, $(R_C \rightarrow S_2)$, $(R_D \rightarrow S_1)$ and $(R_A \rightarrow S_2)$, $(R_B \rightarrow S_1)$, $(R_C \rightarrow S_1)$, $(R_D \rightarrow S_2)$. The first allocation found is arbitrarily chosen as the new data allocation. So, $R_B \Rightarrow S_2$ and $R_C \Rightarrow S_2$. Since the minimum total response time found with two servers is greater than the specified threshold $(216 > 200)$, an additional server is added to the distributed database system.

$S=\{S_1, S_2, S_3\}$: (incremental growth from s=2 to s+1=3 servers)

There are 81 possible allocations of 4 relations to 3 servers. The Exhaustive Search method finds the minimum response time of 182, with the allocations $(R_A \rightarrow S_1)$, $(R_B \rightarrow S_2)$, $(R_C \rightarrow S_3)$, $(R_D \rightarrow S_1)$ and $(R_A \rightarrow S_1)$, $(R_B$

Table 4: System Parameters

Parameter	Value
CPU Rate	50
Network Transfer Rate	100
Threshold	200
Optimization Parameter	Response Time

Table 5: Relations

Relation	Selectivity	Size
R_A	1.0	1000
R_B	0.9	900
R_C	0.8	800
R_D	0.7	700

Table 6: Queries

Queries
Join A, B & C
Join B & D
Join A & C
Join A, B, C & D

Table 7: Exhaustive Search with 4 Relations, 2 Servers

	R_A	R_B	R_C	R_D	R_T
1)	1	1	1	1	307
2)	1	1	1	2	279
3)	1	1	2	1	273
4)	1	1	2	2	242
5)	1	2	1	1	224
6)	1	2	1	2	267
7)	1	2	2	1	216
8)	1	2	2	2	244
9)	2	1	1	1	244
10)	2	1	1	2	216
11)	2	1	2	1	267
12)	2	1	2	2	224
13)	2	2	1	1	242
14)	2	2	1	2	273
15)	2	2	2	1	279
16)	2	2	2	2	307

$\rightarrow S_3$), $(R_C \rightarrow S_2)$, $(R_D \rightarrow S_1)$. Since the response time resulting from adding the third server meets the specified threshold ($182 \le 200$), no additional servers are added. The final data allocation found by Exhaustive Search is $R_A \Rightarrow S_1$, $R_B \Rightarrow S_2$, $R_C \Rightarrow S_3$, $R_D \Rightarrow S_1$ or $R_A \Rightarrow S_1$, $R_B \Rightarrow S_3$, $R_C \Rightarrow S_2$, $R_D \Rightarrow S_1$ with the total response time of 182 ticks.

Partial REALLOCATE

$S = \{S_1, S_2\}$: (incremental growth from s=1 to s+1=2 servers)

There are $R = 4$ reallocation tests required. The response time is computed for each independent allocation (see Table 8). The Partial REAL-LOCATE algorithm finds the lowest response time of 224, with the allocation $(R_A \rightarrow S_1)$, $(R_B \rightarrow S_2)$, and $(R_C \rightarrow S_1)$, $(R_D \rightarrow S_1)$, so $R_B \Rightarrow S_2$. Since $224 > 200$, an additional server is added to the distributed database system.

$S = \{S_1, S_2, S_3\}$: (incremental growth from s=2 to s+1=3 servers)

Again, $R = 4$ reallocation tests are required. The response time is computed for each independent allocation (see Table 9). The Partial REAL-LOCATE algorithm finds the lowest response time of 182, with the allocation $(R_A \rightarrow S_1)$, $(R_B \rightarrow S_2)$, and $(R_C \rightarrow S_3)$, $(R_D \rightarrow S_1)$, so $R_C \Rightarrow S_2$. Since $182 \le 200$, Partial REALLOCATE terminates. The final data allocation found by Partial REALLOCATE is $R_A \Rightarrow S_1$, $R_B \Rightarrow S_2$, $R_C \Rightarrow S_3$, $R_D \Rightarrow S_1$ with the total response time of 182 CPU cycles.

Table 8: Partial REALLOCATE: 2 Servers, 4 Relations

$(R_j \rightarrow S_2)$	Allocation	RT
$(R_A \rightarrow S_2)$	2111	244
$(R_B \rightarrow S_2)$	1211	224
$(R_C \rightarrow S_2)$	1121	273
$(R_D \rightarrow S_2)$	1112	279

Table 9: Partial REALLOCATE: 3 Servers, 4 Relations

$(R_j \rightarrow S_3)$	Allocation	RT
$(R_A \rightarrow S_3)$	3211	188
$(R_B \rightarrow S_3)$	1311	224
$(R_C \rightarrow S_3)$	1231	182
$(R_D \rightarrow S_3)$	1213	206

Full REALLOCATE

$S = \{S_1, S_2\}$: (incremental growth from s=1 to s+1=2 servers)

There are a maximum of $\sum\limits_{r=1}^{R} r = 10$ reallocation tests.

In the first iteration, the response time is computed for $R = 4$ independent allocations (see Table 10). The Full REALLOCATE algorithm finds the lowest response time of 224, with the allocation $(R_A \rightarrow S_1)$, $(R_B \rightarrow S_2)$, and $(R_C \rightarrow S_1)$, $(R_D \rightarrow S_1)$, so $R_B \Rightarrow S_2$. Full REALLOCATE reiterates with R_A, R_C, and R_D (see Table 11). The Full REALLOCATE algorithm finds the lowest response time of 216 with the allocation $(R_A \rightarrow S_1)$, $(R_B \rightarrow S_2)$, $(R_C \rightarrow S_2)$, $(R_D \rightarrow S_1)$, so $R_C \Rightarrow S_2$. Full REALLOCATE reiterates with R_A and R_D (see Table 12).

Since the minimum response time found in this iteration is greater than the response time in the previous iteration (244 > 216), Full REALLOCATE does not reiterate with 2 servers. Therefore, the allocation is $(R_A \rightarrow S_1)$, $(R_B \rightarrow S_2)$, $(R_C \rightarrow S_2)$, $(R_D \rightarrow S_1)$ with a response time of 216 CPU cycles. Since 216 > 200, an additional server is added to the distributed database system.

$S = \{S_1, S_2, S_3\}$: (incremental growth from s=2 to s+1=3 servers)

Even with $S = \{S_1, S_2, S_3\}$, there are still only 10 maximum possible allocations with the Full REALLOCATE algorithm. We start with the best allocation (1221) from the result of Full REALLOCATE at 2 servers.

Again, we independently reallocate each R_j to S_{s+1} and evaluate the

Table 10: First Iteration

$(R_j \rightarrow S_2)$	Allocation	RT
$(R_A \rightarrow S_2)$	2111	244
$(R_B \rightarrow S_2)$	1211	224
$(R_C \rightarrow S_2)$	1121	273
$(R_D \rightarrow S_2)$	1112	279

Table 11: Second Iteration

$(R_j \rightarrow S_2)$	Allocation	RT
$(R_A \rightarrow S_2)$	2211	242
$(R_C \rightarrow S_2)$	1221	216
$(R_D \rightarrow S_2)$	1212	267

Table 12: Third Iteration

$(R_j \rightarrow S_2)$	Allocation	RT
$(R_A \rightarrow S_2)$	2221	279
$(R_D \rightarrow S_2)$	1222	244

resulting response time (see Table 13). The Full REALLOCATE algorithm finds the minimum response time of 182 CPU cycles with the allocations $(R_A \rightarrow S_1)$, $(R_B \rightarrow S_3)$, $(R_C \rightarrow S_2)$, $(R_D \rightarrow S_1)$ and $(R_A \rightarrow S_1)$, $(R_B \rightarrow S_2)$, $(R_C \rightarrow S_3)$, $(R_D \rightarrow S_1)$. Arbitrarily choosing the first allocation, $R_B \Rightarrow S_3$, we now test reallocating an additional R_j to S_3 (see Table 14).

Since $216 > 182$ and $182 < 200$, Full REALLOCATE terminates. The final data allocation found by Full REALLOCATE is $R_A \Rightarrow S_1$, $R_B \Rightarrow S_3$, $R_C \Rightarrow S_2$, $R_D \Rightarrow S_1$ or $R_A \Rightarrow S_1$, $R_B \Rightarrow S_2$, $R_C \Rightarrow S_3$, $R_D \Rightarrow S_1$ with the total response time of 182 CPU cycles.

Summary

In this example, we have demonstrated that for at least some problems, the Full and Partial REALLOCATE algorithms find the same optimal data allocation solution that is found using the Exhaustive Search algorithm. Additionally, we have shown that the Full and Partial REALLOCATE algorithms greatly reduce the problem search space, and hence, the cost of determining the new data allocation. In this particular example, the search space when incrementing from $S = \{S_1\}$ to $S = \{S_1, S_2\}$ was reduced by 75% using Partial REALLOCATE and 37.5% using Full REALLOCATE. Incrementing from $S = \{S_1, S_2\}$ to $S = \{S_1, S_2, S_3\}$, the search space was reduced by 95% using Partial REALLOCATE and 87.6% using Full REALLOCATE. While Exhaustive Search and Partial REALLOCATE test 100% of their search space, Full REALLOCATE tested only 90% of its search space when incrementing from $S = \{S_1\}$ to $S = \{S_1, S_2\}$ and only 70% when incrementing from $S = \{S_1, S_2\}$ to $S = \{S_1, S_2, S_3\}$.

Table 13: Full REALLOCATE: First Iteration

$(R_j \rightarrow S_3)$	Allocation	RT
$(R_A \rightarrow S_3)$	3221	216
$(R_B \rightarrow S_3)$	1321	182
$(R_C \rightarrow S_3)$	1231	182
$(R_D \rightarrow S_3)$	1223	216

Table 14: Full REALLOCATE: Second Iteration

$(R_j \rightarrow S_3)$	Allocation	RT
$(R_A \rightarrow S_3)$	3321	242
$(R_C \rightarrow S_3)$	1331	216
$(R_D \rightarrow S_3)$	1323	246

SIMULATION RESULTS

To simulate incremental growth and reallocation, including the implementation of Partial and Full REALLOCATE, we have developed SimDDBMS. We have run over 5,800 simulation experiments. 1,100 smaller, tractable problems have been run using the Exhaustive Search optimal and 4,700 larger, more realistic problems have been run using only Full and Partial REALLOCATE. The experiments have been run to minimize system response time in the simple query environment.

A "base case" simulation is run for each problem. The "base case" assumes there is only one server in the distributed database system, with all of the relations allocated to this one server. (This parameter can be relaxed for distributed database systems consisting of more than one server.)

The Exhaustive Search algorithm is used for benchmark comparisons. However, due to the exponential growth in the search space of the Exhaustive Search algorithm, Exhaustive Search computations are restricted to a maximum of 4 servers and 5 relations (a combined search space of 1+32+243+1,024 = 1,300 possible allocations). The effect on the system response time of each of the following parameters (as independent variables) is studied: CPU processing rate, network transfer rate, number of queries, number of relations. In all graphs, each data point represents the average cost for 100 randomly generated problems. Fixed parameter values are displayed in a box at the top of each graph.

Effect of CPU Rate

The REALLOCATE algorithms performed very close to optimal across a broad range of CPU rates (see Figure 2). We observed that at the lowest CPU rate, Full REALLOCATE was on average only 4.92% from the Exhaustive Search optimal with a worst case of 28.4% from optimal. Partial REALLO-CATE on average deviated 6.66% from the Exhaustive Search optimal with

Figure 2

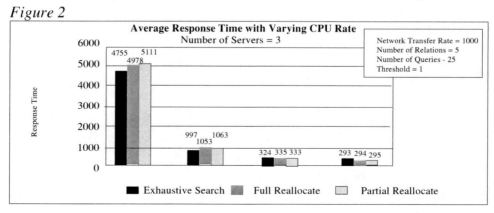

a worst case of 32.53%. As the CPU rate increased, both REALLOCATE algorithms achieved results even closer to optimal. Additionally, Full REAL-LOCATE on average reduced execution time by at least 94.5% when compared to Exhaustive Search and Partial REALLOCATE on average reduced execution time by at least 96.5% compared to Exhaustive Search.

When comparing the results of Full and Partial REALLOCATE with a larger number of relations, we found that Partial REALLOCATE actually performed better than Full REALLOCATE at the lower CPU rates and matched Full REALLOCATE at the higher CPU rates (see Figure 3). Partial REALLOCATE required significantly more servers to achieve these results, often close to double the number the number of servers that Full REALLO-CATE specified.

Figure 3

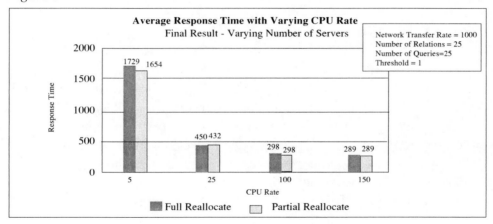

Figure 4

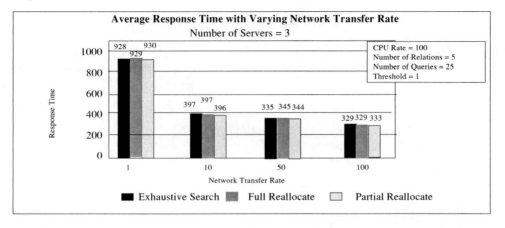

Effect of Network Transfer Rate

As with the effect of varying CPU rates, both Partial and Full REALLO-CATE performed well against Exhaustive Search when varying network transfer rate (see Figure 4). At worst, Full REALLOCATE performed within 3% of optimal and Partial REALLOCATE within 2.7%. As network transfer rate increased beyond 100, the effect of network transfer rate became minimal.

Effect of Number of Queries

When increasing the number of queries (see Figure 5), Full REALLO-CATE achieved solutions on average of only 3.3% worse than the Exhaustive Search optimal, while Partial REALLOCATE achieved solutions averaging 4% worse than optimal. With a larger number of servers and relations, Partial and Full REALLOCATE obtained identical final cost results. Partial REAL-LOCATE, however, required a larger number of servers than Full REALLO-CATE.

Effect of Number of Relations

Varying the number of relations did not effect the comparative results of Partial REALLOCATE and Full REALLOCATE. Once again, Partial RE-ALLOCATE required a greater number of servers than Full REALLOCATE in order to achieve the same cost results. Examining the response time with an equivalent number of servers (Figure 6) showed that Partial REALLOCATE's response time grew linearly as the number of relations increased. Thus, the efficiency of Partial REALLOCATE dropped per server as compared to Full REALLOCATE.

Figures 7 and 8 compare the execution times of the three data realloca-

Figure 5

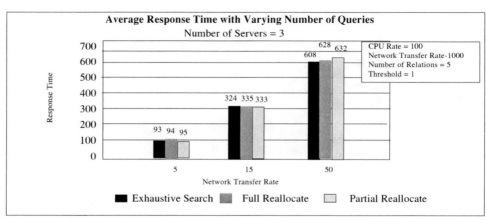

Figure 6

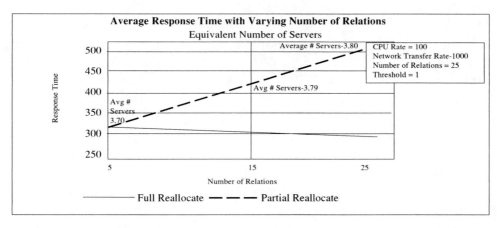

Figure 7

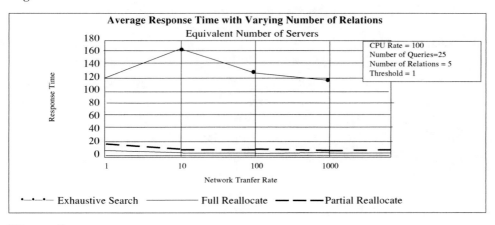

Figure 8

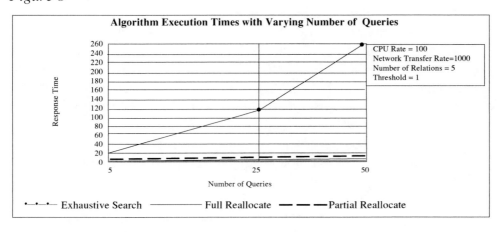

tion algorithms. The network transfer rate is varied in Figure 7 and the number of queries is varied in Figure 8 (varying the other system parameters showed similar results). Figure 7 shows that Full REALLOCATE in the best case, only required 3.58% of the time required by Exhaustive Search, and in the worst case, only required 7.73% of Exhaustive Search. Partial REALLO-CATE, in the best case, only required 1.74% of the time required by Exhaustive Search, and in the worst case, only required 6.16% Exhaustive Search's time. Figure 8 shows similar results with varying number of queries. In the best case, Full REALLOCATE only required 4.03% of Exhaustive Search's time and only 5.75% in the worst case. Partial REALLOCATE varied from a low of 1.78% to a high of 2.81% of Exhaustive Search's time.

Tables 15 and 16, which correspond to the parameters in Figures 7 and 8, compare the average number of tests required for each of the three reallocate algorithms. Each line in the table represents the average of 100 randomly generated problems.

SUMMARY

In summary, the Partial and Full REALLOCATE algorithms have been shown to considerably reduce problem search space, and hence, the cost of testing relation-server combinations. If the cost of each test is one unit, implementing Partial REALLOCATE over exhaustive search results in a cost savings of S^R - R units; implementing Full REALLOCATE over exhaustive search results in a cost savings of

$$S^R - \sum_{r=1}^{R} r \text{ units.}$$

Using SimDDBMS, parametric studies across a range of parameters, including CPU Rate, Network Transfer Rate, Number of Queries, and Number of Relations have been performed. The parametric studies have demonstrated the consistency of the REALLOCATE algorithms across a broad range of parametric values. Additionally, the simulation experiments have shown that Partial REALLOCATE and Full REALLOCATE provide good solutions as compared to exhaustive search optimums.

Partial and Full REALLOCATE have different strengths. As shown in Table 17, if the cost of testing relation-server combinations is high, Partial REALLOCATE is the algorithm of choice. This is because Partial REAL-LOCATE has a much smaller search space than Full REALLOCATE (R vs $\sum_{r=1}^{R} r$, where R is the number of relations in the

distributed database system). If the cost of adding additional servers is high, Full REALLOCATE is the algorithm of choice. As demonstrated in the

Table 15: Comparison of Average Number of Algorithm Tests with Varying Network Transfer Rate

	Network Transfer Rate			
	1	10	100	1000
Partial REALLOCATE	7.02	5.90	5.72	5.90
Full REALLOCATE	11.37	15.15	15.20	15.25
Exhaustive Search	365.34	1,125.92	1,136.16	1,146.40

Table 16: Comparison of Average Number of Algorithm Tests with Varying Number of Queries

	Number of Queries		
	5	25	50
Partial REALLOCATE	6.29	5.90	5.60
Full REALLOCATE	13.85	15.25	15.50
Exhaustive Search	862.63	1,146.40	1,177.12

Table 17: Algorithm of Choice

Cost	Level	Algorithm of Choice
Relation-server testing	High	Partial
	Low	Partial, Full
Additional Server	High	Full
	Low	Partial, Full

simulation experiments, Partial REALLOCATE is a server-hungry algorithm. It generally requires two to three times as many servers as Full REALLOCATE in order to find a comparable solution.

CONCLUSIONS

We have presented an incremental growth framework and two data reallocation heuristics — Partial REALLOCATE and Full REALLOCATE — for incremental growth and reallocation in distributed database systems. Through simple examples and then through parametric studies performed using the SimDDBMS simulator, we have demonstrated the robustness of both data reallocation heuristics. Due to their linear complexity, the Partial and Full REALLOCATE algorithms can be used for large, complex problems while achieving good results as compared to the exhaustive search optimal.

REFERENCES

Apers, Peter M. G. (1988). "Data Allocation in Distributed Database

Systems," *ACM Transactions on Database Systems*, 13(3), September, 263-304.

Blankinship, Rex (1991). "An Iterative Method for Distributed Database Design," Ph.D. Dissertation, University of Maryland at College Park.

Brunstrom, Anna, Scott T. Leutenegger, and Rahul Simha (1995). "Experimental Evaluation of Dynamic Data Allocation Strategies in a Distributed Database with Changing Workloads," CIKM, 395-402.

Carey, Michael J. and Hongjun Lu (1986). "Load Balancing in a Locally Distributed Database System," *Proceedings of the ACM-SIGMOD International Conference on Management of Data, Washington, D.C.*, 108-119.

Ceri, Stefano, Shamkant Navathe, and Gio Wiederhold (1983)."Distribution Design of Logical Database Schemas," *IEEE Transactions on Computers*, SE-9(4),487-504.

Chin, Amita Goyal (1999). "An Optimization Algorithm for Dynamic Data Migration in Distributed Database Systems," *Journal of Computer Information Systems*, 39(4).

Chu, Wesley W. (1969). "Optimal File Allocation in a Multiple Computer System," IEEE Transactions on Computers, C-18(10), 885-890.

Ciciani, Bruno, Daniel M. Dias, and Philip S. Yu (1990). "Analysis of Replication in Distributed Database Systems," *IEEE Transactions on Knowledge and Data Engineering*, 2(2), 247-261.

Cornell, Douglas W. (1989). "On Optimal Site Assignment for Relations in the Distributed Database Environment," *IEEE Transaction on Software Engineering*, 15(8), 1004-1009.

Cornell, Douglas W. and Philip S. Yu (1990). "Relation Assignment in Distributed Transaction Processing Environment," *Proceedings of the Sixth International Conference on Data Engineering*, 50-55.

Date, C. J. (1991). *An Introduction to Database Systems*, Addison Wesley.

Daudpota, Nadeem (1998). "Five Steps to Construct a Model of Data Allocation for Distributed Database System," *Journal of Intelligent Information Systems*, 11(2), 153-168.

Du, Xiaolin and Fred J. Maryanski (1988). "Data Allocation in a Dynamically Reconfigurable Environment," Proceedings of the Fourth International Conference on Data Engineering, 74-81.

Eswaran, K., (1974)."Placement of Records in a File and File Allocation in a Computer Network," *Proceedings IFIPS Conference*, 304-307.

Garey, Michael R. and David S. Johnson (1979).*Compilers and Intractability — A Guide to the Theory of NP-Completeness*, W. H. Freeman and Company.

Ghosh, Deb and Ishwar Murthy (1991). "A Solution Procedure for the File Allocation Problem with File Availability and Response Time," *Computers and*

Operations Research, 18(6), 557-568.

Ghosh, Deb, Ishwar Murthy, and Allen Moffett (1992). "File Allocation Problem: Comparison of Models with Worst Case and Average Communication Delays," *Operations Research*, 40(6), 1074-1085.

Goyal, Amita (1994). "Incremental Growth and Reallocation in Distributed Database Systems," Ph.D. Dissertation, The University of Maryland at College Park.

Hevner, Alan R. and S.B. Yao (1978). "Optimization of Data Access in Distributed Systems," Computer Science Department, Purdue University, Technical Report TR281.

Hevner, Alan R. and S.B. Yao (1979). "Query Processing in Distributed Database Systems," *IEEE Transactions on Software Engineering*, SE-5(3).

Ladjel, Bellatreche, Kamalakar Karlapalem, and Qing Li(1998)."An Iterative Approach for Rules and Data Allocation in Distributed Deductive Database Systems," *Proceedings of the 1998 ACM 7th International Conference on Information and Knowledge Management*, 356-363.

Laning, Lawrence J. and Michael S. Leonard, "File Allocation in a Distributed Computer Communication Network," IEEE Transactions on Software Engineering, Vol. C-32, No. 3, March 1983, pp. 232-244.

Lee, Heesok, and Olivia R. Liu Sheng (1992). "A Multiple Criteria Model for the Allocation of Data Files in a Distributed Information System,"Computers and Operations Research, 19(1), 21-33.

Levin, K.D. (1982). "Adaptive Structuring of Distributed Databases," *Proceedings of the National Computer Conference,* 691-696.

Levin, K. D., and H. L. Morgan (1978). "A Dynamic Optimization Model for Distributed Databases," Operations Research, 26(5), 824-835.

Liu Sheng, Olivia R. (1992)."Optimization of File Migration Policies in Distributed Computer Systems," *Computers and Operations Research*, 19(5), 335-351.

Porcar, H.(1982). "File Migration in Distributed Computing Systems," Ph.D. Thesis, University of California at Berkeley.

Rivera-Vega, Pedro I., Ravi Varadarajan, and Shamkant B. Navathe (1990)."Scheduling Data Redistribution in Distributed Databases,"*Proceedings of the Symposium on Reliability in Distributed Software and Database Systems*, 166-173.

Segall, Adrian (1976)."Dynamic File Assignment in a Computer Network," *IEEE Trans. Automat. Control,* AC-21, April , 161-173.

So, Siu-Kai, Ishfaq Ahmad, and Kamalakar Karlapalem (1998)."Data Allocation Algorithm for Distributed Hypermedia Documents,"*The 1998 IEEE 17th Symposium on Reliable Distributed Systems,* , 473-478.

Son, Sang H. (1988). "Replicated Data Management in Distributed Database Systems," *SIGMOD Record*, 17(4),

Tamhankar, Ajit and Sudha Ram (1998). " Database Fragmentation and Allocation: An Integrated Methodology and Case Study," IEEE Transactions on Systems, Man, and Cybernetics, 28(3), 288-305.

Theel, Oliver E and Henning Pagnia (1996). "Bounded Dynamic Data Allocation in Distributed Systems," The 1996 3rd International Conference on High Performance Computing, 126-131.

Wolfson, Ouri and Sushil Jajodia, and Yixiu Huang (1997). "An Adaptive Data Replication Algorithm," *ACM Transactions on Database Systems,* 22(2), 255-314.

Chapter 8

Using Business Rules Within a Design Process of Active Databases

Youssef Amghar, Madjid Meziane and André Flory
National Institute of Applied Sciences, France

Modeling behavior is an important task of the information system engineering process. This task is especially important when information systems are centered on active databases, which allow the replacement of parts of application programs with active rules. To relieve programmers from using either traditional or ad hoc techniques to design active databases, it is necessary to develop new techniques to model business rules. For that reason, inclusion of rules during analysis and design stages becomes an actual requirement. In this paper, we propose a uniform approach to modeling business rules (active rules, integrity constraints, etc.). To improve the behavior specification, we extend the state diagrams that are widely used for dynamic modeling. This extension is a transformation of state transitions according to rule semantics. In addition, we outline new functionalities of Computer Aided System Engineering (CASE) to take into consideration the active database specificities. In this way, the designer can be assisted to control, maintain, and reuse a set of rules.

Current design methods for information systems do not consider rules at the design level. In systemic methods such as "Structured Analysis Design Technique" (SADT) (Yourdon, 1979), rules are considered as a part of the design process but they are not modeled explicitly. In Object-Oriented methods such as the Object Modeling Technique (OMT) (Rumbaugh, 1991) or Object-Oriented Analysis (OOA) (Booch, 1994), rules are partially represented in dynamic models, particu-

Previously Published in the *Journal of Database Management, vol.11, no.3,* Copyright © 2000, Idea Group Publishing.

larly in state diagrams. Moreover, at the development level, rules are often coded in the application programs implying a hard maintenance of business rules. These methods are generally supported by CASE.

To allow designers to exploit the specificities and features of active databases, it is important to build prototyping and monitoring tools to assist the designer during the design and development stage. This kind of tool offers indicators about choice relevancy and writing of rules. An active database management system (active DBMS) is an extension of a passive (relational or object) DBMS by adding trigger mechanisms. The notion of trigger appeared in the seventies, and has been generalized to the notion of active rule that is based on the Event-Condition-Action (ECA) formalism. The semantics of an ECA rule is as follows: when an event E is produced, if the condition C is satisfied, then the action A is executed. Actions are initiated by the DBMS when appropriate events occur, independently of external requests. These rules allow database designers to specify the active behavior of a database application that provides the enforcement of database integrity.

In the literature, several approaches were proposed to integrate active concepts into databases. For most systems, the knowledge model is based on ECA rules and the execution model on the nested transaction model, which authorizes different coupling modes (immediate, separate, deferred). Other systems use a weakened version of ECA rules. Furthermore, a number of research projects on active databases have focused on the rules' management and their evaluation. Several commercial DBMS include event/trigger mechanism proposed initially by Kotz (1988), such as the Postgres rule system (Stonebraker, 1990), Starburst's production and alert rules (Lohman, 1991), Ariel's production rule system (Hanson, 1989), the (ECA) model of HiPAC (Dayal, 88), and the event-action (EA) model of Ode (Gehani, 1992). In addition, there is a general agreement to consider that the new generation of DBMS systems would include active capabilities (Buchman, 1993) to support non-conventional applications such as documentation, geographic systems, workflow, and project management.

The design issue of active database applications is known as one of the most open research problems. Indeed, to design active database applications, programmers use either traditional or ad hoc techniques, which increases the complexity of applications by forcing the user to defer several modeling decisions concerning the active behavior to the development stage.

To gain benefits of active database capabilities, new approaches require inclusion of rules during both analysis and design stages. Few researchers have addressed the conceptual specification of behavioral aspects of applications independently from any active DBMS. To our knowledge, only IDEA (Ceri, 1993) and SORAC (Peckham, 1995) projects have treated the design of active database. However IDEA methodology is strongly linked to Chimera that is a DBMS developed especially in the framework of IDEA project. In IDEA project, any rules' specification is proposed. Rules, identified from requirement analysis, are directly expressed to the syntax of Chimera. The SORAC model permits the schema designer to specify enforcement rules that maintain constraints on object and relationships to facilitate the task of the designer. With active databases, it is interesting to replace a part of the application programs by using active rules that are stored, detected and executed by the DBMS. This technique called *knowledge independence* allows a database to evolve by managing the rules without altering the program code. But a main problem exists regarding the design of such databases. More precisely, the design methods of information systems do not offer satisfying means to describe active rules that represent active behavior of applications. It is necessary to improve the techniques of active behavior description whether at designing or derivation level.

Our work presents a framework for designing applications for which active behavior needs to be correctly modeled, particularly applications focused on active databases. The main contributions of this paper include:

1. Specification of system behavior at a high level of description. This specification improves the modeling of system behavior with the introduction of the ECA rules' semantics.
2. Derivation process of active behavior specification for relational DBMS's.
3. Definition of an environment for active database design.

This paper is organized as follows: Section *Case Study* presents a case study to support our explanations. Section *Dynamic Description* briefly discusses the techniques currently used to represent the business rules within data models. Section *Specification of System Behavior* proposes to model the behavior of an active object through a specification based on a description language developed initially for telephone switching systems. Section *Derivation Process* describes the derivation process of models elaborated in the design stage for a relational schema. Section *Rule Modularization* presents a strategy for modularizing a set of rules in order to facilitate the rules' maintenance. This section also presents some features of a prototyping tool. Section *Environment for Active Databases* describes the original functionality of the architecture of an environment for active databases. The last section concludes this work.

CASE STUDY

We present a case study to illustrate the paper's propositions. Let us consider an example of a document-loan management system. In this example,

Figure 1: Entity-Relationship model of a borrowing management system

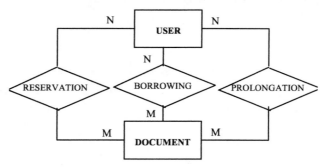

reservation, loan and loan prolongation are managed. Some rules are imposed by the application to fix the number of loans and loan prolongations. Two activities are identified: *document loaning* and *document restitution*. We delimit the application schema to entities described in Figure 1. The two main entities are *user* and *document*. The three relationships indicate the links between a user and a document. Indeed a document can be borrowed or reserved. Let us note that a user can prolong a loan under certain conditions.

Relational Schema

Two main entities constitute the relational schema: *DOCUMENT* and *USER*. Each document is described by the following attributes: *id-doc*: the reference of the document; *doc-name*: the document name; *state*: the availability of the document in the document center; *nb-copies*: the number of copies of the document; and *nb-loans*: the loan number of the document. A reference (id-user) and his name (username) describe each user. Each loan concerns one user (*id-user*) and one document (*id-doc*) and begins at *b-l-date* and would finish at *e-l-date*. The document is effectively returned at *ret-date*. Each reservation, concerning one user (*id-user*) and one document (*id-doc*), begins at *b-reservation-date* and finishes at *e-reservation-date*. The relational schema is comprised of the following relations and their respective attributes:

Document(#id-doc,doc-name,state,nb-copies,nb-borrow),
User(#id-user,name),
Borrowing(#id-doc,#id-user,b-l-date,e-l-date,ret-date),
Reservation(#id-doc,#id-user, b-reservation-date,state).

Note that in this case study, the illustration is simplified by not considering document prolongation. The user requirements provided the basis for the following rules concerning the document object:

R_verif-availability:
on record borrow
   if document exists
   then OK
     else document can
     not be borrowed;

R_verif-nb-loans:
on record borrow
   if user has more than 2 documents
   then document can not be borrowed
   else OK;

The first activity concerns loan management in a document center. This activity consists of checking the existence and availability of the document to loan. Whenever a document can be borrowed, this activity updates the database and records the loan. The second activity considered in this example focuses on the return of documents. This activity either records the document return by updating the database, or triggers the first activity whenever the document is reserved. Rules concerning these two activities are:

R_loan-req
on loan request
if true
then verify possibility to
   loan the document;

R_end-loan
on end of loan verification
if the loan is possible
then mark document as borrowed
else record a reservation;

R_ret-req
on document return
if true
then verify document
   reservation;

R_reservation
on end of reservation verification
if document has been reserved
then mark document as borrowed else
mark document as available;

TECHNIQUES FOR MODELING BEHAVIOR

Business rules represent essential elements in the activity paradigm. They may be expressed using different modeling techniques including data flow and state transition diagrams or Petri-net graphs. Each of these techniques is briefly described. Concerning the modeling approaches, business rules appear through the data and behavior models.

Specification Using Data Flow Diagrams

Data flow diagrams (DFD) are utilized to describe data flow between processes or between a process and an external unit or stored data. The action component of the ECA structure corresponds to a process in the DFD framework. Initially, these diagrams (Yourdon, 1979) could not represent control and temporal events as data flow. Moreover, DFDs do not allow the representation of the synchronization conditions for process execution. In order to avoid these drawbacks several extensions were proposed to model synchronization and temporal aspects in DFD (Eddins, 1991).

Specification Through State Transition Diagrams

State transition diagrams (Davis, 1988; Muck, 1994) allow the representation of the behavioral requirements in terms of states and transitions. Although there are not special symbols to represent ECA rules, all types of rules can theoretically be represented. These diagrams describe inter-dependencies among rules well, but rule effects over objects are not visible. State transition diagrams do not offer explicit symbols for all components of a business rule even in some techniques such as OMT (Rumbaugh, 1991). Though transitions can be labeled with events, conditions and actions, the diagramming notation doesn't support labeling of rules.

Specification with Petri Nets

Petri nets (PN) are widely used to describe and simulate system behavior (Peterson, 1986). There are many kinds of PN such as autonomous, non-autonomous, with predicates, colored, generalized, with priorities, temporized, etc. Sinkless, conflict-free, safe and reachability are properties that characterize PN.

A PN is a bipartite graph in which there is a succession of places and transitions in a path constituted with successive edges. To model business rules, places are used to represent events and/or conditions, and transitions represent actions. Gatzui (1993) proposed the use of PN extensions to describe elementary or complex events. Extended PN's use labeled edges to model alternative results depending on the condition clause. Using these extensions, it is possible to model the structure of all business rules.

The drawback to using PNs, however, is the complexity associated with its specification. The PN doesn't help the user understand the complexity of system behavior.

Dynamics Within the Extended ER Model

In the ER (Entity-Relationship) model, rules are directly expressed through the semantics of the model inclusive of relationships, cardinalities, and existential dependencies. The ER model does not allow the designer to formulate separate events, conditions and actions. A rule in this model can only represent an integrity constraint. Transitions and active rules cannot be modeled. Note that Nijssen's (1989) NIAM model, a derived ER model, models integrity constraints with constructors representing uniqueness, optional, and mandatory constraints. Uniqueness constraints correspond to primary keys of a relational database.

Among the ER extensions to embed the database application behavior, we can cite:

Entity-Relationship-Event-Rule (ER²) is an ER model that includes events and rules (Tanaka, 1992). In this model, events and rules are objects. Relationships between events are represented by precedence relationships, links between rules describe priorities, and relationships between events and rules symbolize triggering relationships. Another association allows the designer to link an event to an entity, expressing that the entity can be affected by the event. The process model associated with ER^2 uses a colored PN to model flow control between processes.

The advantages of this model are: i) the expressiveness of all rules triggered by database operations and ii) the ability to describe the relations between rules and objects. The drawbacks of this model are ii) the sequence of rule invocations is not considered and ii) the events that are included in the model concern only database operations.

The model of Dows et al (1992) is an ER model based on the entity life cycle. This approach focuses on the expression of state changes of entities during their life cycle. The main idea of this model is to describe all events attached to state changes; this concerns all events from object creation to object deletion. This model uses a tree structure representation of which the root corresponds to an entity type and terminal nodes correspond to events affecting this entity type. Intermediate nodes may exist to describe selection and iteration. In this model, conditions are not expressed, that is each event implies an unconditional execution of associated operations. One of the model's strengths is the description of transition rules. However, it has a major limitation of not modeling the effects of a rule over an entity.

Behavior Specification Within the Object-Oriented Context

The object-oriented design requires the utilization of three models: i) a static (or data) model to represent classes and their relationships, ii) a dynamic model to represent the behavior of each object type, and iii) an interaction model for message flow between objects. Business rules may be identified at each level in these models according to heuristic and organizational knowledge that may differ from one organization to another. Previous work concerning the extension of object-oriented methods, has introduced active behavior during the modeling stage (Bichler, 1994; Loucopoulos, 1991).

Business rules within the data model. For each object class, the object model allows for the definition of attributes as well as associations for static aspects and methods for dynamic aspects. Attributes can be viewed as object states and methods as means to define state changes. Moreover, integrity constraints may be expressed at this level to support data coherence by restricting object states as well as dynamic constraints by restricting state transitions. These constraints are a subset of the business rules.

Business rules within the dynamic model. The dynamic model specifies object life cycles through a transition diagram or its derived diagrams (Harel, 1988). Such diagrams implicitly describe business rules. In particular, whenever an object receives a message, it decides, according to its current state, if it is ready to respond. The object executes associated methods to change its state according to its state diagram. It is noted that these diagrams are used to model the behavior of only one class of objects.

Business rules within the interaction model. The interaction model describes messages between objects for a given activity or use case. A popular representation technique for message exchange is the interaction diagram, which specifies an interaction sequence and messages sent by a sender to several receivers. Business rules within this type of model concern message ordering, receiver selection, synchronization modes and temporal constraints (Booch, 1994; Embley, 1992; Liddle, 1992).

Lists of messages and receiver selection determine the message to transmit and the object that receives it. The synchronization mode defines how objects involved in interactions are synchronized, while temporal constraints specify beginning, delay and end of interactions. Thus, an interaction model expresses the global behavior of a system, showing the exchanged messages between application objects.

Discussion

An information system can be described through two components: static and dynamic. Business rules that support theses two components are classified into two main categories: integrity constraints to control the static aspect, and active rules to describe the dynamic aspects. The behavior representation techniques are used to represent the dynamic part of the information system.

All of these techniques dedicated to behavioral specifications present insufficiencies to describe the ECA semantic. The extension of the ER model permits the specification of integrity constraints at the model level but it is hardly exploitable for behavior description. Although object-oriented methodologies allow the designer to describe the two aspects of the information system, the modeling of dynamic aspects uses several different formalisms to elaborate system specifications. We propose to specify, in a uniform way, dynamic aspects (integrity constraints and active rules) through a formalism that is characterized by uniformity and derivability properties.

SPECIFICATION OF SYSTEM BEHAVIOR

The distinction between active and traditional database designs focuses on the active behavior component that can be expressed by the ECA paradigm to represent business rules. Active behavior is described in terms of rules defined as a set of conventions that must be respected by the system. Business rules ensure correct system behavior. They are either descriptive (integrity constraints) or functional rules (derivation rules, active rules).

The popular information systems modeling tools do not permit a high level specification of business rules, except for integrity constraints that are typically taken into account. Though there are currently specification languages for constraint (or rules) modeling, there is little if no interest in their use due to their lack of abstraction capabilities and the complexity of their underlying formalisms.

The work presented in this paper, in keeping with the general framework of the object-oriented approach, proposes a meaningful expression of business rules that can be readily used by designers. Our proposed framework offers the same support as provided by popular DBMS tools. In addition, it offers several advantages primarily at the conceptual level of information systems modeling. These advantages include:

1. The independence between the model definition and its implementation. Indeed, the rules' specification is a high level abstraction.
2. The definition of a user-oriented model. Business rules are widely included in user requirements.
3. The uniform representation of rules. All types of rules are described with the same formalism.

The behavior of a system is expressed in terms of its global behavior and at a more granular object level. Thus, it is necessary to represent system behavior for each of these levels.

The local level allows us to specify the correct behavior of each object. Local modeling focuses on understanding how objects operate inclusive of events that impact the behavior of the object.

The global level specifies how objects communicate with one another. This requires the identification of global rules (or interaction rules) that represent functional behavior at the system level.

Tool for Active Behavior Specification

To model the behavior of active objects (Amghar, 1996), we propose to extend a graphical specification and description language (SDL) defined by the Consultative Committee for International Telegraph and Telephony (Saracco, 1987). Originally, it was designed for external behavior and internal design of telephone switching systems (Davis, 1988). SDL is a super-set of the state chart diagrams in which only state and event components are defined. The extension consists of new elements representing the condition and action of a rule.

Figure 2: The Behavior Automaton

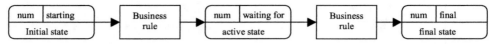

The research goal is to adapt SDL to the ECA rule semantics. The model resulting from this extension is more useful than state diagrams because it permits the description of all components of an ECA rule, and supports the execution semantics. The significance of this graphical language is that it describes a state transition in terms of events, conditions and actions in an explicit way thus facilitating the active behavior specification. By using this approach, a uniform and complete representation of business rules is obtained, which constitutes an important part of information systems. The generic description of the object behavior, through the use of SDL, provides automated support for two key concepts: state and business rules, as depicted in Figure 2.

The graphical model depicted in Figure 2 shows the object states as rounded rectangles. A state is described by: i) an *order number* (*num*) identifying the state in the automaton, ii) a *status (s)* and iii) a *label (l)*. Status is predefined and may be *starting*, *waiting* or *final*. *Starting* state corresponds to an initial state of the object, *waiting* state indicates that the object is waiting for an event, and *final* state indicates the end of the object life cycle. The transition between the *initial* state and *waiting* state corresponds to the initial transaction, while the transition between two *waiting* states does not commit the initial transaction. The transition between the *waiting* state and the *final* state corresponds to the transaction commit or abort. A state label is a comment that describes more precisely the state description and waiting event. For example, the states associated with a document can be: *starting* when a loan request occurs, *waiting* for verification of existence of document, *waiting* for availability of document, and *final* when the document has been returned.

Complete Specification of Object Behavior

An object leaves its current state whenever a rule is triggered by one or more event occurrences. This triggering may lead to a change in state depending on the condition. A business rule that specifies the transition from one state to another is an extended ECA rule type. We use the ECA[2] rule: *on event if condition the action-1 else action-2*, in which the graphical modeling (shown in Figure 3) necessitates the representation of each of the following elements.

Event. An event is considered as an aggregation of three parts and is formally written as a triplet *<type, parameters, designation>* where: *type* is internal (database event, noted I_n_E), *external* (event defined by user, noted E_x_E), or

Figure 3: Graphical Model for Behavior Representation

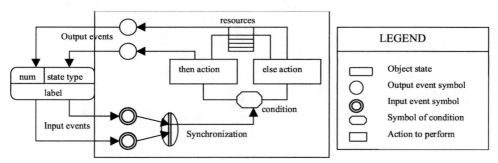

temporal (reference to time in an explicit way, noted T_e_E). *Parameters* correspond to value or references and *designation* is a comment concerning the event to improve readability. The automaton distinguishes between a consumed event (input event) and a produced event (output event). The input event represents the rule trigger, while the output event is raised by the action execution. These two kinds of events are represented differently.

Synchronization. This mechanism is utilized to specify the composite event occurrence. An ellipse in Figure 3 depicts it. It allows the description of a composite event with Boolean operators (disjunction, conjunction and negation), sequence or temporal operators. The synchronization input is a set of elementary events and the synchronization output represents the composite event.

Condition. A condition is a predicate or a query over a database (such as a comparison between object attributes). The condition consists of controlling the action execution. A diamond graphically depicts it. The condition evaluation may necessitate attribute values. This component offers two alternatives according to the evaluation result and renders easy the specification of extended rules. For example, ECA^2 is an extended rule indicating that two actions may be executed alternatively. The first one is executed in the case where the condition is true and the other whenever the condition is false. An extension of this may be denoted by ECA^* which means that various possibilities may be considered depending on the condition value.

Action. The action part of a rule may be seen as an operation or a task to be executed. An action can produce one or more events. Actions are depicted by a rectangle, which contains a brief description of the action or event.

Resources. Resources are necessary for the execution of each rule component. These resources represent either attributes or objects used by both condition evaluation and action. They represent the context of the triggered rules.

Business rules are considered to be the basis for state transitions. A business rule groups one or more input events with one or more output events. For each input event, the event's synchronization, optional condition, and action are included. The input event is mandatory because a rule cannot be triggered without such an event. At least one of the other two components must appear in the rule. The two kinds of rules are: i) *on event if condition then action*, ii) *on event do action* that is equivalent to *on event if true then action*.

Expressiveness of the Graphical Model

The active behavior has to be modeled in a uniform way, which means that activities are also represented through the graphical LDS. Accordingly, a diagram representing the behavior modeling with ECA rules and its relationships is elaborated for each activity. The number of business rules increases as the activity complexity increases thus making comprehension of the diagram more difficult.

To improve the expressiveness of such a representation, a business rule is viewed (or visualized) in terms of three levels of abstraction. *The global level* in which each rule is simply identified by its name and depicted by a rectangle (Figure 2). *The event level* in which a rule is represented as an event that triggers the transition from one state to another. Graphically, the transition is an edge labeled by the event name. *The complete level* in which all rules' components are represented in detail as shown in Figure 3. Within a behavior diagram, rules are represented in one of the levels of abstraction depending on the degree of detail chosen by the designer. These representation levels aid the visualization of the rule design. If we use a menu-based tool, the specification of the behavior is simple.

Example of Behavior Specification

The modeling of interactions between objects and activities of applications is very important to design active databases. Indeed, a system is considered active when objects and activities interact among themselves. The interaction diagram is essential to represent the exchange of messages. It shows the events produced and consumed by each object and each activity. It constitutes a fundamental step before the specification of each object behavior. In order to illustrate this, Figure 4 shows an example of such a diagram as applied to our case study.

Based on that interaction diagram, the behavior is specified for each object of the application. To illustrate a behavior specification let us consider the object *Document* of which active behavior is described in Figure 5. Note that the object *Document* leaves its initial state when the event *I_verif-loan (e2)* is raised by the activity *loan a document*. This event triggers two rules. The first rule *R_verif-nb-loans* verifies the document existence in the database, through the condition *c1*. The second rule *R_verif-availability* verifies the possibility for the user to loan an additional document. That verification is done through the condition *c2*. After that, the activity *loan document* decides the possibility of a loan and produces an event

Figure 4: Interaction Between Objects of the Application

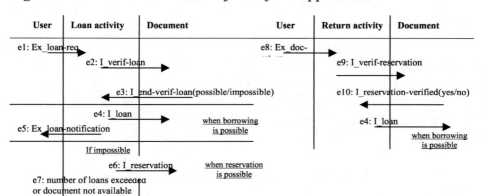

Table 1: Rules Used by the Object Document

rule name	triggering events	condition to test	produced events
R_verif-nb-loans	e2:I_verif-loan	(nb-copies-nb-borrow)	e3:I_end-verif-loan
R_verif-avalability	e2:I_verif-loan	state of document	e3:I_end-verif-loan
R_borrow	e4:I_loan	No	no
R_verif-reservation	e9:I_verif-reservation	state of reservation	e10:I_reservation-verified
R_reservation	e6:I_reservation	reservation is possible?	e7:Ex_notify-user

Figure 5: Document Behavior.

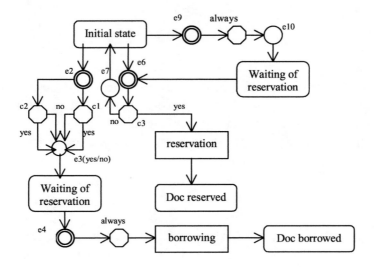

I_end-verif-loan (e3). The activity tests the parameter value of the event *I_end-verif-loan.* The object *Document* reacts to the event *I_loan (e4)* whenever borrowing is possible. The rule *R_borrow* is thus triggered and consists of recording the document loan. Furthermore, whenever the event *I_verif-reservation (e9)* is raised, the object *Document* reacts by activating the rule *R_verif-reservation* that verifies if the returned document was reserved. This rule produces the event *I_reservation-verified (e10)* allowing the activity to reserve the document by triggering the rule *R_reservation.* Table 1 summarizes this behavior as it relates to the behavior of *Document as shown in Figure 5.*

Rules Ordering and Rules Priorities

Rules may share a same triggering event. Thus an occurrence of such an event may trigger the execution of several rules. To determine an execution order, a mechanism is necessary to avoid conflicts between rules. To resolve these conflicts, priority management may be used.

The user defines an order relation between rules. The main approaches used to define priorities are *Total order* and *Partial order.* Whenever a rule is defined, a default priority is assigned to the rule. This priority may be modified. Whenever a rule is defined, "any" priority is assigned. So initially, rules have the same priority. Later the user may specify priorities between couples of rules to determine their execution order. Rules for which "any" priority is specified are executed in their creation order. In our example, the rules *R_verif-availability* and *R_verif-nb-loans* are triggered by the same event *I_verif-loan.* However, no priority is necessary to fix their execution order, because it concerns only a verification of the database state. For this reason, these two rules have the same priority.

DERIVATION PROCESS

This section describes the process used during the derivation step. As shown in Figure 6, the different concepts of our model are mapped into a relational environment. Several relationships are explained below:

[T1]: Each application process (or activity) is represented by a package which can be considered an independent object.

[T2]: Each object of the data schema is transformed into a relational table.

[T3]: An active or derivation rule is translated into a stored procedure.

[T4]: When rules identified at the design level concern integrity constraints, they are mapped either to constraints embedded in the database schema or triggers. Events linked to these rules are database operations (insert, update, and delete).

Figure 6. Metamodel

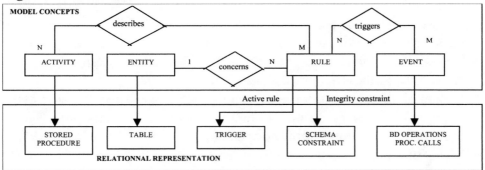

Figure 7: State Diagrams

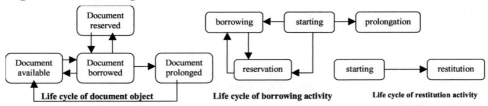

[T5]: The events triggering integrity constraints or derivation rules are considered as database operations, and the events identified in each activity are replaced by procedure calls.

Methodology

The methodology used to model our application is based on object-oriented method such as OMT (Rumbaugh, 1991) and is described as follows:

1. Description of object and relationship through an ER diagram (Section *Case study*).

2. Building of the interaction model. For our case study, Figure 4 of Subsection *Example of behavior specification* is an illustration of such a diagram.

3. Elaboration of state diagrams for each object and each activity. That gives a global view of the application dynamics. For example, state diagrams of document object and the two activities (loaning and restitution) are depicted in Figure 7.

4. Active behavior specification throughout our model as defined in Section *Specification of System Behavior*. This step introduces business rules including integrity constraints in an explicit way.

5. Derivation of specifications for a specific DBMS.

Active Behavior Description

As shown in Figure 5, a document reacts to events produced by the activity *loan document*. The document behavior, as described in Section *Example of Behavior Specification*, is a sequence of steps: is checking the number of documents for a given user and then the availability of the requested document. Table 2 illustrates the different rules used in these activities.

The active behavior of two activities is depicted in Figure 8. The goal of the first activity is the loan management in the document center. This activity, triggered by a user request, is composed of two operations, each one supported by an ECA² rule. The first rule checks the possibility of borrowing the document. The second rule processes the document loan. The second activity concerns the document restitution. Its goal is to manage returned documents. This activity consists of two rules. The first rule identifies whether the returned document was reserved. The second rule marks the returned document as available or records the new loan. Figure 8 depicts the behavior specification of the *loan and return document* activities.

Derivation of Constraints and Rules

The rules associated with objects of the application are considered next. Rules applied to the application schema concerning database coherence are categorized as follows:

1. Value constraints, which concern the values of attributes. This type of constraint is supported by the word: *check*. For example, the value of attribute *state* of entity document is constrained as follows: *Rule R_availability: check (Document.state in ('available', 'not available').*

2. Referential integrity, which supports association between objects. This type of constraint is supported by the word : *references*. For example, a document cannot be borrowed when it doesn't exist in the document center: *R_doc-borrow: Borrow.id-doc references Document.id-doc.*

3. Cardinality constraints, which give the number of entities that may participate in a relationship. Triggers support these constraints.

4. Inter-entity constraints that express a relation between two (or more) attributes belonging to different entities. Triggers also support these constraints (or more generally, these rules). They concern the application and they do not depend on a database schema.

Activity Description

Each activity (loan and restitution) is a mapped package where each activity rule is translated to a stored procedure. Thus, each stored procedure represents a business rule. This mapping allows the designer to consider the rules because of their

Table2: Rules of loan and return activities

Rule name	Triggering event	Condition to test	Produced event
R_verif-loan	e1:Ex_loan-req	No	e2:I_end-verif-loan
R_loan	e3:I_end-verif	c5:parameter of e3 if loan is possible or impossible	e4:I_loan e5:Ex_notification e6:I_reservation
R_doc-return	e1:Ex_doc-return	No	e9:I_verif-reservation
R_reservation	e10:I_reservation-verified	c6:parameter of e10 if borrow is possible	e4:I_loan

Figure 8: Loan and restitution activities

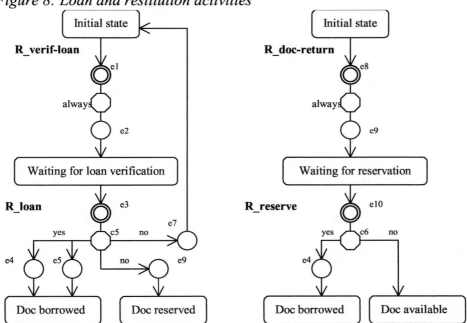

Table 3: Translation of rules to relational DBMS

Rule	Implementation
R_availability, R_doc-borrow	check
existence of the borrowed document	reference
R_nb-borrows, R_verif-availability, R_verif-nbcopies, R_verif-reservation	trigger
R_verif-loan, R_loan, R_doc-return, R_reservation	procedure

modularization into the package's procedures. We summarize the derivation of different rules from our case study. Table 4 shows the translation of each rule into a relational model. Note that rules implemented with relational database system mechanisms are triggered by events dealing with database operations (*insert, update and delete*) and rules represented by procedures are triggered by procedure calls. Table 3 illustrates some rules with their triggering events.

RULE MODULARIZATION

Active rules have the property to react among themselves to build a complex interaction net. In order to facilitate exploitation and maintenance of an important set of rules, several authors (Baralis, 1996; Aiken, 1992; Aiken, 1995) propose to subdivide the rule set into disjoint subsets called strata. Each of them must individually support termination and confluence of rules' stratum.

Termination. Whenever rules are executing, they may trigger themselves. The property of termination is important to warrant that all rules belonging to the same triggering graph terminate. Particularly, if there are no cycles in the graph, termination is guaranteed[*].

Confluence. Whenever two rules must be executed due to the occurrence of the same event, they are said to be confluent whenever their execution order has no influence on the final result on the database. Otherwise, priorities would be given to the rules.

Rule Stratification

The different types of stratification defined by Baralis et al. (1996) are:

Behavioral stratification. A stratum contains rules corresponding to an activity or a task of an application. For each, stratum convergence is described by a metric measuring the progression of rules during activity execution. Strata are ordered according to priorities. The metric is a decreasing numeric function m_i corresponding to a progression of the state of the database to a final state. More precisely the final value of the metric can only converge to a minimum. To verify conservation between strata, any stratum can increase the metric of strata of high level priority.

Assertional stratification. It is used to group rules whose goal is to achieve a compensatory action after a constraint violation. A post-condition is associated with each stratum and whenever stratum rules are activated, they must restore the post-condition. Conservation between strata verifies that any stratum can modify the post-condition value of a stratum of higher priority.

Event-based stratification. Event-based stratification is applicable when it is possible to associate rules with specific events. Rules within a stratum respond to input events and produce output events, therefore each stratum establishes a dependency relationship between sets of events. Event-based stratification requires such a relationship to be no cyclic. Baralis et al. (1996) have shown that behavioral stratification subsumes assertional and event-based stratification and the intersection of the latter two is not empty. Consequently it is possible to define a metric over any type of stratification.

A New Proposal for Partitioning

We propose that the difference between these three stratifications concerns convergence criterion. Indeed behavioral stratification must observe a metric progression, assertional stratification must verify a post-condition (Boolean expression) and event-based stratification implies a hierarchy of strata such that a stratum of a given priority cannot trigger rules of strata of higher priority. The main drawback of these stratifications remains the choice of convergence criterion for a given application. It is difficult to choose between stratification types. Although partitioning criterion for event-based stratification is interesting, the constraint of stratum that does not trigger a stratum of a higher priority is not realistic.

Concerning assertional stratification, it differs from behavioral stratification only by the type of criterion (Boolean in first case and numeric in second case). Moreover the post-condition can be a rule condition. For behavioral stratification, the main problem concerns metric identification, that is the difficulty to find a particular function describing database progression from one state to final state. This function is different according to applications. *To conclude, these types of stratification do not lead to result unity and render any automaton process difficult.*

Partition Based on Triggering Graphs

After these remarks, we propose to partition a rule set according to the triggering graph. This graph is issued from rule chaining triggered by event occurrence. Analysis of automation (object diagram presented in Section *Specification of system behavior*), and particularly of their links, allows the building of a graph in which an oriented link between a node A and a node B means that rules corresponding to A trigger rules corresponding to B. The rule set is subdivided into a set of the partitions. Let us note that partitions obtained are not necessarily disjoint. The partitioning process can be summarized as follows:

1. Choose a node (a rule r_k) from the graph (a rule which is not triggered by another one).
2. Build a triggering graph of this rule as being a set of rules that are activated from r_k directly or in a transitive way.
3. Delete r_k from the initial rule set.
4. Repeat step 1 until the rule set is empty.

Based on Figure 8, three examples of rule stratifications issued from loan and return management of documents can be considered. Each stratum corresponds to a triggering graph. The first stratum corresponds to a set of rules that are executed to respond to the user loan request. Let's us note that the rule *R_verif-availability* may be skipped. There are two alternatives to this stratum because there is no priority between *R_verif-availability* and *R_verif-nb-borrow* corresponding to stratum *s11* and stratum *s12*. The rules *R_verif-availability* and *R_verif-nb-borrows* are thus confluent. Stratum *s2* corresponds to the treatment of the user loan request in the case where the loan is impossible. Stratum *s3* corresponds to the document return.

Metric for a Convergence

A metric allows for the measurement of rule execution progression within a partition. However, it is important to establish a hypothesis warranting convergence and confluence of rules. The convergence translates a distance expressing the progression of database from one state to final state. These hypotheses are:

1. Whenever an event occurs, a transaction is created to execute all rules triggered by this event. Rules can belong to different partitions.

2. To delete cycles, a rule is triggered only once within the same transaction. In other words, a rule is activated for the current transaction. Since a rule cannot be triggered any other time, a cycle is impossible. The rule is reactivated at the commit point of the transaction.

3. A rule can trigger one or more other rules through its action part. Rule action is an operation sequence including database operations.

4. Whenever several rules are in conflict, priorities are applied. The programmer explicitly attributes them or they can be affected, for example, according to the creation order of the rules.

ENVIRONMENT FOR ACTIVE DATABASE DESIGN

The different stages of the design process, with regard to stages used in other object-oriented methods, remain unmodified. However, the models' elaboration within each stage must include the specification of active rules. We have shown in the previous section how active rules can be represented in the specification of an object behavior. Static models would also include integrity constraint descriptions. The proposed environment is designed as a set of functionalities to support all steps of the active database design. It may be considered an extension of existing CASE tools for both designing and generating a set of rules that control the behavioral aspect of a database. Modules required treating dynamic aspects concern mainly:

1. *The validation of both the semantic and the syntactic of the specification* developed in the section *Specification of system behavior*. The first

verification avoids the transition from one state to another without taking into consideration the business rule, while the second verifies that the produced event is done during (or at the end of) the action and after the event which has triggered the action. This module corresponds to a semi-automated process since it interacts with the designer in an entry-correction-validation cycle.

2. *The partitioning of active rules considered as the principle key design to warrant their modularization and control.* Rules are partitioned into subsets so that the designer can abstract the rule behavior by reasoning locally on each individual subset. In order to generate coherent rule sets, rules are organized according to a criterion that consists of grouping rules by call graphs according to the partitioning algorithm (Section *Rule modularization*).

3. *The generation of rules from each rule partition elaborated by the partitioning module using capabilities of the target DBMS.* It is obvious that if the DBMS has active features, the derivation is easier in comparison with a passive DBMS in which rules must be coded as program pieces. The generation can be done towards any kind of DBMS (relational or object-oriented). In the particular case of relational DBMS, rules are essentially used to enforce database integrity and are coded through triggers. Some details were given in the section, *Derivation process*.

CONCLUSION

This paper is a contribution to modeling business rules at the design level as any part of an information system. A business rule is seen as a means to transit from one state to another within the behavior model. The primary interest is to explicitly introduce business rules during the modeling of the different components of a system. In addition, the general architecture of an environment to design active databases and the specifications of theoretical aspects to elaborate a monitoring and debugging tool are presented.

This work addresses more generally the extension of CASE to add active functionalities to existing ones. The rule modularization is important and necessary to abstract all rules identified during the analysis stage. This work contributes to the extension of existing models and tools to take into account active features of a database. Future work will study the correctness of such extensions. For this proposed work, the extended Petri Net seems to constitute an ideal solution because: i) the transformation from state diagrams including ECA rules to Petri Nets is relatively obvious and ii) the formal basics of Petri Nets can be very useful to show for example the trace of a transaction or to verify the termination of a set of rules.

REFERENCES

Aiken, A., Hellerstein, J.M., & Widom, J. (1995). Static Analysis Techniques for Predicting the Behavior of Active Database Rules. *ACM Transactions on Database Systems,* 20(1), USA.

Aiken, A., Widom, J., & Hellerstein, J.M. (1992). Behavior of Database Production Rules: termination, Confluence and Observable Determinism, in *ACM SIGMOD*, ACM Press, San Diego, USA.

Amghar, Y., & Meziane, M. (1996). Designing databases using the activity paradigm. *Third International Work*shop of the Moscow ACM SIGMOD Chapter Moscow, September 10-13, pp 57-65, Russia.

Baralis, E., Ceri, S., & Paraboschi S. (1996). Modularization Techniques for Active Rule Design. ACM Transactions on Database Systems, 21(1), March, USA.

Bichler, P., & Schrelf, M. (1994) Active Object-Oriented Database Design Using Active Object/Behavior Diagrams. In J. Widom and S. Chakravarthy, editors, Proceedings of the 4th Workshop on Research Issues in Data Engineering (RIDE), Active Database Systems. IEEE Computer Society, Houston, Texas, USA.

Booch, G. (1994). Object-Oriented Design with Applications. The Benjamin/ Cummings Publishing Compagny, Inc. RedWood City. San Francisco, California, USA.

Buchmann, A.P. (1993). Active Object System. Proceedings of NATO Advanced Study Institute on Object-Oriented Database Systems, Kusadasi, Turkey, 201-224.

Ceri, S., & Manthey, R. (1993). First specification of Chimera. IDEA Report DD.2P.004.01., Milano, Italy.

Davis, A.M. (1988). A Comparison of Techniques for the Specification of External System Behavior. Communications of the ACM 31, 1089-1115, USA.

Dayal, U. et al. (1988). The HiPAC Project: Combining Active Databases and Timing Constraints. SIGMOD Record, 17(1), 51-70, USA.

Dows, E., Clare, P., & Coe, I. (1992). Structured Systems Analysis and Design Method - Application and Context. 2nd ed., Prentice-Hall, Englewood Cliffs, New Jersey.

Eddins, W.R., Crosslin, R.L. & Sutherland, D.E (1991). Using Modeling and Simulation in the Analysis and Design of Information Systems. In H.G and K.M, vanHee (eds.), Dynamic Modeling of Information Systems, Elsevier, Amsterdam, pp. 89-119.

Embley, D.W., Kurtz, B.D., & Woodfield S.N. (1992). Object-Oriented System Analysis - A Model Driven Approach. Yourdon Press, New York.

Gatziu, S., Geppert, A., & Dittrich, K.R. (1993). Events in an Active Object-Oriented Database System. The 1st Workshop on Rules in Database Systems, Edinburg - Scotland.

Gehani, N.H. et al. (1992). Composite Event Specification in Active Databases: Model & Implementation. Proceedings of the 18th VLDB Conference, Vancouver, Canada.

Hanson, E.N. (1989). An initial report on the design of Ariel: A DBMS With an Integrated Production Rule System. *SIGMOD Record*, 18(3), 12-19, USA.

Harel, D. (1988). On Visual Formalism. *Communications of the ACM*, 31(5), USA.

Kotz, A.M., Dittrich, K.R., & Mulle J.A. (1988). Supporting Semantic Rules by a Generalized Event/Trigger Mechanism. *Advances in databases Technology-EDBT'88,* (write out the conference name and in boldface, vol.303, Springer-Verlag, Venice, Italy, 76-91.

Liddle, S.W. et al. (1992). Analysis and Design for Active Object Bases. *Technical report of the Brigham Young University,* England, 22.

Lohman, G.M. et al. (1991). Extensions of Starburst: Objects, Types, Functions, and Rules. *Communications of the ACM*, 34(10), 94-109, USA.

Loucopoulos, P., Theodoulidis, B., & Pantazis, D. (1991). Business Rules Modeling: Conceptual Modeling and OO Specifications. *Proceedings. of the IFIP TC8/WG8.1 Working Conference on the OO Approach in Information System*, Quebec City, Canada.

Muck, T.A. (1994). Design Support for Initiatives and Policies in Conceptual Models of Information Systems - A Statechart Approach. In: J.F Nunamaker and R.H. Sprague (eds.), *Proceedings of the 27th Annual Hawaii International Conference on System Sciences,* Vol.IV, IEEE Computer Society Press, Los Alamitos, . 743-752.

Nijssen, G.M. & Halpin, T. (1989). *Conceptual Schema and Relational Database Schema.* Prentice Hall, Sydney (Australia).

Peckham, J., MacKeller, B., & Doherty, M. (1995). Data Model for Extensible Support of Explicit Relationships in Design Databases. *Very Large Data Base Journal,* 4(1), 157-191, USA.

Peterson, J.L. (1986). *Petri Nets and the Theory of Modeling Systems.* Englewood Cliffs, NJ(USA) : Prentice Hall, , 230.

Rumbaugh, J., et al. (1991). *Object-Oriented Modeling and Design.* Englewood Cliffs, NJ(USA): Prentice Hall, 500.

Saracco R., & Tilanus A.J. (1987). CCITT-SDL: Overview of language and its applications. *Computer Networks and IDSN System.* 13(2), 65-74, Holland.

Stonebraker, M., et al. (1990). On Rules, Procedures, Caching and Views in Database Systems. *Proceedings. of the ACM SIGMOD International Conference on Management of Data,* 281-290, Atlantic City, New Jersey.

Tanaka, A.K. (1992). On Conceptual Design of Active Databases. Phd-Thesis, Georgia Institute of Technology, December 1992, pp. 172, USA.

Yourdon, E. (1979). Constantine L., *Structured Design.* Prentice-Hall, New Jersey.

ENDNOTE

* With the assumption that the action part of a rule always terminates

Chapter 9

A Methodology for Datawarehouse Design: Conceptual Modeling

José María Cavero and Esperanza Marcos
Universidad Rey Juan Carlos, Spain

Mario Piattini
Universidad de Castilla-La Mancha, Spain

Adolfo Sánchez
Cronos Ibérica, S.A., Spain

Data warehousing and online analytical processing (OLAP) technologies have become growing interest areas in latest years. Specific issues, such as conceptual modeling, schemes translation from operational systems, physical design, etc... have been widely treated, but there is not a general accepted complete methodology for datawarehouse design. In this work, we present a multidimensional datawarehouse development methodology based on and integrated with a Public software development methodology.

INTRODUCTION
The concept of datawarehouse first appeared in Inmon (1993) to describe a "subject oriented, integrated, non-volatile, and time variant collection of data in support of management's decisions". It is a concept very related to the OLAP technology, first introduced by Dr. E.F. Codd in 1993 (Codd, Codd, and Salley, 1993) to characterize the requirements of aggregation, consolidation, view production, formulae application and data synthesis in many dimensions. A datawarehouse is a repository of information mainly coming from on-line transactional processing (OLTP) systems that provides data for analytical processing and decision support.

Previously Published in *Managing Information Technology in a Global Economy,* edited by Mehdi Khosrow-Pour, Copyright © 2001, Idea Group Publishing.

The development of a datawarehouse needs the integration of data mainly proceeding from legacy systems. The process of developing a datawarehouse is, like any other task that implies some kind of preexisting resources integration, profoundly complex. This process will be "labor-intensive, error-prone, and generally frustrating, leading a number of warehousing projects to be abandoned midway through development" (Srivastava and Chen, 1999). OLTP and OLAP environments are profoundly different. Therefore, the techniques used for operational database design are inappropriate for datawarehouse design (Kimball, Reeves, Ross and Thornthwaite, 1998; Miguel et al., 1998).

Although many solutions have been developed "for interesting subproblems like handling multidimensional data as typical requirement for datawarehouses, view maintenance for aggregated data, data integration etc., combining these partial and often very abstract and formal solutions to an overall design methodology and warehousing strategy is still left over to the practitioners" (Gatziu, Jeusfeld, Staudt and Vassiliou, 1999).

Despite the obvious importance of having a methodological support for the development of OLAP systems, the design process has received very little attention of the scientific community and the product providers. Models usually utilized for operational data base design (like E/R model) shouldn't be used without further ado for analytical environments design. Attending only to technical reasons, databases obtained from E/R models are inappropriate for decision support systems, in which query performance and data loading (including incremental loading) are important (Kimball, 1996). Multidimensional paradigm should be used not only in data base queries, but also during its design and maintenance. "To use the multidimensional paradigm during all development phases it is necessary to define dedicated conceptual, logical and physical data models for the paradigm and to develop a sound methodology which gives guidelines how to create and transform these models during the development process" (Dinter, Sapia, Blaschka and Hofling, 1999). In Wu and Buchmann (1997), authors claim for datawarehouse design methodologies and tools "with the appropriate support for aggregation hierarchies, mapping between the multidimensional and the relational models, and cost models for partitioning and aggregation that can be used from the early design stages."

The rest of the chapter is organized as follows: in the next section we briefly present the state of the art related to data warehousing methodologies. The following section outlines the IDEA conceptual multidimensional model, an overall view of the methodology, and will go more deeply into the conceptual modeling activity. Finally, in the last section, we present some conclusions and future works.

STATE OF THE ART

There are several proposals for datawarehouse design. In this section, we summarize the most relevant ones.

Kimball et al. (1998) proposes an approach based on two points: on the one hand, the Datawarehouse Bus Architecture that shows how to construct a series of data marts that, finally, will allow to create a corporate datawarehouse, and, on the other hand, the Business Dimensional Lifecycle - BDL-, whose objective is, starting from the business requirements, the construction of data marts based on dimensional star schemes. It is an iterative methodology in which, after a project planning and a business requirements definition task, different activities are developed. These activities can be grouped in three groups: technology activities, data design activities, and specification and developing of final user applications activities.

Last, there are two activities related to datawarehouse deployment, maintenance and growth. It is a very detailed methodology and, according to the authors, widely tested. However, in our opinion it is very focused from its first phases on the relational model.

In Debevoise (1999) an object-oriented methodological approach is proposed, using UML to detail the methodology steps. Use case diagrams are used to describe the tasks that the team has to carry out to complete each phase. Use cases will specify what every team member has to do to complete each project cycle part. This methodology is less detailed than the previous one, and a bit difficult to follow.

In Cabibbo and Torlone (1998), the authors present a logical model for multidimensional data base design (called MD), and a design methodology to obtain a MD scheme from operational databases. They use as a starting point an ER scheme that describes an integrated view of the operational databases. This scheme will contain every available information for the datawarehouse but in an inappropriate format for this kind of systems. The methodology consists on a series of steps for the MD model scheme construction and its translation into relational models and multidimensional matrices. The methodology is incomplete and starts from an ideal assumption; that is, every information is included in the ER scheme. In our opinion, operational schemes should be simply a support, giving more importance to analytical users requirements.

In Golfarelli and Rizzi (1999) the authors outline a methodological framework for datawarehouse design based on a conceptual multidimensional model of the same authors, called Dimensional Fact Model (DFM). The methodology is still incomplete, and only focused on a relational implementation.

There are many other partial proposals, focused on issues such as models translations, view materialization, index, etc. For example, in Sapia et al.

(1999), using data mining techniques in datawarehouse design phases is proposed (for example, using data mining algorithms for discovering implicit information on data, for conflicts resolution in schemes integration for recovering lost values and incorrect data, etc.).

The problem with all these works is that they propose to use a new different methodology for datawarehouse design, so organizations must use at least two totally different methodologies: one for OLTP environments and one for OLAP environments. We think it is better to integrate datawarehouse design in the existing methodologies, modifying and adding new activities, so that training and learning curve for datawarehouse design was less difficult.

PROPOSAL

The methodology we proposed in this chapter has been developed in the EINSTEIN project. EINSTEIN is a research and development project that applies the experience and knowledge obtained in relational data base system development in the last decade (SQL, ER modeling, CASE tools, methodologies...) to multidimensional database (MDDB) design.

The project proposes a MDDB development methodology analogous to the traditional ones used in relational data base system development. This methodology is supported by a CASE tool that incorporates a graphical interface (Miguel et al., 2000). This tool allows the translation of a conceptual IDEA scheme into a logical scheme based on a model supported by some multidimensional or relational products. Figure 1 shows a tool prototype window, whose graphical notation is based on Golfarelli, Maio and Rizzi (1998).

IDEA multidimensional conceptual model is used to understand and represent analytical users requirements in a similar manner than ER model is used

Figure 1: IDEA CASE tool

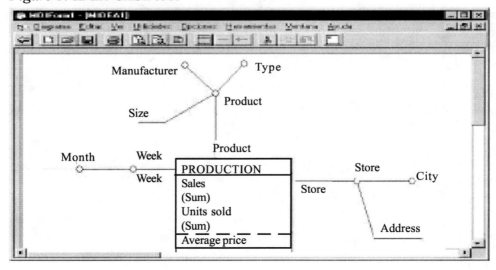

to interact with microdata users. Preexisting OLTP system data scheme and requirements obtained from analytical data users are the main inputs to the construction of IDEA multidimensional conceptual scheme.

Next step is to transform, using a set of methodological rules, each conceptual schema previously defined into a logical scheme based on the model of each product (pure multidimensional or relational with multidimensional issues). The most usual procedure in current projects is to translate directly relational scheme into multidimensional schemes supported by OLAP tools.

EINSTEIN project approach allows reverse engineering of existing specific multidimensional schemes into IDEA conceptual schemes. These schemes could be checked against OLAP users requirements to verify that current datawarehouse satisfies them.

In the same way, contrary to most current approaches, it is possible to create and/or verify elementary ER conceptual schemes using a set of rules contained in the methodology to satisfy analytical users requirements. We think that this approach hasn't been treated enough in previous works, in which usually we can only see one direction on dimensional modeling: the one from the operational data bases to the analytical data bases, but not the contrary, that is, from analytical requirements to operational design.

The methodology uses as a reference framework the Spanish Public Methodology METRICA version 3 proposal (MV3), which is similar to British SSADM or French Merise. MV3 processes considered are those on which the datawarehouse development has more influence, that is, Information System Analysis, Design and Construction (ASI, DSI and CSI). The new processes, modified from the MV3 proposal, have been named as ASI-MD (MultiDimensional), DSI-MD and CSI-MD. Of course, considering only these three processes doesn't mean that the others processes shouldn't be taken into account on a datawarehouse development, but we have considered that the differences shouldn't be significant with respect to any other information system development.

Figure 2 shows an overview of the methodology, showing the scope of its three processes, ASI-MD, DSI-MD and CSI-MD.

Every process is divided into activities and every activity is divided into tasks. The order of the activities doesn't mean a necessary sequential order. The activities can be developed in a different order, or in parallel, overlapping tasks of different activities. However, a process will not be completed until every one of its activities will be completed. In every process, a graphic emphasizing its most important activities will be included.

The methodology is fundamentally focused on data modeling, and doesn't take into consideration the functional part of the development. Therefore, extraction, translation and load functions are not considered.

Figure 2: Methodology overview

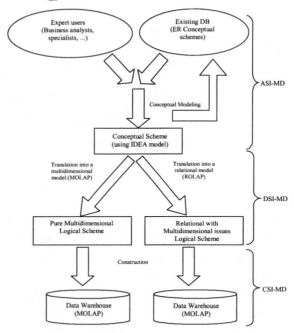

In the following, we will offer a general overview of the IDEA multidimensional conceptual model. As an example, we will describe one of the methodology activities.

General Overview of IDEA Model

IDEA is the multidimensional data model used as conceptual model to get the semantic during the development (Sanchez, Cavero and Miguel, 1999). Figure 3 shows, using the ER formalism (Chen, 1976), the elements that comprise the model.

Figure 3: IDEA metamodel

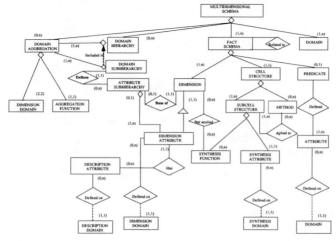

The figure doesn't include relationships between the different kind of domains, which are included on figure 4. To enrich the model semantic, extensions to the original ER model have been used, such as inheritance and generalization hierarchies (Batini, Ceri and Navathe, 1992).

Next, we will describe on a higher level of detail every element of the model.

Multidimensional Scheme

We define the Multidimensional Schema (MS) as a non empty set of domains Dom_i, set of aggregations A_{ij}, set of hierarchies H_i and non empty set of fact schemata FS_i.

$$MS < \{Dom_i\}, \{A_{ij}\}, \{H_i\}, \{FS_i\}> \mid Dom_i \rfloor \angle, FS_i \rfloor \angle$$

Domain

A Domain is a named set of values: $Dom_i < \{v_{ij}\} \mid p(v_{ij}) >$

Where $\{v_{ij}\}$ is the set of values of Dom_i and $p(v_{ij})$ is the predicate which has to be true for all the values of the domain.

There are different types of domains depending on the data they represent (see figure 4):

- **Dimension Domain:** The values of a Dimension Domain may belong either to **an OID Domain** (representing objects) or to a **Category Domain** (representing qualities). Dimension attributes of the fact schema take values from Dimension Domains.

- **Synthesis Domain:** The values of a Synthesis Domain may belong either to a **Quantity Domain** (representing quantities) or to a **Boolean Domain** (representing existence). Synthesis attributes of the structure cells take values from Synthesis Domains.

- **Description Domain:** A Description Domain may be either a Quantity Domain or a Category Domain. It provides complementary information about dimension attributes of a fact schema.

As Figure 4 shows, a Quantity Domain (e.g., "Age") can be transformed into a Category Domain (e.g., "Age Intervals"), by means of a Transformation Function, and vice-versa.

Domain Aggregation, Hierarchy and Subhierarchies

A Domain Aggregation $A_{ij} < f_{ij}, Dom_i, Dom_j >$ consists of an aggregation function f_{ij} between two different Category Domains Dom_i (origin) and Dom_j (destination) that fulfills:

$$f_{ij}: Dom_i \mid\!\!-\!\!-\!\!-\!\!-\!\!-\!\!-\!\!-\!\!-\!\!> Dom_j$$
$$v_{ik} \mid\!\!-\!\!-\!\!-\!\!-\!\!-\!\!-\!\!-\!\!> v_{jl} : (\forall v_{jl} \ Dom_j \exists v_{ik} \ Dom_i : f_{ij}(v_{ik}) = v_{jl})$$

A Hierarchy H_i consists of a set of aggregations that are linked to shape a directed graph. The graph's vertex represents the Dimension Domains of the Hierarchy and the arcs represent the aggregation functions.

Figure 4: A domain defined using the E/R formalism

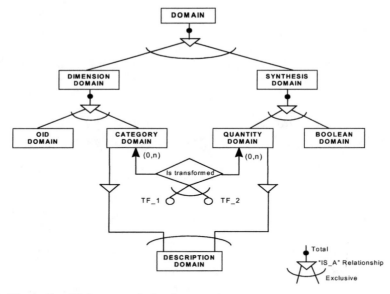

A hierarchy H_n is a graph $G_{Jn}(V_{Jn}, U_{Jn})$:

$V_{Jn:}$ Set of vertex (domains)

U_{Jn}: Set of arcs (aggregate functions).

A Domain Subhierarchy (DSH) consists of a set of Domain Aggregations included in a hierarchy; it is a subgraph of the hierarchies graph. A DSH is identified by its name and may be associated to one or more attribute subhierarchies.

Fact Schema

The Fact Schema (FS) is the description of an n-dimensional space containing relevant information for its analytical processing. Every FS $<\{Atr_i\}, \{D_i\}, CS, p>$ consists of:

- $\{Atr_i\}$: Set of dimension attributes
- $\{D_i\}$: Set of dimensions
- **CS**: Structure of the cell contained in the FS.
- **p**: Predicate associated with the CS.

The attributes, which are always defined on a domain, are used to describe the Fact Schema. Formally an attribute can be defined as the application of a FS into a domain:

$Atr_i : FS_i \varnothing Dom_i$

A dimension D_i of a Fact Schema is a dimension attribute. If an attribute subhierarchy should be related to the dimension, it will be its root.

A Cell Structure $CS_{FS} <\{SCS\}, \{methods\}>$ consists of:

- A SubCell Structure SCS $<$Synthesis Attribute, $\{fs_i\}>$. The Synthesis Attribute is defined on a Synthesis Domain and its extension contains quantitative information about the Fact Schema interesting for the analysis. The Synthesis Functions are applied to a set of data and return a value. Standard synthesis functions are for example frequency, sum, average, maximum, minimum, maximum(n), minimum(n), and so on.

- Method: Procedure applied to one or more SubCell Structures returning one or more values.

A Predicate may be set up for the attributes defined in the Fact Schema, so that the data contained in the extensional Fact Schema will be only the ones which conform to the Predicate.

The Fact Schema is the main structure in IDEA and is similar to the schema of relation in the relational data model and to the entity type in the ER model. Dimensions, cell structures and predicates, as well as attributes, can only exist within the fact schema in which they have been defined.

Next, we will show the "Datawarehouse conceptual modeling" activity. It has seven tasks. Due to space restrictions, input and output artifacts, techniques and participants of every task haven't been specified in this paper.

Activity ASI-MD 3: Datawarehouse Conceptual Modeling

The purpose of this activity is to obtain, using IDEA model, the datawarehouse data multidimensional conceptual schema. We use as inputs the requirements catalog and existing ER schemes.

Task ASI-MD 3.1: Obtaining Preliminary Subcell structures

The first step to obtain the multidimensional conceptual scheme is to obtain a preliminary scheme that will be realized in the first two tasks.

The purpose of this task is to obtain preliminary subcell structures. These subcell structures will model "events occurring dynamically in the enterprise world" (Golfarelli et al., 1998), such as sales of a company, movements in a bank account, etc. At this moment, it is not necessary to detail attributes level and synthesis functions that comprises every subcell structure. We are still only interested in preliminary, generic structures. Necessary information for modeling preliminary subcell structures can come from different sources, such as, expert users opinion. They know which are their problems, and which are the data they need for their daily work. Usually these correspond with numeric, continuously valued, and additive data (Kimball, 1996). On the other hand, if we have a data base ER conceptual scheme, these preliminary subcell structures use to correspond with some of the entities or N:M relationships attributes. We can also use the previous multidimensional conceptual scheme made in activity ASI-MD 1.

Task ASI-MD 3.2: Obtaining Preliminary dimensions

Preliminary subcell structures previously detected represent company interesting variables. The next step is to detect dimensions that will take part on them, that is, how the values detected can be aggregated. In this moment, users have to think about dimensions in a very general manner. They don't need to detail dimensions hierarchy attributes. For example, users will think in dimensions such as time, space, etc., but no in attributes such as days-months-years, delegation-province-country. This descending way of working can be complemented with the study of operational data bases conceptual schemes observing the attributes of entities and relationships connected (directly or by means of others) to those identified as facts in ER scheme. Those attributes could give us clues about hidden dimensions not detected by users. If we have a general multidimensional scheme as output of the process first activity, then it can be used as another information source.

Task ASI-MD 3.3: Obtaining Preliminary Hierarchies

At this point, we have a preliminary scheme with a set of preliminary subcell structures defined over some dimensions. Now we have to identify in a more precise manner dimensions and their hierarchies. We have to identify every dimension, describing (if exists) its subhierarchy and subhierarchy aggregations. It is not necessary at this moment to detail dimension domains of every aggregation, nor aggregation functions. At this point new dimensions could be detected. A typical example is time, which sometimes is not in the elementary databases, but is essential in every datawarehouse.

Task ASI-MD 3.4: Obtaining Detailed Hierarchies

Next step is to refine hierarchies obtained in previous step. This refinement consists in a detailed enumeration of subhierarchy dimension attributes of each dimension. New attributes could be detected, useless attributes eliminated, and hierarchies attributes properties detected and converted into description attributes. For example, telephone or address attributes used to be only dimension attributes properties (description attributes). For every attribute, its domain must be defined, or assigned a previously defined domain. Domain aggregation hierarchy must be specified, detailing aggregation functions.

Task ASI-MD 3.5: Obtaining Detailed Subcell Structures

At this point, we have completely defined dimensions and its hierarchies. Now we have to study the detail of subcell structures. For each subcell structure we must specify its attribute and the synthesis functions. Every synthesis function should be studied with respect to the dimensions that affect it. Perhaps some of them couldn't be applied (for example, it doesn't have sense adding temperatures along time). Usually, synthesis functions will be sums, but also can be taken into consideration mean, maximum, minimum, etc.

Task ASI-MD 3.6: Obtaining Fact Schemes

We have now subcell structures with associated dimensions. The next step is grouping these subcell structures into cell structures, to form fact schemes. Every cell structure belongs to a fact scheme, and every fact scheme has dimensions associated. So, subcell structures that could be joined must be detected. This join can be one of the following:
- Joining two subcell structures into one, because they both represent the same fact (they are duplicated). Its synthesis attributes and dimensions should be the same. The resulting synthesis functions will be the union of the synthesis functions of both subcell structures, deleting those duplicated. Synthesis functions applicability to dimensions and dimension attributes should be revised.
- Aggregation of two subcell structures into one, or one subcell structure into one previously detected. In this case, its dimensions should be similar. We can be interested in joining substructures whose dimensions are not the same. In this case, aggregations must be studied with respect to the new dimensions (to be or not aggregable). Of course, we always have the possibility of join every subcell structures into one (fact scheme), but in this case many of the synthesis attributes could be not aggregable, and the resulting scheme should be illegible.

Task ASI-MD 3.7: Multidimensional scheme verification and validation

In this task, the conceptual multidimensional scheme will be verified and validated, assuring that it is complete, adjusted to requirements catalogue, and to some predefined quality criteria.

Some other verifications should be done, such as availability of data from elementary DB. If those data are not available, perhaps could be planned to modify the elementary DB.

Figure 5 shows a resulting scheme graphically.

CONCLUSIONS

Datawarehouse development has turned into a critical success factor for many companies. This approach is not absolutely new, but there are some contributions in the work carried out in EINSTEIN project, such as:
- verification and construction of analytical schemes starting from analytical data user requirements, using existent operational scheme as support for the creation of conceptual multidimensional scheme.
- reverse engineering for obtaining IDEA schemes from existent specific multidi-

Figure 6: Graphical representation

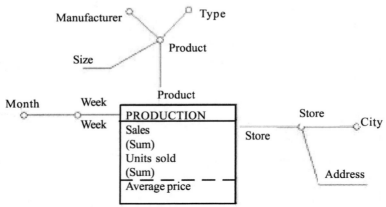

mensional data bases.
- creation of modification of existent operational schemes as a result of analytical users requirements.
- Integration of OLTP and OLAP database design in a unique methodology.

A general multidimensional methodology based on a public Spanish methodology proposal has been developed (Miguel et al., 1998). Part of the methodology is supported by a CASE tool (IDEA-DWCASE). A first prototype of the tool is available and was presented in (Miguel et al., 2000). Its repository structure is the IDEA metamodel, and allows the creation of IDEA multidimensional conceptual schemes, and its translation into different logical schemes directly supported by MOLAP or ROLAP products, such as EXPRESS and ORACLE.

REFERENCES

Batini, C., Ceri, S. and Navathe, S. (1992). *Conceptual Database Design: An Entity-Relationship Approach*, Ed. Benjamin/Cummings.

Cabibbo, L. and Torlone, R. (1998). A Logical Approach to Multidimensional Databases. *Sixth International Conference on Extending Database Technology (EDBT'98)*, Valencia, Spain.

Chaudhuri, S. and Dayal, U. (1997). An Overview of Data Warehousing and OLAP Technology. *ACM SIGMOD Record* 26(1), March.

Chen, P. P. (1976). The Entity-Relationship Model: Towards a Unified View of Data. *ACM TODS*, 1(1).

Codd, E. F., Codd, S. B., and Salley, C. T. (1993). Providing OLAP (On-Line Analytical Processing) to User-Analyst: An IT Mandate. *Technical Report*, E. F. Codd and Associates.

Debevoise, N. T. (1999). *The Datawarehouse Method*. Prentice Hall PTR.

Dinter, B., Sapia, C., Blaschka, M., and Höfling, G. (1999). OLAP Market and Research: Initiating the Cooperation. *Journal of Computer Science and*

Information Management, 2(3).

Gatziu, S., Jeusfeld, M. A., Staudt, M., and Vassiliou, Y. (1999). Design and Management of Datawarehouses - Report on the DMDW'99 Workshop. *SIGMOD Record* 28(4), Dec.

Golfarelli, M., Maio, D. and Rizzi, S. (1998). Conceptual design of datawarehouses from E/R schemes, *31st Hawaii International Conference on System Sciences*.

Golfarelli, M., and Rizzi, S. (1999). Designing The Datawarehouse: Key Steps And Crucial Issues. *Journal Of Computer Science And Information Management*, 2(3).

Inmon, W. H. (1993). *Building the Datawarehouse*, NY: John Wiley & Sons.

Kimball, R. (1996). *The Datawarehouse Toolkit: Practical techniques for building dimensional datawarehouses*. John Wiley & Sons.

Kimball, R., Reeves, L., Ross, M., and Thornthwaite, W. (1998). *The Datawarehouse Lifecicle Toolkit*, John Wiley & Sons, Inc.

Miguel, A. de, et al. (1998). METRICA Version 3: Planning and Development Methodology of Information Systems. Designing a Methodology: A practical experience, *Proceedings of CIICC'98*, Aguascalientes, México, Nov., 264-76.

Miguel, A. de, et al. (2000). IDEA-DWCASE: Modeling mutidimensional databases, EDBT 2000 Software Demonstrations track. Konstanz, Alemania, March.

Sánchez, A., Cavero, J. M., and Miguel, A. de. (1999). IDEA: A conceptual multidimensional data model and some methodological implications. *Proceedings of the CIICC'99*, Cancún, Méjico. 307-318.

Sapia, C., et al. (1999). On Supporting the Datawarehouse Design by Data Mining Techniques, GI-Workshop: Data Mining and Data Warehousing, September 27.-28., Magdeburg, Germany.

Srivastava, J., and Chen, P-Y. (1999). Warehouse Creation - A Potential Roadblock to Data Warehousing. *IEEE Transactions on Knowledge and Data Engineering*, 11(1), Ene/Feb.

Wu, M. C., and Buchmann, A. P. (1997). Research Issues in Data Warehousing. BTW'97, Ulm, March.

Chapter 10

Assessing and Improving the Quality of Knowledge Discovery Data

Herna L. Viktor and Niek F. du Plooy
University of Pretoria, South Africa

Data quality has a substantial impact on the quality of the results of a Knowledge Discovery from Data (KDD) effort. The poor quality of real-world data, as contained in many large data repositories, poses a serious threat to the future adoption of this new technology. Unfortunately, data quality assessment and improvement are often ignored in many KDD efforts, leading to disappointing results.

This chapter discusses the use of data mining and data generation techniques, including feature selection, case selection and outlier detection, to assess and improve the quality of the data. In this approach, redundant low quality data are removed from the data repository and new high quality data patterns are dynamically added to the data set. We also point out that data capturing is part of the social practices of office work, and this fact must be taken into account in designing the data capturing processes.

INTRODUCTION

KDD is an exciting new technology that can be effectively used to obtain previously unknown patterns from large data repositories. However, experience shows that the quality of data in many real-world data repositories is unacceptably poor. According to Redman (1996), error rates of 1-5% are typical, with an estimated immediate cost of about 10% of revenue. These costs are amplified when poor data quality leads to the failure of KDD projects.

Previously Published in *Managing Information Technology in a Global Economy,* edited by Mehdi Khosrow-Pour, Copyright © 2001, Idea Group Publishing.

Poor data quality significantly impacts the application of the KDD process and the quality of the final results thereof. That is, large portions of data, which may contain important knowledge regarding the problem domain, may have to be discarded prior to data mining. The removal of substantial amounts of data may cause data mining tools to fail to find accurate and general concept descriptions. For example, our recent KDD efforts regarding the investigation of traffic accident reports, showed that the quality of the original data was so poor that the application of the discovery techniques could not be completed successfully without initiating new data capturing policies (Nel and Viktor, 1999). The vast amount of available data could thus not alleviate the effect of poor data capturing and preprocessing.

Unfortunately, the importance of assuring high quality data is often understated (Weiss and Indurkhya, 1998). Also, the implicit assumption that the data to be mined does in fact relate to the organization from which it was drawn and thus reflects the organizational processes, is often not tested (Pyla, 1999).

This chapter proposes the use of data mining tools and data generation procedures to assess and improve the quality of organizational data. In this approach, data mining tools are used to identify low quality data. The resultant reduced data set is then used to generate new high quality data instances for subsequent data mining. In addition, we also emphasize the need for improved data capturing procedures.

The chapter is organized as follows. The next section introduces the KDD process and discusses the impact of data quality on the final results of KDD. The following section presents methods to improve the quality of the data through the use of data mining techniques. Finally, the last section concludes the paper.

DATA QUALITY AND THE KDD PROCESS

The KDD process consists of three main stages, as shown in Figure 1. *Data preprocessing* involves the evaluation of the data to determine its appropriateness for the KDD project (Pyla, 1999). Data preprocessing concerns the selection, evaluation, cleaning, enrichment and transformation of the data (Adriaans and Zantinge, 1997; Han and Kamber, 2000; Pyla, 1999). The actual knowledge discovery stage in called *data mining*. Here, one or more techniques, such as decision trees or neural networks, are used to discover knowledge from the data. Finally, the *reporting* stage concerns the presentation of the results by means of a graphical user interface (GUI).

It can be argued that the results of the KDD process reflect the memory of the organization that is being investigated (Robey et al., 1995). That is, data are explored to discover knowledge about the organization, and ultimately, the world (Pyle, 1999). Importantly, the KDD results can be viewed as a reflection of the quality of the data capturing and preprocessing processes. An understanding of

Figure 1: The KDD process (Adapted from [Han and Kamber, 2000])

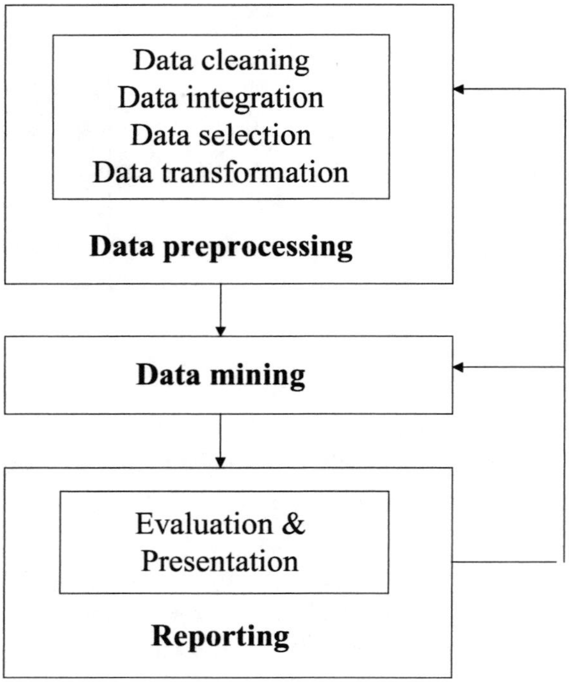

the processes that are used to capture, generate, use and store the data are therefore essential to ensure data quality (Matheiu and Khalil, 1998) and to ensure the meaningfulness of the KDD process.

A survey conducted by Cykana et al. (1996) lists the main causes of poor data quality according to four primary problem areas. These are process problems, systems problems, policy and procedure problems and data design problems. These problem areas are clearly also dependent on the social (work) practices that is followed in organizations and that are involved during data capturing in organizations. The way work is perceived (in the social sense) will determine the way information systems (and thus the associated capturing of data) is designed (Jones 1995; Käkölä, 1995; Pentland, 1995).

The fact that work (and thus data capturing) primarily is a social process is often ignored when information systems are designed. Systems are often approached mechanistically, that is, as a mere automation of current processes and procedures from the viewpoint of the systems designer. In this way, the designed imposes his or her value system (e.g. the way work should be done, and the order in which it should be done) on the data capturer (Du Plooy, 1998). This may not be appropriate to the way the data capturer works or would like to work. It has been acknowledged that systems developers who are to design the data capturing techniques are not equipped (in the sense of the tools they use or the training they receive) to deal with the social processes intrinsic to information systems development (Hirschheim and Newman, 1991).

Rethinking the organization's approach to information system design may counter claims that office work in the information era often reflects Tayloristic work designs, focusing on the individual's task productivity to the exclusion of the social content of the work (Lyytinen and Ngwenyama, 1992; Fitzgerald and Murphy, 1994). Mechanistic automation may result in increased control, but it also affects the autonomy of workers and depersonalises work. The effect of this may be that data capturing is done by rote, following the dictates of the system and thus resulting in erroneous and redundant data since the data capturers have no real interest in what they are doing.

The identification of specific problem areas, through the use of data mining tools, can improve the data capturing processes and thus facilitate organizational learning. The next section examines the use of data mining approaches that can be used to identify poor quality data and the problem areas that caused the creation thereof. The section also discusses how, after the removal of redundancies from the data repository, new high quality data can be generated.

DATA QUALITY THROUGH DATA MINING AND DATA GENERATION

Feature selection concerns the selection of those attributes that are deemed important to describe the data repository. That is, a subset of the features that are considered to be critical in order to adequately describe the data set is selected. Feature selection approaches include statistical analysis, sensitivity analysis and the use of data mining tools such as decision trees or rule induction algorithms to obtain the important features (Han and Kamber, 2000).

Many real-world data sets contain a number of features that are unimportant. When considering a tuberculosis data set containing 345 features, only seven of them were of importance (Viktor et al., 1997). In another data mining effort, approximately ten of the 4000 features considered when describing small business loans were actually important (Weiss and Indurkhya, 1998). The presence of a large amount of redundant data, as identified during feature selection, shows that the data capturing processes are not adequately focused. Rather, the data repository acts as a "data morgue" in which all features, relevant or not, are placed. Storing data in a haphazard and unfocused manner may therefore also have a serious detrimental affect of the usability of this part of the organization's memory. This implies that the organization should rethink the validity of the data that are captured, thus streamlining their operational processes. For example, a traffic accident report should not blindly be streamlined by removing redundant features that are normally discarded by the traffic officers. Rather, the traffic accident and road condition expertise of, for example, construction engineers, rally drivers and medical personal should be used to update the report. This 'rethinking' could well start by examining the manner in which information systems design is approached. If systems are designed in a mechanistic manner, data will also be captured mechanistically, thus robbing the 'data capturer' of the opportunity to remove the redundancy and enhancing the validity.

Case or instance selection is used to eliminate redundant instances from the data repository, mainly to limit the size requirements to store data in memory (Brodley and Friedl, 1996; Cherkauer and Shavlik; 1996). This approach has also been used to reduce decision tree size, thus improving human comprehensibility (Sebban and Nock, 2000). The existence of a large number of redundant and irrelevant instances again indicates that the data repository has not been fine-tuned for data mining and hints to possible organizational problems that may result in poor quality data. The removal of the appropriate poor quality instances from the repository not only improve the quality of the data set, but may be subsequently used when questioning the appropriateness of the data sources and data capturing processes.

Outlier detection highlights surprises in the data, that is data instances that do not comply with the general behavior or model of the data (Han and Kamber 2000). An outlier is a single, or very low frequency, occurrence of a value of a variable that is far away from the majority of the values of the variable (Pyla, 1999). Outliers are detected using statistical tests or data mining tools such as the nearest neighbor algorithms.

Most data mining methods and practitioners discard outliers as noise or exceptions (Pyla, 1999). However, from a data quality perspective, the rare event can be more interesting that the regularly occurring patterns. That is, outlier detection is especially useful to assess the quality of the data, since it may indicate that the organizational processes and subsequent assumption may be wrongfully made. The detection of many diverse outliers often indicates the presence of problems within one or more of the four areas identified in the previous section, leading to poor data capturing processes.

Data generation utilizes the results of feature selection, case selection and outlier detection to produce new data. Here, the data selection approaches produces a reduced data set that contains high quality data that has been shown to be of importance to adequately describe the problem domain. This data set may thus substantially reduce the large data repository to a small set of usable data to be used for data mining. However, experience has shown that many data mining tools have difficulty to generalize well if the number of instances is few. This is especially evident in difficult to learn domains. Data generation addresses this problem through the automating generation of new instances that are based on the high quality data, as contained in the reduced data set identified earlier (Viktor, 2000). The application of this approach to a real-world repository concerning a Human Resources data warehouse, showed that data generation can be used to generate sufficient data for effective data mining, even in domains where the initial data quality was poor (Viktor and Arndt, 2000).

Note that the above-mentioned data mining and data generation processes should be executed with the active participation of the members of the organization and the subsequent adaptation of the organizational processes, where appropriate. In this way, the problem areas can be identified and be rectified as far as possible. If this is not done, KDD may fall into the selfsame trap as information systems design in general, namely, approach the discovery of data mechanistically in the firm belief that the technology alone can take care of things (Postman, 1993).

CONCLUSION

According to Matheiu and Khalil (1998), the improvement of the quality of data in an organization is often a daunting task. This is especially evident in KDD projects, which are often initiated "after the fact." However, it is the opinion of the authors that the assessment and improvement of data quality during KDD can positively influence the organizational processes, highlight problem areas and facilitate organizational learning. This however, is dependent on heading the injunction that information systems design, and thus the design of data capturing processes, is approached less mechanistically and by taking the social context of the work of data capturing into account.

This chapter concerned the use of data mining techniques, namely feature and case selection and outlier detection, to assess and improve the quality of the data. Also, the use of automatic data generation, in order to improve the quality of the data, was discussed. In addition, it was pointed out how ignoring the social side of data capturing may influence the quality of the data. These methods can be effectively used to with inconsistent, noisy and incomplete data that are commonplace in large, real-world data repositories.

REFERENCES

Brodley, C. E., and Friedl, M. A. (1996). Identifying and Eliminating Mislabeled Training Instances, *13th National Conference on Artificial Intelligence*, CA.

Cherkauer, K. J., and Shavlik, J. W. (1998). Growing Simple Decision Trees to facilitate Knowledge Discovery, *Second International Conference on Knowledge Discovery and Data mining*.

Cykana, P., Paul, A., and Stern, M. (1996). US Department of Defense guidelines on Data Quality Management, *Proceedings of the 1996 Conference on Information quality*, Cambridge, MA: pp.154-171.

Debenham, J. (2000). Knowledge Decay in a Normalized Knowledge Base, Data and Expert Systems Applications, Lecture Notes in Computer Science, Vol 1873, pp.417-436.

Fitzgerald, B., and Murphy, C. C. (1994). Introducing Executive Information Systems into Organizations: Separating Fact from Fallacy, *Journal of Information Technology*, 9, pp.288-296.

Han, J., and Kamberen, M. (2000). *Data Mining: Concepts and Techniques*, CA: Morgan Kaufman.

Hirschheim, R. A., and Newman, M. (1991). Symbolism and Information System Development: Myth, Metaphor and Magic, *Information Systems Research*, 2(1), pp 29-62.

Jones, M. (1995). Organizational Learning: Collective Mind or Cognitivist Metaphor? *Accounting, Management & Information Technology*, 5(1), pp. 61-77.

Käkölä, T. M. (1995). Increasing the Interpretive Flexibility of Information Systems through Embedded Application Systems, *Accounting, Management & Information Technology*, 5, 1, pp 79-102.

Liskin, M. (1990). Can you trust your Database? *Personal Computing*, June 29, pp.129-134.

Lyytinen, K., and Ngwenyama, O. K. (1992). What does Computer Support for Cooperative Work Mean? A Structural Analysis of Computer Supported Cooperative Work, *Accounting, Management & Information Technology*, 2 (1), pp. 19-37.

Mathieu, R. G., and Khalil, O. (1998). Data Quality in the Database Systems Course, *Data Quality Journal*, 4 (1), September.

Nel, C., and Viktor, H. L. (1999). Data Mining of Traffic Accident Reports, Progress Report, Department of Informatics, University of Pretoria, Pretoria, South Africa.

Pentland, B. T. (1995). Information Systems and Organizational Learning: The Social Epistemology of Organizational Knowledge Systems. *Accounting, Management & Information Technology*, 5, 1, pp.1-21.

Plooy, N. F. du (1998). An Analysis of the Human Environment for the Adoption and Use of Information Technology, (Unpublished) DCom dissertation, University of Pretoria, South Africa.

Postman, N. (1992). *Technopoly: the Surrender of Culture to Technology*, NY: Vintage Books.

Pyle, D. (1999). Data Preparation for Data Mining, CA: Morgan Kaufman.

Quinlan, J. R. (1994). C4.5: Programs for Machine Learning, CA: Morgan Kaufman.

Redman, T. C. (1996). Data Quality for the Information Age, Norwood, MA: Artech House.

Robey, D., Wishart, N. A., and Rodriguez-Diaz, A.G. (1995). Merging the Metaphors of Organizational Improvement: Business Process Reengineering as a Component of Organizational Learning, *Accounting, Management & Information Technology*, 5(1), pp.23-39.

Sebban, M., and Nock, R. (2000). Contribution of Dataset Reduction Techniques to Tree-simplification and Knowledge Discovery, *International Journal of Computers, Systems and Signals*, December.

Viktor, H. L. (2000). Generating New Patterns for Information Gain and Improved Neural Network Learning, *The International Joint Conference on Neural Networks (IJCNN-00)*, Como, Italy, 24 - 27 July.

Viktor, H. L., and Arndt, H. (2000). Data Mining in Practice: From Data to Knowledge using a Hybrid Mining Approach, *International Journal of Computers, Systems and Signals*, December.

Viktor, H. L., Cloete, I., and Beyers, N. (1997). Rules for Tuberculosis Diagnosis, *Methods for Informatics in Medicine*, 36 (2), pp.160-168.

Weiss, G., and Indurkhya, N. (1998). *Predictive Data Mining: A Practical Guide*, CA: Morgan Kaufman.

Chapter 11

Complementing the Data Warehouse with Information Filtered from the Web

Witold Abramowicz, Pawel Jan Kalczynski and Krzysztof Wecel
The Poznan University of Economics, Poland

The data warehouse is considered to be the best way to organize transactional data. However, as many researches claim data warehouse should be augmented with external textual information. The objective of this chapter is to examine the requirements for profiling in the data warehouse environment. Profiles created in the data warehouse are then utilized to filter information. The goal of the sketched system is to support users in his situated actions. We explore many issues concerning personalization, such as information overflow, user models, and situatedness. We also analyze the factors that influence the filtering process. Finally, we draw some conclusions that should be considered during extension of the evaluated system.

INTRODUCTION

One of the problems, technology has to cope with, is the overflow of information. Users have access to a great deal of information resources through such means as commercial online services, business portals, financial wires, mail messages, electronic bulletin boards, and news articles (Abramowicz, Kalczynski & Wecel, 2001b). Although users of electronic sources have access to a rich body of information, only a small part of information is actually relevant to their interests. Thus, the problem of picking and presenting to the user only documents containing interesting information arises. One solution is to use filters that selectively eliminate the irrelevant information based on user preference (Foltz, 1990).

Another solution to dealing with the increasing flow of data is data warehousing. Data warehousing has grown during the last 10 years into a technology proven in

Previously Published in *Managing Information Technology in a Global Economy,* edited by Mehdi Khosrow-Pour, Copyright © 2001, Idea Group Publishing.

many successful organizations as the best way to organize, store, analyze and report data collected through the course of doing business. The data warehouse stores and manages historical data, and can be reshaped and reused to meet the business requirements as they evolve. Many data warehousing tools exist to extract, transform, store, aggregate, access, present, mine and extrapolate data.

The chances of success in a data warehousing project can be greatly increased by using one of the newest business trends: knowledge management. Knowledge management allows businessmen to make better use of resources, find innovative solutions to business problems, and improve quality of management (Abramowicz, 2001). Data warehousing is, in essence, a form of knowledge management. It promises to improve data quality and integrate internal and external data (Allison, 2000).

This chapter presents the incorporation of information filtering into the data warehouse environment through appropriately defined profiles.

The specific contributions include: (1) exploiting information filtering techniques to supplement the data warehouse with external information, (2) requirements concerning the profiles, (3) suggestion to explore the data warehouse to build profiles.

The rest of this chapter is organized as follows: the next section presents the background of our project. The following section discusses some personalization issues in the data warehouse environment and reviews related work. The section entitled, *The Profiles in a DW Environment*, presents requirements for profiles in a DW. Finally, the last section provides conclusions.

BACKGROUND
Data Warehousing

We assume that the idea of data warehousing is commonly known (Inmon, Hackathorn,1994; Kimball, 1996). For the purposes of our project we use the SAS/Warehouse Administrator™ (SAS Institute, Inc., 1997b) from the SAS Institute (http://www.sas.com).

To be more precise, we briefly describe this specific DW environment. According to the data warehousing paradigm, the repository is organized into a number of *subjects*. A warehouse *subject* can be defined as a collection of data and information concerning a particular issue (e.g. client, product). Each subject must contain a single *detail logical table*. The detail logical table consists of a single multidimensional table or a number of detail tables organized into a star schema.

It is very beneficial that each subject may also contain an *information mart* – a logical grouping of information items. The information mart may contain any information generated from detail data or summary data in the warehouse, and additionally text documents, HTML pages, or spreadsheets.

Other significant feature of the SAS® solution is that the DW metadata is stored in one repository. There is no dispersion of technical and business metadata among different databases. That allows easy and consistent access to metadata through the API (SAS Institute, Inc., 1997a).

Every object in the SAS warehouse environment has its owner and administrator.

Information Filtering (IF)

Selective Distribution of Information (SDI) system is a typical information filter. SDI was introduced by Luhn (1958) in order to improve exchange and distribution of information between scientists. It was then improved by Housman and Kaskela (1970). The goal of SDI system is not to find documents when they are required, but to inform constantly about new documents that may be interesting for users.

Information is filtered against user profiles (representation of user's needs) by measuring similarity between documents and user profiles. Documents that are similar to a particular profile are distributed to its owner (Abramowicz & Ceglarek, 2001).

System Overview

Information filtering aids the user in receiving interesting information, which grows increasingly difficult for a user because of the large amount of material now available electronically. The objective is to search for interesting information automatically to relieve the user of tedious search tasks. In other words we have to help people find what they do not know (Belkin, 2000). In our system personalization is achieved through the profiles. To our knowledge, profiling for information filtering has not been integrated so far into data warehouse environments.

Figure 1: System Overview

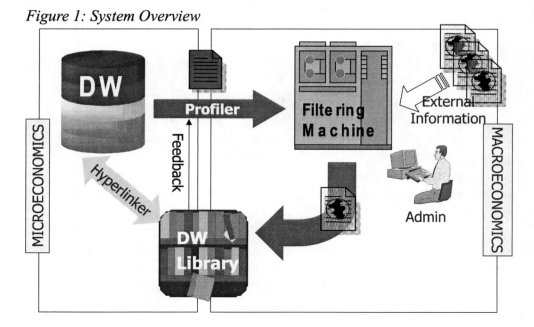

In our earlier projects we analyzed different architectures of our system. State of the art is depicted on Figure 1.

The architecture is determined by the functions of the system, which are the following (Abramowicz, Kalczynski & Wecel, 2002):

- Recognize situation (state of the environment);
- Generate alert; and
- Provide content to react on this alert accordingly to situation.

All these aspects are described in the reminder of this chapter.

As microeconomics we understand everything that regards particular organization, and as macroeconomics – all the economic system (environment). Warehouse profiles have to express internal needs to external sources (Abramowicz et al., 2001b). The role of filtering machine is to filter information accordingly to provided profiles. Data Warehouse Library collects both internal and external information. All the resources that may be of interest to the user are stored *persistently* (Abramowicz & Kalczynski, 2001).

Another important feature is the enhancement of navigation in the DW, e.g. viewing of the report is accompanied by a list of probably relevant documents. A user profile determines which documents should be presented.

Our concept is similar to the Web Farming idea presented in Hackathorn (1999).

PERSONALIZATION IN A DATA WAREHOUSE

Personalization generally refers to making an access to information more responsive to the unique and individual needs of each user. Nowadays in a world of too-many-information personalization is viewed as an important issue, e.g. the whole *Communications of the ACM* from August 2000 (Vol. 43, No. 8) was devoted to this topic.

Why should we personalize? The answer is straightforward – personalization is a mean to cope with information overflow. Nobody would require the personalized services if users received information appropriate to their needs and only such information. And since our needs are different, there is no easy solution.

In the data warehouse environment the question is not whether to personalize but how to personalize. In this chapter we would like to present the determinants of the personalization.

Information Overflow

In today's world, we can observe both information overflow and information deficit. The information overflow is caused by too much general information. The information deficit is caused by the lack of appropriate information.

Information overflow is not a technical problem. As stated in the introduction, many technologies have been developed to cope with this issue, e.g. data warehousing, knowledge management. Some authors claim that the current hype on "information overload" problem on the Internet seems to be more psychological problem (Lueg & Pfeifer, 1997).

It seems that the information problem exist independently from the existence of the Internet and its services. People consider Internet services to be more attractive because they deliver data in the electronic form.

The amount of information that can be accessed in the Internet exceeds the human cognitive capabilities (Lueg et al., 1997). However, this is also true for traditional sources of information – the amount of information provided by books, newspapers, television already exceeds human cognitive capabilities by far (Lueg et al., 1997). "Information overload" seems to be social phenomenon caused by expectations such as always being informed. Professionals seem to spend more and more time searching for information while the overall time available to consume the information will not be extended (Marchionini, 1995). We can induce that time devoted to searching comes at the expense of time for reading (Marchionini, 1995).

Another interesting statement about information overflow can be found in Goldhaber (1997). He states that "information is not scarce – especially on the Net, where it is not only abundant but overflowing... The economy of attention – not information – is the natural economy of cyberspace..." Attention is a scarce resource since each of us has only 16 or so hours per day to devote to all the topics (Hackathorn, 1999).

Because information overflow has a psychological background, technology can only support humans in coping with information overload phenomenon. It is not possible to replace humans. We take this into account in our system.

Today's overload of information often makes information systems ineffective. What is important is to deliver information to the user according to his needs, interests, and expectations. One of the possibilities is to use user models (Allen, 1990). We can help the user by showing them only a few documents. This will protect them from reading too many documents, and having the feeling of wasting time.

To conclude, the system has to supply users accordingly to their actual needs, causing neither information overflow nor information deficit.

Data Warehouse Users

The data warehouse is one of the solutions that help to overcome among others the information overflow problem. First of all, according to the definition, DW is divided into different subjects. Each subject comprises data marts where users can store most frequently used reports or charts. However, this is a case of access to the data warehouse, usually delimited by an administrator in accordance with user role. Our intention is to build profiles that express actual user information needs based on the subject-oriented organization of the data warehouse.

User modeling can be viewed as a classification task (Allen, 1990); users are categorized on the basis of a particular characteristic or group of characteristics, according to features detected in their interaction with the system. In a DW environment, users can be grouped around the warehouse subjects or accordingly to the played role. Such classifications may assign each user to a particular user group (or stereotype).

In the early beginning, data warehouse was used by analysts that prepared reports for top management. Nowadays, the situation is quite different. Making data warehouses accessible from intranets proves that more and more users are interested in a DW content: from president to sales operator.

The problem of choosing an appropriate configuration is in many respects a traditional user modeling problem. The system is required to adapt to individual users whose requirements vary enormously, and it takes responsibility for ensuring successful system-user communication.

Knowledge representation

A profile is a representation of information needs. Under the term *warehouse profile* we understand the information needs' representation of users of the data warehouse. Typical profile usually contains a list of terms with corresponding weights. For purpose of our project we extended the profile in order to represent knowledge gleaned from the data warehouse (Wecel, 2000). Further extensions are required, what is basic because profiles are defined in XML.

Standardization is an important issue. There are many problems with describing the resources. The language of Internet is different from the language of the data warehouse. Therefore we are creating a framework called Common Semantic Layer (Abramowicz, Kalczynski & Wecel, 2001a). It should help to establish semantic interoperability between data warehouse and information space. It would also solve the problem of describing users' interest. We should define the domain and user knowledge as well as mechanisms for manipulating this knowledge.

Our profile is a kind of mediation between this two "worlds". Our knowledge representation integrates Web resources and the warehouse, and allows filtering appropriate information.

Situated information filtering

Situatedness is a very appealing concept (Lueg et al., 1997). The main idea is that users have different needs in different situations. These needs are dynamic, not static. Hence, situation strongly affects personalization.

In this concept, every information has its background, which creates situated environment. Human is not treated as a data processing system but situated agent, which interacts with environment. In this case human should not be replaced but supported by a machine.

Situated design methodology has to take into account the whole environment in which the task has to be performed (Müller & Pfeifer, 1997). The way the user interacts with his environment strongly depends on the individual cognitive capabilities and the user's experience (Lueg et al., 1997). This is especially important in information filtering environment since the meaning of information strongly depends on a person.

PROFILES IN A DW ENVIRONMENT
Representing User Information Needs

As we mentioned earlier, DW users (information consumers) specify their information needs in the profiles. A traditional profile contains a list of terms. Users may define numerous profiles to represent various issues (Abramowicz, 1990). Profiles are encoded in XML. The further incorporation of the RDF is projected (Cingil, Dogac & Azgin, 2000).

Previous work

In our early work, we distinguished two types of profiles (Abramowicz, Kalczynski & Wecel, 2000):
- warehouse subject profile linked to a structure of data warehouse
- user profile linked to a person

The warehouse subject profile represents information needs of a virtual user. Each subject profile is managed by a human, referred to as the profile supervisor. Every user profile had to be assigned to a warehouse subject profile.

In order to enable refining the warehouse profiles we supposed to take advantages of relevance feedback. However, in the DW environment there are too many documents. Also, the goal of the information supply is different. It has slightly evolved. Now a user can be a person, a role, or even a DW element.

Personalization determinants

The main objective of profiling in the DW environment is to support users in his situated actions. Therefore, we define the profiling as a function of:
- situation – we suggest the notion of situatedness (Lueg et al., 1997);
- role of the user (in an organization, data warehouse, workflow (Abramowicz & Stankowski, 2001), etc.); and
- DW structure.

Many researches and our experiments proved that one single profile is not enough to filter proper information to DW. Therefore, we distinguish many different aspects of profiles.

Situatedness

Information needs depend on the actual situation – they are dynamic, not static. We claim that users act different in different situations. In order to cope with this we explore the conception of *situatedness* (Lueg et al., 1997). In the business world, situation is created by environment and is strictly connected to macroeconomics. Macroeconomic situation can be determined by inflation, unemployment, credit rates, etc.

For example during the recession stage of business cycle an executive could be interested in information that will help to cut costs, and during the boom he could seek for new opportunities of increasing income.

Situation cannot be omitted. It should be reflected in profiles as different aspects (subprofiles).

Accuracy Levels

First of all, we have to distinguish two levels of filtering:
a) subject level – more general profile, documents concerning every issue of a warehouse subject
b) role level – more specific profile, fulfilling the needs of specific role

We were motivated by different researches. They prove that filtering algorithm is not as important as representation of profiles and the use of linguistic and hierarchical knowledge in the forming of features. This has a much larger impact than particular classification algorithm (Pazzani & Billsus, 1997).

According to the subject level, the more documents are retrieved the better. Nevertheless, we do not want to force the user to read all documents, but to enhance user in his tasks. All documents filtered on the subject level are stored in DW library. These are then assigned to particular users on the role level. Users access information on a particular activity (e.g., view of report), or situation (e.g., increase in unemployment).

Purposes

Information can be filtered for different targets. We distinguish the following purposes:
a) event alerting (event detection) – to awaken to the need to introspect the situation
b) situation detection – to give a background for user needs
c) solution support – to provide information fulfilling the needs

Managers are accessing the DW on time basis (e.g. every week) or event basis (e.g. marketing campaign). Event alerting can relieve user from doing too much work, and draw his attention to a particular issue only when required. Daily news may contain information for alerting. Governmental reports may provide information about situation. Any other information may help an executive to find a solution to a particular problem indicated by alert, in a given situation.

Building the Profiles

The task of building the profiles is the straight continuation of extracting knowledge from the data warehouse. We distinguish four different possibilities of building warehouse profiles. We can utilize the knowledge from (Abramowicz & Wecel, 2001):

- documents in information marts;
- metadata of the data warehouse;
- data warehouse models; and
- detailed data in the data warehouse.

Building the profiles out of metadata has been studied in greater detail in (Wecel, 2000; Abramowicz & Wecel, 2000).

The challenge is to identify what information is available for the given "learning to personalize" task and what methods are best suited to the available information (Hirsh, Basu & Davison, 2000).

Refining the Profiles

When thinking about refining, there are always questions about user control in refining.

Past research has shown that it is rather difficult for people to state their information needs precisely, but quite easy for them to identify documents that satisfy their information needs. These results suggest that the original statement of information needs (query) should be refined automatically (Abramowicz et al., 2001).

The typical technique for improving retrieval effectiveness is relevance feedback (Rocchio, 1971). Information retrieval systems can modify the original query by analyzing relevance judgments about previously retrieved documents (adding new terms, modifying weights).

Relevance feedback forces users to read all documents. The method of having users rate each article as interesting or not-interesting provides a lot of data, but also requires a lot of effort on the part of the user. In many cases, it is not feasible or even not desirable.

Therefore, many other possible solutions have been developed (Abramowicz, 1990; Callan, 1998). They may, for instance, monitor how much time users spent on an article, how much of an article is read, or just have users occasionally indicate articles that they account to be good examples of what they like or dislike (adaptive filtering).

Automatic improving of user profiles (or queries) takes some of the burden off the user. However, it means that the user model is hidden from the user, which makes it more difficult to be evaluated and modified by its owner.

In our earlier works, we supposed that users judge each filtered document. However, this approach proved infeasible in the data warehousing environment. The reasons for that include: too many documents, management do not have much time, people don't want to read all documents – they just want an access to relevant information.

Our approach to relevance feedback has been revised, and now we have to deeply investigate other techniques, such as Local Context Analysis (Xu & Croft, 1996).

CONCLUSIONS AND FUTURE WORK

We have learned that filtering information to the data warehouse makes sense. To fulfill this purpose personalization based on profiles is employed.

In the DW environment, information filtering is more complex than filtering without underlying system. It is due to the architecture of the warehouse (i.e., division into subjects) and complexity of business management and organization (Abramowicz et al., 2002). The latter involves many problems that are not easily solvable by technology.

We found that information filtering has different goals, among which we mentioned event alerting, situation detection and solution support. Moreover, filtering process should be carried out on two levels: subject level to supply the whole subject of a warehouse, and role level to supply the individual users. We also introduce the problem of refining warehouse profiles and signalize the problem of semantic interoperability.

Our improvement over other solutions include: filtering in the DW environment, taking into account the situatedness, creating enhanced profiles (XML), treating user needs as a function of his role, situation and task he has to perform.

Further work should focus on examining the methods we presented and evaluating their usefulness in real business environment. Currently we are dealing with pharmaceutical industry (Abramowicz et al., 2002). This area requires a substantial amount of work but the idea is enticing.

REFERENCES

Abramowicz, W. (1990). *Hypertexte und ihre IR-basierte Verbreitung*, Humboldt Universität Berlin, 292 +VII.

Abramowicz, W. (2001). Information Filters Supplying Management Information Systems, *WebNet 2001, World Conference on the WWW and Internet, Orlando, Florida*, October, 24-27, invited speaker.

Abramowicz, W. and Ceglarek, D. (2001). Improving Users' Profiles in Selective Dissemination of Information, In A. J. Baborski, R. F. Bonner, and M. L. Owoc (Eds.), *Knowledge Acquisition and Distributed Learning in Resolving Managerial Issues*, Mälardalen University Press, 126-132, ISBN 91-88834-22-0.

Abramowicz, W., and Kalczynski, P. J. (2001). On Supplying the Data Warehouse with Unstructured Contents Filtered from the Internet, In A. J. Baborski, R. F. Bonner, and M. L. Owoc (Eds.), *Knowledge Acquisition and Distributed Learning in Resolving Managerial Issues*, Mälardalen University Press, 133-144, ISBN 91-88834-22-0.

Abramowicz, W., Kalczynski, P. J., and Wecel, K. (2000). Information Filters Supplying Data Warehouses with Benchmarking Information, In W. Abramowicz, and J. Zurada (Eds.), *Knowledge Discovery for Business Information Systems*, Kluwer Academic Publishers, 2000, pp. 1-28.

Abramowicz, W., Kalczynski, P. J., and Wecel, K. (2001a). Common Semantic Layer to Support Integration of the Data Warehouse and the Web, *Proc. of 5th International Conference Human-Computer Interaction – HCI2001*, Gdansk.

Abramowicz, W., Kalczynski, P. J. and Wecel, K. (2001b). Information Ants to Explore Internet Sources of Business Information, *Proc. of ISCA 14th International Conference on Computer Applications in Industry and Engineering - CAINE2001* (A. Chung, Ed.), Las Vegas, NV, pp. 134-137.

Abramowicz, W., Kalczynski, P. J., and Wecel, K. (2002). *Filtering the Web to Feed Data Warehouses*, Springer, London.

Abramowicz, W., and Stankowski, F. (2001). Instancing Workflows with Information Filtered from Internet, In A. J. Baborski, R. F. Bonner, and M. L. Owoc (Eds.), *Knowledge Acquisition and Distributed Learning in Resolving Managerial Issues*, Mälardalen University Press, 2001, 145-155, ISBN 91-88834-22-0.

Abramowicz, W., and Wecel, K. (2000). Building HyperSDI Profiles from Data Warehouse Metadata Repository, In *Proceedings of Conference on Integrated Systems KSW2000*, Polish Academy of Sciences, System Researches, Vol. 26, Warsaw, pp. 54-66.

Abramowicz, W., and Wecel, K. (2001). On Extracting Knowledge from the Data Warehouse for Information Filtering Purposes, In A. J. Baborski, R. F. Bonner, and M. L. Owoc (Eds.), *Knowledge Acquisition and Distributed*

Learning in Resolving Managerial Issues, Mälardalen University Press, 156-172, ISBN 91-88834-22-0.

Allen, R. B. (1990). User models: theory, method, and practice, *International Journal of Man-Machine Studies*, 32:511-543.

Allison, B. (2000). Catching the Next Wave, *DM Direct*, July 14.

Belkin, N. J. (2000). Helping People Find What They Don't Know, *Communications of the ACM*, August, Vol. 43, No. 8, pp. 58-61.

Benaki, E., Karkaletsis, V. A. and Spyropoulos, C. D. (1997). Integrating User Modeling Into Information Extraction: The UMIE Prototype, In A. Jameson, C. Paris, and C. Tasso (Eds.), *User Modeling: Proceedings of the Sixth International Con-ference UM97*, Vienna, NY: Springer Wien New York

Callan, J. (1998). Learning While Filtering Documents, *Proceedings of SIGIR 98*, 22nd International Conference on Research and Development in Information Retrieval, pp. 224-231.

Cyngil, I., Dogac, A. and Azgin, A. (2000). A Broader Approach to Personalization, *Communications of the ACM*, August, Vol. 43, No. 8, pp. 136-141.

Foltz, P. W. (1990). Using Latent Semantic Indexing for Information Filtering. In R. B. Allen (Ed.), *Proceedings of the Conference on Office Information Systems*, Cambridge, MA, pp. 40-47.

Goldhaber, M. H. (1997). Attention Shoppers, *Wired*, December.

Hackathorn, R. D. (1999). *Web Farming for the Data Warehouse*, San Francisco, CA: Morgan Kaufmann.

Hirsh, H., Basu, C., and Davison, B. D. (2000). Learning to Personalize, *Communications of the ACM*, August, Vol. 43, No. 8, pp. 102-106.

Housman, E. M. and Kaskela, E. D. (1970). State of the art in Selective dissemination of information, *IEEE Transactions on Engeeneering Writing and Speech*, Vol. 13, pp. 78-83.

Inmon, W. H., and Hackathorn, R. D. (1994). *Using the Data Warehouse*, NY: John Wiley & Sons

Kimball, R. (1996). *The Data Warehouse Toolkit - Practical Techniques for Building Dimensional Data Warehouses*, NY: John Wiley & Sons, Inc.

Lueg, C. and Pfeifer, R. (1997). Cognition, Situatedness, and Situated Design, *Proc. 2nd Internationall Conference on Cognitive Technology*, Aizu, Japan, August.

Luhn, H. P. (1958). A Business Intelligence System, *IBM Journal of Research and Development*, Vol. 2, No. 2, pp. 159-165.

Marchionini, G. (1995). Information Seeking in Electronic Environments, *Cambridge Series in Human-Computer Interaction,* Cambridge, University Press.

Müller, M. and Pfeifer, R. (1997). Developing effective computer systems supporting knowledge intensive work: Situated Desing in a paper mill, In M.

Khosrow-Pour and J. Liebowitz (Eds.) *Cases in Information Technology Management in Modern Organizations*, Hershey, PA: Idea Group Publishing.

Pazzani, M., and Billsus, D. (1997). Learning and Revising User Profiles: The Identification of Interesting Web Sites, *Machine Learning 27*, Kluwer Academic Publishers, pp. 313-331.

Rocchio, J. (1971). *Relevance Feedback in Information Retrieval*, Prentice-Hall Inc., ch. 14, pp. 313-323.

SAS Institute Inc. (1997a). *SAS/Warehouse Administrator™ Metadata API Reference, Release 1.2*, Cary, NC: SAS Institute Inc., 86 pp.

SAS Institute Inc. (1997b). *SAS/Warehouse Administrator~ User's Guide, Release 1.1, First Edition*, Cary, NC, SAS Institute Inc., 142 pp.

Wecel, K. (2000). *Knowledge Discovery for Building HyperSDI Profiles in Data Warehouses*, Master Thesis (with summa cum laude), The Poznan University of Economics, Faculty of Economics, Poland.

Xu, J. and Croft, W. B. (1996). Query Expansion Using Local and Global Document Analysis, In *Proceedings of the 19th International Conference on Research and Development in Information Retrieval (SIGIR 96)*, Zurich, Switzerland, pp. 4-11.

Chapter 12

Justification of Data Warehousing Projects

Reinhard Jung and Robert Winter
University of St.Gallen, Switzerland

Project justification is regarded as one of the major methodological deficits in Data Warehousing practice. As reasons for applying inappropriate methods, performing incomplete evaluations, or even entirely omitting justifications, the special nature of Data Warehousing benefits and the large portion of infrastructure-related activities are stated. In this chapter, the economic justification of Data Warehousing projects is analyzed, and first results from a large academia-industry collaboration project in the field of non-technical issues of Data Warehousing are presented. As conceptual foundations, the role of the Data Warehouse system in corporate application architectures is analyzed, and the specific properties of Data Warehousing projects are discussed. Based on an applicability analysis of traditional approaches to economic IT project justification, basic steps and responsibilities for the justification of Data Warehousing projects are derived.

INTRODUCTION

An empirical analysis (Helfert, 2000) of large companies' research needs in the field of Data Warehousing shows that Data Warehouse project justification is regarded as a major issue which requires a considerable research effort. As a consequence, only 53% of the participating companies tried to set up a Data Warehousing business case at all. Of those companies that performed an evaluation of costs and benefits, 58% used multi-attribute utility techniques, 33% used investment techniques, and 17% used various other approaches (Helfert, 2000). Superficial or missing analyses of Data Warehousing projects are usually attributed to the special nature of those projects, e.g., to the "obvious impossibility" to

Previously Published in *Managing Information Technology in a Global Economy*, edited by Mehdi Khosrow-Pour, Copyright © 2001, Idea Group Publishing.

assess "intangible benefits" (McKnight, 1999). If estimations are made, the return on investment (ROI) ranges from -1857% to an incredible 16,000% with an average of 401% (IDC study cited in McKnight, 1999).

In analogy to the term database system, the term Data Warehouse system denotes the entire range of applications and databases that is needed to utilize a Data Warehouses for business purposes. Data Warehousing then denotes all activities that are linked to the development, utilization, and operations of the Data Warehouse system.

Several facts contribute to the problems that companies are facing when they try to calculate ROIs for Data Warehousing projects:

- The Data Warehouse system is a complex middleware architecture built up incrementally by several Data Warehouse development projects.
- If a large number of data sources is integrated and a large number of applications is supported by the Data Warehouse, a huge investment is necessary, and lots of internal and external side-effects may be influencing the project(s).
- The Data Warehouse system comprises various components which are utilized by different business units in a different manner while the investment maybe has to be made jointly. While data consuming components (e.g., interfaces to decision support applications or horizontal applications) can be assigned quite easily to "consuming" business units, no such assignment can be made for infrastructural components (e.g., the core Data Warehouse, interfaces to source applications, meta data management).
- Due to the dynamic nature of many management processes, the Data Warehouse system is subject to frequent changes. From an investment theoretical point of view (Jung, 1998, p.38), diversification investments have to be taken into account in addition to initial investments.
- Although less frequently, not only information consuming applications, but also source applications are subject to changes (e.g., migration to standardized software packages).

In this chapter, the economic justification of Data Warehousing projects is analyzed, and first, descriptive results from a large academia-industry collaboration project in the field of non-technical issues of Data Warehousing are presented. As conceptual foundations, the role of the Data Warehouse system in corporate application architecture is discussed, and the specific properties of Data Warehousing projects are analyzed in the next section. In the following section, the applicability of traditional approaches to economic IT project justification is discussed. Based on that analysis, basic justification elements (i.e., tasks and responsibilities) for Data Warehousing projects are derived in the next section entitled, *Methodological and Organizational Aspects of Data Warehousing Project Evaluation*, and summarized in the last section.

CONCEPTUAL FOUNDATIONS
The Role of the Data Warehouse System in Corporate Application Architecture

Data Warehouse systems are widely accepted as a new middleware layer between operational applications and decision support applications, thereby decoupling systems focused on efficient handling of business transactions from systems focused on efficient support of business decisions. Such a middleware layer is necessary because the direct, individual access of decision support applications to data of operational, transaction oriented applications has proved to be technically or economically infeasible. Data quality problems and complex integration requirements usually make it impossible to supply consistent, integrated data real-time to various decision support applications. Even if technically feasible, the development and maintenance of mn interfaces between m Decision Support applications and n transactional applications cannot be economically useful. As an intermediate systems layer, the Data Warehouse system is decoupling decision support applications and operational applications, thereby reusing integration mechanisms and derived data for various decision support applications and allowing maintenance to be focussed on few, well-defined interfaces.

In Nagel (1990) a high-level application architecture model is proposed that locates applications along the dimensions "function," "product (group)," and "process." The dimension "function" lines up the various functional areas of the corporation (e.g., order processing, materials management, financials). The dimension "product (group)" lines up the various divisions or product groups of the corporation (e.g., loans, cash deposits, custody). The dimension "process" represents the course of business processes (e.g., information request, negotiation, contract, fulfillment/clearing, archiving). Most operational applications comprise modules that cover all functional aspects of a (more or less) complete business process for a specific product, product group, or division (Imhoff, 1999, p.2-3). Hence, the application architecture comprises a relatively small number of components that can be designated "vertical" applications due to their optical appearance in the model.

While the transfer of functions like customer data management or product configuration and pricing from vertical applications into dedicated cross-product applications has started in the 1990's, channel-specific functions have not been transferred into dedicated channel-specific applications until recently. This is due to the fact that a strong demand for multi-channel (i.e., face-to-face, letter-based, phone-based, and electronic) access to corporate applications is associated with increased mobility and the recent advent of electronic business and widespread access to the Internet. Channel-specific applications integrate access and/or distribution functions which are specific for a certain channel, but may be implemented identically for different products or product groups. If access and/or distribution channels have to be flexibly assigned to products or services, channel-specific functions, product-specific functions, and cross-product functions should be implemented in separate applications.

The clustering of channel-specific functions into applications is determined by the respective access media. As a consequence, vertical applications have to be complemented by alternative, channel-specific application add-ons like Call Center support, WWW portal, WAP portal, Letter Center/Document Management support, ATM support, and traditional, inhouse transaction applications. These applications may differ not only by supporting a different access and/or distribution channel, but also by different security mechanisms. In the application architecture model, channel-specific applications are represented by cubes that comprise various products for selected functions and for a certain portion of the underlying business processes. Due to their optical appearance, channel-specific applications can be designated as "horizontal" applications.

The positioning of vertical applications, cross-functional applications, horizontal applications, the Data Warehouse system, and finally decision support applications in corporate application architecture is illustrated in Figure 1.

Figure 1: The Role of the Data Warehouse System in Corporate Application Architecture

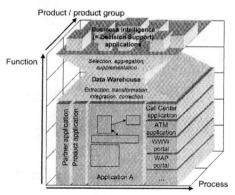

Data Warehousing Development Projects

In contrast to development projects for mature corporate IT platforms that are often 20 to 30 years old, Data Warehousing development projects are still characterized by an immature, work-in-progress IT platform. One the one hand, this immaturity creates opportunities that do not exist for traditional IT projects, examples being the recent inclusion of Operational Data Stores and horizontal operational applications into corporate information architecture. On the other hand, "early" development projects using a novel IT platform have to pay a significantly higher portion of infrastructure costs. This phenomenon can be observed for every novel IT platform, e.g., real-time applications in the 70's/early 80's or intranets in the early 90's. Figure 2 illustrates a typical development of a new IT platform. With every additional IT project, usually a lesser amount has to be spent for the development of the IT platform (light gray cost curve) because synergies can be used and significant IT platform development efforts have been paid for by earlier projects. When using a mature IT platform (i.e., IT development project in t_1, left part of Figure 2), the infrastructure costs I_1 usually are very small compared to the actual application development costs A_1. When building a new IT platform (i.e. IT development project in t_2, right part of Figure 2), the ratio of infrastructure costs I_2 and actual application development costs A_2 is more unfavorable.

Figure 2: IT Platform Maturity vs. IT Development Costs

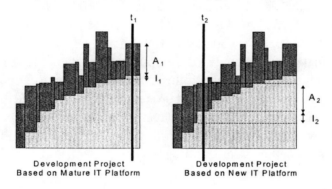

From these considerations, an important consequence for the economic justification of Data Warehousing projects follows: high infrastructure costs resulting from the immaturity of the IT platform must be carefully differentiated from application-related development costs. Based on a decision-oriented paradigm, only actual application development costs should be at the expense of business-driven Data Warehousing projects, while infrastructure-related costs should be allocated to corporate projects like "central IT infrastructure." If a cost split is not possible, development projects could be credited platform grants to avoid an unfair competition for financial and other resources between Data Warehousing projects and other IT projects.

APPLICABILITY OF TRADITIONAL JUSTIFICATION APPROACHES

The justification of IT development projects usually comprises the estimation of expected costs and the estimation of expected benefits. The term "benefit" is used instead of "revenue" because IT applications often create results that cannot be measured directly. This is particularly true for Data Warehousing projects because most applications do not directly affect value-creating business processes and, therefore, cannot directly be assigned to profit centers. In the following, we analyze traditional approaches to cost and benefit estimation with regard to their applicability for Data Warehousing projects.

Estimation of Costs

Due to the volume and significance of many IT development projects, a large number of methods have been proposed (cf. overviews in Baumoel (1999, 167ff.) and Jung, (1998, 61ff.)). However, the applicability of traditional cost estimation approaches to Data Warehousing projects is limited because (1) a function or process centric phase model of application development is assumed and (2) specific requirements are regarded as given and elicitable from business users. Moreover, often only initial development costs are analyzed although total costs of ownership could be significantly higher due to the long-term utilization of the Data Warehousing infrastructure (Thomason, 1998).

1) In contrast to most traditional IT development projects, we have not observed that Data Warehousing projects follow a certain sequence of distinct phases. Since nearly the entire development process is centered around data/information structures, modularization and development strategies like top-down or bottom-up have much less significance. Instead, activities like architectural planning, meta data management, end-user involvement, and project marketing become key issues for successful projects.

2) Due to the nature of many management processes, objective information requirements of managers are often not explicitly known when Data Warehousing projects start. In contrast to most traditional IT development projects, therefore, requirements have to be elicited incrementally from business users.

Estimation of Benefits

A very comprehensive analysis of benefit estimation for IT projects can be found in Nagel's work (1990). Two fundamental types of estimation approaches are differentiated:

- Single and two dimensional methods use one or two types of input variables (e.g., revenues and costs) to derive an output variable (e.g., profitability). A well-known example of this type of methods is the net present value method by which (input) net revenues at different points in time are aggregated to one (output) net present value using some discounting rate.

- Multi-dimensional methods are used to evaluate choice options regarding a set of quantitative as well as qualitative attributes. A well-known example is the multi-attribute utility analysis that is e.g. used to evaluate creditworthiness or standardized software packages.

While traditional cost estimation approaches in general do not seem to be applicable to Data Warehousing projects, most benefit estimation methods are successfully applied by companies to Data Warehousing projects. In the following section, methodological and organizational aspects of an appropriate justification approach for Data Warehousing projects are discussed, and open issues are identified.

METHODOLOGICAL AND ORGANIZATIONAL ASPECTSOF DATA WAREHOUSING PROJECT EVALUATION

Whatever the method is that is used to estimate project costs or project benefits, it is important that those persons and/or organizational units are involved in the project justification that own the management processes or operational processes that have to be supported. The involvement of process owners is not only important because application benefits can be estimated most precisely by business experts, but also because project commitment is much higher when being involved in early project stages.

In addition, it has proven to be useful to document results from a first, rough-cut requirements analysis together with cost and benefit estimations by means of a business case (Ewen, Levan-Shultz, Medsker, Smith, Dusterhoff and Gottschall, 1998). Business cases are not only used as a basis for investment decisions, but can also be used for project controlling purposes.

Estimation of Costs

Regardless of the type of application supported by the Data Warehouse, cost estimations for Data Warehousing projects should by guided by the following rules:

- Like the development project itself, cost estimations should be decomposed into clear modules ("components" or "increments," cf. (Jung and Winter, 2000, 15 ff.)).
- If analogies to similar projects in the respective company cannot be used to derive cost estimations, external consultants with large practice databases should be brought in.

The following Data Warehousing project component types can be differentiated:

1) Decision support applications (e.g., a Controlling Data Mart) and horizontal operational applications (e.g., a Customer Relationship Management application);

2) Core Data Warehouse including interfaces to vertical operational applications; and

3) Meta data management system.

Since components of type (1) are linked to management and operational processes, respectively, they create both costs and added-value. In contrast, components of type (2) and (3) have to be considered as infrastructural components which create costs, but no direct added-value. Costs for infrastructural components should either be regarded as (IT) overhead costs or should be apportioned and assigned to components of type (1) corresponding to their respective infrastructure utilization (which can be measured, e.g., by total data consumption).

Estimation of Benefits

In his general analysis of IT project benefits, Nagel (1990) differentiates "cost reduction," "productivity/quality gain," and "competitive advantage" as basic benefit categories. While cost reductions can be calculated, quantitative effects of productivity and quality gains can only be estimated. Quantitative effects of competitive advantages can neither be calculated nor estimated so that respective decisions have to be based on personal judgement. Benefits of Data Warehousing projects can be structured in a similar way. While direct operational benefits by supporting horizontal operational applications can be calculated (e.g., reduced amount of parallel mailings to the same customer), estimated (e.g., increased response rates to individualized marketing campaigns), or decided (e.g., higher customer intimacy), benefits by supporting decision support applications may only be estimated (e.g., higher customer retention by churn management) or decided (e.g., consistent corporate reporting).

Figure 3: Application Type vs. Evaluation Procedure

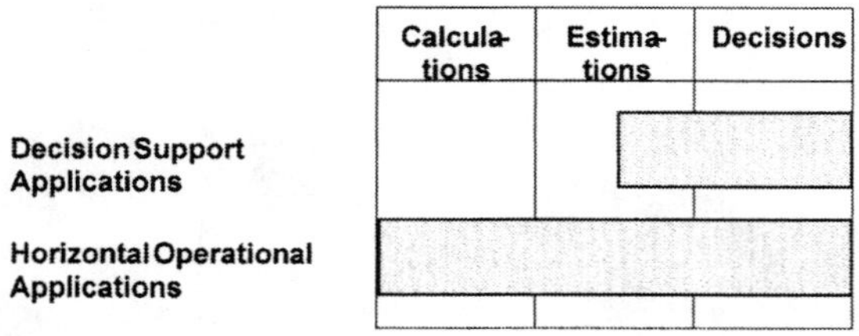

CONCLUSIONS

While their actual applicability depends on the type of supported applications, benefit estimation approaches are applicable to Data Warehousing projects in principle. Large-scale cost estimation approaches proposed for traditional IT projects, however, should not be applied to Data Warehousing projects. Our recommendation is to decompose Data Warehousing projects and use adapted cost estimation methods for estimating project component costs instead.

After all, the organization of Data Warehousing project justification seems to be even more important than the particular methods in use: Table 1 assigns the most important steps of project justification to the dominant organizational roles "IT" and "business sponsor." The division of responsibilities between IT and business sponsors has not only led to a more precise benefit estimation by business experts, but has also created a higher commitment by the business side for project critical tasks like requirements analysis, meta data elicitation, and systems utilization.

Table 1: Organizational Responsibilities for Data Warehouse Project Justification Steps

| Step | Responsibility | |
	IT	Business Sponsor
1. Identification of business sponsor, creation of commitment of business sponsor	✓	
2. Analysis of decision processes, demonstration of Data Warehousing potentials	✓	
3. Definition of application scope		✓
4. Benefit estimation		✓
5. Cost estimation	✓	
6. Putting together the Business Case (including results from steps 3 through 5	✓	✓
7. Aggregation of benefit and cost estimations, final decision		✓

ACKNOWLEDGEMENTS

This chapter is a result of the Competence Center "Data Warehousing Strategy" (CC DWS). CC DWS was founded at the University of St.Gallen, Switzerland, in January 1999, and it was a joint, two-year research project of the Institute of Information Management and ten large German and Swiss companies from the insurance, logistics, telecommunications and consulting industry, and the Swiss department of defense. The project is being continued as Competence Center "Data Warehousing 2" (CC DW2; datawarehouse.iwi.unisg.ch).

REFERENCES

Baumoel, U. (1999). *The Application of Target Costing to Software Development*, Vahlen: Munich (in German).

Ewen, E.F., Levan-Shultz, K., Medsker, C.E., Smith, J.L., Dusterhoff, L.E., and Gottschall, M.A. (1998). Data Warehousing in an Integrated Health System; Building the Business Case, In *Proc. ACM First International Workshop on Data Warehousing and OLAP* (DOLAP'98).

Helfert, M. (2000). *An empirical investigation of data warehousing research issues from the industrie's perspective*, Research Report BE HSG/CC DWS/05, University of St.Gallen. Available at http://datawarehouse.iwi.unisg.ch/arbeitsberichte.htm (in German).

Imhoff, C. (2000). The Corporate Information Factory, *DM Review*, December 1999, http://www.datawarehouse.com/dmreview, downloaded 03-29.

Jung, R. (1998). *Reverse Engineering of Conceptual Data Schemas*, Deutscher Universitaets Verlag: Wiesbaden (in German).

Jung, R., and Winter, R. (2000). Data Warehousing – Application, Reference Architecture and Process Model, In Jung, R., and Winter, R. (Eds.): *Data Warehousing Strategie*; Springer, Berlin et al., pp. 3-21 (in German).

McKnight, W. (1999). Data Warehouse Justification and ROI, *DM Review*, November 1999, http://www.datawarehouse.com/dmreview, downloaded 12-08.

Nagel, K. (1990). *Benefits of Information Processing*, 2nd edition, Oldenbourg: Munich (in German).

O'Donnell, J.H., and Sanders G.L. (2000). *Is Data Warehousing Increasing Your Firm's Value?*, *Journal of Data Warehousing*, 5(1), pp. 24-29.

Thomason, P. (1999). *ERP and Data Warehousing: The Cost of Ownership debate*, One Concept White Paper, October 1998; http://www.one-concept.com, downloaded 12-08.

Watson, H., and Haley, B. (1998). Managerial Considerations, *Communications of the ACM*, 41(9), pp. 32-37.

Winter, R. (2000). *The Current and Future Role of Data Warehousing in Corporate Application Architecture*, Research Report BE HSG/CC DWS, University of St.Gallen; available at http://www.iwi.unisg.ch/publications.

Chapter 13

A Survey of Spatial Data Mining Methods Databases and Statistics Point of Views

Karine Zeitouni
PRiSM Laboratory
University of Versailles

This chapter reviews the data mining methods that are combined with Geographic Information Systems (GIS) for carrying out spatial analysis of geographic data. We will first look at data mining functions as applied to such data and then highlight their specificity compared with their application to classical data. We will go on to describe the research that is currently going on in this area, pointing out that there are two approaches: the first comes from learning on spatial databases, while the second is based on spatial statistics. We will conclude by discussing the main differences between these two approaches and the elements they have in common.

INTRODUCTION

The growing production of maps is generating huge volumes of data that exceed people's capacity to analyze them. It thus seems appropriate to apply knowledge discovery methods like data mining to spatial data. This recent technology is an extension of the data mining applied to alphanumerical data on spatial data. The main difference is that spatial analysis must take into account spatial relations between objects.

The applications covered by spatial data mining are decisional ones, such as geomarketing, environmental studies, risk analysis, and so on. For example, in geomarketing, a store can establish its trade area, i.e., the spatial extent of its

Previously Published in *Challenges of Information Technology Management in the 21st Century,* edited by Mehdi Khosrow-Pour, Copyright © 2000, Idea Group Publishing.

customers, and then analyze the profile of those customers on the basis of both their properties and the properties related to the area where they live.

In our project, spatial data mining is applied to traffic risk analysis (Zeitouni, 1998). The risk estimation is based on the information on the previous injury accidents, combined to thematic data relating to the road network, population, buildings, and so on. The project aims at identifying regions with a high level of risk and analyzing and explaining those risks with respect to the geographic neighborhood. Spatial data mining technology specifically allows for those neighborhood relationships.

Nowadays, data analysis in geography is essentially based on traditional statistics and multidimensional data analysis and does not take account of spatial data (Sanders, 1989). Yet the main specificity of geographic data is that observations located near to one another in space tend to share similar (or correlated) attribute values. This constitutes the fundamental of a distinct scientific area called "spatial statistics" which, unlike traditional statistics, supposes inter-dependence of nearby observations. An abundant bibliography exists in this area, including well-known geostatistics, recent developments in Exploratory Spatial Data Analysis (ESDA) by Anselin and Geographical Analysis Machine (GAM) by Openshaw. For a summary, refer to Part 1.c of (Longley, Goodchild, Maguire, and Rhind, 1999). Multi-dimensional analytical methods have been extended to support contiguity (Lebart, 1984 & 1997). We maintain that spatial statistics is a part of spatial data mining, since it provides data-driven analyses. Some of those methods are now implemented in operational GIS or analysis tools.

In the field of databases, two main teams have contributed to developing data mining for spatial data analysis. The first one, DB Research Lab (Simon Fraser University, Vancouver), developed GeoMiner (Lu, Han and Ooi, 1993), which is an extension of DBMiner. The second one (Munich University) devised a structure-of-neighborhood graph (Ester, Kriegel, Sander and Xu, 1997), on which some algorithms are based. They have also worked on a clustering method based on a hierarchical partitioning (extension of DBSCAN with a R*Tree), classification (extension of ID3 and DBLearn), association rules (based upon an efficient spatial join), characterization and spatial trends. STING (University of California) uses a hierarchical grid to perform optimization on the clustering algorithm (Wang, Yang and Muntz, 1997). We might also mention work on Datawarehouse dedicated to spatial data (University of Laval) (Bedard, Lam, Proulx, Caron and Letourneau, 1997).

This chapter will describe data mining methods for Geographic Information Systems and highlight their value in performing spatial data analysis. It will survey both statistical approaches and those involving inference from databases.

It is structured as follows. In the next section, we define spatial data mining and subdivide it into generic tasks. Then in following section, we classify spatial data mining methods, whether drawn from the realm of databases, statistics or artificial intelligence, in terms of these different tasks. We go on to compare the statistical analysis approach with the spatial database approach, with the aim of emphasizing their similarities and complementarity. Lastly, we conclude and discuss research issues.

DEFINITION OF SPATIAL DATA MINING

Spatial data mining (SDM) consists of extracting knowledge, spatial relationships and any other properties which are not explicitly stored in the database. SDM is used to find implicit regularities, relations between spatial data and/or non-spatial data.

The specificity of SDM lies in its interaction in space. In effect, a geographical database constitutes a spatio-temporal continuum in which properties concerning a particular place are generally linked and explained in terms of the properties of its neighborhood. We can thus see the great importance of spatial relationships in the analysis process. Temporal aspects for spatial data are also a central point but are rarely taken into account.

Data mining methods (Fayyad et al., 1996) are not suited to spatial data because they do not support location data nor the implicit relationships between objects. Hence, it is necessary to develop new methods including spatial relationships and spatial data handling. Calculating these spatial relationships is time consuming, and a huge volume of data is generated by encoding geometric location. Global performances will suffer from this complexity.

Using GIS, the user can query spatial data and perform simple analytical tasks using programs or queries. However, GIS are not designed to perform complex data analysis or knowledge discovery. They do not provide generic methods for carrying out analysis and inferring rules.

Nevertheless, it seems necessary to integrate these existing methods and to extend them by incorporating spatial data mining methods. GIS methods are crucial for data access, spatial joins and graphical map display. Conventional data mining can only generate knowledge about alphanumerical properties.

SPATIAL DATA MINING TASKS

As shown in Table 1, spatial data mining tasks are generally an extension of data mining tasks in which spatial data and criteria are combined. These tasks aim to: (1) summarize data, (2) find classification rules, (3) make clusters of similar objects, (4) find associations and dependencies to characterize data, and (5) detect deviations after looking for general trends. They are carried out using different methods, some of which are derived from statistics and others from the field of machine learning.

The rest of this section is devoted to describing data mining tasks that are dedicated to GIS.

Spatial data summarization

The main goal is to describe data in a global way, which can be done in several ways. One involves extending statistical methods such as variance or factorial analysis to spatial structures. Another entails applying the generalization method to spatial data.

Statistical analysis of contiguous objects

Global autocorrelation

The most common way of summarizing a dataset is to apply elementary statistics, such as the calculation of average, variance, etc., and graphic tools like histograms and pie charts. New methods have been developed for measuring neighborhood dependency at a global level, such as local variance and local covariance, spatial auto-correlation by Geary, and Moran indices (Geary; Moran, 1948).

These methods are based on the notion of a contiguity matrix that represents the spatial relationships between objects. It should be noted that this contiguity can correspond to different spatial relationships, such as adjacency, a distance gap, and so on.

Table 1: Comparison between statistical and machine learning approaches to SDM

SDM Tasks	Statistics	Machine Learning
Summarization	Global autocorrelation Density analysis Smooth & contrast analysis Factorial analysis	Generalization Characteristic rules
Class identification	Spatial classification	Decision trees
Clustering	Point pattern analysis	Geometric clustering
Dependencies	Local autocorrelation Correspondence analysis	Association rules
Trends & deviations	Kriging	Trend rules

Density analysis

This method forms part of Exploratory Spatial Data Analysis (ESDA) which, contrary to the autocorrelation measure, does not require any knowledge about data. The idea is to estimate the density by computing the intensity of each small circle window on the space and then to visualize the point pattern. It could be described as a graphical method.

Smooth, contrast and factorial analysis

In density analysis, non-spatial properties are ignored. Geographic data analysis is usually concerned with both alphanumerical properties (called attributes) and spatial data. This requires two things: integrating spatial data with attributes in the analysis process, and using multidimensional data to analyze multiple attributes.

To integrate the spatial neighborhood into attributes, two techniques exist that modify attribute values using the contiguity matrix. The first technique performs a smoothing by replacing each attribute value by the average value of its neighbors. This highlights the general characteristics of the data. The other contrasts data by subtracting this average from each value.

Each attribute (called variable) in statistics can then be analyzed using conventional methods. However, when multiple attributes (above tree) have to be analyzed together, multidimensional data analysis methods (i.e., factorial analysis) become necessary (Lebart, 1984). Their principle is to reduce the number of variables by looking for the factorial axes where there is maximum spreading of data values. By projecting and visualizing the initial dataset on those axes, the correlation or dependencies between properties can be deduced.

In statistics and especially in the above methods, the analyzed objects were originally considered to be independent. The need to look at spatial organization spawned several research studies (Benali and Escofier, 1990; Lebart, 1984). The extension of factorial analysis methods to contiguous objects entails applying common Principal Component Analysis or Correspondence Analysis methods once the original table is transformed using smoothing or contrasting techniques.

Generalization

This method consists of raising the abstract level of non-spatial attributes and reducing the detail of geometric description by merging adjacent objects. It is derived from the concept of attribute-oriented induction as described in (Lu et al., 1993). Here, a concept hierarchy can be spatial (like the hierarchy of administrative boundaries) or non-spatial (thematic) (Han, Cai and Cerone, 1992). An example of thematic hierarchy in agriculture can be represented as follows: "cultivation type (food (cereals (maize, wheat, rice), vegetable, fruit, other))". That kind of hierarchy can be directly introduced by an expert in the field or generated by an inference process related to the attribute. A spatial hierarchy may preexist, like the administrative boundaries one, or it may be based on an artificial geometric splitting like a quad-tree (Samet, 1990), or it may result from a spatial clustering.

There are two kinds of generalization: non-spatial dominant generalization, where we first use a thematic hierarchy and then merge adjacent objects; and spatial dominant generalization, which is based on a spatial hierarchy to begin with, followed by the aggregation or generalization of non-spatial values for each generalized spatial value. The complexity of the corresponding algorithms is O(NlogN), where N is the number of actual objects.

This approach could be treated as a first step towards a method of inferring rules, such as association rules or comparison rules.

Characteristic rules

The characterization of a selected part of the database has been defined in Ester, Frommelt, Kriegel and Sander (1998) as the description of properties that are typical for the part in question but not for the whole database. In the case of a spatial database, it takes account not only of the properties of objects, but also of the properties of their neighborhood up to a given level.

Consider a subset S of objects to analyze. This method uses the following parameters: 1) significance (relative frequency to the database in S); 2) confidence (ratio of objects in S which satisfy the significance threshold in the neighborhood) ; and 3) the maximum extension max-neighbors to the neighbors. This method throws up the properties $pi = (attribute, value)$, the relative frequency factors *freq-fac i* (higher than the significance parameter) and the number *ni* of neighbors on which the frequency of the property is extended. The characterization can be expressed by the following rule:

   $S\ p\ 1\ (n\ 1\ ,freq\text{-}fac\ 1\ )\ ...\ p\ k\ (n\ k\ ,freq\text{-}\ fac\ k\ ).$

Class identification

This task, also called supervised classification, provides a logical description that yields the best partitioning of the database. Classification rules constitute a decision tree where each node contains a criterion on an attribute. The difference in spatial databases is that this criterion could be a spatial predicate and, because spatial objects are dependent on neighborhood, a rule involving the non-spatial properties of an object should be extended to neighborhood properties.

In spatial statistics, classification has essentially served to analyze remotely-sensed data, and aims to identify each pixel with a particular category. Homogeneous pixels are then aggregated in order to form a geographic entity (Longley et al., 1999).

In the spatial database approach (Ester, Kriegel and Sander, 1997), classification is seen as an arrangement of objects using both their properties (non-spatial values) and their neighbors' properties, not only for direct neighbors but also for the neighbors of neighbors and so on, up to degree N. Let us take as an example the classification of areas by their economic power. Classification rules are described as follows:

High population ^ neighbor = road ^ neighbor of neighbor = airport =>
high economic power (95%).

In GeoMiner, a classification criterion can also be related to a spatial attribute, in which case it reflects its inclusion in a wider zone. These zones could be determined by the algorithm, whether by clustering or by merging adjacent objects, or it could arise from a predefined spatial hierarchy.

A new algorithm (Koperski, Han, Stefanovi, 1998) extends this classification method in GeoMiner to spatial predicates. For example, to determine high level wholesale profits, a decision factor can be the proximity to densely populated districts.

Clustering

This task is an automatic or unsupervised classification that yields a partition of a given dataset depending on a similarity function.

Database approach

Paradoxically, clustering methods for spatial databases do not appear to be very revolutionary compared with those applied to relational databases (automatic classification). The clustering is performed using a similarity function which was already classed as a semantic distance. Hence, in spatial databases it appears natural to use the Euclidean distance in order to group neighboring objects. Research studies have focused on the optimization of algorithms. Geometric clustering generates new classes, such as the location of houses in terms of residential areas. This stage is often performed before other data mining tasks, such as association detection between groups or other geographic entities, or characterization of a group.

GeoMiner combines geometric clustering applied to a point set distribution with generalization based on non-spatial attributes. For example, we may want to characterize groups of major cities in the United States and see how they are grouped. Cluster results will be represented by new areas, which correspond to the convex hull of a group of towns. A few points could stay outside clusters and represent noise. A description of each group may be generated for each attribute specified.

Many algorithms have been proposed for performing clustering, such as CLARANS (Ng and Han, 1994), DBSCAN (Ester, Kriegel, Sander and Xu, 1997) or STING (Wang et al., 1997). They usually focus on cost optimization. Recently, a method that is more specifically applicable to spatial data, GDBSCAN, was outlined in (Knorr and Ng, 1996). It applies to any spatial shape, not only to points data, and incorporates attributes data.

Statistic approach

Clustering arises from point pattern analysis (Fotheringham and Zhan, 1996; Openshaw, Charlton, Wymer and Craft, 1987) and was mainly applied to epidemiological research. This is implemented in Openshaw's well-known Geographical Analysis Machine (GAM) and could be tested by using the K-function (Diggle, 1993). The clusters could also be detected by the ratio of two density estimates: one of the studied subset and the other of the whole reference dataset.

Spatial data dependencies

One way to reflect how data are related is the local autocorrelation method. The other typical for data mining yields association rules and has been adapted to spatial data.

Local autocorrelation

Local auto-correlation is concerned with the assessment of the degree of spatial dependence using the notion of spatial weight matrix (Cliff & Ord, 1973; Ord & Getis, 1992, 1995). This makes it possible to measure the difference between the actual spatial distribution of variable values and a random one. Thus, it is equivalent to a residual test in regression analysis. When the matrix consists of one column, association is sought between one point and all the others.

Association rules

This method is well known in data mining and is applied to market analysis by looking for items that are frequently associated in a commercial transaction (Fayyad et al., 1996). It has been extended to deal with spatial data to express rules like:

$A_1 {}^\wedge A_2 ... {}^\wedge A_m \wedge$ *Spatial Relations* $=> B_1 {}^\wedge ... {}^\wedge B_n \wedge$ *Spatial Relations [s, c]*

where Ai and Bj are predicates like attribute=constant_value , s is the rule support and c the rule confidence. These rules are used to find associations between properties of objects and those of neighboring objects.

For example, the rule :

is_a (x, gas_station) $^\wedge$ *within (x, rural_area) -> close_to (x, highway) [65%, 80%]*

expresses the fact that gas stations that are located in rural areas are also close to highways at 80% and represent the majority (65%) of gas stations near highways.

Searching for association rules can involve the whole spatial database, as for example: "What kind of spatial objects are close to each other in California ?" with object types such as towns, forests, hydrology, roads, etc. The result is expressed by rules like:

is_a (x, big_town) $^\wedge$ *intersect (x, highway)* $\varnothing$ *adjacent_to (x, river). [7%, 85%]*

The main difficulty is to determine spatial relationships efficiently. The algorithm proposed in GeoMiner uses a concept of generalized predicates enabling spatial predicates to be evaluated in two phases (Koperski, 1999; Koperski & Han, 1995). The first one performs an approximate test and generates candidates for performing an exact test of this spatial predicate in the second phase.

Extension to multi-level association rules

These associations can be generalized or detailed for forming a hierarchy of concepts. Spatial hierarchies or a conceptual hierarchy of attributes are refined or aggregated (like the subdivision into regions, then departments and municipalities). In relational databases, a current method entails aggregating classes of objects before looking for association rules in order to generate more general and relevant rules. An example of hierarchical association in a spatial database is to express the fact that 64 percent of houses are about 500 meters from schools, two-thirds of which are primary schools and one-third secondary, or high, schools.

Group proximity rules

Suppose we have a cluster containing groups of private houses. The user wants to express the fact that the location of these groups is defined by the nearest particular spatial objects. For example, we can determine that 65 per cent of these houses are close to lakes, beaches or mountains.

Knorr and Ng (1996) propose a variation of association rules. The principle of this method is to discover the classes of objects which are frequently close to predefined groups. An algorithm CRH is used to make an efficient computation of the proximity of an object to a group (for example, aggregating the distances between this object and all the points in the group). Then another algorithm, called GenCom, is used to deduce the proximity rules and combine them with generalized attributes when a hierarchy of concepts is known.

Trend and Deviation Analysis

In relational databases, this analysis is applied to temporal sequences. In spatial databases, we want to find and characterize spatial trends.

Database approach

Using the process described in Ester et al. (1997), which is based on the central places theory, the analysis is performed in four stages. The first one involves discovering centers by computing local maxima of particular attributes; in the second, the theoretical trend of these attributes is determined by moving away from the centers; the third stage determines the deviations in relation to these trends; and finally, we explain these trends by analyzing the properties of these zones. One example is the trend analysis of the unemployment rate in comparison with the distance to a metropolis like Munich. Another example is the trend analysis of the development of house construction.

Geostatistical approach

Geostatistics is a tool used for spatial analysis and for the prediction of spatio-temporal phenomena. It was first used for geological applications (the geo prefix comes from geology). Nowadays, geostatistics encompasses a class of techniques used to analyze and predict the unknown values of variables distributed in space and/or time. These values are supposed to be connected to the environment. The study of such a correlation is called structural analysis. The prediction of location values outside the sample is then performed by the "kriging" technique (Isobel, 1987).

It is important to remember that geostastics is limited to point set analysis or polygonal subdivisions and deals with a unique variable or attributes. Under those conditions, it constitutes a good tool for spatial and spatio-temporal trend analysis.

COMPARISON OF SDM APPROACHES

One interest of this study is to bring together the whole body of research relating to the analysis and extraction of spatial data. The research was carried out either in the field of statistics, or in the field of database learning, but most of the time they ignored each other. One thus has to be able to compare and analyze them with the same analytical goal. After classifying them by task and distinguishing between the different methods arising from these two approaches, this section will seek to make a comparison of all these methods and identify the points they have in common. Here is a résumé:

Graphical methods and semantic methods

Some methods are based solely on the graphical aspect of the data, as in the exploratory analysis of spatial data (density and relative cluster). The result is often visual.

Others utilize a semantic representation of spatial relations such as graphs and neighbor matrices. Apart from clustering, which remains a graphical method, most of the methods derived from the database approach fall into this category. In the statistical approach, one may describe auto-correlation tests, smoothing, and smoothed or contrasted factorial analysis as semantic methods.

Taking account of contiguity

There are substantial differences in the use of neighborhood semantics. In the learning approach, spatial relationships are clearly represented, as though it were a question of properties in their own right. Conversely, in the statistical approach these neighborhood relationships are either integrated in formulas, as in the case of auto-correlation, or used to rectify the initial data, as in smoothed analysis.

Furthermore, in the statistical approach, these relationships are exclusively intra-thematic, which is to say among objects of the same theme, whereas they can also be inter-thematic (between several layers) in the learning approach. This is important, especially in an explanatory model where surrounding objects may intervene, whatever the theme. As an example, rainfall and population density layers are highly correlated.

Inter-thematic relationships are retrieved using joint operators with various spatial criteria. Since these operators are complex and time consuming, one needs to try and optimize them (Gunther, 1990; Yeh, 1999).

Interpretation

In addition, the learning approach, like generalization, enables the data to be summarized and synthesized by aggregating them and combining their geographic locations. This approach generates classifications with very little intervention on the part of the user and produces association rules that non-specialists can understand.

Graphical methods forming part of exploratory analysis offer a very high degree of readability and require relatively little knowledge to use them.

As for factorial analysis, it also synthesizes the data, but, contrary to generalization, it does not reduce the number of objects, which may be a handicap for large amounts of data. The result may be of great interest for an enlightened user of these techniques who is capable of interpreting them, but not for a neophyte in data analysis.

Complementarity

These differences result in a degree of complementarity that is extremely valuable from an analytical viewpoint. For example, a generalization phase would enable the data to be reduced and simplified in order to prepare them for smoothed or contrasted factorial analysis.

It would also be interesting to undertake generalization prior to characterization, the search for associations or classification rules. Similarly, characterization or the search for associations may be used to explain a localized concentration.

Another approach is that described in (Sander et al., 1998). It would entail carrying out a density analysis to find centers, then contrasting the real trend with a theoretical trend in order to detect deviations, and finally looking for properties that are characteristic of the places of these deviations.

CONCLUSION AND RESEARCH ISSUES

Different methods of data mining in spatial databases have been outlined in this chapter, which has shown that these methods have been developed by two very separate research communities: the Statistics community and the Database community.

We have summarized and classified this research and compared the two approaches, emphasizing the particular utility of each method and the possible advantages of combining them. This work constitutes a first step towards a methodology incorporating the whole process of knowledge discovery in spatial databases and allowing the combination of the above data mining techniques.

Among the other issues in the area of spatial data mining, one approach is to consider the temporality of spatial data, while another is to see how linear or network shape (like roads) can have a particular influence on graphical methods. In any event, it remains essential to continue enhancing the performance of these techniques. One reason is the enormous volumes of data involved, another is the intensive use of spatial proximity relationships. In the case of graphical methods, these relationships could be optimized using spatial indexes. In regards to the other methods that use neighborhood structures, instanciation of the structure is costly and should be pre-computed as far as possible.

ACKNOWLEDGEMENTS

This research forms part of a national PSIG project of the CASSINI network, dealing with the traffic risk analysis. My thanks to the participants in this project and especially to Sylvain Lassarre from INRETS (the French national institute for transport and safety research) and Florence Richard from the THEMA laboratory for their contribution to this study.

REFERENCES

Bédard, Y., Lam, S., Proulx, M.J., Caron, P.Y., and Létourneau, F. (1997). Data Warehousing for Spatial Data: Research Issues, *Proceedings of the International Symposium Geomatics in the Era of Radarsat (GER'97)*, Ottawa, May, pp. 25-30.

Benali, H., and Escofier, B. (1990). Analyse factorielle lissée et analyse factorielle des différences locales, *Revue Statistique Appliquée, XXXVIII* (2), pp 55-76.

Cliff, A.D., and Ord, J.K. (1973). *Spatial autocorrelation*, Pion, London.

Diggle, P.J. (1993). Point process modeling in environmental epidemiology. In Barnett V., and Turkman K. (Eds), *Statistics for the Environment*, Chichester, John Wiley & Sons, pp 89-110.

Ester, M., Frommelt, A., Kriegel, H.-P., and Sander, J. (1998). Algorithms for Characterization and Trend Detection in Spatial Databases, *Proc. 4th Int. Conf. on Knowledge Discovery and Data Mining*, New York, NY.

Ester, M., Kriegel ,H.-P., Sander, J., and Xu, X. (1997). Density-Connected Sets and their Application for Trend Detection in Spatial Databases, *Proc. 3rd Int. Conf. on Knowledge Discovery and Data Mining*, Newport Beach, CA, pp. 10-15.

Ester, M., Kriegel, H.-P., and Sander, J. (1997). Spatial Data Mining: A Database Approach, *Proc. 5th Symp. on Spatial Databases*, Berlin, Germany.

Fayyad et al. (1996). *Advances in Knowledge Discovery and Data Mining*, AAAI Press / MIT Press.

Fotheringham, S., and Zhan, B. (1996). A comparison of three exploratory methods for cluster detection in spatial point patterns, *Geographical Analysis*, Vol. 28, n° 3, pp. 200-218.

Gatrell, A., Bailey, T., Diggle, P., and Rowlingson, B. (1996). Spatial point pattern analysis and its application in geographical epidemiology, *Transactions of the Institute of British Geographers*, n° 21, pp. 256-274.

Geary, R.C. The contiguity ratio and statistical mapping, *The Incorporated Statistician*, 5 (3), pp 115-145.

Gunther, O. (1990). Efficient Computation of Spatial Joins, *Proc of Data Engineering*, Vienna, Austria, April, pp. 50-59.

Han J., Cai, Y. & Cerone, N. (1992). Knowledge Discovery in Databases; An Attribute-Oriented Approach. *Proceedings of the 18th VLDB Conference*. Vancouver, B.C., August, pp. 547-559.

Isobel, C. (1987). Practical geostatistics, Applied Science Publisher, Reprinted. Also at URL: <http://curie.ej.jrc.it/faq/introduction.html>

Knorr, E. M., and Ng, R. T. (1996). Finding Aggregate Proximity Relationships and Commonalities in Spatial Data Mining, *IEEE Transactions in Knowledge and Data Engineering*, Vol 8(6), December.

Koperski, K. (1999). A Progressive Refinement Approach to Spatial Data Mining', PhD Thesis, the School of Computing Science, Simon Fraser University, April.

Koperski, K. and Han, J. (1995). Discovery of Spatial Association Rules in Geographic Information Databases, In *Advances in Spatial Databases* (SSD'95), pp. 47-66, Portland, ME, August.

Koperski, K., Han, J., and Stefanovic, N. (1988). An Efficient Two-Step Method for Classification of Spatial Data, In Proc. International Symposium on Spatial Data Handling (SDH'98) , pp. 45-54, Vancouver, Canada, July.

Lebart L. et al. (1997). Statistique exploratoire multidimensionnelle, Editions Dunod, Paris, 439 p.

Lebart, L. (1984). Correspondence analysis of graph structure. Bulletin technique du CESIA, Paris:2, 1-2, pp 5-19.

Longley P. A., Goodchild M. F., Maguire D. J., and Rhind D. W. (1999). *Geographical Information Systems - Principles and Technical Issues*, John Wiley & Sons, Inc., Second Edition

Lu, W., Han, J. and Ooi, B. (1993). Discovery of General Knowledge in Large Spatial Databases, In *Proc. of 1993 Far East Workshop on Geographic Information Systems (FEGIS'93)*, Singapore, June, pp. 275-289.

Mathsoft Inc. (1988). S-Plus for ArcView GIS - Users Guide Version 1.0 and S-Plus Spatial Stat., Data Analysis Products Division, Seattle, Washington, April.

Moran, P.A.P. (1948). The interpretation of statistical maps, *Journal of the Royal Statistical Society*, B: 10, pp 234-251.

Ng, R. and Han, J. (1994). Efficient and Effective Clustering Method for Spatial Data Mining, In *Proc. of 1994 Int'l Conf. on Very Large Data Bases (VLDB'94)*, Santiago, Chile, September, pp. 144-155.

Openshaw, S., Charlton, M., Wymer, C., and Craft, A. (1987) A mark 1 geographical analysis machine for the automated analysis of point data sets, *International Journal of Geographical Information Systems*, Vol. 1, n° 4, pp. 335-358.

Ord, J.K., and Getis, A. (1992). The Analysis of Spatial Association by Use of Distance Statistics, *Geographical Analysis*, Ohio State University Press, Vol. 24, n° 3, pp. 189-206.

Ord, J.K., and Getis, A. (1995). Local Spatial Autocorrelation Statistics : Distributional Issues and an Application, Geographical Analysis, Ohio State University Press, Vol. 27, n° 4, pp. 287-306.

Samet, H. (1990). *Design and Analysis of Spatial Data Structures: Hierarchical (quadtree and octree) data structures*, Addison-Wesley Edition.

Sander, J., Ester M., Kriegel H.P., and Xu X. (1988). Density-Based Clustering in Spatial Databases: The Algorithm GDBSCAN and its Applications, In *Data Mining an Knowledge Discovery, An International Journal*, Kluwer Academic Publishers, Vol. 2 (2).

Sanders, L. (1989). L'analyse statistique des données en géographie, GIP Reclus.

Wang, W., Yang, J., and Muntz, R. (1997). STING : A Statistical Information Grid Approach to Spatial Data Mining, Technical Report CSD-97006, Computer Science Department, University of California, Los Angeles, February.

Yeh T. S. (1999). Spot: Distance based join indices for spatial data, *ACM GIS 99*, Kansass City, 5-6 November.

Zeitouni, K. (1998). Etude de l'application du data mining à l'analyse spatiale du risque d'accidents routiers par l'exploration des bases de données en accidentologie, Final report of the contract PRISM -INRETS, December, p.33.

Chapter 14

Efficient Query Processing with Structural Join Indexing in an Object Relational Data Warehousing Environment*

Vivekanand Gopalkrishnan and Qing Li
City University of Hong Kong

Kamalakar Karlapalem
University of Science and Technology, Hong Kong

In an Object Relational Data Warehousing (ORDW) environment, the semantics of data and queries can be explicitly captured, represented, and utilized based on is-a and class composition hierarchies, thereby resulting in more efficient OLAP query processing. In this chapter, we show the efficacy in building semantic-rich hybrid data indexes incorporating Structural Join Index Hierarchy (SJIH) on the ORDW views. Given a set of queries, we use a hill-climbing heuristic algorithm to select (near) optimal SJIHs, thereby embedding query semantics into the indexing framework. Finally, by a cost model, we analyze the effectiveness of our approach vis-a-vis the pointer chasing approach.

INTRODUCTION

Data warehouse (DW) equips users with more effective decision support tools by integrating enterprise-wide corporate data into a single repository from which business end-users can run reports and perform ad hoc data analysis (Chaudhuri and Dayal, 1997). As DWs contain enormous amount of data, often from different sources, we need highly efficient Indexing structures (Sarawagi, 1997; Gupta, Harinarayanan, Rajaraman and Ullman, 1997), materialized (stored) Views (Roussopoulos, 1997), and query processing techniques (Gopalkrishnan and

Previously Published in *Challenges of Information Technology Management in the 21st Century,* edited by Mehdi Khosrow-Pour, Copyright © 2000, Idea Group Publishing.

Karlapalem, 1999) to efficiently answer *on-line analytical processing (OLAP)* queries. Materialized Views represent integrated data based on complex aggregate queries, and should be available consistently and instantaneously. Maintaining the integrity of these Indexes and Views (Mohania and Kambayashi, 1999) imposes a challenging problem when the source data changes frequently, when the size of the DW keeps growing, and/or when the user queries become more and more complex. An extensible framework that can accommodate *dynamic warehousing* (Dayal, 1999) of changing data gracefully, and have adaptive handles for processing OLAP queries efficiently is needed.

In Gopalkrishnan, Li and Karlapalem (1998), we showed that besides establishing a semantically richer framework for multi-dimension hierarchies, the Object Relational View (ORV) model provides excellent support for complex object retrieval. In Gopalkrishnan et al. (1999), we presented the Object Relational Data Warehousing (ORDW) approach to address some of the issues discussed in Gopalkrishnan et al. (1998) on data warehousing. More specifically, we devised a translation mechanism from the star/snowflake schema to an object oriented (O-O) representation. In particular, we have also studied some query processing strategies utilizing vertical partitioning (Karlapalem and Li, 1998) and SJIH indexing techniques (Fung, Karlapalem and Li, 1998) for complex queries on complex objects.

In this chapter, we show the efficiency of building semantic-rich hybrid data indexes incorporating Structural Join Index Hierarchy (SJIH) on the ORDW views. Given a set of queries, we run a hill-climbing heuristic algorithm to select (near) optimal SJIHs, thereby embedding query semantics into the indexing framework. Finally, by a cost model, we analyze the effectiveness of our approach vis-a-vis some other existing techniques.

To put our research in perspective, we review some related work and briefly outline our previous work in the field of ORDW and SJIH on OODBs in the next section. We further motive our study by presenting on the ORDW schema some sample queries whose patterns are classified based on DW operations and by OO concepts. Obtaining an optimal indexing scheme to process this set of queries is the main focus of the following section, where we employ a hill-climbing heuristic algorithm to select a (near) optimal SJIHs. This algorithm is *profiling driven,* and can also be further extended to incorporate other semantics. In the section entitled, SJIH Evaluation, we compare results of retrieval costs using the SJIH versus other retrieval methods. Finally we conclude in the last section, and briefly state our future work.

BACKGROUND AND MOTIVATING EXAMPLE
Related Work

Some extensive research has been done in recent years in the field of indexing OLAP data and query optimization. (Sarawagi, 1997) provided a good survey of existing indexing methods, discussing their advantages and short comings in the realm of OLAP databases. It also proposed extensions to conventional multidimensional indexing methods to make them more suitable for indexing OLAP data. Gupta et al. (1997) studied the problem of view selection together with index selection at the same time, and provided a set of algorithms with their performance studies. O'Neil and Quass (1997) presented a family of indices to speed up queries in the read-mostly environment of data warehousing, along with their space-time tradeoffs among these indices.

Also recently, we have conducted some preliminary studies on developing an object-relational data warehouse framework. In Gopalkrishnan et al. (1998), we showed that the ORV (Object Relational View) model offers inherent features that are conducive to managing a data warehouse. We listed the various issues that arise during the design of an OR-DWMS (Object Relational Data Warehouse Management Systems). Here, OR means an object-oriented front-end or views to underlying relational data sources. Based on the issues discussed in Gopalkrishnan et al. (1998), we put forward a three phase design approach in Gopalkrishnan et al. (1999), which also provided a query-driven translation mechanism from the star/snowflake schema to an object oriented (O-O) representation. Some query processing strategies utilizing vertical partitioning and SJIH techniques for complex queries on complex objects were also identified, which are to be refined and evaluated in this paper. Additionally, Karlapalem et al. (1998) presents a framework for devising partitioning schemes based on different types of methods and their classification, including horizontal and vertical partitioning and their variants. The issue of fragmentation transparency is addressed by considering appropriate method transformation techniques. Fung et al. (1998) and Fung (1998) present the Structural Join Index Hierarchy (SJIH) cost models and selection algorithms for complex object retrieval in object oriented databases.

Motivating Query Examples

To further motivate our subsequent discussions, let us consider the sample ORDW schema as shown in Figure 1, taken from Gopalkrishnan et al. (1999). This schema is a simple single-star/snowflake schema, for a sales application. As seen in the figure, dimension tables are connected by solid arrows (composition hierarchies) to the main fact table (Sales). Also, there are other inter-dimension hierarchies (as obtained by vertical partitioning), and other composition links. More-

Figure 1: The ORDW Schema. The figure shows the class composition hierarchy for the Time dimension, and the is-a hierarchy (shaded area) for the Customer dimension.

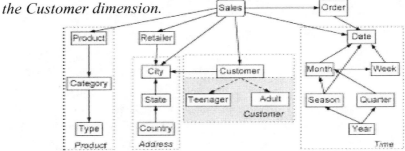

over, we also demonstrate is-a hierarchies (denoted by dotted lines) obtained by horizontally partitioning the ORDW schema.

A Fact is the "subject" of the OLAP queries, and is quantified by its dimensions and "values." Dimensions can be hierarchical and composite in nature, whereas Values are numerical data. When a Dimension is complex enough to contain various other components which can themselves be classified as Dimensions and Values, then that Dimension can be a "Fact" of another OLAP query. In this case, we can consider the schema to be that of "Nested Fact" or "Fact within Fact."

Whereas when two (or more) Facts share (one or more) Dimensions, then the OLAP queries can be considered as "Inter-Fact." To support OLAP applications, we define a group of OLAP queries *OQG*, which are invoked as a set (not necessarily in an order). Query patterns in the *OQG* may not be restricted to a particular composition hierarchy or inheritance hierarchy. The access paths may involve multiple paths emanating from the same complex object, as well as interact with entities in completely unrelated complex objects.

For this discussion, queries involving Nested Facts can be considered as subsets of inter-Fact queries. They are distinguished by the presence of a semantic disjointness between the Facts involved. It must be noted though that this

Table 1 : Sample OLAP queries - OQG

No.	Query	Query type
Q1	Sales by Prod by State	Only along **cch** (pivot)
Q2	Sales by Prod by State by Year	-> Drill-down
Q3	Sales by Prod	-> Roll-up
Q4	Sales by Prod by City	Only along **cch**, Drill-down
Q5	Sales by Prod by Country	Only along **cch**, Roll-up
Q6	Sales by Prod by Teenagers by State	Only along **cch**, Slice_and_dice
Q7	Sales of Prod **1** compared with Sales of Prod **2** to Teenagers	Only along **cch**, Drill-down, Slice_and_dice
Q8	% increase in Sales to Teenagers over Sales to Adults, of Prod **1 / 2**	Combination of **is-a** & **cch**, Drill-down, Slice_and_dice

disjointness does not preclude the Facts from sharing the same component objects. A query processing scheme based on indexing that is built on separate Facts will inadvertently need costly joins. This inefficiency is highlighted for queries with low selectivity and high frequency. This calls for a need for an indexing scheme that transcends Facts and is not restricted by the hierarchies mentioned.

Based on classifications by DW operations & by OO concepts, we consider the following queries listed in Table 1 as our sample *OQG* for subsequent discussions.

SJIH SELECTION METHODOLOGY

The Structural Join Index Hierarchy (SJIH) is a comprehensive framework for efficient complex object retrieval in both forward and reverse directions (Fung et al., 1998). It is a sequence of OIDs that provides direct access to component objects of a complex object, possibly located on different paths. We employ the SJIH on our ORDW schema, and propose to extend its applicability from class composition hierarchies to also include is-a hierarchies, thereby encompassing the Complete Warehouse Schema (CWS) in the ORDW.

SJIH cost model

The total cost of the SJIH framework can be broadly categorized as storage cost, index retrieval cost and index maintenance cost. In this chapter, we also incorporate *query-centric* information including *selectivity* to determine the selection of forward and backward paths (> 2 paths) during creation (storage) and retrieval of SJIH.

As shown in Figure 2, a sample SJIH is built on objects from first level classes C_0, C_2^1, C_1^2, and C_2^3 in the class composition hierarchy (CCH). As class C_1^2 is

Figure 2: SJIH on the Is-a & Class Composition Hierarchies

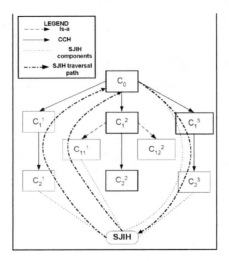

subclassed into C_{11}^2 and C_{12}^2, the SJIH now involves is-a along with CCH. The implicit link supported by the O-O system between classes and their subclasses provides the needed link from the complex object (e.g., C_0) to the specializations (e.g., C_{11}^1) of its component objects (C_1^2). Thus the SJIH can also utilize this is-a link along with the CCH links already exploited by previous work. Note here that the class composition hierarchy in this example is denoted by the superscript of the first level class, such as j in C_1^j; whereas the (sub) is-a hierarchy is denoted by the subscript (such as 11) and the superscript of the specialized class, such as C_{11}^2 and C_{12}^2.

The minimization of storage cost and index retrieval cost requires the determination of an optimum traversal path between the objects. In a case where the SJIH is based on objects belonging to p paths (p>2), one path would be traversed in the forward direction and the other (p-1) would be traversed in the reverse directions. The cost is proportional to the cardinality of the Join Index.

As shown in our *OQG*, the OLAP queries we consider in this chapter are assumed to retrieve the *subject matter*, i.e. Sales; hence the class composition hierarchy can be considered to be rooted at "Sales" or (C_0). Other queries which do not involve the "Sales" table and instead have another *subject* as the *fact*, can be considered separately as in another *star* hierarchy and/or in a *nested / multi star* hierarchy (The discussion of such nested/multi-star hierarchy queries is currently beyond the scope of this chapter).

According to the cost model defined in Fung et al. (1998), the Cardinality of a join index is given as :

$n = \|C_0\| \infty$ MF for a forward query and

$\quad \|C_i^p\| \infty$ MF for a backward query for the *i*th class in the *p*th path.

$\qquad$ where MF is the Multiplying factor.

Some important parameters affecting MF are *constraints* and *degree of sharing*. *Constrained pair-up* (between two classes C_1 and C_2), means that there are constraints on the pairing up of actual objects (between classes C_1 and C_2), in which case the SJIH involving C_1 and C_2 will contain less tuples than in the case of *unconstrained pair-up* where the objects between the two classes can be paired up freely without any constraint. *Degree of sharing* reflects the number of *composite references* between two objects of the classes. An exclusive composite reference from an object O_2 of C_2 to an object O_1 of C_1 means that O_2 is a part of only O_1; whereas a shared composite reference means that O_2 is a part of O_1 and possibly other objects.

With these in mind, the Multiplying factor has upper or lower bounds given below:

Upper bound
$$i+h-1$$
$MF = P f_k$; for a JI involving h+1 *unconstrained pair-up* classes in a path.
$$k = i$$
Lower bound
$$i+h-1$$
$MF = Max(f_k)$; for a JI involving h+1 *constrained, exclusive pair-up*
classes in a
$$k = i \quad path.$$

By including selectivity (*s*) from the query patterns and the nature of class composition hierarchy we determine the multiplying factor (MF). After that, we can determine the cost for traversing each path as :
$$n_i = s_i \infty \|C_i{}^p\| \infty MF$$
Hence fwd and bwd traversal costs can be compared and the best combination of paths can be chosen.

SJIH selection procedure

We apply the hill-climbing heuristic SJIH selection algorithm (HCHSSA) as presented in Fung et al. (1998), which was developed for finding optimal or near-optimal SJIH based on the input of database characteristics and query characteristics. This algorithm uses the concepts of *pair-ups* and is illustrated as follows:

Input : ORDW schema and *OQG* query set.

Output : Optimal or near-optimal SJIH

Step 1 : Construct the Query Graph (QG) from the ORDW Schema Graph (SG) and the query characteristics.

Step 2 : Apply branch separation to the QG and obtain a set of simpler QGs (SQG). The separation is guided by the information about the constrained / unconstrained *pair-ups* between the different branches in the QG derived in Step 1.

Step 3 : For each QG in the SQG, perform a hill-climbing heuristic process to find the minimum cost SJIH. This process is guided by the cost model.

Step 4 : Collect the SJIs in all SJIHs obtained in Step 3, into a new SJIH as the final or near-optimal SJIH.

The Query Graph (QG) for the queries in *OQG* is given in Figure 3. As shown in the figure, there are 5 distinct paths, from the root (*Sales*) for the four dimensions (*Product, City, Customer, Date*).

From the semantics of our ORDW schema and *OQG*, the three branches (*Product-1* and *Customer-2*) are *constrained* pair-up branches, whereas the other two branches (*Date* and *City*) are *unconstrained* pair-up branches. So

Figure 3: The Query Graph (QG).

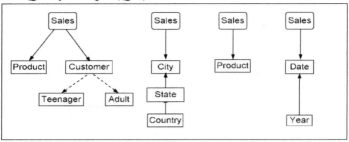

Figure 4: Optimal SJIH generated from the HCHSSA.

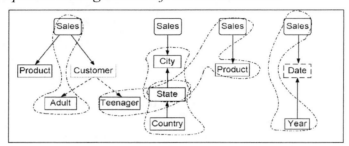

after branch separation in Step 2, we obtain the 4 simpler QGs as shown in Figure 4. This resultant set of simpler query graphs is denoted by SQG.

In Step 3 of the HCHSSA algorithm, we start the hill-climbing process. As this requires an initial guess, we start with an SJIH (as shown in Figure 5) which completely covers all the classes in the most significant query. By most significant, we mean that among the queries in *OQG,* the query that is executed most frequently, the query which needs the shortest response time, or the query with the highest query processing cost. For example, in our OQG, Q1 is "*Total Sales by Product by State*". This query involves 3 classes, *Sales, Product* and *State*. It is spread over two paths (3 and 4), and the classes involved are unconstrained pair-up. Hence, our first SJIH is SJI-1 (S,P,S). Such an initial guess will be closer to the real optimal SJIH and hence is preferred over any random guess. We can consider the first query (Q1) to be the most important query. Then for each consecutive query, we repeat the process of finding the next guess with lower processing cost. In each iteration, SJIs are merged, split, transferred or deleted to form the SJIH with the lowest query processing cost.

Continuing the example, we take the next queries Q2 "Sales by Prod by State by Year" and Q3 "Sales by Prod" from the OQG (both are along the same CCH). We can either add a CSJI (Sales, State, Product, Year) which is the complete SJIH for the given queries; or a SJI (Sales, Date, Month, Year); or a DJI (Sales, Year). It is seen that the DJI (Sales, Year) has the lowest query processing cost, and hence it is selected at this stage of the algorithm. Similarly taking query Q4

"Sales by Prod by City" and Q5 "Sales by Prod by Country", we have the options of adding Base SJIs : BJI (Sales, City), BJI (City, State), BJI (State, Country) or a SJI (Sales, City, State, Country). At this stage, it is seen that the SJI has a lower query processing cost and is selected over the BJIs. But processing the next query, Q5 "Sales by Prod by Teenagers by State", we see that by splitting up the SJI along the Address CCH, into BJIs (City, State) and (State, Country) combined with an extension or merging of the initial SJI into (Sales, Product, State, Teenager) and the DJI (Sales, Year) is the most efficient SJIH. Similarly we repeat the process for the remaining queries in the OQG.

The final SJIH is obtained after step 4, by merging all the SJIs at the end of step 3. This gives us the optimal/near-optimal SJIH, as shown in Figure 4.

As shown in the figure, the final (near optimal) SJIH contains several SJIs: namely, SJI-1 (*Sales, Product, Teenager, State*), DJI-1(*Sales, Adult*), BJI-1(*City, State*), BJI-3(*State, Country*), DJI-2(*Sales, Year*). Note that this result is due to our initial assumptions of *constrained* pair-ups between Customer and Product, and our choice of most significant query.

SJIH EVALUATION

In this section, we analyze the index retrieval cost for processing queries in *OQG* using SJIH. A comparison of the results with that of plain query processing approach using pointer chasing is then conducted.

Index retrieval cost

SJIH as described earlier is a set of OIDs. Hence to facilitate retrieval of the correct tuples from the SJI, indices are built on them. We can regard the OIDs of the SJI to be stored in the form of tuples in the leaf level of a clustered B+ index. This clustered index is built, in the case of our ORDW, on the root class, i.e., *Sales.* Note that other non-clustered indices on the SJI tuples can also be built as needed.

For Clustered Index According to Fung et al. (1998), the estimation of disk accesses in case of a clustered index is given by the following:

Index retrieval cost =   Disk access for leaf-level nodes +
                              Disk access for non leaf–level nodes.

where :

Disk access for leaf-level nodes = $Y(k, m, n)$;
Disk access for non leaf–level nodes = $Y[Y(k, m, n), Ym/BTF\sim, m]$;
Y is an auxilliary function defined as :
$Y(k, m, n) = Yao(k, m, n)$; when node size <= page size;

$$= m * k / n; \text{ when node size} > \text{page size.}$$

$$\text{and } Yao\,(k,\,m,\,n) = m * \sum_{i=1}^{k} [1 - P\,(nd - i + 1) / (n - i + 1)]\,, \text{ where}$$

n is the no. of tuples uniformly distributed into m pages ($1 < m <= n$);
k tuples ($k <= n$) are to be randomly selected from these n tuples;
$d = 1 - 1 / m;$
and BTF is the fan-out of the B+ tree.

For Non-clustered Index The index retrieval cost for a non-clustered index is given by:

Index retrieval cost = Disk access for leaf-level nodes of the clustered index +
Disk access for non leaf – level nodes of the non-clustered index.

where :

Disk access for leaf-level nodes of the clustered index = $Y(k, m, n)$;
Disk access for non leaf – level nodes of the non-clustered index =

$Y[k, \cup n / BTF ..., n] + Y[Y(k, \cup n / BTF ..., n), \cup \cup m / BTF ... / BTF ..., \cup n / BTF ...]$

Pointer traversal cost

In the case of no SJIH or partial indexing mechanism provided, one has to traverse the ORDW schema paths by means of *pointer chasing*. For instance, if we have u OIDs of a class C^p_{i+1}, we need to traverse backward from the class C^p_{i+1} to the root class along the path p. Then in the absence of further indices, we have to traverse in the forward direction towards the classes in the select clause.

When there are reverse pointers along the path, the cost of pointer chasing is given in Fung et al. (1998) as follows:

$$\sum_{j=i}^{0} Y(\,\text{bwd}\,(j, j + 1, u, p\,),\,|C^p_j|,\,\|\,C^p_j\,\|\,)$$

where the bwd( ) term [FKL98] provides an estimate of the average number of distinct objects in C^p_j referencing a set of u objects in C^p_{j+1}.

If there are no reverse pointers, the cost is much higher as all the objects in all the classes will have to be scanned.

Comparing SJIH retrieval cost with pointer traversal cost

In this section, we compare the pointer traversal cost with the retrieval cost using the SJIH selected from the HCHSSA algorithm (cf., Figure 4). The performance metric, Cost Ratio (CR) is defined as:

CR = Cost of using SJIH for complex object retrieval

Cost of using Pointer Traversal for complex object retrieval

Note that a CR value of less than 1, implies that using SJIH is more beneficial than following pointer chasing.

Figures 5a – 5d show the result plots for cardinality of the classes involved in the query v/s Cost Ratio for the respective queries from *OQG*.

Figure 5a: Cost Ratio comparison for Q1 and Q2.

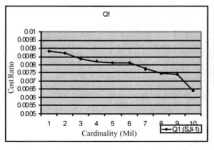
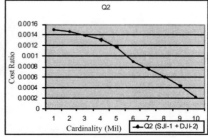

Figure 5b: Cost Ratio comparison for Q3 and Q4.

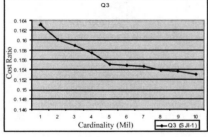
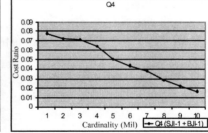

Figure 5c: Cost Ratio comparison for Q5 and Q6.

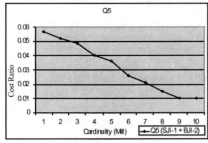
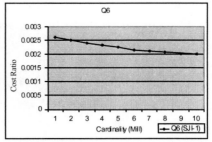

Figure 5d: Cost Ratio comparison for Q7 and Q8.

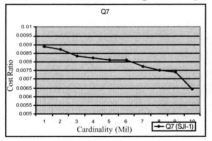
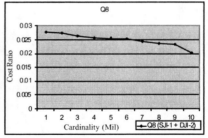

Overall, it can be seen from the result plots that the SJIH is a vast improvement over pointer chasing.

The specific observations are as follows :

1. Retrieval costs using SJIH are less than retrieval costs using Pointer Traversal by a factor of 10 - 5000.
2. As the cardinality of the classes involved in the queries increases, the Cost Ratio improves. This can be attributed to the fact that though SJIH costs increase, the pointer traversal mechanism has to visit considerably more objects and hence the SJIH is better suited for higher loads.
3. Some queries (eg, Q2), though use a SJI-DJI combination, have better Cost Ratios (700-5000). This is because the pointer traversal scheme suffers due to the semantics of the query. In this particular case, the query involves objects from deeply nested classes (Year and State). Hence the SJIH which provides direct access to complex objects is very efficient in this case.
4. Some queries (eg, Q3), though involved with only one SJI, are not as efficiently accessed as the other queries in *OQG*. (It must be noted that the performance gain is nevertheless > 6). Again, the semantics of the query indicate that this is a simple query involving only two adjacent classes (Sales and Product). Hence the pointer traversal mechanism has to only navigate from one class object to the next.
5. Queries Q6 & Q7 are very efficiently serviced by the SJIH. In these cases, the Cost ratio is between 125-500 even for simple queries. The reason is that an effective "horizontal partitioning" has been achieved by the SJIH on the class *Customer (Teenager & Adult)*. Hence the costs for the queries involving *Teenager,* show a marked reduction as the SJIH is built on a fragmentation of the *Customer* class. This advantage is not available to the pointer traversal mechanism or to any other indexing techniques which do not incorporate these semantics.

CONCLUSIONS AND FUTURE WORK

OLAP queries in Data Warehouse systems are essentially complex queries, involving multiple dimensions and their specializations. We have demonstrated the need to incorporate additional semantics, and provided the ORDW environment to explicitly capture, represent, and utilize the query and data semantics based on is-a and class composition hierarchies. We presented a *query-driven* indexing approach based on structural join index hierarchy (SJIH) mechanism (Fung et al., 1998). Specifically, by using a hill-climbing heuristic algorithm, a near-optimal SJIH incorporating query semantics can be generated and used for efficient OLAP query processing. Through analytical studies using a cost model, we have demonstrated the tremendous efficiency of employing SJIH over plain pointer chasing approach in our ORDW environment.

To provide better support of *dynamic data warehousing* (Dayal, 1999), it is instrumental to incorporate more semantics into the indexing mechanism, and to provide an adaptive and extensible indexing framework (such as SJIH). Currently, we're investigating ways to supplement the SJIH with efficient bit-vectoring indices (O'Neil et al., 1997). We are also in the process of building an experimental ORDW prototype system, upon which empirical studies based on classified benchmark queries (such as TPC-H) will be conducted to validate our approach.

REFERENCES

Chaudhuri, S., and Dayal, U. (1997, March). An Overview of Data Warehousing and OLAP Technology, *ACM SIGMOD Record*, 26(1), pp. 65-74.

Codd, E. F., Codd, S. B., and Salley, C. T. (1993). Providing OLAP (on-line analytical processing) to user-analysts: An IT mandate, Technical report.

Dayal, U. (1999). Dynamic Data Warehousing, *First International Conference on Data Warehousing and Knowledge Discovery (DaWaK)*.

Fung, C. (1998, December). Vertical Class Partitioning and Complex Object Retrieval in Object Oriented Databases, PhD. Thesis, Department of Computer Science, HKUST.

Fung, C., Karlapalem, K., and Li, Q. (1998). Structural Join Index Hierarchy: A Mechanism for Efficient Complex Object Retrieval, *Proc. FODO Conference 1998*, pp. 127-136.

Gopalkrishnan, V., Li, Q., and Karlapalcem, K. (1998). Issues of Object-Relational View Design in Data Warehousing Environment, *IEEE SMC Conference 1998*, pp. 2732-2737.

Gopalkrishnan, V., Li, Q., and Karlapalem, K. (1999). Star/Snow-flake Schema Driven Object-Relational Data Warehouse Design and Query Processing Strategies, *First International Conference on Data Warehousing and Knowledge Discovery (DaWaK'99) 1999*, pp. 11-22.

Karlapalem, K., and Li, Q. (1998). A Framework for Class Partitioning in Object-Oriented Databases, *Distributed and Parallel Databases*, Kluwer Academic Publishers, accepted in Sept. 1998 (to appear).

Gupta, A. and Mumick, I. S. (1995). Maintenance of Materialized Views: Problems, Techniques, and Applications, *Data Engineering Bulletin*, June 1995.

Gupta, H., Harinarayanan, V., Rajaraman, A., and Ullman, J. D. (1997). Index Selection for OLAP, *ICDE 1997*, pp. 208-219.

Mohania, M., and Kambayashi, Y. (1999). Making Aggregate Views Self-Maintainable, *Journal of Data and Knowledge Engineering*, 1999 (to appear).

O'Neil, P., and Quass, D. (1997). Improved query performance with variant indexes, *Proc. ACM SIGMOD '97*, pp. 38-49.

Roussopoulos, N. (1997). Materialized Views and Data Warehouses, *KRDB 1997*, pp. 12.1-12.6.

Sarawagi, S. (1997). Indexing OLAP Data, *Bulletin of the Technical Committee on Data Engineering*, 1997, 20:36-43.

Yang, J., Karlapalem, K., and Li, Q. (1997). Algorithms for Materialized View Design in Data Warehousing Environment, *VLDB 1997*, pp. 136-145.

NOTE

* This work has been supported by City University of Hong Kong under grant no.7100078.

Chapter 15

An Electronic Commerce Framework For Small and Medium Size Enterprises

Anne Banks Pidduck
University of Waterloo, Ontario, Canada

Quang Ngoc Tran
TurboLinux

The accessibility of the Internet and the World Wide Web has provided an excellent means for presenting, disseminating and distributing information. As well, this is a new and convenient channel for businesses to reach customers and other businesses. In this chapter, we describe an electronic commerce framework for small business. We discuss various services that a typical small business may want to provide its customers. Possible technologies to implement the services are examined and, finally, a prototype to generate such a model will be suggested.

INTRODUCTION

We have developed a generic electronic commerce model for small business. The framework provides a template for the quick and easy development of electronic commerce sites, in particular, for those firms who do not have a lot of money, time or web expertise. A pilot implementation is currently underway on a local community information network.

Previously Published in *Managing Information Technology in a Global Economy,* edited by Mehdi Khosrow-Pour, Copyright © 2001, Idea Group Publishing.

The Waterloo Information Network

The base for our electronic commerce framework is the Waterloo Information Network (WIN), developed by researchers in the Computer Systems Group at the University of Waterloo (Cowan et al., 1998; Cowan, 1998). This is a next generation community network, providing a large repository of valuable information and services. The WIN design is based on an advanced open architecture to achieve easy scalability and ease of information maintenance. It uses databases to store the information in the community network, and uses the Web to deliver and display the information (Cowan et al., 1997). It also utilizes advanced hypermap technology to provide better representation of data and information.

Current community groups presented by Yahoo and Alta Vista, for example, normally return queries with a random collection of facts and little or no context. Unlike these models, WIN takes a uniform approach to present community information. WIN's architecture satisfies the open concept in the sense that the technologies used in the network can be expanded or replaced without rebuilding the entire community network.

This innovative community network uses hypermap to display locations on a map image. Objects in the hypermap are associated with meaningful data to provide users with detailed information about the objects. Users navigate in the network via hyperlinks and tables of contents. More important, text and hyperlinks are stored in databases rather than flat files. This helps to automate the process of maintenance and cuts the cost of insertion and deletion in the table of contents. Hyperlink integrity is also kept at a constant cost. In addition, storing data in the databases makes searching easier and more extensive. The WIN pilot project built for the City of Waterloo can be found at http://www.city.waterloo.on.ca.

Goals

Our main goal is to provide an electronic commerce framework for small businesses in next generation community networks. Our current focus is the customer-to-business and business-to-customer (B2C) commerce. The more complex business-to-business orientation will be examined in the future once we successfully implement our B2C model.

We want to have a secure and complete model for this type of business. Many controversial issues such as digital certificate distribution, security features, services handled by the community networks, and so on will be identified for discussion. In many cases, we do not propose a unique valid answer but rather a range of possible answers that can be customized to best fit the business interests and requirements.

We also want to implement a program to generate such a framework. The program should be accessible via the Web so that a typical small business can go there and build their Web sites to boost their current business quickly. Although there are issues that may need to be taken care of by people, we would like to automate the whole process as much as possible.

Assumptions about Small Business

When designing the electronic commerce framework, we made generalized assumptions about the small businesses using our system. These assumptions serve as a frame of reference and our model is only realistic with these settings. Any changes in presumption mean that we may have to redesign or modify the framework.

The assumptions are as follows:

1. People who run businesses are not necessarily highly computer literate. They may know how to use simple application software and browse the Web, but they do not know or need to know all the technical details such as the operating system, system architecture, programming languages, HTML, CGI, middleware, and so on.
2. Typically, they do not have their own server to house the Web sites and the database, nor do they have the expertise to maintain these infrastructures.
3. They are willing to pay a small fee to reach a broader base of customers and experience a new way to do business.
4. They want the Web sites to be up and running as soon as possible to get competitive advantage.
5. Things they want to offer on-line include advertising, providing information about their businesses, buying and selling, booking appointments and reservations, searching, and transferring confidential information.

THE E-COMMERCE FRAMEWORK

In our model, we use the notion of an account as a basic unit associated with a business. The framework identifies all the components of an account, a secure mechanism for account creation and account access, and an architecture for the e-commerce server. Below we describe each component in detail.

An Account

An account is a virtual representation of the business in the Internet. To be more concrete, an account consists of a collection of Web sites that provide various services such as advertising, providing information about the business, buying and selling, booking, searching, and transferring confidential information. Customers look in the account pages to access the above services. Figure 1 illustrates a set of pages in an account.

Figure 1: A Set of Web Pages in An Account

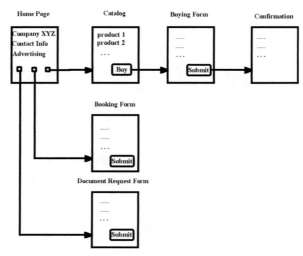

Next, we discuss each type of service that may be offered by an account.

Advertising

This feature is simply to store, arrange and display information. An account holder should be able to edit the content of information that he/she wants to include in the Web sites. The information could be an introduction about the business, contact information, press conferences, special offers, a map showing how to get to the company, and so on. These data are not limited to text but can be images, sounds, multimedia, or animations to further enhance the appearance of the Web sites and to attract more customers to come back. In addition, we use databases to store documents and hyperlinks instead of flat files. This makes hyperlink management much easier and faster and reduces complexity. Consequently, we want to build a set of automated tools for hypertext management.

Selling

This feature is probably the one of most interest to small business. It is vital to have a complete and secure method for selling things on-line (Cain, 1995). We provide a catalog of products or services offered by the account holder. An item in the catalog should include fields such as name, description, image and price. To help customers find what they want easily we have designed some searching capabilities. Customers can search items by name, price, description, or any combination of those. Customers can select items and add them to their baskets (or shopping carts) when browsing through the catalog. The catalog itself and searching capabilities are naturally augmented with the mature database technologies.

When finished shopping, customers will have to fill in order forms and make their payments as with current commercial sites. This information is then transferred back to the Community Network servers using SSL technology (Luotonen, 1998; MacGregor et al., 1996; Yeager, 1996). Once the servers receive the order, a confirmation (similar to a receipt) is sent back to the customer for future reference purposes.

Security

Note that for selling we do not need the customers to identify themselves in order to establish a secure selling channel (Shaffer and Simon, 1995; Stallings, 1995). Only the account holder has to do so because customers want to make sure that the account holder is who they claimed to be. Customers are typically very skeptical about giving out their credit card numbers, and they do not want those numbers to go to the wrong place. Each account holder should have a digital certificate, the Internet equivalent form of a passport, to identify his/her entity. A digital certificate has two keys, a *public* one and a *private* one. The public key is listed in on-line directory services similar to the yellow pages version of the phone book, while the private key is stored in the account holder's account. When a secure selling channel needs to be established (i.e., when the customers click to the form pages), the following steps happen:

1. The Web browser generates a *session key*.
2. The Web browser retrieves the account holder's *public key* from a directory service.
3. The Web browser encrypts the *session key* using the account holder's *public key* and sends it to the server.
4. The server (acting for the account holder) uses the account holder's *private key* to decrypt the message and obtain the *session key.*
5. Two parties now can communicate securely by encrypting their messages (symmetric key cryptography) using the *session key*.

Account Holder Notification

Now the orders (together with the credit card numbers) are already in the Community Network servers, but the account holder does not have any sales information yet. We provide three options for the account holder to get the orders. The account holder must choose one of the three options at the time the account is set up, but he/she can change the option anytime. The options are:

1. Encrypt the orders using the account holder's *public key* and then send them via secure email.

2. Send a notification email to the account holder, and provide a view-order capability via the Web. This requires the account holder to authenticate himself with the system. The authentication mechanism is discussed in the Account Access section of this chapter.

3. This option is similar to option 2, but the view-order is limited only to the order parts. No credit card numbers appear in the view. The Community Network acts as a middleman to take care of the financial transaction with this option and later credits the account holder's checking account. This option was proposed because many small businesses do not want to be involved in the financial transaction process. By subscribing to this option, the account holder frees himself/herself from money matters and can concentrate on producing and delivering goods and services to customers.

Booking Appointments and Reservations

There is a design dilemma for this feature. Ideally we would like to implement the whole booking system accessible via the Web for the account holder and customers. Customers are capable of making their own reservations, while account holders are allowed to update the booking capacities, states, and so on. However this approach encounters some serious difficulties. For example, if the server is somehow shutdown for a few hours, the business will not be able to do any booking. When the system is up again, the booking system must be reinitialized to update all reservation states. Any delay in reinitializing the system can cause erroneous functionality. Concurrency is also another big issue that needs to be controlled when multiple parties try to access the system.

As a result, we only provide a notification service to the account holder when there is a booking. We leave the account holder the responsibility to arrange bookings and contact back to the customers if such a reservation is not possible. The obvious disadvantage with this approach is that customers won't know instantly if their bookings are accepted.

Transferring confidential information

As with the **Booking** feature, we provide a notification service to the account holder when there is a request to retrieve confidential information such as medical records, credit ratings, personal financial portfolios, and so on. Typically, a customer who wants to use such a service should first register with the account holder to verify his identity due to the importance and confidentiality of these documents. Also the customer should have a digital certificate so that documents sent to him can be encrypted using his *public key*. Then, only the customer can decrypt the documents since he has the *private key*. Digital certificates are distributed by many Certificate Authorities (CAs) such as RSA, VeriSign, VISA, Master, and enTrust. These certificates can be used for many purposes other than just sending and receiving confidential documents. The price for digital certificates is quite affordable. For example, VeriSign charges $14.95 US for an individual digital certificate.

Searching

By storing documents and hyperlinks in the databases rather than flat files, we can use available advanced indexing and searching techniques. This allows searching for Web pages according to contents, keywords, categories, items, locations, and many more criteria.

Account Access

Account access is a mechanism that allows the account holder to login, initialize, view, and make any necessary changes in the account. An account holder should have a digital certificate installed in his Web browser to access his account pages. This is to ensure the security of the account. In addition, a simple user ID and password scheme is also used to safeguard the situation where the business has many employees but only certain personnel are entitled to access the system. Note that the userid and password scheme alone would not be sufficient. Attackers can easily write a script to break this scheme due to its availability in the Web. Therefore, the digital certificate is to prevent advanced attackers, while the userid and password prevent low-tech attackers. The latter are often ordinary employees who may have access to the computer with the digital certificate installed.

An account holder is able to login to his account, as shown in Figure 2. He can view, edit or delete any pending orders, booking requests, document requests, or advertising information in his account.

Figure 2: Account Access Pages

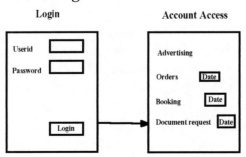

Account generating program

The account generating program is a program used to create new accounts. Once a business registers with the Community Network and provides all the necessary information, the account will be automatically generated. This program is a script written either in Perl or C/C++. The look-and-feel of this program interface is shown in Figure 3.

Figure 3: Account Setup Pages

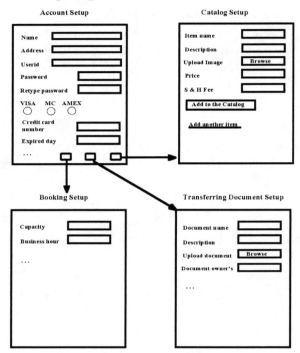

CONCLUSIONS

This chapter has presented a flexible, working model for e-commerce implementations that will be of interest to any small business considering this technology. It provided an overview of the various features that can be offered, and gave some insight into the different challenges and how they are approached from an implementation point of view. There is also a concise explanation of the use of encryption technology for secured transactions.

We have developed a template for small business electronic commerce sites. The prototype implementation will be working shortly, so that we can test the suitability of this framework for a number of businesses.

REFERENCES

Cain, A., and McGrath, R. E. (1995). Digital Commerce on the Web, *NCSA Access*, (9:2), Summer, pp. 36-39.

Cowan, D. D., German, D. M., and Mackie, E. W. (1997). LivePAGE – A multimedia database system to support World Wide Web development, *Proceedings of the Second Australian Document Computing Symposium*, Melbourne, Australia, April.

Cowan, D. D., Mayfield, C. I., Tompa, F. W., and Gasparini W. (1998). New Role for Community Networks. *Communications of the ACM*, April, 61-63.

Cowan, D. D. (1998). Community Networks – A Next Generation. *Technical Report*, University of Waterloo.

MacGregor, R. S., Aresi, A., and Siegert, A. (1996). *WWW.Security: How to Build a Secure World Wide Web Connection*, Upper Saddle River, NJ: Prentice Hall PTR.

Luotonen, A. (1998). *Web Proxy Servers*, Upper Saddle River, NJ: Prentice Hall PTR.

Shaffer, S. L., and Simon, A. R. (1995). *Network Security,* Academic Press, Inc.

Stallings, W. (1995). *Network and Internetwork Security*, Englewood Cliffs, NJ: Prentice Hall, Inc.

Yeager, N. J., and McGrath, R. E. (1996). *Web Server Technology*, San Francisco, CA: Morgan Kaufmann Publisher, Inc.

Chapter 16

The VLEG Based Production and Maintenance Process for Web-based Learning Applications

Jörg Schellhase and Udo Winand

Universität Gh Kassel, Fachbereich Wirtschaftswissenschaften

For the realization and maintenance of high quality and complex Web-based applications, there is a need to use sound Web-engineering principles. This chapter presents an application for the realization, management and maintenance of Web-based learning applications. Web-based learning applications are very important for the area of E-Learning, which is a field of increasing importance for E-Commerce.

INTRODUCTION

In many cases there is a lack of systematic approaches to the development of Web-based systems (Murugesan, Deshpande, Hansen & Ginige, 1999). Due to the increasing complexity of Web-based applications, there will be an increasing demand for methods and tools that support the efficient development of Web-based applications. By using adequate methods and tools, the costs and time to develop and maintain a Web-based application can be decreased enormously. Furthermore, the quality of the resulting Web-based applications will be much higher (Chen, Zhao & Fan, 1999).

This chapter introduces an architecture of a special kind of Web-based application, a Web-based learning application, the production process of the Web-based application, the architecture of a tool that plays an important part in the production process and the overall process model. The product model of the

Previously Published in *Managing Information Technology in a Global Economy,* edited by Mehdi Khosrow-Pour, Copyright © 2001, Idea Group Publishing.

Web-based learning application is modelled with the well known OOHDM method. The process model can be applied to different kinds of Web-based applications. The importance to differentiate between a product model and a process model is stressed in Ginige (1998) and Lowe and Hall (1999). The tool that plays a very important part in the production process is called the *Virtual Learning Environment Generator* (VLEG). It is a tool for the realization, management and maintenance of Web-based learning applications. Examples of products produced by the VLEG are Web-based learning applications of the project WINFOLine. WINFOLine is a well known german teaching cooperation of the universities of Göttingen, Leipzig, Kassel and Saarbrücken. The following Figure 1 shows the situation at the beginning of the WINFOLine project, after the requirements of the Web-based applications had been defined. Figure 2 shows briefly the development method chosen to produce and maintain the Web-based applications.

Figure 1: The situation at the beginning

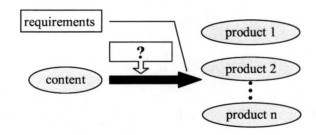

Figure 2: The chosen development method

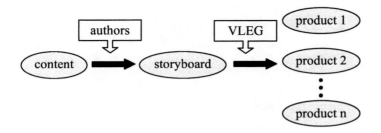

ARCHITECTURE OF THE WEB-BASED LEARNING APPLICATIONS

This section presents the architecture and some typical features of Web-based learning applications that are produced by the VLEG.

Features of the Web-based learning applications

The Web-based learning applications contain the content, communication services and numerous features to support the learning process. Students are able to configure the Web-based learning application according to their learning styles. One of the most important possibilities to configure the Web-based learning application is that students can choose between several output alternatives, e.g. slides, slides and audio, slide and text or slides, text and audio. The following figure shows a sample configuration with slide and text.

The learning process is supported in different ways. Due to the fact that in many hypertexts users tend to become disoriented, the Web-based learning application offers a wide variety of instruments that help avoiding the problem of disorientation. The Web-based learning application consists of several chapters, every chapter consists of several sections, and every section consists of several units. Depending on the user configuration, a unit can be just a slide, a slide and a separate text that explains the slide, a slide with an audio file or a slide with an audio file and a text that explains the slide. To the student, it is always transparent to which section and chapter the current slide belongs. Every slide has got a heading and a number. Students can get a list of learning goals and important keywords for every section.

There are up to 18 different types of hyperlinks. Every type of hyperlink is characterized by a small icon in front of the hyperlink or by brackets. Most internal and external hyperlinks offer a kind of textual and graphical preview. While the students are following referential hyperlinks, they are working in a special mode. In order to continue a linear learning process, they can terminate the special mode

Figure 3: Screenshot of a VLEG product (http://winfoline.wirtschaft.uni-kassel.de/intranet.htm)

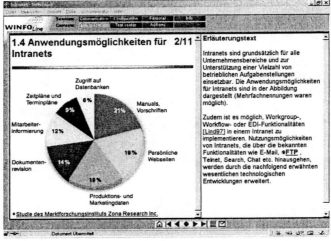

whenever they want to. Additional information is provided by several types of pop-ups.

The communication is supported by a number of means. Every slide offers the possibility to send a contextual email to the tutor, which indicates where the question of the student occurred. In addition, there exists a Web-based forum with a kind of list-server functionality. Furthermore, it is possible to make public and private annotations. There are several types of self-learning exercises, such as multiple-choice questions, crossword puzzles, one-word responses and long text answers.

Product model of the Web-based learning applications

This section shows the conceptual model and the context schema of the VLEG products and gives an abstract description of the used product model.

The essential conceptual objects of the VLEG products are chapters, sections, units, tests, glossaries, bibliographies, bookmarks, printouts and index pages. Specializations of printouts are printouts for slides, printouts for text and printouts for slides and text. Specializations of units are units with slides containing keywords, units just containing the learning material and units with exercises. The following figure shows the **conceptual model** of the VLEG products in OOHDM notation.

All classes of the conceptual schema, except for the class chapter, belong to the **navigation class schema** as well. Every navigation class corresponds to a certain type of web page of the VLEG products. The navigation class section

Figure 4: Conceptual model of the VLEG products

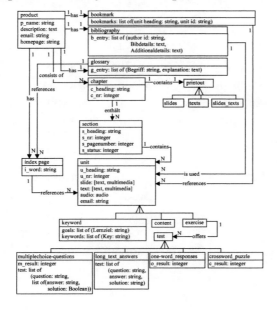

contains some additional attributes of other conceptual classes.

The numerous access structures, which allow to access the content of the VLEG products from different perspectives, are shown in the following **context schema** in OOHDM notation.

Figure 5: Context Schema for the Web-based learning application

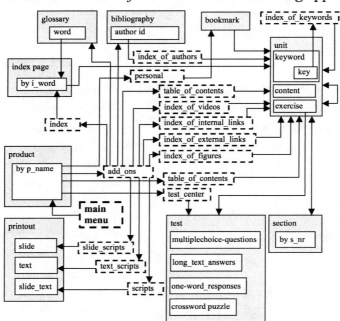

THE PRODUCTION PROCESS AND ARCHITECTURE OF THE VLEG

The basis for the production of the VLEG products are storyboards and multimedia assets. The storyboards are written by means of WYSIWYG HTML editors like Netscape Composer. The development and production process of the VLEG products were designed with the following main goals in mind:

- Separation of the production of content and the production of the final products.
- Authors should concentrate on the production of the content.
- The production of the final products should be automated.

The automation of the production process has many advantages: faster production of the final products; separation of content, layout and technical realization; easier reuse of content; easier production of different variants and versions; high quality of the final products; a common look and feel.

The structure of the storyboards

For a VLEG product several storyboards can exist. In a kind of meta storyboard several storyboards can be combined. For the structuring of the storyboards VLEG specific tags are used. These tags are used to mark headers, slides, texts, pop-ups and many other semantic units. The following figure shows a typical part of a storyboard illustrating the separation of a slide from the explaining text.

Figure 6: A unit of a storyboard

The production process

Authors of VLEG products write, modify and manage storyboards. In the meta storyboard the authors decide which storyboards to combine in order to produce a VLEG product. The following figure shows the input and output relation of the VLEG:

Figure 7: Input and output relation of the VLEG

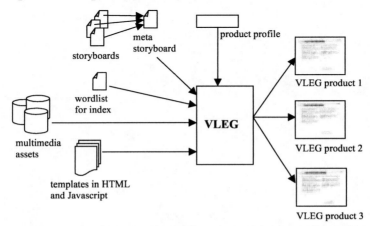

The product profiles are used for the setting up and the management of product configurations. A given product configuration determines the production process of a certain VLEG product. Template files and resource files can be changed by the authors. Therefore it is possible to change the look and feel as well as the functionality of the resulting VLEG products. The VLEG can handle several different sets of template files and resource files. Authors can develop special sets of template files and resource files for Web-based documentations, catalogues and other types of Web-based applications.

The VLEG is able to manage different variants of products. These variants can share resource intensive objects like multimedia assets. The VLEG product for the university course intranet for instance corresponds to a manuscript of 200 pages. The product intranet contains about 50 internal and 50 external hyperlinks that were manually inserted in the corresponding storyboards. By producing the VLEG product intranet, the VLEG created a hypertext with about 800 notes and 5000 hyperlinks. All internal hyperlinks were validated and all the hyperlinks within the slides and texts were semantically enriched by the VLEG during the production phase.

THE PROCESS MODEL

The process model shown in the following figure contains the authoring process for VLEG products as well as the development process for the VLEG tool and the template files.

Figure 8: Development process for the VLEG products

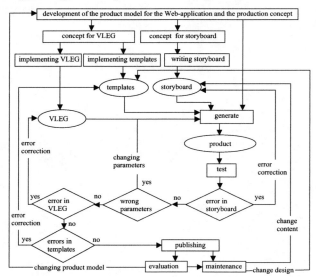

After implementing the VLEG, programming the template files and writing storyboards, it was possible to produce the described type of Web-based applications. Every Web-based application that is produced by the VLEG should be tested, before it is published. The following types of errors could occur:

1. error in storyboard (author)
2. wrong parameters in the product profile (author)
3. error in template files (author or programmer)
4. error in the VLEG tool (programmer)

Errors of type 3 will only occur if new template files are tested. Errors of type 4 could occur if the programmer tests new features for the VLEG tool. If errors of type 3 or 4 occur in other situations as well, this means that either the new template files or the VLEG tool have not been tested properly. After the final tests have been made, the VLEG product can be published. The VLEG products function on web servers and CD-ROMs. There is no need to do any web server specific or operating specific tests. The VLEG products are maintained by changing the storyboard and in rare cases by changing the template files.

The following figure shows the **authoring process**. The main task of an author is to write the storyboard. For the realization of the final Web-based learning application the author executes the VLEG tool, selects the appropriate product profile and activates the production process. If the author notices any mistakes in the storyboard he has to correct them, afterwards he has to restart the production process.

Figure 9: Authoring process for the VLEG products

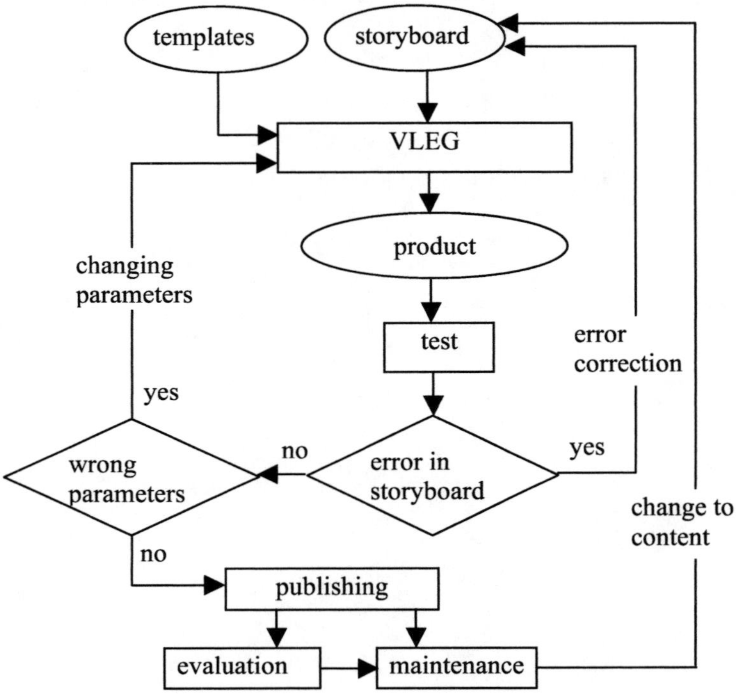

CONCLUSION

For the realization and the management of highly complex and sophisticated Web-based applications the utilization of adequate software tools is necessary. The presented tool VLEG can be used to produce flexible, configurable Web-based learning applications as well as some other types of Web-based E-Commerce applications. The VLEG helps to reduce the development expense for Web-based learning applications significantly. In addition, the maintenance process is simplified. The VLEG products automatically have many sophisticated features and are especially well suited for Web-based learning. Two years of experience with the VLEG products and product evaluations show that they are highly accepted by different kinds of users.

REFERENCES

Chen, J., Zhao, W., and Fan, X. (1999). A Content-centric Modeling Approach for Web-based Applications. *Asian Pacific Web Conference*. Hong Kong

Ginige, A. (1998, December). Methodologies for developing large and maintainable Web based Information Systems. In *Proceedings of IEEE International Conference on Networking India and the World*. Ahmedabad, Indien, 9(12).

Lowe, D., and Hall, W. (1999). *Hypermedia and the Web – An Engineering Approach*. New York: Wiley.

Murugesan, S., Deshpande, Y., Hansen, S., and Ginige, A. (1999). Web Engineering: A New Discipline for Web-Based System Development. *International Conference on Software Engineering, ICSE'99*. First ICSE Workshop on Web Engineering.

Schwabe, D., and Rossi, G. (1998). Developing Hypermedia Applications using OOHDM. Workshop on Hypermedia Development Processes, Methods and Models, Hypertext'98. Pittsburgh, USA 20.-24. June 1998. http://www.telemidia.puc-rio.br/oohdm/oohdm.html, 2000-12.

Chapter 17

Specification of Components Based on the WebComposition Component Model

Martin Gaedke
University of Karlsruhe, Germany,

Klaus Turowski
University of the Federal Armed Forces, Munich, Germany

Developing application systems that use the World Wide Web (WWW, Web) as an application platform suffers from the absence of disciplined approaches to develop such Web-applications. Besides, the Web's implementation model makes it difficult to apply well-known process models to the development and evolution of Web-applications. On the other hand, component-based software development appears as a promising approach that meets essential requirements of developing and evolving highly dynamic Web-applications. With respect to Web-applications, its main objective is to build Web-applications from (standardized) components. Founded on these insights and based on a dedicated component model, we propose an approach to a disciplined specification of components.

WEBCOMPOSITION COMPONENT MODEL

The *WebComposition* component model (Gellersen & Gaedke, 1999) describes the way of composing Web-applications from components. It bridges the gap between design and implementation by capturing whole design artifacts in components of arbitrary granularity. The resolution of a component is not preset but can vary depending on the level of detail required by the design concept in

Previously Published in *Managing Information Technology in a Global Economy,* edited by Mehdi Khosrow-Pour, Copyright © 2001, Idea Group Publishing.

question. A component may represent, e.g., an atomic feature such as the font size attribute, a complex navigation structure, implementations of hypermedia design-patterns, or simply compositions of other components. In this way, WebComposition supports the bridging of the gap between the design and the implementation model by offering a high-resolution implementation model relying on code-abstractions. We construct complete target language resources by compiling compositions of these components. In the following sub-sections, we describe the WebComposition approach, which is based on the WebComposition component model. The complete WebComposition approach defines a disciplined procedure of composing Web-applications with components (Gaedke, 2000). It is a synthesis of a component-oriented process model with a dedicated Web-application framework, reuse management, and a dedicated component-technology.

Figure 1: Dimensions of a Web-application's evolution space

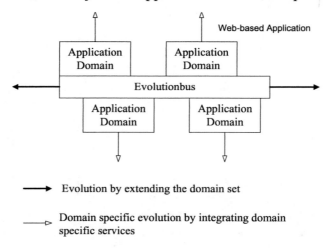

Evolution by extending the domain set

Domain specific evolution by integrating domain specific services

WebComposition Process Model

The requirements for a software system change as time goes by. It is obvious that many kinds of influences are responsible for this, e.g., new regulations, changes in corporate identity or an extension of functionality. Such maintenance tasks are difficult to handle if we did not design the application with the possibility of later changes and extensions in mind.

The *WebComposition Process Model* focuses on the evolution of Web-applications by reusing components. It consists of three main-phases. The phases are derived from the common phases of (object-oriented) process models as well as solutions addressing the need of software reuse, and taking the principles of the

Web into account. The process model follows a spiral consisting of evolution analysis and planning, evolution design and the execution of evolution. The first phase deals with common problems in strategic planning of the applications' functionality respectively with Domain Engineering. *Domain Engineering* has been described as a process for creating a competence in application engineering for a family of similar systems. The last two phases reflect the two different views towards reuse: consumer view (*development with reuse*) and producer view (*development for reuse*). We facilitate the evolution of an application following these phases by a framework, which maps the results of each phase directly to components. We explain the process in the following.

To allow for a disciplined and manageable evolution of a Web-application in the future, it makes sense not to design the initial application on the basis of the concrete requirements identified at the start of the project. Instead, the initial application should be regarded as an empty application that is suitable for accommodating functionality within a clearly defined evolution space.

This approach is based on domain engineering. During the analysis phase, we determine the properties of an application domain. During the design phase, we transform this information into a model for the application domain. From this, we can determine the required evolution space and, during the implementation phase of the domain engineering process, we can construct the initial application as a framework ready to accommodate any kind of functionality that lies within the evolution space of the domain.

Figure 2: Complete evolution process

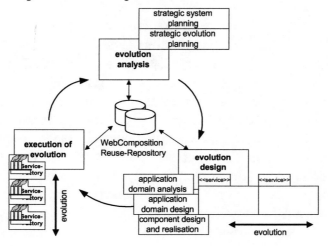

We can extend this view to several application domains. Therefore, we use the term *evolutionbus* for the basic architecture of a Web-application. The evolutionbus is the initial application for all abstract application domains of a Web-application, cf. Figure 1.

The evolutionbus enables the management and collaboration of domain-components, i.e., components that implement specific application domains such as Web-based procurement, reporting, or user driven data exchange. These domain-components (also called *Services* within the WebComposition approach) also represent prototypes for future services of the same application domain. The evolution can take place in two clearly defined ways:

· *Domain specific evolution (evolution design)* – The extension of a domain through new services, e.g. by prototyping an existing service of a domain. Another possibility is that the domain itself changes or that it receives more functionality, which requires the modification of the domain's initial service that serves as a prototype for other services.
· *Evolution of the domain set (evolution execution)* – The evolution of an application is also possible through the modification of the domain set. The extension of an application's functionality by adding a new application domain takes place, e.g., when a shopping basket and corresponding functionality is added to a Web-based product catalog. The integration of a new domain is realized by connecting a new initial service to the evolution bus (this mechanism can be facilitated using dedicated editors or automated by factories, cf. Factory design-pattern).

Figure 2 gives a detailed overview of the complete process.

Reuse Management

It is hoped that growing numbers of components increase the probability that a component fitting a certain purpose exists. On the other hand, the difficulty associated with finding such a component also increases with larger numbers of components. As soon as a lot of components are available finding appropriate components becomes one of the main problems of code reuse and of the CBSE (*component-based software engineering*) approach especially. In short, this so-called *component dilemma* states that the probability to own a component that can be used to solve a specific problem increases with the number of available components while at the same time the effort needed to locate such a component within the set of available components increases as well. The retrieval of components in libraries is therefore a widely discussed problem. Component repositories can be an answer to problems posed by a situation in which a human developer cannot be acquainted with all of those components (let alone know all the details about them).

Repositories intended for reuse can employ different methods for the classification and representation of components to improve the chance of finding a component matching a given development problem and to present an augmented perspective of the stored components. The commonly used representation methods usually belong to (at least) one of the following categories: *controlled and uncontrolled indexing* or *methods that contain semantic information*. Also *hypertext-based systems* are mentioned sometimes.

In the WebComposition Process Model, the *WebComposition Repository* is the responsible tool for the administration of reusable components (cf. Figure 2). There is no single program, which constitutes the repository. Instead, the basic mode of operation is the cooperation of at least three system entities: a component store, at least one *Metadata Store*, and a search or browsing tool *(Repository Tool)*. The tool can utilize the information stored in the Metadata Stores to provide advanced retrieval abilities or it can display information from the Component Store augmented with additional information provided by the Metadata Stores. We shape tools to work with the information of certain sets of Metadata Stores. Furthermore, we propose a disciplined approach to specify components in a consistent and reuse friendly way.

Dedicated Component Technology for the Web

The *Web Composition Markup Language* (WCML) was introduced in Gaedke, Schempf, and Gellersen (1999) to offer a convenient way to define and represent components. WCML is an application of the *eXtensible Markup Language* (XML) and allows a (tag-based) definition of components, properties, and relationships between components on top of WebComposition's object-oriented prototype-instance-model (Gellersen & Gaedke, 1999). As an application of XML the WCML is platform independent and easy to parse, it is rigorous in terms of well-formed or valid documents.

Within the WCML model, we describe a Web-application as a composition of components. From the perspective of the progress of different processes, Web-applications can consist of a hierarchy of components that each correspond to whole parts of Web-applications with resources or fragments of resources. On the other hand, for certain parts of a Web-application, only information from analysis or design may exist. Components within the WCML-model are identifiable through a *Universally Unique Id* (UUID). They contain a state in the form of typed attributes, called properties, which resemble simple name-value-pairs. Furthermore, the value of a property can be defined through static text or WCML language constructs and must correspond to the data-type of the property.

The before mentioned concept of developing component software by composition is realized with WCML language constructs. Each component can be based on any number of other components and use their behavior by referencing them or by using them as prototypes. A modification of a component can therefore consistently change all components that use it.

SPECIFYING WEBCOMPOSITION COMPONENTS

To store components in a repository and to further retrieve and reuse them, we have to describe their interface and behavior in a consistent and unequivocal way. In short, we have to *specify* them. *Software contracts* offer a good solution to meet the special requirements of specifying components. Software contracts go back to MEYER, who introduced contracts as a concept in the *Eiffel* programming language. He called it *programming by contract* (Meyer, 1988).

Figure 3: Software contract levels

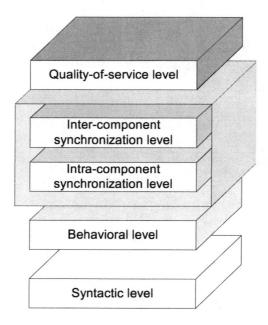

Software contracts are obligations to which a service donator (a component) and a service client agree. There, the service donator guarantees that

· a service it offers, e.g. calculate balance or determine demand,
· under certain conditions, which have to be met by the service client, e.g., the provision of data necessary to process the service,
· is performed in a guaranteed quality, e.g., with a predetermined storage demand or with an agreed response time, and
· that the service has certain external characteristics, e.g., the specified interface.

· Figure 3 shows contract levels according to Turowski (1999). At syntactic level, we conclude basic agreements. Typical parts of these agreements concern names of services (offered by a component), names of public accessible attributes, variables, or constant values, specialized data types (in common based upon standardized data types), signatures of services, as well as the declaration of error messages or exception signals. To do so, we use, e.g., programming languages or *Interface Definition Languages* (IDL) like the IDL that was proposed by the Object Management Group (OMG). The resulting agreement guarantees that service client and service donator can communicate with each other. With this, we put the emphasis on enabling communication technically. Semantic aspects remain unconsidered.

Agreements at behavioral level serve as a closer description of a component's behavior. They enhance the basic agreements of the syntactic level, which mainly describe the syntax of an interface. Agreements at syntactic level do not describe how a given component acts in general or in borderline cases.

As an example, we could define an invariant condition for a component *stock keeping* at behavioral level, which says that the reordering quantity for each (stock) account has to be higher than the minimum inventory level. Known approaches to specify behavior are based on approaches to *algebraic specification* of abstract data types (cf. e.g., Ehrig & Mahr, 1985). To describe behavior, we extend the specification of an abstract data type by conditions. These conditions describe the abstract data type's behavior in general (as *invariant conditions*) or at specific times (*pre conditions* or *post conditions*). In general, conditions are formulated as equations, and as axioms they become part of the specification of an abstract data type. The *Object Constraint Language* (OCL) (Rational Software et al., 1997) is an example for a widespread notation to specify facts at the behavioral level. It complements the *Unified Modeling Language* (UML).

Agreements at intra-component synchronization level regulate the sequence in which services of a specific component may be invoked or navigated to, and synchronization demand between its services. Here, e.g., we may lay down that a minimum inventory level has to be set before it is allowed to book on a (stock) account for the first time, or that it is not allowed to carry through more than one bookkeeping entry at the same time for the same account.

At inter-component synchronization level, we come to agreements that regulate the sequence in which services of *different* components may be invoked. Here, e.g., we may define that a certain service, which belongs to a component *shipping*, and which refers to a certain order, may only be processed after a service, which belongs to a component *sales*, and which refers to the same order, has been processed at any time before.

There exist various approaches to specify components at the synchronization levels. These approaches base, e.g., on using *process algebras, process calculi*, or on using *temporal logics*. In addition, (semi formal) graphical notations are in use, e.g. Petri net-based notations.

As an extension to functional characteristics, we have to describe *non-functional* characteristics of components. Non-functional characteristics are specified at the quality-of-service level. Examples for these characteristics are the distribution of the response time of a service or its availability.

We propose to use the OMG IDL or WCML-prototypes (syntactic level), the UML OCL (behavioral level), and the UML OCL with temporal extension (inter- and intra-component synchronization level) to specify WCML components. At the quality-of-service level, we so far use natural language. These specifications are encapsulated in standardized XML markup to ease its use in the Web environment.

Figure 4 shows an example of how we specify the process component *PrintInvoice* as part of a WCML service *OrderProcessing* at behavioral level. There, we use a pre-condition for the component *PrintInvoice*. It ensures that printing an invoice is allowed, if and only if the corresponding order was delivered before. Furthermore, there is a post condition that explains in detail, how the invoice amount was calculated.

Figure 4: Examples for the XML-based specification of components at behavioral level using OCL

```
<Service>
  <UUID>OrderProcessing</UUID>
  <ProcessComponent>
   <UUID>OrderProcessing</UUID>
  <BehavioralLevel>
   <Method>
     <Name>PrintInvoice</Name>
     <Signature><Name>at</Name><Type>Order</Type></Signature>
   </Method>
   <OCL>
    <PRE>
     self.Order->exists(a:Order | a = at and at.Delivered = True)
    </PRE>
    <POST>
     at.InvoiceAmount =
       at.OrderPositions->iterate(p:Position; b:Amount = 0 |
       b + p.Quantity * p.PiecePrice * (1 – p.Discount)) * (1 – at.Discount)
    </POST>
   </OCL>
  </BehavioralLevel>
  </ProcessComponent>
...
      </Service>
```

In this example we use WCML-interfaces for prototypes on the syntactical level as shown in Figure 5. The WCML markup uses an official Document Type Definition that describes the grammar of the WCML components. For reasons of simplicity we do not use schemas and namespaces in this example (even though the WCML-compiler supports these). The WCML-component may be used as prototype for other components and for syntax checking in the WCML-Compiler.

Figure 5: The specification of a component at syntactical level using WCML-prototypes

```
<?xml version="1.0" encoding="UTF-8" ?>
<!DOCTYPE wcml SYSTEM "http://webengineering.org/REC/wcml/wcml2.dtd">
<wcml>
 <component uuid="Order" referable="false">
    <property name="TechnicallyPracticable" mode="interface" type="boolean" />
    <property name="Delivered"                mode="interface" type="boolean" />
    <property name="InvoiceAmount"            mode="interface" type="double" />
    <property name="Discount"                 mode="interface" type="double" />
    ...
 </component>
      </wcml>
```

CONCLUSION

We have pointed out that the coarse-grained implementation model of the Web hinders the representation of abstract design concepts in actual code. The resulting gap between implementation and design model is a burden to the use of modern software engineering practices in Web projects. The WebComposition approach with its implementation technology WCML bridges this gap and allows designing for reuse by a dedicated process model.

The WebComposition Process Model describes a consistent approach to the development of Web-applications as component software. It introduces the concept of an evolution-oriented process model that allows for the integration of components using the abstract concept service. In this view, a Web-application is a set of services that are grouped by certain domains. The services are modeled as components with the WebComposition Markup Language. WCML is an application of XML and is in concordance with the basic principles of the Web. The application domains are described through services that correspond to domain-components. The evolution by application domains is a central part of the process model and is described through the so-called Evolutionbus, a framework for the integration of domain-components. In this chapter we proposed a standardized way to describe components on a software contract level architecture. The use of a standardized approach like presented in this chapter is essential for a disciplined evolution of Web-applications.

The WebComposition Process Model has been successfully applied to several real world applications. The advantages for the evolution could be verified in a three-year project for a large international Web-application "E-Victor Procurement Portal" at the company Hewlett-Packard that has been developed according to the process model, and using the described component technologies.

EXAMPLES

For information about the WCML-Compiler and the WebComposition approach please feel free to browse: http://webengineering.org

REFERENCES

Ehrig, H., & Mahr, B. (1985). *Fundamentals of Algebraic Specification 1: Equations and Initial Semantics*. Berlin: Springer.

Gaedke, M. (2000). *Komponententechnik für Entwicklung und Evolution von Anwendungen im World Wide Web*. Aachen: Shaker Verlag.

Gaedke, M., Schempf, D., & Gellersen, H.-W. (1999, May 11-14, 1999). WCML: An enabling technology for the reuse in object-oriented Web Engineering. Paper presented at the *Poster-Proceedings of the 8th International World Wide Web Conference (WWW8)*, Toronto, Ontario, Canada.

Gellersen, H.-W., & Gaedke, M. (1999). Object-Oriented Web Application Development. *IEEE Internet Computing, 3*(1), 60-68.

Meyer, B. (1988). *Object-Oriented Software Construction*. Englewood Cliffs: Prentice Hall.

Rational Software, Microsoft, Hewlett-Packard, Oracle, Sterling Software, MCI Systemhouse, Unisys, ICON Computing, IntelliCorp, i-Logix, IBM, ObjecTime, Platinum Technology, Ptech, Taskon, Reich Technologies, & Softeam. (1997). *Object Constraint Language Specification: Version 1.1, 1 September 1997*. Available: http://www.rational.com/uml [1999, 04-17].

Turowski, K. (1999). *Standardisierung von Fachkomponenten: Spezifikation und Objekte der Standardisierung*. Paper presented at the 3. Meistersingertreffen, Schloss Thurnau.

Chapter 18

The Development of Ordered SQL Packages to Support Data Warehousing

Wilfred Ng
Hong Kong University of Science and Technology, Hong Kong

Mark Levene
University of London, UK

Data warehousing is a corporate strategy that needs to integrate information from several sources of separately developed Database Management Systems (DBMSs). A future DBMS of a data warehouse should provide adequate facilities to manage a wide range of information arising from such integration. We propose that the capabilities of database languages should be enhanced to manipulate user-defined data orderings, since business queries in an enterprise usually involve order. We extend the relational model to incorporate partial orderings into data domains and describe the ordered relational model. We have already defined and implemented a minimal extension of SQL, called OSQL, which allows querying over ordered relational databases. One of the important facilities provided by OSQL is that it allows users to capture the underlying semantics of the ordering of the data for a given application. Herein we demonstrate that OSQL aided with a package discipline can be an effective means to manage the inter-related operations and the underlying data domains of a wide range of advanced applications that are vital in data warehousing, such as temporal, incomplete and fuzzy information. We present the details of the generic operations arising

Previously Published in the *Journal of Database Management, vol.12, no.4*, Copyright © 2001, Idea Group Publishing.

from these applications in the form of three OSQL packages called: OSQL_TIME, OSQL_INCOMP and OSQL_FUZZY.

Data warehousing is a corporate strategy that addresses a broad range of decision support requirements such as querying information over its underlying databases and managing ordered data for the purpose of analysis. One of the main characteristics of data warehousing is that in order to build its foundation, it should consist of integrated data from several sources of separately developed information systems. The transmission of data relies on the network system which connects all these information systems. As a result, the integrated database has the following important features:

- **It involves huge amounts of historical data.**

Data warehouse is described as a "subject-oriented, integrated, non-volatile, time variant" collection of data which is intended to support management decisions (Inmon, 1996). It is widely recognised that the underlying database in a data warehouse should capture transactions and snapshots in time in an efficient manner in order to carry out the activities of market forecast and strategic planning (McCabe & Grossman, 1996).

- **It is usually incomplete.**

This is due to two main reasons. First, some sources of the databases may be incomplete in order to protect sensitive data or to improve the speed of the process of data downloading via a network. Second, it has been observed in Libkin (1995) that even if each source of the database is complete, the integrated database may still not be complete. Hence, incompleteness may show up in the integrated database or in the answer to users' queries.

- **It is mainly used for decision support in an enterprise.**

However, many management professionals may not necessarily have good knowledge about the technical aspects of a data warehouse. As a result, their queries over the database are sometimes fuzzy in nature due to the ambiguity of natural languages. For example, they may ask to find the "best performed" shares in the Hong Kong stock market this month in order to carry out some share trading activities.

Many database researchers have recently recognised that ordering is inherent to the underlying structure of data in many database applications (Maier & Vance, 1993; Libkin, 1995; Buneman et al., 1997) including temporal information (Tansel et al., 1993), incomplete information (Codd, 1986) and fuzzy information (Buckles & Petry, 1982). However, current relational Database Management Systems

(DBMSs) still confine the ordering of elements in data domains to only a few kinds of built-in orderings. SQL2 (or simply SQL) (Date, 1997), for instance, supports three kinds of orderings considered to be essential in practical utilisation: the *alphabetical ordering* over the domain of strings, the *numerical ordering* over the domain of numbers and the *chronological ordering* over the domain of dates (Date, 1990). Let us call these ordered domains *system domains* or alternatively, domains with *system ordering*.

With the advent of the *Internet* technology, there is strong evidence that the limited support for ordering provided by current relational DBMSs is inadequate for future commercial applications. For example, a large proportion of the useful business information available in global Web sites is available only in hypermedia format. Hypermedia information normally consists of a very large amount of image data and thus resolution is an effective means to manage the size of data domain element. We illustrate this concept with the following simplified multi-resolution domain: { 'Null' < 'Black and white icon' < 'Black and white raster' < '8-bit Colour raster' < '24-bit Colour raster' }. This domain consists of five distinct levels of resolution and thus the users can select the appropriate level to save the transmission time for downloading a hypermedia document. However, the semantics of RESOLUTION_LEVEL cannot be captured by any one of the system orderings.

In order to alleviate the above-mentioned problems, we have extended SQL to Ordered SQL (OSQL) by providing the facility of user-defined orderings over data domains (Ng & Levene, 1997), which we refer to as *semantic orderings*. Queries in OSQL are formulated in essentially the same way as using standard SQL. We demonstrate this mode of querying with the following example, which shows how OSQL simplifies the specification of certain queries which might be useful in business decisions. We note that the following queries are not easy to formulate in SQL due to the fact that they must involve non-trivial use of aggregate functions and nesting (see Sections 25.1 and 26 in Celko (1995) and Section 9 in Pascal (2000)).

Example 1 In this example we assume that the attributes in their respective relation schemas are linearly ordered.
1. Get the third and sixth lowest share prices from a stock market.
   (Q_1) *SELECT* (SHARE_PRICE) (3,6) *FROM* STOCK_MARKET.
2. Get the names of exactly five participating banks from a syndicated loan record.
   (Q_2) *SELECT* (BANK_NAME) (1..5) *FROM* SYNDICATED_LOAN.
3. Get the names of all bosses of John.
   (Q_3) *SELECT* (EMPLOYEE_NAME) (*) *FROM* EMPLOYEE_TABLE
   WHERE EMPLOYEE_NAME > 'John' *WITHIN* EMP_RANK.

Although we have not yet formally introduced OSQL, the meaning of the above statements is quite easy to understand, assuming that the reader has some knowledge of standard SQL. For instance, the clause (3,6) in the query (Q_1) means that the third and sixth tuples, according to the order of SHARE_PRICE, are output and the clause (1..5) in the query (Q_2) means that the first to fifth tuples, according to the order of BANK_NAME, are output. The keyword *WITHIN* in the query (Q_3) specifies that the comparison EMPLOYEE_NAME > 'John' is interpreted according to semantic ordering of the domain EMP_RANK.

The usual way to tackle the above problems is to use a programming approach such as embedded SQL. However, as most data warehouses are built upon a *client-server* architecture, the programming approach has to pay the performance penalty in the *data extraction* process, if there are too many calls from the programming level to the relational level. In this respect, OSQL offers the advantage that it can help to relieve the burden of the bandwidth of a network system and the loads of *client processes*, if such kinds of queries can be performed in the *database server* instead of the client platform.

Herein we investigate the introduction of a package discipline into OSQL, which allows us to modularise a collection of generic operations on an ordered data domain. These operations can then be called from within OSQL whenever the package they belong to is loaded into the system. For example, the OSQL statement (Q_4) uses the function SNAPSHOT provided by the OSQL package OSQL_TIME, which returns the prices of shares of the temporal relation STOCK_MARKET in 1990.

(Q_4) *SELECT* (SHARE_PRICE) (*) *FROM* SNAPSHOT(STOCK_MARKET, 1990).

Table 1: The Brief Description of Three OSQL Packages

Package Name	Brief Description
OSQL_TIME	Provides support for temporal information in ordered databases. For example, finding the historical information pertaining to a relation for a given year.
OSQL_INCOMP	Provides support for incomplete information in ordered databases. For example, comparing two tuples in order to decide which one contains more information than another.
OSQL_FUZZY	Provides support for fuzzy requirement in ordered databases. For example, finding the most suitable tuples in a relation according to a given fuzzy requirement.

The package discipline makes it easier to formulate queries relating to the underlying ordered domains of the package and allows us to extend OSQL with powerful operations, which enhance its applicability and expressiveness. We demonstrate that OSQL aided with a package discipline is extremely powerful and has a very wide range of applicability. In particular, we demonstrate that OSQL is very useful in managing the three advanced database applications described in Table 1.

The use of packages is very popular and successful in many existing software systems such as *PL/SQL* in *Oracle* and most recently in *Latex2e* and *Java*. Similar to the usage of packages in other systems, OSQL packages, supported by OSQL language constructs, enjoy many of the benefits of using modularisation techniques as a management tool. For instance, a top-down design approach is adopted for the grouping of related operations in an OSQL package, within which constraints can be enforced and supported by a language construct called *enforcement*. Thus, the operations in an OSQL package can be controlled in a more coherent manner. OSQL packages can also hide the implementation details of the code of their operations. The database administrator has the flexibility to decide whether an operation should be *public* or *private*.

Related Research

A related approach is to use abstract data types to define domains and their associated operations, which can then be treated as an integral part of the data type. This approach is basically an object-oriented extension of the relational model, resulting from the strong trend of object-oriented programming in the 1980s. Examples of commercial products that conform to this approach are Illustra's DataBlades and IBM's Database Extenders. However, it is not clear that how the optimisation of programs can be carried out when using these systems if the code of the operations is introduced to the execution engine at run time. If the optimisation can be carried out at compile time, to our knowledge there has been very little research done on how these systems provide syntactic and semantic compatibilities with SQL.

The most recent version of SQL (SQL3 or SQL:1999) has the provision for a procedural extension of SQL (Melton, 1996), which allow users to define functions in abstract data types. However, the issue of ordering abstract data type instances in SQL3 is still unclear (Melton, 1996). Our work here can be employed as a useful reference point which explores the issue of incorporating order into SQL. We emphasise that our approach is novel. First, we regard partial ordering as a fundamental property of data which is captured explicitly in the ordered relational model. It results in more efficient operations than those using the programming approach to embed this property into an application program. Second, our approach adheres to the principle of upwards compatibility, since OSQL packages are provided as additional utilities to be used rather than replacing any standard features of a relational DBMS. Third, our approach provides maximum flexibility for users and allows the design of optimisation strategies for the execution engine of a relational DBMS.

The remainder of the paper is organised as follows. In the next section we briefly describe the ordered relational model, the query language OSQL and its package discipline. Then it follows the section which we describe in detail the contents and the uses of three OSQL packages for temporal (OSQL_TEMP), incomplete (OSQL_INCOMP) and fuzzy (OSQL_FUZZY) information. In the last section we conclude with discussion on the implementation issue of OSQL packages.

A PACKAGE DISCIPLINE FOR ORDERED DATABASES

In this section we briefly describe the ordered relational data model and its query language OSQL. Within this model, we demonstrate how OSQL packages can be applied to solve various problems that arise from many advanced applications.

The Ordered Relational Model

We assume the reader is familiar with the relational model as presented in Ullman (1988) and Levene & Loizou (1999). A basic assumption of this model is that elements in a data domain have no explicit relations amongst them. In the ordered relational model, however, partial orderings (or simply orderings when no ambiguity arises) are included as an integral part of data domains. Without an explicit specification by the user, we assume that the domains of databases have the *system ordering* attached to them.

As an illustration we assume a domain consisting of three employee names: Ethan and Nadav being the subordinates of their boss Mark. Viewing this domain as a conceptual domain, all three elements are indistinguishable with respect to their ordering. On the other hand, viewing this domain as a system domain, the alphabetical ordering is imposed onto the conceptual domain resulting in a linear ordering of the three names. Finally, viewing this domain as a semantic domain, the boss-subordinate relationship can be explicitly captured. The three different views of this domain are depicted in the diagram shown in Figure 1.

Figure 1: Domains with Different Kinds of Ordering

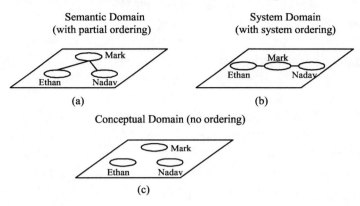

An important notion in our model is that given a conceptual domain, apart from the system ordering assumption, we can declare one or more semantic orderings which override the default system ordering. Furthermore, the orderings of domains can be extended to tuples so that tuples in an ordered relation are ordered according to the *lexicographical ordering* of the domains associated with the attributes present in the underlying relational schema. Therefore, any change in the order of attributes in a relational schema may affect the order of tuples in an ordered relation. For the formalism of this model, readers may refer to the recent research presented in Ng (1999) and Ng, Levene & Trevor (2000).

OSQL

Ordered SQL (OSQL) is an extension of the Data Definition Language (DDL) and Data Manipulation Language (DML) of SQL for the ordered relational model. In addition to the extended DDL and DML, OSQL provides a Package Definition Language (PDL), which will be detailed later on. Herein we just describe the *SELECT* statement of the DML and the *CREATE DOMAIN* statement of the DDL; the sample of OSQL can be found in the Appendix and the detailed BNF for OSQL can be found in Appendix B in Ng (1998).

1. The DML of OSQL
SELECT < lists of attributes > [ANY | ALL] < levels of tuples > [ASC | DESC]
FROM < lists of ordered relations >
WHERE < extended predicates >

An *attribute list* above is a list of attributes similar to the usual one, except that it provides us with an option that an attribute can be associated with a semantic domain by the syntax *attribute name WITHIN domain name*. The purpose of declaring a *WITHIN* clause is to override the system ordering with semantic ordering specified by the domain name. When the *WITHIN* clause is missing then the system ordering will be assumed.

A tuple level, which is a set of positive numbers, with the usual numerical ordering, can also be written in some short forms (see Appendix B1 in Ng (1998)). As a set of tuples in a linearly ordered relation $r = \{t_1,...,t_n\}$ is isomorphic to a set of linearly ordered tuples, we interpret each number i in a tuple level as an index to the position of the tuple t_i, where $i = 1,...,n$ and $t_1 <...< t_n$. In addition, a user can specify the retrieve of *ALL* the tuples or *ANY* one of the tuples in a specified level l_j when the output of a relation is partially ordered as a tree, having levels $\{l_1,...,l_m\}$.

Following the FROM keyword is a comma separated list of all relations used in a query. The meaning of the usual comparators $<, >, <=, >=$ is extended to include semantic comparison as we have mentioned earlier. A typical form of a semantic comparison is:

$<$ attribute $> <$ comparator $> <$ attribute $>$ *WITHIN* $<$ semantic domain $>$.

Without the optional *WITHIN* clause, the comparison is just the conventional one and is based on the relevant system ordering.

Example 2 Let us examine at the following OSQL statements:
(Q$_5$) *SELECT* (NAME, SALARY) (*) *FROM* EMPLOYEE.
(Q$_6$) *SELECT* (SALARY, NAME) (*) *FROM* EMPLOYEE.
(Q$_7$) *SELECT* ((NAME *WITHIN* EMP_RANK), SALARY) (*) *FROM* EMPLOYEE.

Note that the ordering of tuples in an output relation depends on two factors: first on the ordering of domains of individual attributes, and second on the order of the attributes in an attribute list. The attribute list of the query (Q$_5$) is (NAME, SALARY), and thus tuples in the output answer are ordered by NAME first and only then by SALARY (see Figure 2(a)). Therefore the ordering of tuples is, in general, different to that of query (Q$_6$), whose list is specified as (SALARY, NAME), since the output of (Q$_6$) is ordered by SALARY first and then by NAME (see Figure 2(b)). It will also be different from that of (Q$_7$) whose list is ((NAME

Figure 2: An Employee Relation EMPLOYEE with Different Ordering

NAME	SALARY
Ethan	28K
Mark	27K
Nadav	28K

(a)

SALARY	NAME
27K	Mark
28K	Ethan
28K	Nadav

(b)

NAME	SALARY
Ethan	28K
Nadav	28K
Mark	27K

(c)

WITHIN EMP_RANK), SALARY), where the ordering of NAME is given by the semantic domain EMP_RANK shown in Figure 1 (see Figure 2(c)).

2. The DDL of OSQL

The syntax of OSQL allows users to define semantic domains using the *CREATE DOMAIN* command as follows:

CREATE DOMAIN < domain name > < data types > *ORDER AS* < ordering specification >.

The first part of the statement is similar to the SQL standard statement that declares a domain. Following the *ORDER AS* keywords is a specification of the ordering of a semantic domain. The basic syntax of the *ordering-specification* is: (<data-pair>, <data-pair>,...) where *data-pair* is of the form, *data-item* B < *data-item* A, if and only if *data-item* A is greater than *data-item* B in the semantic domain.

Example 3 The definition of the semantic domain shown in Figure 1(a) can be written as follows:
(Q$_8$) *CREATE DOMAIN* EMP_RANK *CHAR*(5) *ORDER AS*
('Ethan' < 'Mark', 'Nadav' < 'Mark').

For a large and complex domain, this syntax may be tedious. Thus OSQL provides a useful short forms { } and the keywords *OTHER* for those data items not mentioned explicitly to make the task of formulating queries easier (see Appendix B in Ng (1998) for detail). For instance, (Q$_8$) can be rewritten as follows:
(Q$_9$) *CREATE DOMAIN* EMP_RANK *CHAR*(5) *ORDER AS*
  ({'Nadav','Ethan'} < 'Mark').

Four major practical benefits of using OSQL in database applications can be summarised as follows: First, with few syntactical modifications to the basic form of standard SQL, OSQL provides us with new facilities that can be interfaced to existing relational DBMSs to compare attributes according to semantic orderings, in addition to the usual system orderings. Second, OSQL incorporates some of the suggestions put forward by Date (1990) to improve SQL-type query languages, mainly concerning the support of the wider use of "<" operator. Third, OSQL provides an easy way to control the number of output tuples without having to do low level programming. This facility is both necessary and convenient for database users, especially for those who are non-programmers, when querying over a data warehouse. Fourth, partial ordering is a formal concept which has a simple interpretation in terms of real world entities. Due to this simplicity, OSQL can easily gain acceptance from a broad range of users.

Implementation of Ordered Domains

We now discuss two strategies in deploying an ordered domain. First, an ordered domain is implemented by using a conventional database system such as the Oracle DBMS. This strategy is attractive due to the known robustness and wide availability of conventional DBMSs. Another strategy is based on an object-oriented system such as IBM Smalltalk (Smith, 1994), which is an efficient programming language offering an *OrderedCollection* class to manipulate ordered data.

Using the first strategy the semantic domain EMP_RANK described in Figure 1 can be easily maintained by using a binary relation to represent the ordering. After executing the CREATE DOMAIN statement written as (Q_8), the OSQL system generate an internal relation called ORDERING_EMP_RANK with two attributes ORDERING_SMALL and ORDERING_LARGE to represent the semantic domain EMP_RANK.

There are still two possibilities to represent ORDERING_EMP_RANK. One possible way is to use *transitive reduction* as the representation of the semantic domain. In this method, the binary relation ORDERING_EMP_RANK, consisting of two attributes over ORDERING_SMALL and ORDERING_LARGE, implements the orderings between pairs of elements. This approach caters for space reduction, i.e., we use the minimal numbers of tuples describing the semantic ordering of a given domain. The transitive closure can be easily obtained by the command *CONNECT BY* in Oracle, which essentially performs a closure operation.

Another way is to use the transitive closure as the representation of semantic ordering. This method has the advantage of minimising the cost of query execution time. Although these two approaches, the *transitive reduction* representation and the *transitive closure* representation, are equivalent in the sense that they represent the same partial ordering of a semantic domain, they have different implications in updating semantic domains. If we delete a tuple in the transitive reduction representation, then in the meantime it *implicitly* removes the ordering relationship between the two elements in the ordered pair. We also note that in this approach we have freedom to delete any tuple. In contrast, if we delete the same tuple in the transitive closure representation, it preserves the semantics of orderings of other elements in the domain. However, it may not possible to delete a particular tuple in such a method.

We remark that in most cases it is not necessary that all the values in a semantic domain be explicitly stored in the database because many of these values are unordered relative to each other (recall the keyword *OTHER* to represent those values which are not mentioned). We can also use the Oracle SQL command *CREATE VIEW* to form the necessary intermediate relations, and thus should not burden the system with large space usage overheads. Moreover, the dynamic SQL routine guarantees that the translated SQL program runs efficiently.

We now briefly discuss the implementation of a semantic domain based on an object-oriented (O-O) system; in this approach we can represent a given partial ordered domain as a set of *linear extensions* of the domain. Informally, the set of linear extensions representing a given ordered domain satisfies the criterion that it can precisely generate all the ordered pairs in the domain by imposing intersection on all linear extensions. An O-O system usually supports a rich set of linearly ordered types. For example, the programming language *Smalltalk* (Smith, 1994) provides two ordered classes called *OrderedCollection* and *SortedCollection*. When using the *OrderedCollection* class the ordering is determined by a sequence of the insertion and modification operations. When using the *SortedCollection* class users can formally state the sorting criterion by means of a *sort block*, which is a two-parameter Boolean-returning block for comparing successive ordered pair of data elements corresponding to a partially ordered set. The sort block can be specified explicitly at creation time, once the sort block is changed the entire collection is re-sorted according to a new sorted block.

Using OSQL in Advanced Applications

We now show that how OSQL can be applied to solve various problems that arise in relational DBMSs involving applications of temporal information, incomplete information and fuzzy information under the unifying framework of the ordered relational model. Let us consider the following relation EMP_DETAILS shown in Figure 3.

- **Temporal Information:**

    We assume that SALARY_TIME is a time attribute whose values are timestamps of the tuples in the relation EMP_DETAILS (for simplicity in presen-

Figure 3: An Employee Relation EMP_DETAILS

NAME	SALARY	PREVIOUS_WORK	EDUCATION	SALARY_TIME
Ethan	12K	UNK	MSc	1994
Mark	10K	NI	MBA	1990
Mark	18K	NI	MBA	1996
Nadav	15K	Programmer	BA	1995

tation, we also assume that the time stamping denotes valid time (Tansel et al., 1993)). For instance, we can see that Mark had salary 10K in 1990 and his salary increased in 1996. Note that we do not record Mark's salary if there had been no change since the year it was last updated. We can use the keyword LAST to find the last time the tuple was updated, since the domain of the attribute SALARY_TIME is linearly ordered. With the following query, we show how to find the salary of Mark in 1993 as follows.

(Q_{10}) *SELECT* (SALARY_TIME, SALARY) (*LAST*) *FROM* EMP_DETAILS *WHERE* NAME = 'Mark' *AND* SALARY TIME <= 1993.

- **Incomplete Information:**

     Suppose we have the domain INCOMPLETE_DOMAIN as in Figure 5 to capture the semantics of different null values; in this figure all known data values are more informative than the null symbol UNK (UNKnown), and UNK and DNE (Does Not Exist) are more informative than another null symbol NI (No Information) (we will address this point in detail in the next section). Let us define a semantic domain called INCOMPLETE_DOMAIN for the attribute PREVIOUS_WORK as follows:

(Q_{11}) *CREATE DOMAIN* INCOMPLETE_DOMAIN *CHAR*(10) *ORDER AS* ('NI' < 'DNE', 'NI' < 'UNK' < *OTHER*).

     We emphasise that users have the freedom to use a semantic domain or not for comparison in an extended predicate. So it needs to specify the target semantic domain in the DML, in addition to declaring the existence of a semantic domain in the DDL. Now, we illustrate this idea by the following query, which finds the name and previous work of those employees whose previous work is more informative than NI:

(Q_{12}) *SELECT* (NAME, PREVIOUS_WORK) (*) *FROM* EMP_DETAILS *WHERE* (PREVIOUS_WORK > 'NI' *WITHIN* INCOMPLETE_DOMAIN).

- **Fuzzy Information:**

     Suppose we have a semantic domain called QUALIFY to capture the semantic of the requirement "good science background in academic qualification" which is formulated as follows:

(Q_{13}) *CREATE DOMAIN* QUALIFY *CHAR*(10) *ORDER AS* ({'BA', 'MBA'} < 'MSc').

     We can formulate the query of finding the names of employees with good science background in academic qualification as follows:

(Q$_{14}$) *SELECT* ((EDUCATION *WITHIN* QUALIFY), NAME) (*,*) *DESC*
   FROM EMP_DETAILS.

The OSQL statements in (Q$_{10}$) to (Q$_{14}$) reveal the potential of using OSQL to support the above-mentioned three advanced applications. In order to make use the capabilities of OSQL in a more systematic manner, we define a variety of generic operations with respect to these advanced applications and classify them into three OSQL packages: OSQL_TIME, OSQL_INCOMP and OSQL_FUZZY. Using these packages, we now show how the mentioned queries can be formulated in a simpler manner by embedding the operations of the OSQL packages into OSQL.

Using the package OSQL_TIME, the query (Q$_{10}$) can be simplified as follows:

(Q$_{15}$) *SELECT* (SALARY) (*,*) *FROM* SNAPSHOT(EMP_DETAILS, 1993)
   WHERE NAME = 'Mark'.

Using the package OSQL_INCOMP, the query (Q$_{12}$) can be simplified as follows:
(Q$_{16}$) *SELECT* (NAME, PREVIOUS_WORK) *FROM* EMP_DETAILS
   WHERE MORE INFO(PREVIOUS_WORK, 'NI').

Using the package OSQL_FUZZY, the query (Q$_{14}$) can be simplified as follows:
(Q$_{17}$) *SELECT* (IMPOSE_FUZZY(EDUCATION, QUALIFY), NAME) (1)
   FROM EMP_DETAILS.

Although we have not yet introduced the details of OSQL packages, the meaning of the operations are quite easy to understand. For instance, the operation IMPOSE_FUZZY in (Q$_{17}$) returns the appropriate tuples arranged in a list such that it satisfies the imposed fuzzy requirement "good science background in academic qualification".

The Structure of OSQL Packages
We now introduce the building blocks of an OSQL package; the full syntax of the PDL is given in Appendix B3 in Ng (1998). An OSQL package is defined by the following statement:

PACKAGE < package name >
< package body >
END PACKAGE.

The package body consists of the following five basic PDL *language constructs*:

1. Parameter constructs.
2. Function constructs.
3. OSQL constructs.
4. Program constructs.
5. Enforcement constructs.

The parameter component in an OSQL package is organized as a sequence of *parameter constructs* followed by the keyword *PARAMETER* as follows:

PARAMETER: parameter construct [parameter construct]...

where a parameter construct is of the form *package data type*: *variable names*, declaring the global variables used in the function and enforcement components. For example, VARCHAR, INT and BOOL are package data types representing characters, integers and boolean values, respectively.

The function component in a package is organized as a sequence of *function constructs* followed by the keyword *FUNCTION*. A function construct is a block structure which is defined as follows:

```
< function name >< input variables >
< parameter list >
DEFINE
< function body >
RETURN [á output variables ñ]
```

where *parameter list* is a sequence of parameter constructs and where the variables are local to the function. The *function body* describes the operation of the function consisting of an *OSQL construct* or a *program construct*. An OSQL construct is simply an OSQL statement such that its variables have been declared either within a function (i.e. local variables) or in the parameter component at the beginning of the package (i.e. global variables). A function in a package returns a list of zero or more values.

As the expressive power of OSQL is limited (Ng, Levene & Trevor, 2000), we enhance OSQL with a *program construct* in OSQL, which is of the form *AS PROG program name*. The program name is the path location and the name of a program, which is written in C programming language, which allows SQL statements to be embedded in it. This program performs the operation of the function.

For example, the program construct "AS PROG \usr\Prog\time.strip" in a function body specifies that the C program *time.strip* found in the directory \usr\Prog\ implements the function.

The enforcement component in a package is organized as a sequence of *enforcement constructs* followed by the keyword *ENFORCEMENT*. An enforcement construct, which is similar to a function construct, is also a block structure as follows:

    < enforcement name >
    DEFINE
    < enforcement body >
    END

where the body of an enforcement construct is formulated by a program construct which implements some constraints over the functions of an OSQL package. For example an enforcement construct can be implemented to ensure that the identified domain is indeed linearly ordered. We reserve the enforcement, ENFORCE_INIT, to be used by the system for the initialization of an OSQL package.

Note that there is an important difference between using an OSQL construct and a program construct in a function. The OSQL statement in an OSQL construct can be decomposed and restructured by the query execution engine of a relational DBMS for optimisation purposes. For instance, the query (Q_{15}), which uses the package function SNAPSHOT, is equivalent to the query (Q_{10}), which is an ordinary OSQL statement not using any functions. On the other hand, an external program specified in a program construct is "opaque" with respect to a relational DBMS, in the sense that its code can only be integrated into its associated OSQL statement at run time and thus allows no possibility of optimisation at compile time. As a result, operations defined by OSQL constructs are, in general, more efficient to implement than those defined by program constructs.

OSQL PACKAGES FOR ADVANCED APPLICATIONS

In this section we present in detail of the three OSQL packages for temporal information, incomplete information and fuzzy information, respectively. The OSQL packages can be predefined and thus made available for the database users as built-in facilities. The functions in an OSQL package can be embedded in an OSQL statement, provided that the data types of the input and output variables of a function comply with the syntax of OSQL.

OSQL_TIME: A Package for Temporal Information

The underlying semantics of time used in this OSQL package is that time is considered to be linearly ordered. In our implementation an ordered relation is

Figure 4: An Employee Relation EMP_TIME Stamping with Time Intervals

NAME	SALARY	FROM_TIME	TO_TIME
Bill	15K	1991	1995
Bill	18K	1995	1996
Bill	20K	1996	1997
Mark	25K	1992	1995
Mark	30K	1995	1997

employed to maintain the data elements of a time domain, which are non-empty, finite, linearly ordered, and of the same data type. This relation can only be accessed by the operations of the package and the comparison of time data can be applied only over the time domain.

One of the many approaches (Tansel et al., 1993) in the literature to manipulating temporal data is to use an attribute, which we call a *time attribute*, and to *timestamp* the attribute values of this attribute with either *time instants* or *time intervals* (Tansel et al., 1993). We assume temporal data is timestamped with the time interval during which it is valid. For example, the relation EMP_TIME in Figure 4 uses the attributes FROM_TIME and TO_TIME to denote time intervals. We can see that, for instance, Mark had salary 20K in the time interval 1992 < YEAR < 1995 (note that in our formalism the year 1995 is not included in the time interval).

The advantage of using time intervals in modelling time data is that it can save storage space. However, there are some complications arising from using time intervals in modelling time data. For example, they cannot directly support the update or retrieval of tuples at a particular time instant and some useful operations such as the *snapshot* operation obtaining the temporal relation in a particular year, cannot be carried out in a direct manner. To solve this problem, two operations *EXTEND* and *COALESCE* have been suggested in the literature (Tansel et al., 1993). It can be shown that these two operations can be formulated in OSQL, with the assumption that an ordered relation is maintained for the time domain used in OSQL_TIME. Therefore, in this sense, we can claim that the expressive power of OSQL_TIME is *temporally complete* (see Chapter 5 in Tansel et al. (1993)).

We assume that DATE (i.e. DAY-MONTH-YEAR) is the default domain to be used in the package unless the function IDENTIFY is used to specify another time domain. Other standard domains available in OSQL_TIME include YEAR, MONTH, DAY, HOUR, MINUTE, SECOND. Note that these time domains support the need of using *multidimensional* databases in data warehousing (Inmon, 1996).

Note that we have not required that in OSQL_TIME contain some of the common temporal operators, such as *overlaps* and *contains* (see Chapters 4, 5

Table 2: The Description of the Operations in OSQL_TIME

Operations	Brief Description
IDENTIFY function	To IDENTIFY a given domain as the time domain used in OSQL_TIME.
CURRENT function	To return all the CURRENT tuples in a temporal relation.
HISTORY function	To return all tuples which are not valid at present.
SNAPSHOT function	To return all tuples which were valid at a given time instant.
SUCC function	To return the SUCCessor of a given time instant in the time domain used in OSQL_TIME.
PRED function	To return the PREDecessor of a given time instant in the time domain used in OSQL_TIME.
DURA function	To calculate the DURAtion between two time instants in the time domain used in OSQL_TIME.
EXPAND function	To convert interval-stamped tuples in a given relation into instant-stamped tuples.
COALESCE function	To convert instant-stamped tuples in a given relation into interval-stamped tuples, i.e. the reverse of the EXPAND function.
TIME_RES function	To create a time domain whose time scale is defined by the users.
VERIFY function	To VERIFY that the identified time domain satisfies the requirements for a time domain.
STRIP_TIME function	To project out the time attributes FROM_TIME and TO_TIME from the relational schema for a given relation and return the remaining attributes.
ENFORCE_ INIT enforcement	To enforce the initialization which identifies the domain DATE to be used as the time domain of OSQL_TIME.
ENFORCE_IDENTIFY enforcement	To enforce the verification over the identified domain given by the function IDENTIFY.

and 6 in Tansel et al. (1993)), which can be explicitly defined in order to compare time intervals, since they can be quite easily formulated in an OSQL comparison predicates. We now present the following description of the operations in OSQL_TIME in Table 2. The reader can consult Appendix for the declarations of the operations Appendix A in Ng (1998) for the full reference of the declarations pertaining to all OSQL packages.

Example 4 We use the relation EMP_TIME shown in Figure 4 whenever it is necessary.

1. IDENTIFY(YEAR) identifies the standard domain YEAR, which specifies the ordered set {1900 < ... < 2000} and IDENTIFY(MONTH) identifies another standard domain {*JAN* < ... < *DEC*}. If the user has used the function TIME_RES(100, HUNDRED) to create a domain HUNDRED, then IDENTIFY(HUNDRED) identifies this user-defined domain, which specifies the ordered set {0 < ... < 99}.
2. Find the current salaries of all employees.
   (Q_{18}) *SELECT* (NAME, SALARY) (.) *FROM* CURRENT(EMP_TIME).
3. Find the salary history of Mark.
   (Q_{19}) SELECT (.) (.) *FROM* HISTORY(EMP_TIME) *WHERE* NAME = 'Mark'.
4. Find the salary of Bill in 1994.
   (Q_{20}) SELECT (SALARY) (.) *FROM*
   SNAPSHOT(EMP_TIME, 1994)
      WHERE NAME = 'Bill'.
5. Find the names of those employees who have worked for more than two years.
   (Q_{21}) *SELECT* (NAME) (.) *FROM* EMP_TIME
      WHERE DURA(FROM_TIME, TO_TIME) > 2.

OSQL INCOMP: A Package for Incomplete Information

In this OSQL package, we classify the incompleteness into three unmarked *null symbols* whose semantics is given in (Codd, 1986).
1. UNK: Value exists but is UNKnown at the present time, for example some employees do not want to disclose their ages.
2. DNE: Value Does Not Exist, for example a fresh graduate does not have any previous work experience.
3. NI: No Information is available for the value, for example we may not have any information available as to whether an employee has previous working experience. The employee either has no previous working experience or it is unknown at the present time.

We use the notion of *more informative* values, which allows us to deduce useful information available from a relation having incomplete data (Libkin, 1995). The diagram in Figure 5 shows a partial ordering, say <, based upon the relative information content in a domain augmented with the three null values we have introduced. We can extend this partial ordering to tuples by defining a tuple t_1 to be less informative than another tuple t_2, if for all attributes A in the relational schema, $t_1[A] < t_2[A]$.

The ordering of null values is captured by the standard incomplete domain called INCOMP provided by OSQL_INCOMP. Recall that the domain can be

Figure 5: A Partial Ordering on a Data Domain

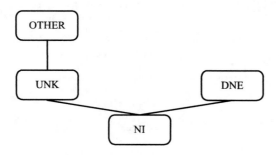

formulated by the OSQL statement in (Q_{11}). As we would like to make the domain INCOMP standard, we do not allow any user-defined incomplete domains in OSQL_INCOMP.

Note that the function IDENTIFY in this OSQL package is declared to be *private*, since the users are not allowed to change the meaning of various null symbols. This is to prevent the users from defining a casual notion of incompleteness, since the issue of missing information is much more difficult to handle than it appears (c.f. see Chapter 10 in Pascal (2000) for the problems of using SQL2 to handle null values). The functions COMPLETE_VAL, PARTIAL_VAL, DNE_VAL, NI_VAL and UNK_VAL provide users with the ability to manipulate various types of incomplete information based on the notion of being "more informative". The functions MORE_INFO and LESS_INFO provide users with the ability to semantically compare tuples in incomplete databases. We now present the following description of the operations in OSQL_TIME in Table 3.

Example 5 We use the relation EMP_INCOMP in Figure 6 whenever it is necessary.

1. Find the name and previous work of those employees whose previous work is less informative than unknown (i.e. UNK).

(Q_{22}) *SELECT* (NAME, PREVIOUS_WORK) (*) *FROM* EMP_INCOMP *WHERE* LESS_INFO(PREVIOUS_WORK, 'UNK').

2. Find the name and previous work of those employees whose information of previous work is not complete.

(Q_{23}) *SELECT* (NAME, PREVIOUS_WORK) (*) *FROM* PARTIAL_VAL(EMP_INCOMP, PREVIOUS_WORK).

Table 3: The Description of the Operations in OSQL_INCOMP

Operations	Brief Description
COMPLETE_VAL function	To return all tuples which contain only known values of an attribute in an incomplete relation.
PARTIAL_VAL function	To return all tuples which contain a null value of an attribute in an incomplete relation.
DNE_VAL function	To return all tuples which contain the DNE value of an attribute in an incomplete relation.
NI_VAL function	To return all tuples which contain the NI value of an attribute in an incomplete relation.
UNK_VAL function	To return all tuples which contain the UNK value of an attribute in an incomplete relation.
MORE_INFO function	To check whether tuples are more informative than a given attribute value.
LESS_INFO function	To check whether tuples are less informative than a given attribute value.
IDENTIFY function	To IDENTIFY the domain INCOMP as the incomplete domain used in OSQL_INCOMP.
VERIFY function	To VERIFY that the domain INCOMP satisfies the requirements for an incomplete domain.
ENFORCE_INIT enforcement	To enforce the initialization which identifies the domain INCOMP as the incomplete domain used in the package.

Figure 6: An employee relation EMP_INCOMP

NAME	PREVIOUS_WORK
Mark	UNK
Ethan	DNE
Nadav	Administrator
Bill	Programmer
John	NI
Simon	NI

3. Find the name and previous work of those employees whose previous work does not exist (i.e. DNE).

(Q_{24}) *SELECT* (NAME, PREVIOUS_WORK) (∗) *FROM*
    DNE_VAL(EMP_INCOMP, PREVIOUS_WORK).

OSQL FUZZY: A Package for Fuzzy Information

There is a strong correspondence between ordering and fuzziness. Assuming that the comparison, $<$, indicates linear ordering, the semantic comparison $x_1 < x_2$

can be used to represent the fact that the data value x_1 is fuzzier than the data value x_2. The smaller the value is with respect to an ordered domain, the fuzzier the value is relative to a given fuzzy requirement. For example, the more junior an employee is with respect to the ordered domain EMP_RANK, the "better chance" this employee has to be promoted.

The advantage of using such an association is that it is not necessary to define a *membership function* for a fuzzy set of data values as adopted by the traditional approach in fuzzy set theory. Therefore, we can avoid measuring the fuzziness of data in terms of an exact number, which is in practice difficult and sometimes unnatural.

In OSQL_FUZZY we provide functions for users to impose fuzzy requirements on a relation. Users can obtain the most suitable information based on the defined requirements in the OSQL package. We assume that for each fuzzy requirement, there is a domain called fuzzy domain, which captures the semantics of the requirement. For example, we have shown in (Q_{14}) the fuzzy requirement "good science background in academic qualification" can be captured by the fuzzy domain QUALIFY. Therefore, the requirement can be referred to by the name of its corresponding fuzzy domain. If there are several fuzzy requirements to be imposed on a relation, then their priorities can be defined by the function ORDER_FUZZY and tuples can be ordered and then retrieved according to the priorities of fuzzy requirements. This strategy can be employed by an expert system to support users' decision based on fuzzy information.

We now present the description of the operations in Table 4. The priorities of a set of fuzzy requirements are system defined (system ordered) if they are not specified. The function ORDER_FUZZY can be used to arrange the priorities of requirements. There is a parameter called order, which is a natural number describing the relative priority of the requirement defined in the second parameter fuzzy domain. The information about the priorities is maintained by the relation called FUZZY_DICT, whose relational schema consists of the attributes FUZZY_REQ and PRIORITY, containing all the name information of the fuzzy requirements and their priorities. The users can use the function LIST_REQ, which returns the relation FUZZY_DICT, to check for the priorities of all fuzzy requirements.

Example 6 Let us consider the relation EMP_FUZZY in Figure 7 whenever it is necessary, and suppose that there is a project which requires an employee with a good science background in his/her academic qualification and strong connections in the research community. We use two fuzzy domains called QUALIFY and CONNECT to capture these semantics of the requirements.

Table 4: The Description of the Operations in OSQL_FUZZY

Operations	Brief Description
IDENTIFY function	To IDENTIFY a fuzzy domain to be used to capture the semantic of a fuzzy requirement.
IMPOSE_FUZZY function	To IMPOSE a FUZZY requirement on an attribute.
ORDER_FUZZY function	To order the relative priorities of a set of fuzzy requirements which are currently used in OSQL_FUZZY.
LIST_REQ function	To list all the fuzzy requirements used in OSQL_FUZZY.
VERIFY function	To verify that the given domain satisfies the requirements for a fuzzy domain.
ENFORCE_INIT enforcement	To enforce the initialization which prepares an empty relation called FUZZY_DICT to maintain the fuzzy requirements.
ENFORCE_IDENTIFY enforcement	To enforce the verification over the identified fuzzy domain given by the function IDENTIFY.
ENFORCE_IMPOSE enforcement	To enforce the priorities of the identified fuzzy requirements.

Figure 7: An Employee Relation EMP_FUZZY

NAME	EDUCATION
Bill	MSc
Ethan	MSc
John	BSc
Mark	PhD
Nadav	MBA
Simon	A-Level

1. The fuzzy domain QUALIFY has been formulated in (Q_{13}) and the fuzzy domain CONNECT is given as the statement (Q_{25}) below.

   (Q_{25}) *CREATE DOMAIN* CONNECT *CHAR*(10)
   ORDER AS (OTHER < 'Mark' < 'Ethan').

2. Find the names of those employees with good science background in academic qualification and strong connection in the research community.

   (Q_{26}) *SELECT* (IMPOSE_FUZZY(NAME, CONNECT), IMPOSE_FUZZY (EDUCATION, QUALIFY) (*) *FROM* EMP_FUZZY.

A list of employees in which Mark appears to be the top one (the most preferred candidate) will be returned as the answer for this query.

3. We now use the functions ORDER_FUZZY(CONNECT, 1) and ORDER_FUZZY(QUALIFY, 2) to change the priorities of the requirements, i.e. the requirement CONNECT should be considered first and then QUALIFY the second. The employee Ethan appears on the top of the returned list as the answer for the query (Q_{26}) on this occasion.

4. Finally the fuzzy requirements can be listed as below by the function LIST_REQ().

FUZZY_REQ	PRIORITY
CONNECT 1	
QUALIFY 2	

CONCLUSIONS

We have presented a new query language, namely OSQL, for querying ordered relational databases and a modularisation package discipline, which supports three applications of: (1) temporal information, (2) incomplete information and (3) fuzzy information. These applications are fundamental to develop data warehousing, since we have to integrate data from dynamic information sources. An OSQL package has the advantage that it integrates all of the useful operations with respect to a particular application in a more coherent and systematic way. Thus we could better adapt the data content in the data warehouse.

In Figure 8, we show our design of the system architecture, which allows OSQL statements to be entered via the front-end interface with a Decision Support System (DSS). The OSQL system can easily fit into a data warehousing strategy by offering various useful packages for deriving data required in DSS analysis. Moreover, users have the flexibility to define other customised OSQL packages tailored to the needs of an enterprise, in addition to those already mentioned, which represents as *package slots* and *domain slots* as shown in the figure. The DDL, DML and PDL of OSQL which operate over ordered relational databases have been implemented using an *Oracle8i* server for low level data management.

We are in the process of improving the system in order to make it possible to load more than one package into the system at the same time to support data warehousing strategy; in this case the parser is much more complex than the one that caters for a single package. All the functions of the loaded packages, which are qualified by their corresponding package names, can be applied directly in formulating a query. For example, the query "find the name and salary of the employees in 1996, the information about whose work is less informative than 'UNK'", which involves the application having temporal and incomplete informa-

Figure 8: Architecture of the OSQL System in Data Warehousing

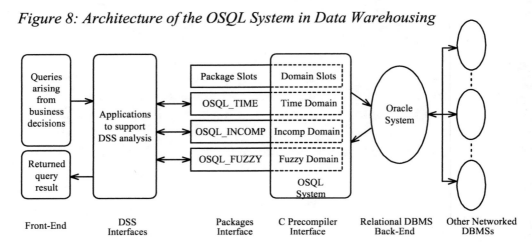

| Front-End | DSS Interfaces | Packages Interface | C Precompiler Interface | Relational DBMS Back-End | Other Networked DBMSs |

tion can be formulated in a unified manner by using two OSQL packages. (The relation EMP_DETAIL has been shown in Figure 3.)

(Q_{27}) *SELECT* (NAME, SALARY) (∗)
 FROM OSQL_TIME.SNAPSHOT(EMP_DETAIL, 1996)
 WHERE OSQL_INCOMP.LESS_ INFO(PREV_WORK, 'UNK').

Admittedly, the current version of OSQL is not without its weaknesses when compared to those database languages which are specialised to only one particular application. In comparing to most proposed temporal extensions to define a richer set of specialised operators in handling temporal information; for instance, the six Allen's operators such as *overlaps*, *contains* and *meets* are defined in HSQL (c.f. Chapter 5 in Tansel et al. (1993)) as the primitive operations in order to compare time intervals. Such a *specialised approach* facilitates better understanding of the needed operations tailored to the specialised databases. In comparing to general fuzzy SQL extensions, we can see that, apart from those ordering information embedded in fuzzy domains, OSQL does not support users to define an algebraic function of membership (Buckles & Petry, (1982)). So the information about the numerical degree values of fuzzy quantities such as TALL, OLD and MANY cannot be directly formulated by using the basic OSQL constructs.

We emphasise that our extension to SQL is *a uniform approach*, since we provide a unified model as a basis for investigating robustness and efficiency of a set of *generic* operations and their new possible applications. Thus, an important on-going research issue is, in a formal manner, to compare OSQL with those extended SQLs specialised to handle temporal, incomplete and fuzzy information. Another limitation of using OSQL is that as a research prototype our system has not yet been developed to the standard of a fully-fledged version. In particular, we still need to study the implementational issues of how to integrate the facilities of user-defined orderings into the kernel of DBMSs at the physical level. We also need to further study those applications involving more complex types involving ordering, in such cases we have the problem of defining a large but elegant class of complex ordered types in the system. Finally, the problem of updating ordered databases has not been discussed in this paper. It can be further investigated in terms of the algorithms and formal semantics of updating ordered domains.

ACKNOWLEDGMENTS

I sincerely thank the editor and anonymous referees for their important comments and suggestions, through which this paper can be greatly improved.

REFERENCES

Buckles, B. P., & Petry, F. E. (1982). A Fuzzy Representation of Data for Relational Databases. *Fuzzy Sets and Systems* 7, 213-226.

Buneman, P., Davidson, S., Fernandez, M., & Suciu, D. (1996). Adding Structure to Unstructured Data. *Technical Report* MS-CIS 96-21, CIS Department, University of Pennsylvania.

Casanova, M. A., Furtado, A. L., & Tucherman, L. (1991). A Software Tool for Modular Database Design. *ACM Transactions on Database Systems* 2, 209-234.

Celko, J. (1995). *SQL For Smarties: Advanced SQL Programming*. Morgan Kaufmann Publishers.

Codd, E.F. (1986). Missing Information (Applicable and Inapplicable) in Relational Databases. *ACM SIGMOD Record* 15(4), 53-58.

Date, C.J. (1990). *Relational Database Writings 1985-1989*. Addison-Wesley.

Date, C.J. (1997). *A Guide to the SQL Standard (4th edition)*. Addison-Wesley.

McCabe, M. C. & Grossman, D. (1996). The Role of Tools in Development of a Data Warehouse. In: *Proceedings of the 4th International Symposium on Assessment of Software Tools*, 139-145.

Inmon, W. H. (1996). *Building the Data Warehouse*. John Wiley & Sons.

Levene, M. & Loizou, G. (1999). *A Guided Tour of Relational Databases and Beyond*. Springer Verlag.

Libkin, L. (1995). A Semantics-Based Approach to Design of Query Languages for Partial Information. In: *Proceedings of the Workshop on Semantics in Databases*, 63-80.

Lu, H., Chan, H. C., & Wei, K. K. (1993). A Survey on Usage of SQL. *SIGMOD Record* 22(4), 60-65.

Maier, D. & Vance, B. (1993). A Call to Order. In: *Proceedings of the Twelfth ACM Symposium on Principles of Databases Systems*, 1-16.

Mattos, N., & DeMichiel, L. G. (1994). Recent Design Trade-offs in SQL3. *ACM SIGMOD Record* **23**(4), 84-89.

Melton, J. (1996). An SQL3 Snapshot. In: *Proceedings of the International conference on Data Engineering*, pp. 666-672.

Ng, W., & Levene, M. (1997). An Extension of OSQL to Support Ordered Domains in Relational Databases. In: *IEEE Proceedings of the International Database Engineering and Applications Symposium*, Montreal, Canada, 358-367.

Ng, W. (1998). OSQL Grammar. *http://www.comp.polyu. edu.hk/~csshng/ JDBM.html.*

Ng, W. (1999). Ordered Functional Dependencies in Relational Databases. *Information Systems* **24**(7), 535-554.

Ng, W., Levene, M., & Fenner, T. I. (2000). On the Expressive Power of the Relational Algebra with Partially Ordered Domains. *International Journal of Computer Mathematics* **74**(3-4), 53-62.

Pascal, F. (2000). *Practical Issues in Database Management*. Addison-Wesley.

Smith, D. (1994). *IBM Smalltalk: The Language*. Benjamin/Cummings.

Tansel, A. et al. (editors) (1993). *Temporal Databases: Theory, Design and Implementation*. Benjamin/Cummings.

Ullman, J. (1988). *Principles of Database and Knowledge-Base Systems, Vol I*. Rockville, MD., Computer Science Press.

APPENDIX SAMPLE OF OSQL GRAMMAR AND THE OSQL_TIME PACKAGE

Data Definition Language (DDL)
1. *CREATE DOMAIN* < domain-name >< data-type > [*ORDER AS* < ordering-specification >]
< ordering-specification > ::= (< data-pair >[, < data-pair >]...)
<data-pair > ::= [data-item | {{data-item,...}}] < [data-item | {{data-item,...}}]
2. *CREATE DOMAIN* < domain-name > *AS* < domain-name >

Data Manipulation Language (DML)
1. *SELECT* < attribute-list > [{*ANY* | *ALL*}]< tuple-list > [{*ASC* | *DESC*}] *FROM* < relation-list >
[*WHERE* <condition >]
< attribute-list > ::= (< extended-attribute > [,< extended-attribute >]...)
<extended-attribute > ::= {attribute-name | (attribute-name *WITHIN* < domain-name > | *)}
< tuple-list > ::= ({#n [, #n]) | *LAST* | #n1. . . #n2 | *})
< condition > ::= < attribute-name | value> < comparator > <{attribute-name | value}>
[*WITHIN* < domain-name >]   < comparator > ::= {<|>|>=|<=|<>}

APPENDIX SAMPLE OF OSQL GRAMMAR AND THE OSQL_TIME PACKAGE (CONTINUED)

Package Definition Language (PDL)

1. *PACKAGE* <package-name > < package-body > *END PACKAGE*
< package-body > :: = { *PARAMETER*: < parameter-list >
FUNCTION: < function-list > *ENFORCEMENT*: < enforcement-list > }
2. < parameter-list > :: = { < parameter-construct > [< parameter-construct >]...}
< parameter-construct > :: = < package-data-type >: variable-name [,variable-name]...
< package-data-type >:: = { *VARCHAR | INT | BOOL | REL* }
3. < function-list > :: = { < function-construct > [< function-construct >]...}
< function-construct > :: = [{*PRI | PUB*}] < function-name > variable-names < parameter-list >
DEFINE < function-body > *RETURN* variable-names
< function-body > :: = [< program-construct > | < OSQL-construct >]
< program-construct > :: = *AS PROG* program-name pseudocode
< OSQL-construct > :: = [DDL statements | DML statements]
4. < enforcement-list > :: = { < enforcement-construct > [< enforcement-construct >]...}
< enforcement-construct > :: = < enforcement-name > *DEFINE* < program-construct > *END*

OSQL_TIME Package and its Operations *PACKAGE* OSQL_TIME
PARAMETER:
   VARCHAR: time_domain, ext_relation, time_instant_1, time_instant_2,
NOW Non_time_schema, ext_domain
   INT: granularity, duration
   BOOL: bool_val
   REL: result_relation
FUNCTION:
PUB IDENTIFY(ext_domain)
PUB CURRENT(ext_relation) *RETURN* result_relation
PUB HISTORY(ext_relation) *RETURN* result_relation
PUB COALESCE(ext_relation) *RETURN* result_relation
PUB SUCC(time_instant_1) *RETURN* time_instant_2
PUB PRED(time_instant_1) *RETURN* time_instant_2
PUB DURA(time_instant_1, time_instant_2) *RETURN* duration
PUB SNAPSHOT(ext_relation, time_instant_1) *RETURN* result_relation
PUB EXPAND(ext_relation) *RETURN* result_relation
PUB TIME_RES(granularity, ext_domain) *RETURN*
VERIFY(time_domain) *RETURN* bool_val
STRIP_TIME(ext_relation) *RETURN* non_time_schema
ENFORCEMENT:
   ENFORCE_INIT()
   ENFORCE_IDENTIFY()
END PACKAGE

About the Editor

Dr. Shirley A. Becker received her MS and Ph.D. in Information Systems from the University of Maryland, College Park, Maryland. Dr. Becker is a full professor of software engineering at Florida Institute of Technology, Melbourne, Florida and director of its E³ Web Technologies Research Group. Dr. Becker's funded research includes E-commerce, web usability and testing, web-enabling tools and technologies, and database systems. She has edited several books and published over sixty articles and book chapters in these areas. Dr. Becker served as editor and currently is an associate editor of the *Journal of Database Management*. She is a section editor for the *Informing Science Journal*, and serves on several editorial review boards. She is a member of IEEE, IRMA, and ACM.

Index